D0821163

Postsocialist Europe

EASA Series
Published in Association with the European Association of Social-Anthropologists (EASA)

1. LEARNING FIELDS
Volume 1
Educational Histories of European Social Anthropology
Edited by Dorle Dracklé, Iain R. Edgar and Thomas K. Schippers

2. LEARNING FIELDS
Volume 2
Current Policies and Practices in European Social Anthropology Education
Edited by Dorle Dracklé and Iain R. Edgar

3. GRAMMARS OF IDENTITY/ALTERITY
Edited by Gerd Baumann and Andre Gingrich

4. MULTIPLE MEDICAL REALITIES
Patients and Healers in Biomedical, Alternative and Traditional Medicine
Edited by Helle Johannessen and Imre Lázár

5. FRACTURING RESEMBLANCES
Identity and Mimetic Conflict in Melanesia and the West
Simon Harrison

6. SKILLED VISIONS
Between Apprenticeship and Standards
Edited by Cristina Grasseni

7. GOING FIRST CLASS?
New Approaches to Privileged Travel and Movement
Edited by Vered Amit

8. EXPLORING REGIMES OF DISCIPLINE
The Dynamics of Restraint
Edited by Noel Dyck

9. KNOWING HOW TO KNOW
Fieldwork and the Ethnographic Present
Edited by Narmala Halstead, Eric Hirsch and Judith Okely

10. POSTSOCIALIST EUROPE
Anthropological Perspectives from Home
Edited by László Kürti and Peter Skalník

Postsocialist Europe

Anthropological Perspectives from Home

Edited by

László Kürti and Peter Skalník

Berghahn Books
New York • Oxford

Published in 2009 by
Berghahn Books

www.berghahnbooks.com

©2009 László Kürti and Peter Skalník

A C.I.P. catalog record for this book is available from the Library of Congress

British Library Cataloguing in Publication Data

A catalogue record for this book is available from the British Library
Printed in the United States on acid-free paper.

ISBN: 978-1-84545-474-6 (hardback)

Contents

List of Illustrations

Preface

Sociocultural anthropology is spreading around the world in such a way that it articulates with local history, social conditions and scholarly styles. The 'other Europe' is other in a different way than when it used to be out of bounds for 'capitalist foreigners'. After 1989 revolutionary changes East-Central and Southeastern Europe has entered the post-communist era. Some call it post-socialism, depending whether they believe in the existence of socialism under communist rule. Internationally known anthropological writing on the countries situated between Western Europe and Eastern Europe has been dominated by researchers coming from Western Europe and North America. Without vetting these outputs our volume offers an alternative, a 'perspective from home.' We firmly believe in this perspective's justification because we experience varieties of daily life of post-communism as insiders, citizens whose professional training allows us to examine critically social relations from the position of scholarly analysis. In many ways the result will (have to) be different from outsiders' viewpoint. Let us express the hope that the mentioned difference will be a welcome change and that our 'self-study' ethnographies will find legitimacy even among those who (still) believe in anthropology as strictly studying the exotic others. Actually our volume is an example of studying otherness while studying ourselves as the changes taking place after the fall of communist rule: they are unprecedented, unexpected as well as culturally shocking also for us.

This volume has been the result of countless discussions, preparatory talks and years of correspondence. It should also be seen as one of the products of the Anthropology of Europe, an exciting area study re-invigorated after 1990. For the former 'Other Europe' is now open, rapidly being integrated into the West, in a sense becoming 'European' as any other parts of Europe. The obvious dependency path, however, modifies our east-central and southeastern Europeanness and we are happy to declare that we have something substantial to say to the world community of anthropologists and all those interested in what anthropology has to say to humankind. Some of us met first thanks to the various annual and biannual conferences organised by the European Association of Social Anthropologists (EASA), an association to which we all belong. We started to formulate our ideas at various EASA gatherings in Copenhagen, Cracow and Vienna but there were other forums as well, such as 'thinktanks' at Florence, NIAS at Wassenaar,

Wissenschaftskolleg in Berlin, or the Collegium Budapest. The present team of contributors formed in Dolní Roveň in 2003 and the commitment to putting together this collective volume was made in September 2004 at Litomyšl, in the Czech Republic, where an exploratory workshop on the Anthropology of Europe was funded by the European Science Foundation. The gestation of the book is of course a long process and several participants at these workshop eventually dropped out or could not finish their promised chapters. Nevertheless what we present to the reader here is to much extent representative of the topics which move the post-communist scene in East-Central and Southeastern Europe.

The publication of this edited volume was made possible by the Executive Committee of EASA (2004–2006, 2007–2009), an expert body providing moral support and encouragement from the very beginning. We wish to thank all those who gave us support and believed in the usefulness of our efforts. They certainly know who they are and therefore we will refrain from putting down their names. We trust that the work on the volume was for all of the contributors a satisfactory activity. The editors did their purely honorary/voluntary work with enthusiasm and if there were some disappointments then it is also the fault of less than stable situation around our institutions still experiencing the fall-out of post-communist times and the newly created difficulties as membership in the European Union for many of our states became a reality. It will be on the readers to judge whether our work was worthwhile and the perspective from home justified.

László Kürti and Peter Skalník

Chapter 1

Introduction: Postsocialist Europe and the Anthropological Perspective from Home

László Kürti and Peter Skalník

Now that twenty years have passed since the collapse of the Eastern bloc of "socialist" states there is a need to understand and theorize what took place since that historic date and where we are at the moment. The question of whether a democratic Eastern Europe does or does not exist because of the collapse of the Soviet bloc cannot be discarded. It is a complex issue for at least two reasons. Firstly, it must be ascertained how the varied legacies of state socialism differ from country to country. Second, for the core members of the EU, the traditional West, new members will remain part of East-Central Europe, or Eastern Europe, for obvious economic, political and cultural reasons. Regionalism across political boundaries is another important issue here but pan-European politics still centre on nation-state policies. Whilst the Eastern bloc was implicitly and sometimes explicitly conceptualized as a unified region, anthropologists have long been involved in debunking notions of homogeneity, arguing as they have for the interconnectedness as well as the unboundedness of its various parts. Now that the EU has expanded to twenty-seven states, and further expansion is underway, new regional hierarchies overshadow the former subdivisions. This, however, does allow for the inclusion of new tropes while maintaining ties with earlier historical boundedness. Thus, united Europe will remain a disunited entity for some time especially after the French and the Dutch rejection of the European constitution treaty (Gillingham 2003; Herrmann, Risse and Brewer 2004).

For obvious reasons, not all post-Soviet bloc countries could be included in this study even though they deserve scholarly scrutiny. But the creation of new nation states from the Baltic to the Balkans, from East-Central Europe to Central Asia and the Caucasus, has resulted in the creation of new scholarly areas and (sub)disciplines. The case studies published here do not address disciplinary developments, topics exhausted in recent works (Skalník 2002; Dracklé, Edgar and Schippers 2003; Dracklé and Edgar 2004; Khittel, Plankensteiner and Six-Hohenbalken 2004; Pink, Kürti, and Afonso 2004). Anyone willing to browse recent contributions by scholars working in Eastern Europe could just simply look at the literatures cited in these contributions to see the similarities and differences. Nor do we want to conceptualize now the much-debated notions of 'transition', East European or Central European 'otherness', and 'civil society' – topics that have seen much light in the past decade and half (Buchowski 2001; Neumann 1999). It is clear, however, that the years between 1989 and 1992 are still referred to by many as the period of transition from state socialism to a capitalist, multi-party democracy. Moreover, it is certain that this phase may now be viewed either as a temporal and geographical frame, or as a cultural rhetorical device used to analyse this time period (Gready 2003). Yet, nobody among us would want to argue that East-Central Europeans still live in the transitory period, and that this time should be referred to as an appendage to the 'long decades of state socialism'. On the contrary, we are pleased that we are in the phase we may label as post-transition, postcommunist or postsocialist, a possibility which allows us to engage in debates that address new questions and examine current processes that are inimical to our scholarly interests including our everyday lives. That this post-transitory period is anthropologically very interesting is supported by the argument that the new political-economic system is now again stabilized – even though there are many cracks in it – and therefore ready for a thorough study (cf. Sampson 2002).

Assumptions that all socioeconomic and political difficulties are attributable to the transtitional period have so permeated research on East-Central Europe, that it is difficult to break free of their premises and legacies. Many current perspectives on East-Central European processes, both during and after the transformative years, are based on 'Western' notions of how transformations ought to occur instead of what actually occurred at the local level. Another confusing factor in comprehending the details of socioeconomic and cultural change is that a considerable emphasis has been placed on short visits and a multi-sited approach by a single researcher on the lookout for social problems. Misreadings emanating from these are difficult to correct. Given current knowledge about the period following the 1989–1992 transformation, it is timely that these assumptions were rigorously and entirely deconstructed.

Thus, our postcommunist/postsocialist local framework is predicated upon specific dimensions and commonalities that arise from historical, cultural, regional and theoretical backgrounds that serve as qualifiers. Historical first because all the countries analysed here, as Milan Kundera (1984) asserts in his influential article , 'The Tragedy of Central Europe', had their share in major European (in fact world) events. It is a fact that the eastern part of Europe was involved in all the major intellectual and artistic movements of Europe, like the Renaissance, Baroque, and Enlightenment, not to mention the two world wars. Consequently, there are large scale historical and ideological underpinnings we must commonly deal with: the end of empires and monarchies, the rise of fascism, Nazism and Stalinism, and events leading to the collapse of the entire Soviet bloc (Ramet 1998). Other studies also support this: state myths, rituals and personality cults often existed side by side with conflicting meanings as, for example, that surrounding Tito (Dubinskas 1983) and Zhivkov (Kaneff 2004). Similarly, the name of the Croatian national hero, Ban Jelačič (Marks 2004), who was instrumental in suppressing the Hungarian revolution of 1848–49, has a rather different ring to Hungarian and Croatian ears. In contrast, Otto von Habsburg is a newly invented Hungarian historic cult figure, scion of a defeated empire and now a champion of democracy, Europeanness and human rights in postsocialist Hungary.

At the moment, one of the most serious challenges seems to be the ideological divides separating more advanced countries, actually the founders of the European Union, from those joining in 2004, and, further, from those who are still awaiting membership. In 2004, many of the former East bloc countries arrived at a new historical turning point because of EU enlargement from the original fifteen to twenty-five member states. As several studies have shown, the years immediately before this date and following it are crucial in the political life of all countries involved (Drulák 2001; Hohnen 2003; Meštrović 2003; Rausing 2004). Participation in the political and socioeconomic processes leading up to EU membership did not take place similarly across the entire region even though certain strands seem to be present in the former Eastern bloc countries, as the recent collections edited by Borneman (2004) and Brunnbauer (2004) so aptly reveal. Nobody can guess what new economic and social system will result from EU enlargement, but if the processes of the past fifteen years are any indication then we can say with certainty that they will be both unique and specific to the countries involved. At the same time, the differences between the various countries (those in, and those waiting to join) may bring serious social as well as cultural friction based on either the continuation of previously implemented policies or, alternately, on brand new political processes resulting from EU membership.

The cultural interconnectedness of our kind of anthropological project may be highlighted by asking what is and what is not included in the common baggage we call culture, language, religion, literacy, and tradition. We all have differing answers to these questions but it is certain that commerce, linguistic borrowing, rites of passage, religious and artistic movements have been at work connecting neighbouring states in varying fashions from the Baltic to the Balkans (cf. Bitušíková 1996; Busch and Kelly-Holmes 2004; Hohnen 2003; Jovanovič, Kaser and Naumovič 1999; Krasteva 1998; Müller and Schultz 2002; Rausing 2004). Thus our project is both a critique of the isolationist paradigm seeking to view all cultural matters as strictly national, and, at the same time, a warning to those who tend to view these as based on borrowing or diffusion – mythicized today as one aspect of globalization – and argue that national cultures are only negotiated symbols.

We are fully aware, however, that with regard to the native culture concept, there are at least three dangers facing anthropologists studying their own society. The first is superficiality, which operates with a rather mythopoetical image of knowing everything that has taken place and occurring in the present. Nativeness often carries the implication of naivety: that is, an information avalanche difficult to explain to those whom it concerns the most, both everyday citizens and scholars alike. This entails a continual presence of the image of 'nativist anthropology', an extreme form of anthropological enterprise rightly criticized by Kuper (1994). Just like the natives who are unable to explain the rules of the grammar of their language, so too are anthropologists baffled when certain rites – their historical, comparative and symbolic aspects – have to be explained to those who are involved in making them happen. Spending many years, sometimes a whole lifetime, in trying to understand particular processes and culture complexes is often dismissed by foreign scholars as leading to unnecessarily detailed knowledge with which the rest of the world cannot do much. Moreover, intimate knowledge of local phenomena is often dismissed as naive navel gazing, with meticulously collected data seen as marginal to more fashionable high-theorizing and existential philosophizing. Thus, it seems that local scholars must engage in discussions to make their voices heard both by Western scholars and more traditional practitioners at home, a work that places a double burden on us as different audiences require different sorts of production and interpretation.

The second danger arises from giving the culture concept too much credit for making people what they really are and not seeing that the cultural is also a collage of historical, economical and political, legal and paralegal, individual and communal complexes. None of the nation states described here are monolingual, adhere to a single religion, or can claim ethno-national purity. The current situation will certainly alter considerably under the weight of the newly constructed European Union and as local scholars we have to face this challenge by seeking those intertwined mechanisms that link our communities one way or another to larger national or transnational processes.

Finally, the third danger involves what scholars call a community, village or local group. Despite all attempts to claim or imply the contrary, none of these terms are, nor have ever been, bounded, standardized or clearly definable. No authors in this collection are ready to defend their study based on these concepts. Yet, and this is noticeable in the following chapters, anthropologists living and working in the same community they study are constantly asked by fellow academics if they can answer in a precise manner what kind of culture their group or locality has and what are the differences by which their community can be distinguished from neighbouring ones.

Obviously, there are questions scholars ask each other, but there are equally important exchanges that scholars have with locals. Local individuals will ask very different questions because they take their own culture for granted and are aware of ongoing phenomena which do not have to be explained to them. For instance, one constant question has to do with the utility or function of what anthropologists do. In answering this, scholars often resort to explanations they would never dare to offer to fellow anthropologists. What this linguistic switch masks lies at the heart of living in a locality that one studies: a mode of discourse that constantly separates the scholar as an outsider specialist from the local population. Similarly, it often creates a rather haphazard and elitist answer to people who know very well the answers to their questions. This is the 'we-all-know' syndrome that we may fall into from time to time. As local scholars we may commit such errors with the added advantage that we may – if we wish to – correct such imbalances quite quickly by visiting our research site or having a more immediate contact with our informants.

Regionality is another issue that must be viewed with care, especially when it is coupled with nationalized concepts such as space, territory and borders. Notions of 'Eastern Europe', 'Central Europe', the 'Balkans', the 'Mediterranean' – or even smaller ones – like 'Silesia' or 'Transylvania' – cannot be simply prolonged as constantly essentialized natural terrains without regard to current events that significantly altered these as both real and imagined entities (Čiubrinskas 2004; Feldman, Prica, and Senjković 1993; Hammond 2004; Kürti 2001; Savoniakaité 2002). Yet, and this also provides a strong theoretical foundation here, we do realize that regions are interconnected in multiple ways, not the least of which are the contested terrains and border regions that have been so fundamental in rekindling nationalist controversies. This connectedness is also a unique feature of the region under the influence of both EU integration and its backlash. As Andre Gingrich aptly puts it: 'From a wider point of view, EU enlargement and integration may be seen as both a variant of, and an adaptation to, the current phase of globalization, whereas the rise of racism, xenophobia, and neo-nationalism in Europe is a powerful reaction against it. Everywhere, these wider tendencies interact with varying local factors' (Gingrich 2004: 174).

These global and local factors are not always visible everywhere and with the same intensity. The concepts themselves are also understood and utilized differently in different disciplines. Globalization, however, is not a concept unique to the twenty-first century, nor does it solely involve the geographic region described by the awkward terms Eastern, East-Central, or Eastern and Central Europe. While it is true, as Sassen writes, that 'Globalization – as illustrated by the space economy of advanced information industries – denationalizes national territory' (Sassen 1999: 186), it is equally valid to see nation states receiving varied signification as subjects of new capital ventures, financial benefits or political prestige. To top this, the EU enlargement has shifted the 'European borders' from the borders of Austria and Germany much farther to the east, where now EU border control is between newly formed states and nations. Thus, Russia, Belarus, Ukraine, Moldova, Serbia and Croatia are now finding themselves in a new environment in which they are immediate neighbours of the new EU member states with which they were allies during state socialism. As new states receive new signification from transnational polities, so too are new social processes, both wanted and unwanted, put into motion. These create unforeseen difficulties as new cross-border trades emerge, transnational migrants enter newly invented (sometimes referred to as dangerous) border zones, and co-nationals are subject to different policies from the mother countries across state borders. In this new oscillating geography of centrality and marginality, European states are realigning themselves according to their newly found place inside or outside the EU. How this political and cultural realignment takes place and what really happens at the community levels, and with what repercussions, needs to be studied so we can understand better the interconnectedness between the global and the local as these are played out in a cultural environment. We as local scholars are especially prone to feel these repercussions on a daily basis and we are well situated to make them intelligible for political, economic or scholarly use.

Theoretical questions abound in this area: is there a need to reject or uphold the notion of 'postsocialism' as both a necessary and a valid concept simply to mean an ongoing legacy without changes and differences across both time and space? Some studies published so far seem to offer a one-sided explanation: socialist policies and values continually plague these countries, providing a rather gloomy picture that the former Soviet bloc countries are necessarily mortgaged to a tradition with which they cannot or do not wish to break. It could also be argued that postcolonialism and postsocialism may have a lot in common, and by looking at the former we can benefit when we want to understand the emergence of postsocialism, its origin, what it entails and its utility as a concept. Recently, many scholars have investigated the former and have asked new questions about decolonization and postcolonial processes (Mudimbe-Boye 2002; Goldberg and Quayson 2002; Bauman and Gingrich 2004). Yet, while postsocialism has received attention by Western colleagues, it has rarely been theorized from within (for an exception, see Drulák 2001). Indeed, the concept 'postsocialism' may be seen as an imposition from the West in the postcommunist world (cf. Skalník 2002: 193–194, note 3).

We could compare many aspects of postcolonial studies to postsocialist studies as showing similarities. A word of caution is in order, however. While postcolonial studies started with the first appearance of work by such writers as Nkrumah, Fanon and later Spivak, Bhabha and others, the postsocialist project started to mushroom in the 1980s with critical reflections on the workings of the Soviet-dominated world order from within. Names such as R. Bahro from East Germany, G. Konrad and I. Szelényi from Hungary, not to mention the literary attempts – mostly of the translated works by Milan Kundera and Alexander Solzhenitsyn – spring immediately to mind. Anthropologists, however, only belatedly joined the theorizing attempts when after 1989 new questions were asked by Western scholars. Both the British and the American schools, even though some do not care to admit it, have been preoccupied with the notion of debunking the myth that the postsocialist period has been a result of a natural or popular movement from below. Instead, they argued that the velvet revolutions should be viewed with caution for several reasons. To be fair to them, not all aspects of the socialist/post-socialist upheavals were legitimate and orderly, let alone democratic. But undoubtedly the people decided to make a difference.

To return to postcoloniality, the similarities and difficulties are striking. For one, the world, and especially the European continent, today, is not what it was during the 1960s and 1970s. The East-West divide that determined the fate of hundreds of millions after the Second World War has been relegated to the annals of history. Instead, global financial capital runs amok, bringing havoc to the most isolated settlements of Eastern and Southern Europe, albeit there have been some genuine attempts, both by locals as well as concerned foreign individuals, to work together to create means to cope with such economic and social crises. It is one thing to argue, as some have done, against direct foreign involvement in local economies and social processes. But it is quite another, as some of these studies propose, to work together in order to bring some solution and manageable conditions to communities facing everyday hardships.

Another issue that needs to be considered in the relationship between globalization, postolonialism and postsocialism, is that globalization is not a unified process. Globalization cannot be defined without particular reference to the local events and processes that support or subvert it. At least in Europe, world-wide movements of goods and people have been around for more than a millennium, a fact that cannot be disregarded in the theoretical arguments about the current wave of political-economic transformations (cf. for example, Mudimbe-Boye 2002). Nobody can question that the collapse of Gorbachev's perestroika and glasnost was a welcome addition to the democratic climate of European transformation. Since we cannot really know for sure what Gorbachev's reforms would have produced now if they had succeeded, it is more fruitful to ponder what came after and how.

The world has taken another turn than that envisioned by the prime movers and shapers of the popular movements in and around the former Soviet bloc. Nobody could imagine that the joyous working-class people of Poland who celebrated the victory of the Solidarity movement in 1990 would later turn against one of its own (Lech Wałęsa). Similarly, Hungary's centre-right governments – celebrated with tremendous happiness by some – lost an election both in 1994 and 2002 when the majority of the people decided that flagrant and dubious nationalistic policies were just not what they really wanted. The citizens of the Romanian town Cluj easily sacrificed their megalomaniac mayor (Funar) during the municipal elections in 2004 for a liberal candidate who promised a more reasonable and peaceful existence during the bumpy road to EU accession. In Belgrade, political corruption and crime has made such deep scars – especially with the assassination of the popular mayor – that the situation will be very difficult to remedy.

Theoretically, it has to be emphasized that there is a strong belief among anthropologists that we are a unique brand among social scientists, because we are privileged to offer perspectives on the societies we study from first-hand local observations that differ considerably from those written by sociologists, political scientists and economists, who use statistics and questionnaires instead of qualitative fieldwork. This difference is perhaps less accented in more recent fashionable disciplines like ethnic, cultural, media and gender studies. Certainly, our anthropological views in this volume are informed by these perspectives but this does not entail that we are not critical of them while, at the same time, able to utilize what is generally acceptable for our investigations. We seek to understand what makes us different from those colleagues studying Third or Fourth World peoples, or from those who are citizens of the region referred here as the West (cf., for example, Crowley and Reid 2002; Reid and Crowley 2000; Svašek 2006). As social scientists we must maintain a comparative framework, but as anthropologists there is nothing in sight that would force us to abandon our original mission: to better understand the human condition in its diversity and complexity by offering minute details of the daily struggles of our co-nationals. In order to do so, we – anthropologists working at home – must engage in specific fieldwork practices in order to provide first-hand accounts of people's lives at the local level. When such studies are juxtaposed with those conducted elsewhere, then the comparative and theoretical aspects of our enterprise will receive a tremendous boost. We are not searching for remote locations, faraway tribes, strange and exotic rituals just for the sake of carrying an anthropological badge, even though some of us have conducted research outside Europe; for many of us there are now, we must stress here, pressing issues present in our very own backyards deserving of attention (cf. Kürti 2006).

Theoretically and methodologically, our starting point is that anthropologists living and working in the society they study may offer alternative views concerning their home countries compared to those who visit for the single purpose of conducting fieldwork research at a particular moment in time. This alternative perspective may serve as a departure from the work of those colleagues who only research a community for a brief period but do not live there permanently. The recognition of this difference connects us to common notions of citizenship, nationality and/or economic (class) interests that are not relevant to anthropologists who may spend months at a research site but do not have these fundamental affiliations or obligations to deal with.

Anthropologists as permanent residents, voters, military recruits and as tax-paying citizens should not be a novel idea: all of us as scholars and researchers encompass all these — at home. And that is our point. This may sound banal after two decades of reading Benedict Anderson, but nationality or ethnicity belong to what Balibar calls 'fictive' community affiliation (1999: 208) but which is not comparable to some sort of fictive citizenship. On the contrary, citizenship, even for as large an entity as the European Union, entails a state or a group of states to which one belongs, and anthropologists do reside in a state, a country, a region, a local community when not 'in the field'; others reside at home while 'in the field'. This presents equally interesting cases to analyse and we proudly declare that we are ready to engage in a new discussion about the pros and cons of this recognized if contested situatedness.

Situated Local Scholarship

There are very few volumes in which native and foreign researchers address the common pitfalls and advantages of their scholarship as well as citizenship. More often than not the former has been theorized in an uneven fashion, the latter being relegated to the pages of autobiographies. No accounts exist — as for instance the book by Ramet (2005) — which would compare accounts, events and theories of key issues, institutions and individuals from a diverse perspective. Decades have passed since the discourse of separation between 'Western' and 'native' scholars — and what they represent — took place in the late 1960s. At that time anthropological (known as *Völkerkunde*) and ethnographic (known as *Volkskunde*) orientations were highlighted as different research and theoretical approaches. However, as Honigsheim pointed out earlier (1942: 336–338), European anthropology had its distinctive features and track of development from American anthropology. These distinctions did not disappear, but only became more muted and slightly altered by three new strands: (1) neo-Marxist and materialist orientations stemming from the influence of the Frankfurt School; (2) the emergence of French structuralism and post-structuralism (largely the works of Lacan, Foucault, and Bourdieu); and (3) postmodernism. At the beginning of the third millennium it is not our purpose to rekindle any debates between the American and European traditions, nor the contestation between the Völkerkunde and Volksunde schools. Especially the second opposition is palpable in our region. We are aware of the persistent influence of German academic ethos reaching from the Rhine to Vladivostok which includes such coveted but hardly understandable procedures as Habilitation without which one is not recognized as a scholar and as apt to lecture at university level. Both Volkskunde and Völkerkunde brands however are comparatively small in numbers of adherents and marginal as to importance in all of the countries discussed in this volume. As Dunja Rihtman-Auguštin (1996: 102) has put it, writing about Croatian ethnology (but whose point could be well extended to East-Central European scholarship): small countries have small ethnographies (cf. Prica 2001). Could it be that this 'smallness' (in size and theory) has been one of the main reasons for the straightforward neglect of local enthnographies on the part of anthropologists writing in English, who dismiss almost everything published by local scholars as too particular (not to mention peculiar) to warrant serious attention? It is possible that this is what Michael Herzfeld had in mind when he described what he called the 'parochial statism of nationalistic ethnologies' (1987: 13). Naturally, to consider all European indigenous scholarship as such would be an overgeneralization. Yet it exists, and one wonders whether Mary Douglas's notion of 'dirt' (as matter out of place) is an apt concept to characterize such neglect. Moreover, it should be emphasized that it is not only in Eastern Europe that we find such peculiarities of the *Volkskunde* brand: in the West there are similar schools relegated today to ethnology and folkloristics (Stahl 1998).

Anthropological neglect often means a relegation of most studies as banal contributions within the *Volkskunde* tradition, as practised by local 'ethnographers' (Rihtman-Auguštin 2004). Meanwhile Western anthropologists accomplish their fieldwork 'by assuming the guise of an 'ethnographer'' (Hann 1987: 150). This is not exactly conducting 'anthropology at home'. This subject positioning adds considerable weight to the already poisoned antagonistic relationship (see for example Buchowski 1997: 8–12) that divides anthropologists and local practitioners. What seemed true in the 1980s seems to linger on today: Western anthropologists conduct empirical work in Eastern Europe because they are more able to understand the 'political realities' than native scholars (Hann 1987: 148). How naive! Long gone are the days when anthropologists claimed that they could go 'native', yet there continues to be a tendency in Eastern Europe to claim that foreign anthropologists bring new and different knowledge that is not (readily?) available to native scholars. Recently an enlivened exchange took place between Buchowski and Hann in the pages of the *Anthropology of East Europe Review*, a non-refereed journal published in the U.S. mostly by graduate students and post-doctorates (Buchowski 2004; Hann 2005). Hann accused Buchowski of insufficient quality of fieldwork and found his allegations of Western self-righteous writing on Eastern Europe indefensible. One would like to know how this charge would stand up against the local anthropological tradition of the Ljubljana kind?

Obviously, debates between native and foreign anthropologists are not special to Eastern and Central European scholarly discussion: several regions are also known for debating such paradoxes. In Indian sociology the concerns with conducting anthropology at home have offered detailed and often heated debates in academic communities (Peirano 1998: 115). Current debates launched by the journal of *Critique of Anthropology* and electronic journal *World Anthropologies Network* contrast the dominant 'Franglus'[French, British, American] anthropology with the variety of world anthropologies. The differences between anthropologists studying

Iceland from both an outsider and insider perspective are also well known (Hastrup 1996; Kristmundsdóttir 1996). Similarly, such dialogue has been instigated by Greek and non-Greek anthropologists with regard to the 'discovery' of Greece and Macedonia as an ethnographic paradise since the 1950s (e.g., Agelopoulos 2003; Argyrou 1998; Bakalaki 1997; Gefou-Madianu 1993; for non-Greek anthropologists see Campbell 1992; Cowan 1990; Herzfeld 2004; Hirschon 1998). Then, of course, there are those 'halfies', to use the phrase introduced by Lila Abu-Lughod (1991:141), or 'hybrids' as Narmala Halstead referred to her own position (2001: 310): those in-between anthropologists who are of native origin but who live outside their nation state and do not have an everyday communication with their subject/object of study. For instance, studies by anthropologists of mainland European background from the U.S., the U.K. and Australia are numerous (e.g., Baldassar 2001; Karakasidou 1997; Loizos 1975, Serementakis 1991).

Noteworthy also is a special position of returnee anthropologists, who, after living, training and working abroad for quite a while, often in countries with strong anthropological traditions, return home for good, often in order to promote sociocultural anthropology in their country of origin. Such is the case for the two editors of this collection, as well as that of Hana Červinková and Vytis Čiubrinskas. Červinková, however, did not really return home after the completion of her fieldwork 'at home', as she subsequently made her life across the Czech border, in neighbouring Poland, while often visiting her family and friends in the Czech Republic. Still another case is that of Alexandra Bitušíková who grew up, trained and worked in Slovakia but subsequently moved to the West from where she continues monitoring developments in her native country.

For the 'insiders', the dangers of knowing everything, or taking our own culture at face value and being immersed into the daily existence of our population, are immense. Often we are viewed with suspicion by foreign colleagues because of our seeming superiority complex for 'knowing it all'. Moreover, outsider anthropologists feel that they must deconstruct this knowledge and the 'taken-for-granted' world of native scholars (Halstead 2001: 310).

Clifford Geertz's famous dictum – that "the anthropologist is a member, however marginal, of the world's more privileged classes " (2000: 31) – and the poststructuralist and postmodern turn in anthropology, means studying at home and being at home are rather different concepts today than before (Peirano 1998). The first study of 'home' still meant that American and French or British anthropologists studied Europe, mostly Western Europe (Jackson 1987). Obviously, there is no simplistic insider/outsider divide, locating the foreign anthropologists in outright opposition to native ethnographers. This is also because native ethnographers either changed by self-educating themselves into the champions of anthropology or decided to train, at least partially, in the style of western social or cultural anthropology. Such conversion is the case of another author in this volume, Zdeněk Uherek, who became an adherent of social anthropology via his studies of culturology and his association with Ernest Gellner during the latter's Prague period (1993–95). Uherek, at the same time, works successfully within the idiom of *národopis*-type 'ethnology' which remains the ruling paradigm in his Prague workplace, where he moreover fulfils the position of director.[1]

Clearly, we do not hold that a globetrotting anthropologist is a viable model these days (even though the phrase 'multi-sited fieldwork' is in vogue). Similarly, nobody among us would accept that sitting in the office all day reading internet information is sufficient to write about one's own society any more. One of the fundamental differences in our argument from the one that Chris Hann offers (Hann 2002, 2005) has to do with fieldwork in the more classical sense of the term. Hann urges young anthropologists to conduct fieldwork away from home, a nice but somewhat questionable proposition especially in light of the economic and financial difficulties involved in the largely homogenized and still state-controlled East-Central European academy. Mortgaged to the romantic idea of fieldwork he defines this as 'at least one full year in a single "community" that is small enough for one to get to know it extremely well, "from the inside"' (2002: 14). A year? Small community? To know extremely well? From the inside? Surely these only scratch the surface of Malinowskian functionalism, or to use another well-known phrase the 'fetishism of fieldwork' (Boon 1982: 5). The more serious problem has to do with the notion 'from the inside' and 'one year' for this is at the heart of what separates native scholars and Western fieldworkers. As local scholars we live the everyday realities from the inside, our foreign colleagues only experience this for the duration of their fieldwork. Moreover, they leave the field after the research period expires, sometimes never returning. Surely, anthropologists working today are free to choose multi-sited fieldwork locations (itself not an idea to be thrown out), or simply abandon their previously studied communities in order to embark upon completely different projects on the other side of the globe. But those living and working at home do not only live with their informants for nine to twelve months but share a life-long commitment as co-nationals, citizens and tax-payers. Sometimes we have extended family relations in the field, and sometimes these relatives assist in conducting fieldwork, an element that may be part of the fieldwork of those 'halfies' discussed above.

We are more than just visitors and our responsibilities lie elsewhere: as anthropologists we must be serious enough about what we study or want to achieve with the data collected. This involves both the local community we study as well as the academic community within which we work. To work with locals who are co-nationals goes one step beyond the usual sympathy and empathy with which foreign colleagues approach their informants. They have more empathy than is called for, we may have less than is needed. Yet foreign colleagues may not have the will to assist local knowledge, or engage in local politics, an aspect of our existence we can hardly avoid. As Ulf Hannerz suggests, authors of 'macro-scenarios' (political scientists, sociologists, international relations specialists) do not pay much attention to each others' materials (Hannerz 2003: 174), but – even more severe – foreign anthropologists do not seem to care much about the miniscule details of ethnographies that we as local scholars may hold precious. Such symbiosis hardly exists. Is it worth adding that, first of all and above all, they do not pay any attention to local ethnological theories and discourses among indigenous scholars? Are these details or intimate knowledge what makes us so dangerous that our foreign colleagues in the West have to simply disregard or marginalize us? Buchowski clearly states: 'Western anthropological publications on CEE [i.e.Central and Eastern Europe] show a remarkable shortage of references to local ethnographies, not to mention theories' (2004: 6). Similarly, the Slovene anthropologist, Rajko Muršič, argues that foreign anthropologists rarely consider the work of Central and Eastern European scholars 'worth reading, turning instead to the works of historians or political scientists' (2005: 8).

Therefore, some words are in order to qualify the notions of margins and indigenousness as categories of separation. Neither of them is well received these days as both are laden profusely with diverse semantic associations that beg further definitions and explanations. We use 'margin' to ask further questions not only about periphery per se but also about centrality and the relation between them. By margins it is meant that interconnectedness and complicity must be brought to the surface, that the notion of centre and margin is not identical with importance and meaninglessness, that they are not about genuineness and falsity. Neither does this dichotomy stand for stability and fragility, powerlessness and exploitation. On the contrary, from our perspective marginality shifs both in time and space, it is conceptualized as a continuum between two poles of the same line. Similarly, centre and centrality are also notions that travel.

But marginality has another, much less kind, meaning attached. Since the early 1970s, social anthropology started on the bumpy road of turning toward Europe (Boissevain and Friedl 1975), or coming 'part-way home' to use the pioneering phrase of John Cole (1977). This redirection, prompted largely by the decreasing accessibility of former colonies, pushed some scholars to work in Europe. These erstwhile Africanists or Americanists were influential in creating a subdiscipline, the social anthropology of Europe (Boissevain 1975). As this field of study resulted in more and more legitimate ethnographies and as fresh ideas emerged, other anthropologists were forced to realize that they had to take Europe and Europeanists more seriously.

However, there was a less welcome side effect: namely, an emerging hierarchy between the often quite pleasant, Western and Southern part of Europe more suitable for research and the backward and ideologically dangerous East (and of course Africa, or Latin America). Europe was pretty much a buzzword among anthropologists visiting the fashionable Mediterranean areas for research: for them 'home' meant Europe from a

Western perspective (Jackson 1987). A few did turn towards Eastern and Central Europe but it was a drop in the ocean compared to the outpouring of anthropological monographs on Western and Southern Europe. Interestingly, this turn also resulted in high-level theorizing concerning oral poetry, music and folklore, areas of inquiry which especially highlighted the Balkan region (Lord 1995; Rice 1994; Sugarman 1997). Consequently, another hierarchy has developed between the visiting foreign anthropologists and native scholars: local scholars have acted as guides and informants to 'legitimate' anthropologists visiting from the 'West,' mostly from the U.S. and the U.K. Little or no ideas that offered alternatives to Western anthropological theories were allowed to surface in publications resulting from these trips. Western theories were confirmed, and confirmed too was the idea that Eastern European ethnographers had no serious theories to offer. Thus, local scholars became second-class anthropologists and their data only made it into the bibliographies or in the acknowledgement sections of major Western monographs. If at all. Actually, we now need to consider seriously the rights of intellectual property because 'much indigenous knowledge is appropriated yet not compensated for' (Carneiro da Cunha 1998: 113). More than that, European anthropology of the 'other kind' – similarly to other less known traditions around the world, as Krotz rightly argues (2006: 233–234) – should not be thought of simply as 'echoes' or 'replicas' of dominant and hegemonic Western anthropology, but rather as anthropological traditions in their own right, mortgaged to specific political, cultural and academic milieu.

Local scholars are made to feel even more inferior when they are compared to scholars from centres of knowledge, or when visiting such centres. In these, British or French theories are continually rehashed in addition to home-grown theories. As more and more of these are being reproduced in different monographs and edited works, many of us feel the need in our own work to repeat these: otherwise we are not considered scholarly. It is not that scholars working in Eastern Europe are openly told to reproduce American or Western theories, but somehow they still feel the pressure to live up to the model accepted, produced and published by colleagues in the West.

Living and working on the margins entails some embarrassing facts. Some international connections do exists and multi-authored works and international conferences attest to the success of such collaborative ventures (e.g., Gingrich and Fox 2002; Dyck and Archetti 2003; Verdery and Humphrey 2004). Not one of these edited collections, however, has a co-editor from the marginalized Eastern parts of Europe! Buchowski (2004: 7) argues similarly with reference to four edited American volumes published between 1999 and 2001 (2004: 7). Alternatives are few and far between (see, e.g., Buchowski, Conte and Nagengast 2001; Pink, Kürti and Afonso 2004).

The marginalization of scholars from Eastern and Central Europe is not only confined to co-edited works. Major journals published in anthropology

– *Annual Review of Anthropology, American Ethnologist, Identities, Journal of the Royal Anthropological Institute, American Anthropologist* and *Anthropological Forum* – suffer from a similar myopia. The last three, for example, do not even have international editorial or advisory boards. For the journal *Identities*, places inside Europe other than the U.K. simply do not exist. Such an exclusivist approach to scholarship is also the hallmark of journals such as *Anthropological Theory* and *Critique of Anthropology*. It could be argued that many of these journals are American, British or Australian and that is the reason for the sole presence of American, British or Australian editors. But who would agree that in today's climate of global scholarship such an argument remains tenable? The morbid fact is that these and a host of other lesser known journals function without the acknowledgement of Central and Eastern European anthropologists and their contribution to anthropological scholarship. In this respect *Critique of Anthropology* is interesting for more than one reason: it purports to be a European journal but without the inclusion of Eastern European scholars on the editorial board. Nevertheless it boasts about fifteen anthropologists from the U.S. (five from the City University of New York alone!)

To counter such an imbalance of knowledge production, there are other European journals, namely *Social Anthropology*, published by the European Association of Social Anthropologists, *Ethnos, Focaal. European Journal of Anthropology* (edited in Holland but published by Berghahn Books in the U.K.), and *AJEC* (Anthropological Journal of European Cultures). These notable exceptions may be congratulated for all having a (token?) individual from the eastern part of Europe on their international editorial board. But tokenism can and should be questioned just like overt marginalization, and conscious or unconscious manipulation. There is no question that the U.S. is the single largest knowledge production economy in anthropology at the moment but its overwhelming presence on the global anthropological market is worrying to say the least. It is true that the sheer size of the U.S. publishing industry and number of practising anthropologists is immense. All this is supported by one of the largest academic industries in the world with over 3,200 universities and colleges. In Europe, the number of anthropology departments in the United Kingdom, France, Scandinavia and Germany far outweigh the number of departments in East-Central or Southeastern Europe. Although not as large as their U.S. counterparts, knowledge centres nevertheless exist in Europe, such as the Max Planck Institute for Social Anthropology in Halle/Saale, the Ecole des Hautes Etudes en Sciences Sociales in Paris, and others in the U.K. and elsewhere. Why such centres do not or cannot exist in Eastern or Southeastern Europe is not a question our colleagues in the West would want to consider. Barely a tenth of the membership of the European Association of Social Anthropologists hails from the formerly communist part of Europe.

No doubt this regional weight is a considerable ideological force that cannot easily be pushed aside. Yet there must be some reasons why – despite the developments of the past fifteen years – such a deep-seated territorial division continues to exist in a discipline championing cross-culturalism, comparison, and siding with the underdog. A few years ago there was a faint attempt on the part of Central European University management in Budapest, Hungary, to invite anthropologists from Europe and North America to discuss the feasibility of a newly implemented program in sociocultural anthropology. More or less, the program was installed but the many useful ideas of the participants fell on deaf ears: the program is based on Western scholars offering courses on short-term or part-time contracts to East European students. Not exactly a novel idea.

From the Baltic to the Balkans, we as local scholars must face the dilemma of either trying to fit into the hierarchy set by colleagues who are at the forefront of organizing workshops and conferences, and produce volumes on particular topics, or face the harsh realities of attempting to do the same on our own. The rate of success benefits the former as funding and support for conferences organized in the East largely arrive from the West. Eastern and Central European scholars can only be participants in EU-funded programs as second-class citizens because their involvements in these programs are reduced to a minium. The best they can hope for is a researcher status in a multinational project that has been successfully implemented by a Western project leader.

We are aware of the recently launched world-wide discussion about the hierarchies of knowledge in anthropology, the dominant and marginal anthropologies (Yamashita, Bosco and Eades 2004; *World Anthropologies Network*, an electronic journal coming out since 2005; Ntarangwi, Mills and Babiker 2006; Ribeiro and Escobar 2006; *Anthropological Journal of European Cultures*, 16[1], 2007). We anthropologists living and working in Central and Eastern Europe feel part of the inequities within anthropology and have tried to contribute to this discussion. One of our authors, Michal Buchowski, has even started one fairly hot exchange with Chris Hann which attracted interest in Europe and beyond (Buchowski 2004; Hann 2005). Another was the article by Hann on the future of anthropology in Eastern Europe which called forth a vivid response by a host of anthropologists who are at home in the region (Hann 2007).

In terms of publishing projects, most of us working in the eastern half of Europe must realize that our projects, when published in our native tongues, can hardly if ever receive credit from outside a small scholarly community within the national boundary. Given the marginalized state of anthropology, many do not even get any recognition within their own academic community. There are many reasons for this. One has to do with the fact that anthropology, as recent collections testify (Baiburin and Kelly 2004; Dracklé, Edgar and Schippers 2003; Dracklé and Edgar 2004; Skalník 2002), has, especially in former Eastern-bloc countries, been a newly emerging discipline carving out with great difficulty its well-deserved space in the often bureaucratic hegemonic academic environment.

The other, a more deeply fundamental problem, is the scholarly division that exists in European academes caused by the political divide plaguing the new democracies of the East. An added feature is the half-hearted assistance of visitors from the West who either do not or do not want to understand the serious divisions between schools, research institutions and national academies. Recognition often occurs at a cost: we have to travel to these knowledge centres and participate in activities not of our own making.

Naturally, an argument could be made that recognition would be more forthcoming and more rapid if we would care to publish in English, something which is becoming more and more a conventional norm (e.g.,, Torsello and Pappová 2003; Skalník 2000, 2002, 2005; Baer 2003; Buchowski 1996, 1997, 2001; Brunnbauer 2004; Červinková 2006; Čolović 2002; Genov 2004; Guy, Uherek and Weinerová 2004). The problem of linguistic hegemony in international anthropological scholarship that many of us face is simple: publish in English or perish. This places a double burden on us even though we are forced to realize the necessity of this unnatural state of affairs. There could be another way to counter such 'Third Worldism' by switching to the German-speaking anthropological tradition (see e.g., Hauschild 2003 Kokot and Dracklé 1996). But is this really an option? German colleagues too are operating within the English-speaking publishing and research market and they are similarly involved with carving out an identity of their own. The only option is switching to the Anglo-American anthropological tradition, and begging for recognition. This, however, is hindered by a three-pillared system that is firmly established throughout the former Eastern bloc countries. 1) the extremely atomized national scholarly communities existing in isolation; 2) the limited number of national funding agencies with their powerful insider and outsider expert bodies; and 3) the existence of centralized state apparatuses with their various highly bureaucratic organizations.

In Central and East European countries, scholars must produce locally because in the eyes of this three-pillared system knowledge is still locally produced (in the local language), used and funded as well as recognized. A further difficulty is that more often than not the prime movers of this three-pillared system are selected from the same core group: thus the same individuals are responsible for the accreditation system (i.e. what may be taught by whom), decisions concerning the academic labour market, and advancement within the university system. Moreover, many of them are connected to the moguls of academic media empires who both monitor and enjoy public media support. In the tiny, and since 1990 even smaller, countries of the East, such as Lithuania, the Czech Republic, Croatia, Estonia, Slovakia, or Slovenia, these national power-bodies consist of not more than just a few dozen individuals (Muršič 2005: 10). Even in relatively larger countries, such as Poland, Hungary, Romania or Bulgaria, the academic environment is regulated by those power–holders, who are intricately connected to each other and battling over the same resources.

It is difficult but necessary to admit: openness, democracy and multi-party systems in politics, now all essential ingredients anchored in the constitutions of postsocialist democracies, did not take root in the academic communities across the region. Moreover, opening more universities and the establishment of new research institutions – many with Western aid such as the Central European University and the Habsburg Research Institution in Hungary – did not result in a more progressive and liberal scholarly climate for the general educational milieu. It is a question whether the Bologna process will eventually change all this in the long run or, on the contrary, cement the existing inequities of the already atomized national academic communities.

There is a difficulty as well with regard to the production of new ideas and areas of interests by disciplines akin to anthropology. In cultural, gender, transnational, media and ethnic studies more and more volumes are being published (Buchli 1999; Crowley and Reid 2002; Pilkington 2002; Roman 2003; Forreser, Zaborowska and Gapova 2004), relegating anthropology to a mere collection of cultural curiosities, out of synch with the postmodern mainstream by exoticizing cultural aspects of social life out of all proportion. At the same time, more and more anthropologists feel the sneed to publish in these collections for the lack of better possibilities which are closed off from them for the reasons mentioned above.

Against this it is necessary to argue that the flow of anthropological theories of socialist and postsocialist societies is still overwhelmingly unbalanced and unidirectional. Therefore, marginality here serves to subvert high-level theorization that emanates from the West, a unidirectionality that has already been noticed (Kürti 2000). Unfortunately, others, even those who are more prone to understand the colonialist ideology embedded in this, may also fall (consciously? unconsciously?) into this trap. Hann, for instance, urges young East European anthropologists as follows: 'Those attracted to the new styles of anthropology coming from the West may want to apply their new models to their home society, in order to highlight the novelty of their approaches as compared with the older national ethnographer' (Hann 2002: 14). Would it be possible that U.S. and British colleagues might 'realize' that there are 'new styles of anthropology' already existing here, and we do not necessarily have to be 'attracted' to models and theories emanating from the West? To continue this line of reasoning: would it be possible to envision a situation in which U.S. and 'Western' colleagues begin their theoretical discussions by highlighting the works of local scholars (more often than not written in native languages) before they turn to the usual and fashionable practice of name dropping and elite theorizing? The acknowledgements provided to local assistance and scholarly help in the preface of monographs produced in different parts of the world are noteworthy, but still a minute part of the work published, which relegates local knowledge and scholarship to the margins at best.

Debates about the differences between the scholarship of foreign and native anthropologists are not novel. We do accept that researchers can be both, or alternatively they can transcend these categories altogether. In fact, working at home – whether in Hungary, Poland, Romania or Slovenia – we as researchers also have to qualify ourselves in the eyes of those we study, and we have to define and redefine our subject and object of study not only for them, but also for friends, relatives and local bureaucrats or policemen. Yet, and there is a validity in this claim, in working at home as one local among many we may select aspects of the community not found in other anthropological narratives. Empathy, sympathy or antipathy is all part of our everyday proceedings but anyone who lives and works in a community may feel more responsibility as a citizen and tax-payer from those who are neither. With the fundamental transformation of life-worlds in the twenty-first century, even in a small town of ten thousand there may be firms, institutions, subcultures and networks that are unfamiliar to a university-educated intellectual from a nearby town. The notion of home, as Moore argues (2004: 81), is always transformed. If this is so, and there is no reason to think otherwise, then it is exactly this problem foreign anthropologists need to understand with regard to the native scholar in a local setting. In some context, he or she may feel quite an outsider – distanced by gender, ethnic, class or religious difference. But anthropologists know well that, in order to conduct research, distance is experienced not only in terms of actual miles. Even as a citizen of the same country, a researcher cannot wear a mask twenty-four hours a day. He or she must realize that as a researcher he or she needs to evaluate and negotiate identity with others in his or her local community. This negotiation is based on different understanding from that of a foreign scholar. In this sense then the idea of a 'native' scholar may blur real divisions between those who study and those who are studied. Politically, to play the marginal/native card may be dangerous, but at the same time not taking cognizance of it is outright silly. It is certainly a challenging task, but one of the challenges we are ready to accept.

If anything, as scholars of these case studies, we raise important issues with regard to our own societies, some critical, others more positive, but never losing sight of the possibility that we too are part of the society that we wish to reform and see developing in the future. All too often, negative and stereotypical examples abound but rarely do we meet analyses that manage a healthier balance. We also believe that the case studies published here point to new departures that frame our topics in more substantiated and local perspectives than those afforded by scholars not living and working in the societies studied. This belief – if agreed on by some of us – should be critically grounded in our perspectives and case studies. Alternative voices are also welcome but they too need to be theorized overtly instead of leaving them muted or submerged in our narratives. This edited volume offers perspectives by anthropologists living and working at home who are well situated to offer first-hand accounts of ongoing current processes in their societies, but who are also familiar with, if not enchanted by, theories and models offered by colleagues do not make part of the society they study.

This collective work aims to balance the rather unfortunate view that scholars living and working in their own countries must necessarily be at a disadvantage. This is based on a literary and theoretical inferiority complex, however defined, if compared with those scholars living and researching in the 'West', however this notion is defined. While it may be true that our budget could well be an iota of that of our colleagues, that our institutions may suffer severe cutbacks or face extinction, and travel possibilities (despite the availability of passports) are limited by lack of funding, we do not think that all these setbacks warrant our second-class status in the global scholarly discourses that seem to favour non-Eastern European scholars. Despite this, or perhaps because of it, we are confident that the situation at hand could change drastically in the near future, an optimism based on the experience from other fields.

Thus, with this collection, our aim is to provide a critical but a fairly balanced picture of current developments in the other Europe by looking at social processes from below, from the perspective of local scholars. From the poor in Hungary to the youth in Slovenia, from the women in the new NATO army to migrant workers in Central Europe, citizens and transnational workers are finding new ways of wrestling with questions of money, identity and survival. These case studies show how people are responding differently to recent socioeconomic and political transformations. The important question to raise has already been proposed by Nairn and James (2004) when they ask how are we to understand new and old nations in the context of changes across the late twentieth century into the present? Our departure is that since the mid to late 1990s many former communist countries entered NATO, and since 2004 quite few became members of the EU as well. Others, however, remain outside and must wait. How do memberships in NATO and the EU affect these two sorts of countries? Are there any visible or hidden signs explaining these 'ins' and 'outs'? What have been the new processes and developments taking place in communities influenced by new governmental policies catering to the directives set by NATO, EU and others transnational players? Does membership and non-membership create a new regional and political division between them and how are these differences felt on the local level by the people we study? What are the results, if anything, of the wait-and-see tactics on the communities we study?

The Contributions

The chapters in this volume analyse cultural, political and socioeconomic aspects of selected countries in East Central Europe from the perspective of local scholars. The authors examine actions, institutions, and processes which they have observed on the local level but which have often been neglected in the larger anthropology of Europe produced by foreign scholars. Our aim with this collection of case studies is not to put a wedge between local and foreign scholarly production, but we do wish to deepen appreciation for the range of specificities and diversities available to us as both scholars and citizens of societies we live in and study at the same time. In the following chapters we offer a whole range of examples where we represent views of our co-nationals and their, as well as our own, experiences by including interview segments in our work.

One of the key concerns in this volume is to understand changing gender relations and gender roles following the collapse of the monolithic state socialist gender ideology and to examine what paths they have taken with the emerging economic and political situation. Červinková addresses this issue by focusing on the Czech military, in particular the ways in which men who have been serving in the Czech Air Force are now fully part of the NATO war-machine. For Červinková, 'In their displacement, the Czech Air Force officers merge with their Soviet planes and the socialist Air Force, indistinguishable from each other in their melancholic disappearance.'

In their chapter, Bitušíková and Koštialová dispel the traditional and stubbornly homogenizing notion that the new political climate has affected women only negatively while it has placed men in more advantageous economic and political positions. In the Slovak Republic, there are many female mayors, mostly in smaller settlements, but with a political motivation and power unmatched by men in similar political positions. Grażyna Kubica investigates gay and lesbian identity politics in traditionally Roman Catholic Poland in order to ask larger questions about scholarship, identity and gender. While traversing between critical anthropology and some kind of postmodern performative ethnography, she argues that as a native scholar her role has been 'to show support for gay and lesbian demands of respect and space in the public sphere', a motivation that carried her throughout her entire fieldwork. The result is a daring first-rate ethnography of Polish gay-rights activism, a topic also serving as a window of opportunity for her in teaching gender courses at her university.

Both Uherek and Čiubrinskas have taken a more global view as they investigate national as well as transnational phenomena in the Czech Republic and in Lithuania respectively. For Uherek, Czech labour relations have been altered by the influx of migrant labourers from neighbouring Ukraine. As expected, this new form of migration has caused mixed reactions in the majority population as Czechs view Ukrainians as mainly economic migrants and do not, as a rule, mix with them. Čiubrinskas's chapter is concerned with Lithuanianness both from the perspective of 'locals' and 'co-nationals' who return from the West to settle in Lithuania.

In contrast to Uherek and Čiubrinskas, Kürti begins with a smaller place – the town he now lives in and its environs, a place experiencing enormous political-economic change since the collapse of state socialism in 1990.

He focuses on the way in which family farming has been altered by the establishment of a Swiss meat-packing factory. His concern is to shed light on how this foreign company has brought new technology and agriculture to a region where agro-industry all but collapsed after that historic date. At the same time, he sees coeval alterations of local community life in the wake of successful capitalistic developments as a difficult but necessary path to follow.

By focusing on Polish privatization processes in agriculture, Michat Buchowski's contribution is also rooted in a specific locality – Dziekanowice, in the Wielkopolska region of Poland. He is concerned with property, privatization and reprivatization, terms that have undoubtedly become one of the most debated topics in the anthropology of postsocialist Europe in recent years.

Following in Kürti's steps, Gabriel Stoicu focuses on the ways in which Romanian and French workers have experienced industrial restructuring at the local level. Romanian workers, similarly to Kürti's Hungarian rabbit farmers, opt for secure employment instead of quick and easy money to be made. Yet, both in Hungary and in Romania, economic reorganization of former state firms and the creation of new foreign companies offer diverse, often contradictory, labour relations and practices for workers.

Rajko Muršič reminds us of the fragile anthropological enterprise, especially in its East-Central European setting, as he searches for an alternative or, in his term, punk anthropology. As a proud local scholar and an experimental musician himself, he offers a comprehensive view of the Slovenian situation by focusing on the vibrant aspect of youth musical subculture. His intervention suggests that the alternative music scene – mentioned profusely in most case studies produced by foreign scholars since the 1980s – is still alive and well in some parts of the postsocialist world today.

The transformation of the political scenery is explored by Peter Skalník, who looks at the contrasting images of democracy and pluralism in the Czech Republic. Questioning the homogenizing notion of political culture, Skalník's investigation leads him to a bleak conclusion: 'that whereas local politics is actively embraced because it is based on individual qualities of local public figures, the national and to some extent urban politics is devoid of participation of citizens/voters.' In contrast to the findings of many foreign or local observers, who argue that citizens' apathy has been ubiquitous and salient in postsocialist Europe, Skalník reveals that an increasing cleavage has emerged in Czech society between generations as well as rural and urban citizens. A similar but a somewhat more pessimistic conclusion is reached by Terézia Nagy, who finds that the postsocialist era has started with an awkward twist in Hungary. Based on her fieldwork among the homeless in Szeged, a large town at the southernmost tip of Hungary, she shows that the country is mortgaged to the heritage of state socialism with the survival of old, or 'hidden poverty', a phrase used since the 1970s to describe the real but ideologically unrecognized army of the poor. At the same time, the 1990s created a new phenomenon, or 'new poverty', a destitute and marginalized group of people created by unemployment, homelessness, the welfare system or drug abuse. As always, timing here is crucial: the more time the homeless spend on the streets, the less possibility they have to reintegrate themselves into mainstream society.

It is obvious that in our volume these case-studies, oscillating between cautious optimism and tamed pessimism, provide a slice of daily life in postcommunist East-Central Europe that we have not experienced before. Poverty, gender and class divides, political and cultural antagonisms, are by no means unexpected or necessary consequences of any major transformation of the scale experienced in the countries of the former Soviet bloc. As local scholars, we are well aware of our task: to build better, more equal and more humane societies while we pursue specific goals within our discipline. This is one of the ways to remain true to our vocational and citizenship vows.

Notes

1. For a well-informed discussion of ethnographic traditions in Czechoslovakia, the German Democratic Republic, Hungary and Poland as they developed and changed during the 'socialist era', see Hann, Sárkány and Skalník (2005).

References

Abu-Lughod, L. 1991. 'Writing against Culture', in R. Fox (ed.) *Recapturing Anthropology: Working in the Present*. Santa Fe, NM: School of American Research Press, pp.137–62.

Agelopoulos, G. 2003. 'Life among Anthropologists in Greek Macedonia', *Social Anthropology* 11(2): 249–64.

Anthropological Journal of European Cultures, 16[1], 2007. Oxford: Berghahn.

Argyrou, V. 1998. *Tradition and Modernity in the Mediterranean: The Wedding as Symbolic Struggle*. Cambridge: Cambridge University Press.

Baer, M. 2003. *Women's Spaces: Class, Gender and the Club. An Anthropological Study of the Transitional Processes in Poland*. Wrocław: Wydawnictwo Uniwersytetu Wrocławskiego.

Baiburin, A. and C. Kelly (eds). 2004. *Cultural Anthropology: The State of the Field*. St. Petersburg: Russian Academy of Sciences.

Bakalaki, A. 1997. 'Students, Natives, Colleagues. Encounters in the Academy and in the Field', *Cultural Anthropology* 12: 502–26.

Baldassar, L. 2001. *Visits Home: Migration Experiences between Italy and Australia*. Melbourne: Melbourne University Press.

Balibar, E. 1999. 'Is European Citizenship Possible', in J. Holston (ed.) *Cities and Citizenship*. Durham, NC: Duke University Press, pp.195–215.

Baumann, G. and A. Gingrich (eds). 2004. *Grammars of Identity/Alterity*. Oxford: Berghahn.

Bitušíková, A. 1996. 'A Brief History of the Jewish Community in Banská Bystrica', *Ročník* 44(2): 202–11.

Boissevain, J. 1975. 'Introduction: Towards a Social Anthropology of Europe', in J. Boissevain and J. Friedl (eds), *Beyond the Community: Social Process in Europe*. The Hague: Government Printing and Publishing Office, pp. 9–18.

Boissevain, J. and J. Friedl (eds). 1975. *Beyond the Community: Social Process in Europe*. The Hague: University of Amsterdam by the Department of Education Science of the Netherlands.

Boon, J. 1982. *Other Tribes, Other Scribes: Symbolic Anthropology in the Comparative Study of Cultures, Histories, Religions and Texts*. Cambridge: Cambridge University Press.

Borneman, J. (ed.) 2004. *Death of the Father: An Anthropology of the End of Political Authority*. Oxford: Berghahn.

Brunnbauer, U. (ed.) 2004. *(Re)Writing History: Historiography in Southeast Europe after Socialism*. Münster: LIT.

Buchli, V. 1999. *An Archeology of Socialism*. Oxford: Berg.

Buchowski, M. 1996. 'The Shifting Meanings of Civil and Civic Society in Poland', in C. Hann (ed.) *Civil Society: Challenging Western Models*. London: Routledge, pp.79–98.

———. 1997. *Reluctant Capitalists: Class and Culture in a Local Community in Western Poland*. Berlin: Centre Marc Bloch.

———. 2001. *Rethinking Transformation: An Anthropological Perspective on Postsocialism*. Poznan: ABEDIK.

———. 2004. 'Hierarchies of Knowledge in Central-Eastern European Anthropology', *Anthropology of East Europe Review* 22(2): 5–14.

Buchowski, M., E. Conte and C. Nagengast (eds). 2001. *Poland Beyond Communism: 'Transition' in Critical Perspective*. Fribourg: Fribourg University Press.

Busch, B. and H. Kelly-Holmes (eds). 2004. *Language, Discourse and Borders in the Yugoslav Successor States*. Clevedon: Multilingual Matters Ltd.

Campbell, J. (ed.) 1992. *Europe Observed*. London: St. Martin's Press.

Carneiro da Cunha, M. 1998. 'Exploitable Knowledge belongs to the Creators of It: A Debate', *Social Anthropology* 6(1): 111–15.

Červinková, H. 2006. *Playing Soldiers in Bohemia: An Ethnography of NATO Membership*. Prague: Set Out.

Cole, J. 1977. 'Anthropology Comes Part-way Home: Community Studies in Europe', *Annual Review of Anthropology* 6: 349–78.

Čolović, I. 2002. *The Politics of Symbol in Serbia: Essays in Political Anthropology*. Trans. C. Hawkesworth. London: Hurst.

Cowan, J. 1990. *Dance and the Body Politic in Northern Greece*. Princeton: Princeton University Press.

Crowley, D. and S. Reid (eds). 2002. *Socialist Spaces. Sites of Everyday Life in the Eastern Bloc*. Oxford: Berg.

Čiubrinskas, Vytis. 2004. 'Transnational Identity and Heritage: Lithuania Imagined, Constructed and Contested', in U. Kockel and C. Máiréad (eds) *Communicating Cultures*. Münster: LIT, pp.42–66.

Dracklé, D., I. Edgar and T. Schippers (eds). 2003. *Educational Histories of European Social Anthropology*. Oxford: Berghahn.

Dracklé, D. and I. Edgar (eds). 2004. *Current Policies and Practices in European Social Anthropology Education*. Oxford: Berghahn.

Drulák, P. (ed.) 2001. *National and European Identities in EU Enlargement*. Prague: Institute of International Relations.

Dubinskas, F. 1983. 'Leaders and Followers: Cultural Patterns and Political Symbolism in Yugoslavia', *Anthropological Quarterly* 56(2): 95–99.

Dyck, N. and E. Archetti (eds). 2003. *Sport, Dance and Embodied Identities.* Oxford: Berg.

Feldman, L., I. Prica and R. Senjković (eds). 1993. *Fear, Death, and Resistance: An Ethnography of War: Croatia 1991–1992.* Zagreb: Institute of Ethnology and Folklore Research.

Forreser, S., M. Zaborowska and E. Gapova (eds). 2004. *Over the Wall/After the Fall: Post-Communist Cultures through an East-West Gaze.* Bloomington: Indiana University Press.

Gefou-Madianu, D. 1993. 'Mirroring Ourselves through Western Texts: The Limits of an Indigenous Anthropology', in H. Driessen (ed.) *The Politics of Ethnographic Reading and Writing: Confrontations of Western and Indigenous Views.* Saarbrucken: Verlag Breitenbach, pp. 160–77.

Geertz, C. 2000. *Available Light. Anthropological Reflections on Philosophical Topics.* Princeton: Princeton University Press.

Genov, N. (ed.) 2004. *Ethnic Relations in South Eastern Europe.* Münster: LIT.

Gillingham, J. 2003. *European Integration, 1950–2003.* Cambridge: Cambridge University Press.

Gingrich, A. 2004. 'Concepts of Race Vanishing, Movements of Racism Rising? Global Issues and Austrian Ethnography', *Ethnos* 69(2): 156–76.

Gingrich, A. and R. Fox (eds). 2002. *Anthropology by Comparison.* London: Routledge.

Goldberg, D. and A. Quayson (eds). 2002. *Relocating Postcolonialism.* Oxford: Blackwell.

Gready, P. (ed.) 2003. *Political Transition: Politics and Cultures.* London: Pluto Press.

Guy, W., Z. Uherek and R. Weinerová (eds). 2004. *Roma Migration in Europe: Case Studies.* Münster: LIT Verlag.

Halstead, N. 2001. 'Ethnographic Encounters: Positioning Within and Outside the Insider Frame', *Social Anthropology* 9(3): 307–22.

Hammond, A. (ed.) 2004. *The Balkans and the West: Constructing the European Other, 1945–2003.* Aldershot: Ashgate.

Hann, C. 1987. 'The Politics of Anthropology in Socialist Eastern Europe', in A. Jackson (ed.) *Anthropology at Home.* London: Tavistock, pp.139–53.

———. 2002. 'The anthropology of Eurasia in Eurasia.' Max Planck Institute for Social Anthropology Working Papers No. 57. Halle/Saale.

———. 2005. 'Correspondence: Reply to Michal Buchowski', *Anthropology of East Europe Review* 23 (1): 194–97.

Hann, C. 2007. *Anthropology's Multiple Temporalities and Its Future in East-Central Europe. A Debate.* (With comments by a number of scholars from Central and Eastern Europe and Hann's reply.) Max Planck Institute for Social Anthropology Working Paper No. 90. Halle. Originally published in a special issue of *Czech Sociological Review*, vol. 43(1), 2007.

Hann, C., M. Sárkány and P. Skalník (eds). 2005. *Studying Peoples in People's Democracies: Socialist Era Anthropology in East-Central Europe.* Münster: LIT Verlag.

Hannerz, U. 2003. 'Macro Scenarios: Anthropology and the Debate over Contemporary and Future Worlds', *Social Anthropology* 11(2): 169–88.

Hastrup, K. 1996. 'Anthropological Theory as Practice', *Social Anthropology* 4(1): 75–82.

Hauschild, T. 2003. *Magie und Macht in Italien.* Gifkendorf: Merlin Verlag.

Herrmann, R., T. Risse and M. Brewer (eds). 2004. *Transnational Identities: Becoming European in the EU.* Lanham, MD: Rowman and Littlefield.

Herzfeld, M. 1987. *Anthropology through the Looking-glass: Critical Ethnography in the Margins of Europe.* Cambridge: Cambridge University Press.

––––––. 2004. *The Body Impolitic: Artisans and Artifice in the Global Hierarchy of Value.* Chicago: University of Chicago Press.

Hirschon, R. 1998. *Heirs of the Greek Catastrophe.* Oxford: Berghahn.

Hohnen, P. 2003. *A Market Out of Place? Remaking Economic, Social, and Symbolic Boundaries in Post-communist Lithuania.* Oxford: Oxford University Press.

Honigsheim, P. 1942. 'The Philosophical Background of European Anthropology', *American Anthropologist* 44: 376–87.

Jackson, A. 1987. 'Reflections on Anthropology at Home and the ASA', in A. Jackson (ed.) *Anthropology at Home,* London: Tavistock, pp.1–15.

Jovanovič, M., K. Kaser and S. Naumovič (eds). 1999. *Between the Archives and the Field: A Dialogue on Historical Anthropology of the Balkans.* Graz: Institut für Geschichte der Universität Graz.

Kaneff, D. 2004. *Who Owns the Past? The Politics of Time in a 'Model' Bulgarian Village.* Oxford: Berghahn.

Karakasidou, A. 1997. *Fields of Wheat, Hills of Blood.* Chicago: University of Chicago Press.

Khittel, S., B. Plankensteiner and M. Six-Hohenbalken (eds). 2004. *Contemporary Issues in Socio-cultural Anthropology.* Wien: Löcker.

Kokot, W. and D. Dracklé. 1996. *Ethnologie Europas: Grenzen, Konflikte, Identitäten.* Berlin: Reimer.

Krasteva, A. (ed.) 1998. *Communities and Identities.* Sofia: Petekston.

Kristmundsdóttir, S. 1996. 'Culture Theory and Anthropology of Modern Iceland', *Social Anthropology* 4(1): 61–74.

Krotz, E. 2006. 'Towards Unity in Diversity in World Anthropology', *Critique of Anthropology* 26(2): 233–38.

Kundera, M. 1984. 'The Tragedy of Central Europe', *New York Review of Books,* 26 April.

Kuper, A. 1994. 'Culture, Identity and the Project of Cosmopolitan Anthropology', *Man* 29: 537–54.

Kürti, L. 2000. 'Uncertain Anthropology: Ethnography of Postsocialist Eastern Europe', *Ethnos* 65(3): 403–20.

––––––. 2001. *The Remote Borderland: Transylvania in the Hungarian Imagination.* Albany: State University of New York Press.

––––––. 2006. 'Symbolism and Drama within the Ritualisation of the Hungarian Parliament', in E. Crewe and M. Müller (eds), *Rituals in Parliaments.* Frankfurt am Main: Peter Lang, pp.41–64.

Loizos, P. 1974. *The Greek Gift: Politics in a Cypriot village.* Oxford: Blackwell.

Lord, A. 1995. *The Singer Resumes the Tale.* Ithaca: Cornell University Press.

Marks, L. 2004. 'Ban Josip Jelačić in Croatian Oral Legends: Between History and Myth', *Narodna Umjetnost* 41(1): 7–21.

Meštrović, M. (ed.) 2003. *Globalization and its Reflection on (in) Croatia.* New York: Global Scholarly Publications.

Moore, H. 2004. 'Global Anxieties: Concept-metaphors and Pre-theoretical Commitments in Anthropology', *Anthropological Theory* 4(1): 71–88.

Mudimbe-Boye, E. (ed.) 2002. *Beyond Dichotomies: Histories, Identities, Culture and the Challenge of Globalization.* Albany: State University of New York Press.

Muršič, R. 2005. 'Between Discursive Fitness and Parochialism', *Anthropology News,* 8 December, p.10

Müller, U. and H. Schultz (eds). 2002. *National Borders and Economic Disintegration in Modern East Central Europe.* Berlin: Arno Spitz.

Nairn, T. and P. James. 2004. *Global Matrix: Nationalism, Globalism and State-terrorism.* London: Pluto.

Neumann, I. 1999. *Uses of the Other: 'The East' in European Identity Formation.* Minneapolis: University of Minnesota Press.

Ntarangwi, M., D. Mills, and M. Babiker (eds). 2006. *African Anthropologies. History, Critique and Practice.* New York: Zed Books.

Peirano, M. 1998. 'When Anthropology Is at Home: The Different Contexts of a Single Discipline', *Annual Review of Anthropology* 27: 105–28.

Pilkington, H. et al. (eds). 2002. *Looking West? Cultural Globalization and Russian Youth Cultures.* University Park: Pennsylvania State University.

Pink, S., L. Kürti and A. Afonso (eds). 2004. *Working Images.* London: Routledge.

Prica, I. 2001. *Mala europska etnologija.* Zagreb: Golden Marketing.

Ramet, S. 2005. *Thinking about Yugoslavia.* Cambridge: Cambridge University Press.

Ramet, S. (ed.) 1998. *Eastern Europe: Politics, Culture, and Society since 1939.* Bloomington: Indiana University Press.

Rausing, S. 2004. *History, Memory, and Identity in Post-Soviet Estonia.* Oxford: Oxford University Press.

Reid, S. and D. Crowley (eds). 2000. *Style and Socialism: Modernity and Material Culture in Post-war Eastern Europe.* Oxford: Berg.

Ribeiro, G.L. and A. Escobar (eds). 2006. *World Anthropologies.* Oxford: Berg.

Rice, T. 1994. *May it Fill Your Soul: Experiencing Bulgarian Music.* Chicago: University of Chicago Press.

Rihtman-Auguštin, D. 1996. 'A National Ethnology, its Concepts and its Ethnologists', *Ethnologia Europaea* 26: 99–106.

——— . 2004. *Ethnology, Myth, and Politics: Anthropologizing Croatian Ethnology.* J. Capo Zmegac (ed.) Aldershot: Ashgate.

Roman, D. 2003. *Fragmented Identities: Popular Culture, Sex, and Everyday Life in Postcommunist Romania.* Lanham, MD: Lexington Books.

Sampson, S. 2002. "Weak States, Uncivil Societies and Thousands of NGOs." Western Democracy Export as Benevolent Colonialism in the Balkans." http://www.anthrobase.com/Txt/S/Sampson_S_01.htm. (accessed September 23, 2008).

Sassen, S. 1999. 'Whose City Is It? Globalization and the Formation of New Claims', in J. Holston (ed.) *Cities and Citizenship.* Durham, NC: Duke University Press, pp.177–95.

Savoniakaité, V. 2002. 'Traditional Textiles and Economic Development: Lithuanian Groups in Latvia's Border Regions', in U. Kockel (ed.) *Culture and Economy: Contemporary Perspectives*. Aldershot: Ashgate, pp.109–23.

Serementakis, N. 1991. *The Last Word: Women, Death and Divination in Inner Mani*. Chicago: University of Chicago Press.

Skalník, P. (ed.) 2000. *Sociocultural Anthropology at the Turn of the Century: Voices from the Periphery*. Prague: Set Out.

Skalník, P. (ed.) 2002. *A Post-Communist Millennium: The Struggles for Sociocultural Anthropology in Central and Eastern Europe*. Prague: Set Out.

Skalník, P. (ed.) 2005. *Anthropology of Europe. Teaching and Research*. Prague: Set Out.

Stahl, P. (ed.) 1998. *Name and Social Structure: Examples from Southeast Europe*. Trans. C. de Bussy. New York: Columbia University Press.

Sugarman, J. 1997. *Engendering Song: Singing and Subjectivity at Prespa Albanian Weddings*. Chicago: University of Chicago Press.

Svašek, M. (ed.) 2006. *Postsocialism. Politics and Emotions in Central and Eastern Europe*. New York – Oxford: Berghahn Books.

Torsello, D. and M. Pappová (eds). 2003. *Social Networks in Movement: Time, Interaction, and Interethnic Spaces in Central and Eastern Europe*. Dunajská Streda: Lilium Aurum.

Verdery, K. and C. Humphrey (eds). 2004. *Property in Question: Value Transformation in the Global Economy*. Oxford: Berg.

Yamashita, S., J. Bosco, and J.S. Eades, (eds). 2004. *The Making of Anthropology in East and Southeast Asia*. Oxford: Berghahn.

World Anthropologies Network. An electronic journal edited by WAN group. 2005– (three issues published thus far). www.ram-wan.org/e-journal

Chapter 2

Gender and Governance in Rural Communities of Postsocialist Slovakia

Alexandra Bitušíková and Katarína Koštialová

Postsocialist transformations in the countries of Central and Eastern Europe and the processes of European enlargement and integration have been accompanied by increasing involvement of women in decision making at all levels. During socialism, the emancipation of women in Slovakia was proudly proclaimed as one of the victories of the regime. Women's political and economic participation was high, but only because it was manipulated and controlled by the Communist Party. Quotas of thirty per cent for participation and representation of women in all political institutions from local to national levels were introduced, and celebrated by the dominant ideology as real proof of equality of women and men. This was part of communist policies aimed at equalization of all citizens and the elimination of all social distinctions including gender. After the fall of the Iron Curtain, the number of women in decision making dropped drastically, but since the 1990s, women's representation in civic and political life has been slowly increasing.

This chapter deals with the questions of women's participation in decision making by examining the example of female mayors in two rural communities in postsocialist Slovakia, a recently formed independent country where selected villages represent the most numerous administrative units in terms of size (less than 1,000 inhabitants)[1]. To place the role of women's representation in a broader societal context, in this study we combine data from the national level with ethnographies of everyday life in two communities. Ethnographic methods of face-to-face structured in-depth interviews, participant observation, media articles, archive materials and documents of non-governmental organizations, as well as quantitative data, are used in order to demonstrate the complex picture of reconstructing women's roles and status in postsocialism. The use of in-depth interviews as a main method has often been criticized in women's studies as exploitative (e.g., Cotterill 1992), but it still remains the main research method in ethnographies and when combined with other methods it may be one of the best ways to find out about people's everyday lives. According to Reinharz (1992), combining multiple research methods allows us to link individual stories and experience with wider social frameworks. Using various methods and data from macro- and micro-levels helps us to validate or redefine our theories.

Anthropological literature on postsocialist transition in Central and Eastern Europe has covered various topics and regions since 1989, but Slovakia has attracted the attention of foreign scholars less often than other countries. One of the reasons for this is that Slovakia is a young state that was only established in 1993 after the split of Czechoslovakia. It was usually known as the second half (and often as the second-class half) of former Czechoslovakia. After the separation from the Czech part, Slovakia was left without the famous city of Prague, and without the national flag and institutions: thus it had to start creating its own national symbols and images and promoting the country abroad. In addition, there is another reason for Slovakia's low presence in literature and media. Unlike, for example, Hungary or the Czech Republic, Slovakia does not have any strong and famous academic personalities of Slovak origin living abroad who would write about the country and put in on the map of the world. Last, but not least, Slovak ethnological/anthropological institutions do not create the necessary conditions for attracting well-known foreign scholars to Slovakia to carry out research or to cooperate in various research projects. As a result, Slovakia is often missing from research networks active in countries with strong anthropological traditions.

Postsocialist Slovakia is not well known in anthropological journals or books, and domestic anthropological/ethnological productions on postsocialism published in the Slovak language similarly marginalize the country. Slovak ethnologists still prefer to focus on pre-1989 or presocialist periods. In the main Slovak ethnological journal *Slovenský národopis* (*Slovak Ethnology*), only a few authors have published studies on the problems of post-1989 transformation (Danglová 2001; Krekovičová 1999, 2002; Podoba 2003), although research on various aspects of postsocialism in Slovakia has intensified in recent years (mainly to do with issues connected with forming and building the newly independent Slovakia, such as ethnicity and ethnic relations, identity, national symbols and myths, nationalism, etc.). Only a handful of Slovak ethnologists and anthropologists have published chapters in books written in English and edited by Western editors (e.g., Bitušíková 2000, 2002; Podoba 1998, 2000, 2005), but none of them has produced a monograph on postsocialist Slovakia in Slovak, English or any other language available to a larger international readership. Western anthropological productions on postsocialist Slovakia are also very sparse and in English-language books on the postsocialist transition which cover Slovakia, the most frequent topic seems to be ethnicity, often related to Hungarian and Roma minorities in Slovakia. Other topics such as gender appear sporadically. In Burawoy and Verdery's *Uncertain Transition* (1999), Andrew Lass writes about computerization of the Czech and Slovak library systems and sociocultural approaches towards reorganization in the early transition period, but this does not really reveal much information about Slovakia except for a few general comments. Skalník, who has worked in the Slovak village of Šuňava from 1970 onwards (Skalník 1979, 1986), has a chapter published in Hann's *Socialism – Ideals, Ideology and Social Practice* (1993) which discusses the reactions of north Slovak villagers to the changes shortly after the demise of communist rule in terms of inertia and continuity (Skalník 1993). Torsello and Pappová's *Social Networks in Movement* (2003) offer more studies concerning Slovakia but most of the authors deal with ethnic relations on the Slovak-Hungarian border (Arendas 2003; Danter 2003; Toth 2003; Szarka 2003; Liszka 2003), the Roma migration from Slovakia (Szep 2003; Weinerová 2003) or other issues such as trust (Torsello 2003). All the articles in the book that deal with the sensitive topic of Slovak-Hungarian ethnic relations are, moreover, written by Hungarian or Hungarian Slovak authors from a Hungarian point of view, quoting almost exclusively Hungarian literature, and arguments concerning the pre-Second World War borders and territories of the Hungarian Monarchy (Upper Hungary).[2] A rare example of a postsocialist monograph dealing with Slovakia is Torsello's *Trust, Property and Social Change in a Southern Slovakian Village* (2003), a book whose main objective is to study an important aspect of postsocialist transformation – property issues. He chooses a predominantly Hungarian-speaking village in southern Slovakia as the main locus of the research. He also uses mainly English and Hungarian literature and ignores numerous Slovak ethnographies written on villages in the same Slovak-Hungarian region. The work is original, rich and a well-written contribution to anthropology of postsocialism, but as an ethnography of a Hungarian-speaking village situated in Slovakia it offers yet another example of the interest of foreign anthropologists in Hungarian parts of Slovakia rather than in those Slovak regions which constitute a majority of the Slovak territory.

Gender has become one of the new research topics in postsocialist countries. Feminism and feminist discourse of any kind was not developed or discussed in the pre-1989 period. Any gender perspective during socialism was ideologized, and Western feminist theories were greeted with hostility. After 1989 numerous gender and women's studies projects dealing with Central and Eastern Europe emerged, and several monographs were published (e.g., Funk and Mueller 1993; Einhorn 1993; Gal and Kligman 2000; Haukanes 2001). Many misunderstandings appeared in the East-West feminist dialogue resulting from the different backgrounds and historic experiences on which Western and Eastern European women drew. Funk and Mueller's (1993) publication tried to overcome this problem by giving a large space to women writers from Eastern Europe. The collection includes studies on former Czechoslovakia and the postsocialist Slovak Republic (Heitlinger 1993; Kiczková and Farkašová 1993; Šiklová 1993). In other Western publications Slovakia has been sparsely mentioned – for example, in Gal and Kligman's (2000) edited volume Slovakia appears three times but in rather marginal comments. It is high time to challenge this one sidedness.

Women in Pre-1989 Slovak Society: Exploited or Emancipated?

For centuries, gender stereotypes have strongly influenced Slovak society. Traditional patriarchal family values strictly determined gender roles: women were placed in the private sphere, responsible for the care of children, household, family and religious life. They were not supposed to work or be involved in politics. Men were the main (often the only) breadwinners and the ones who were expected to enter the public sphere – the world of politics and public affairs. History, culture, religion and ethnicity have all had a big impact on gender roles, attitudes, norms and values. Slovakia was a part of the multi-ethnic Hungarian Monarchy for almost a thousand years. It was a rural area with a strong patriarchal family system and values. Roman Catholicism as the dominant religion defined women as submissive and family-oriented, and discouraged them from entering higher education or working outside the home. The situation was slightly different in Lutheran Protestant and Jewish families, where girls were often encouraged to complete secondary or even university education, especially from the second half of the nineteenth century onwards.

In 1918 Slovakia became a part of Czechoslovakia. Women's de jure equal political status was recognized and women's suffrage introduced in Czechoslovakia in 1919. As the only parliamentarian democracy in Central and Eastern Europe, the inter-war Czechoslovak Republic opened more opportunities for women and women's movements than other countries, partly because of the authority of the first president of Czechoslovakia, Tomas Garrigue Masaryk, who was an active promoter of women's equality and women's rights (Šiklová 1998: 34).[3]

During the socialist period (1948–1989), the equality of women and men was officially proclaimed in the constitution. Women were encouraged to enter the labour market, but this forced equality resulted in unequal working conditions (Regulska and Roseman 1998: 27). Women became an important part of an ideological attempt to create 'the new socialist man' and a source of cheap labour required by industrialization and the five-year economic plans. By the 1980s, almost fifty per cent of the work force in Czechoslovakia were women, which means that about ninety-four per cent of Czech and Slovak women were employed (Šiklová 1993: 75), most of them full time. While becoming an economic force visible in the public sphere, women's full responsibility for household and family remained unchanged.

The positive side of this process which is often underestimated was that giving work to women went hand in hand with the rise of their social rights and education. Employment for all women, a guaranteed job for every mother after a long maternity leave, extensive social benefits, and free and accessible services for all families with children, created prime conditions for the new independence of women. In terms of education, more women in Czechoslovakia completed higher education than men in the 1970s-1980s, much earlier than women in Western European countries.

As with other socialist countries, the political participation of women in Slovakia (Czechoslovakia) was high, but formal and ineffective as a result of the hegemony of the dominant ideology and Communist Party top-down control. There were a few women Communist Party members in top political positions, who represented the Association of Czechoslovak Women and its two national branches (Czech and Slovak), but they became more a target of jokes than of respect. The quota system was utterly discredited during socialism. The memory of unwanted and obligatory quotas given to women 'from above' has remained alive and has negatively influenced public opinion in the later postsocialist period.

Women in Postsocialist Slovakia:
Do Not Poke Your Noses into Politics!

Since the 1990s, several legislative steps have been taken to promote gender equality, but their implementation and enforcement have been insufficient and far too slow. Gender awareness in society has risen thanks to a number of women's non-governmental organizations and journals. After 1989, about seventy women's initiatives and associations were established (Bútorová et al. 1999: 303). The majority of them were based on different concepts than the ones women in Western Europe developed. Women in Central and Eastern Europe did not have to fight for their rights because they gained them during socialism without any struggle and took them for granted. They were fed with communist ideology every day of their lives and were organized from their childhood in pioneer organizations, socialist youth unions and associations of women. No wonder that after 1989 most women in postsocialist countries did not find Western feminist theories and intellectual gender perspectives inspiring and interesting. On the contrary, they considered them hostile towards women's real needs. Any ideology and any form of organized movement reminded women of socialism. The family, the only island of freedom, privacy and true identity during socialism, also remained very important after 1989. Western feminists and anthropologists could not understand this obsession of women in Central and Eastern

Europe with family and motherhood . They did not see (and we, women from 'the other side of the fence', did not explain to them) that the private sphere meant something else for us than it did for them, something that was not necessarily connected with gender, but with an escape from the oppressive nature of everyday public life under socialism.

It seems that public opinion on the role of the family, gender and gender equality has been changing very slowly, and women's social identities in Slovakia have remained closely connected with motherhood. Childcare, family and housework are still viewed as women's priority and responsibility, albeit mainly among members of the older generation, less educated people and residents of smaller municipalities (Bútorová et al. 1999: 280). The younger generation of women and men, that does not carry the historic experience of socialism, is more positive about women's rights and equal opportunities for women and men than their parents and grandparents, but still values the family very highly.

The economic activity of women has remained high despite various predictions of experts, conservative political representatives or Christian activists who expected that once women got a chance to stay at home, they would do so. The majority of women decided to stay at work and build their professional careers. However, unemployment as a new phenomenon has had a significant impact on women's situation especially in small communities which do not create many jobs. Women are the first to lose a job, as many of them hold less qualified and less highly paid positions, and they are also considered more 'problematic' workers due to their family duties and childcare responsibilities. As in many other countries, occupational segregation and income inequality remains a problem. Women dominate lower paid sectors (education, health care, light industry, services, insurance or public administration), and income inequality has been increasing since the 1990s. Slovak women earn almost thirty per cent less than men for equal work. Opinion polls show that women consider unequal pay the most dissatisfying factor in terms of inequality (Gyárfášová and Pafková 2002). Lower incomes mean lower pensions and with the increasing life expectancy of women this leads to a feminization of poverty. Despite the new Labour Code (2001) that enforces the principle of equal pay for both men and women, many employers, mainly in the private sector, find a way to overcome the law. Stereotypes also dominate this sphere as men's higher earnings are often seen as related to men's duty to be the breadwinner.

When looking at the civic and political participation of women in Slovakia, the marginalization of women is profound and visible. Public opinion is that the participation of women in political life is not generally approved of and accepted. A widespread prejudice that women should not 'poke their noses into politics' is stronger among men and women with less education, older people and rural inhabitants (Bútorová et al. 1999: 301), and has been reflected in women's and men's differential involvement in civil society after 1989. We can agree with Gal and Kligman that throughout

Central and Eastern Europe national politics is still viewed with suspicion. In contrast, smaller non-governmental initiatives and associations promise to make a real difference in everyday life. It seems that national politics has remained a male realm and civil society has become an arena for women's civil and political action. Some statistics suggest that by the mid-1990s, a majority of non-governmental organizations in Central and Eastern Europe were headed by women (Gal and Klingman 2000: 93–95).

Although women represent 51.4 per cent of the Slovak population, their participation in national politics is low. Compared with 29 per cent of women in the Parliament in 1985–90, the percentage of women MPs in the 1990–92 term dropped to 12 per cent. Since then it has increased to 15.3 per cent in 1992–94, 14.7 per cent in 1994–98, 14 per cent in 1998–2002 and 19 per cent in 2002–2006. The participation of women in local politics (so called 'small politics') reflects the situation in 'high politics', but shows a faster and more sustained increasing rate. Since the implementation of regional reform in 2002–2004, leading to wide decentralization of public administration, Slovakia has had a two-grade territorial self-administration: 1) higher territorial units (*vyšší územný celok* – VÚC); and 2) towns and villages (municipalities). Municipalities, as highly independent forms of local government, have gone through wide reforms and changes in recent years. There are 2,924 municipalities in Slovakia with an average size of 1,800 inhabitants; out of them only 175 have the status of a town or town district (Štatistický úrad SR 2002). Small municipalities with less than a thousand inhabitants represent over two-thirds of all municipalities. The percentage of women mayors and lord mayors in municipalities (called *starostky* in small municipalities and *primátorky* in towns and cities) has been slowly increasing since 1994 (Table 2.1).

Table 2.1 Municipalities *(Miestne / Mestské zastupiteľstvo) after 1990*

Year	Number of mayors	Number of women mayors in villages	Number of women mayors in towns	% of women mayors total
1990–1994	no data	no data	no data	no data
1994–1998	2866	415 / 15.2%	3 / 2.2%	418/ 14.5%
1998–2002	2867	478 / 17.5%	6 / 4.4%	484/ 16.8%
2002–2006	2787	538/ 20.3%	3/ 2.2%	541/ 19.4%

Women have mainly been successful in elections for mayors in small villages. In the case of the eight regional cities (centres of regional VÚCs), no woman has been elected since 1990; and only a few women have been mayors in district cities and towns. The data from the interviews show that women can identify themselves more easily with municipal politics as they feel more familiar with the problems of the community and feel they can be more useful in finding direct solutions. The fact that as municipal politicians women can stay with their families, and harmonize family duties with their work, is one of the important factors in their decisions to stand. On the other hand, the relatively high number of women mayors in small villages is also a result of the lower interest of men in these positions. In small municipalities the mayor has only a very limited amount of financial and human resources, which makes this position less attractive in terms of power and money.

According to opinion polls[4], 45.2 per cent of men and 33.6 per cent of women consider women's participation in local politics sufficient; 25.6 per cent of men and 42.1 per cent of women find it insufficient.

An Ethnographic Profile of the Villages Studied

Ethnographic research was undertaken in autumn 2004 and spring 2005 in two villages: Ostrá Lúka and Veľká Lúka, situated in the Central Slovak region (VÚC) of Banská Bystrica. Both villages belong to the category of small localities with less than a thousand inhabitants, and the majority of these inhabitants are ethnic Slovaks. The villages became Lutheran Protestant after the Reformation in the sixteenth century, but today they are religiously mixed (half of the inhabitants are Roman Catholics and half are Lutherans). Despite the numbers, inhabitants perceive themselves and their villages as Lutheran (especially in Ostrá Lúka).

Ostrá Lúka is a settlement founded in 1280 where farming and fruit growing were the main professions of the inhabitants for centuries. The village is famous for its Renaissance castle with an inscription engraved on a stone: 'Let this house stand until an ant drinks the sea and a tortoise goes round the world'. This exceptional castle belonged to the noble family of Ostrolúcky, whose estate was confiscated after 1948 by the state, when it became the seat of the State District Archives. Since 1999 the castle has been empty and unused, remaining state property as there are no heirs of the Ostrolúcky family in Slovakia who could claim its restitution. The local municipality would like to buy it, but they have not yet explored the possibility. According to the regional territorial planning office, the castle should be used for tourist and commercial purposes, with the rooms used for workshops and a museum of the Ostrolúcky family. However, it needs reconstruction work, which has not started due to lack of funds.

In Ostrá Luká there are 256 inhabitants, of which 130 are women. There are 155 inhabitants between the ages of 15 and 59, 34 of whom are children under the age of 15 and 67 of whom are over 60. The majority of the inhabitants are ethnic Slovaks, two are Hungarians, two are Roma and one is of Czech nationality (Štatistický úrad 2001). During the socialist period most inhabitants worked in the nearby city of Zvolen or on the local State Farm, which went bankrupt and was dissolved after 1995. Today there are almost no work opportunities in the village and the majority of the inhabitants must commute to work in Zvolen. There is a new small enterprise for bottled mineral water, *Ostrolúcka*, managed by a businessman from Zvolen, where five local people have found work. The kindergarten and primary school were abolished in the 1990s and the children have to visit facilities in other villages (Dubové and Budča). There is only one small grocery shop in the village, so most inhabitants do their shopping in Zvolen.

The village is situated on a steep hill with a beautiful view of the Hron River valley and villages and cities around. There is a bus connecting the village with the nearby village of Budča and the city of Zvolen, which goes several times a day. Most families have a car. People are also used to walking downhill to Budča, but it is not so easy to walk back uphill. Because everyone knows everyone, most drivers stop when seeing a walker and offer a lift. People are generally very friendly. Architecturally, the village contains traditional rural houses from the first half of the twentieth century (farm houses, *gazdovské domy*; Figure 2.1), socialist family houses, called 'cubes'

Figure 2.1 Traditional farm house, 1st half of the 20th century. Photo by Katarína Koštialová in 2005.

Figure 2.2 *Kocka* (the cubic) – typical family house of the socialist period. Photo by Katarína Koštialová in 2005.

(*kocky*; Figure 2.2), because of their shape, and new family houses on the edges of the village, which were built after 1980 mainly by new settlers from Zvolen (Figure 2.3).

The other settlement where we carried out fieldwork, Veľká Lúka, was founded in 1281. It is situated in the Hron valley between two cities – Zvolen and Banská Bystrica. The village has 393 inhabitants (194 men and 199 women). Of these, 251 are aged 15–59, there are 57 children under the age of fourteen, and 85 people are aged over 60. The majority of the inhabitants are ethnic Slovaks, while eight are Roma and two Czech (Štatistický úrad SR 2001). The traditional profession of the inhabitants was agriculture. The socialist State Farm was dissolved in the 1990s and most inhabitants these days work in the neighbouring cities and Vlkanová village, where several private enterprises operate. The village has a kindergarten for small children, but older children go to school in the small spa town of Sliač, a twenty-five minute walk away. There are two grocery shops in the village, open every day. The village profits from being close to two cities (10 km) and having a good public transport system (bus and train connections). The look of the village is more 'socialist' than that of Ostrá Lúka, with most family houses having been built in the 1950s–1970s in the catalogue 'cube' style of those days. Veľká Lúka feels more vibrant than Ostrá Lúka. It has a wide asphalt road to Sliač, which is now rarely used by cars because there is a parallel motorway connecting Zvolen and Banská Bystrica. The road is used by inhabitants of the village and both cities for cycling and roller skating. There is a golf drive near the village with the prospect of a golf course in the future, which may put the village on the golf map of Europe.

Figure 2.3 New post-1989 architecture. Photo by Katarína Koštialová in 2005.

Portraits of the Two Female Mayors

Both female mayors of the villages have been in their positions for two electoral periods. The mayor of Ostrá Lúka, Mirka, is thirty-nine. She was born in western Slovakia, but used to come to Ostrá Lúka for holidays at her grandparents' house, and that is how she met her husband. They have been living in Ostrá Lúka for eighteen years. Before becoming mayor, she worked in the school canteen. After her second child was born, she decided to run for the position of a mayor as an independent candidate. Mirka is an active and communicative person and she was happy to talk to us about her experience.

The mayor of Veľká Lúka, Valika, is fifty-nine years old and was born in the village. Previously, she worked in the human resource department of a local company. Since 1986 she has been a member of the local government committee. She ran for mayoral office for the first time as a member of the Slovak Democratic Left and at the next election as a member of the Communist Party. She stresses, however, that she has never mixed politics with her mayor's position.

> I am convinced that we have to work for the citizen regardless of what party we represent. There were four candidates in my first election. In a small village, people cannot recognize who will be the best for the position. There are family ties that are important here. I campaigned with this in my mind – everyone had the same chance because everyone had a similar number of relatives, neighbours and friends. Then in the second election, I was the only candidate.

When asked about the main reasons for their motivation to become mayor, both women strongly emphasized their identification with the village; their positive relationships and solidarity with the inhabitants; a desire to help and to change things for the better; and personal self-satisfaction. Desire to win power or better their financial situation did not have a place in their decision making.

> I wanted to help the village. I had some experience in working with people; I have been doing it all my life. The situation in small villages is bad, the economy is low, people need help and support. (Veľká Lúka mayor).

> I am of that type – a leader. I always was a leader at school, I like organizational work. I cannot imagine sitting in the office for eight hours doing the same work. I am happy in the field, with the people. Meeting people, helping people. There are a lot of various problems here, but I really like this work. (Ostrá Lúka mayor).

Neither mayor has been aware of a gender dimension to their public representation. They did not consider the fact that they were women as an important one, and did not think it had an impact on the election results or on the way they were treated by other citizens.

From the interviews, it seems that, unlike in 'high' politics, political affiliation and activism do not play a significant role in municipal politics although many mayoral candidates in Slovakia are members of a political party. According to surveys, independent candidates are more trusted and in elections they receive more votes than candidates who represent a political party (Bernátová et al. 2001: 247). Political agendas have not been a decisive factor in the municipal elections in the studied communities, either. Inhabitants of both villages seem to represent a wide spectrum of political opinions and there is no strong political antagonism visible in the communities as it is in some other regions and villages in Slovakia. Both mayors view their work as a community service, rather than as a political post. This was reflected in the election results, which were not influenced by political agendas, but by the personal characteristics of the candidates.

It seems obvious from our data that female mayors are more often successful in small villages than in larger settlements. Both interviewees agree that the position of mayor in small places is not as attractive and financially rewarding as it is in big villages or towns. Mayors in Slovakia are paid according to the size of the village (number of inhabitants). Therefore, in small villages the salaries are low and responsibilities large as there are usually only one or two paid employees working in the local government in addition to the mayor. That is the reason, according to the mayors, that there are fewer male candidates for the position of mayor in small rural communities, and on the contrary, more women candidates who are motivated by a desire to make a change, and to help their community.

> Here in Veľká Lúka, there is a tradition of female mayors. But when you go to nearby Sliač [a little spa town], it is different. They only have male mayors. The conditions are not comparable. You know, in bigger villages and towns, it is all about money. No female candidates have ever been successful in Sliač. (Veľká Lúka mayor).

Barriers to Women's Representation: Harmonizing Work and Family

Family still has a crucial, most important place in the value hierarchy of the Slovaks, as opinion polls show. It is the conflict between the family and public/political activities that is considered the main barrier to women's political participation. According to an opinion poll taken by the Institute of Public Affairs in 2002, 79 per cent of women and 70 per cent of men think that it is mainly family duties that prevent women from entering politics (Institute of Public Affairs 2002; quoted in Filadelfiová, Bútorová and Gyárfášová 2002: 256). The rural-urban divide and the generation gap also play a role in shaping opinions about women in decision making and their family roles.

In the case of the two mayors, the generation gap is visible in the approach to family and family duties. Gender stereotypes are stronger in the family of the Veľká Lúka mayor (who is older), which reflects a more traditional model of gender roles and duties than in the family of the Ostrá Lúka mayor (who is younger). As the Veľká Lúka mayor puts it:

> Every woman who takes this position [of mayor], sacrifices her family, her privacy, everything if she wants to do it well and effectively. If you want to solve every problem in a responsible way, you suffer a lot. Especially a woman ... Women do not do careers like men. Women are busy. They have more activities ... Simply, family duties are much more time consuming for women than for men ... For me, I just do not have time, do not have time. I come home at about six, now it's dark. I can do some work at home, but not in the garden. I have not even had time to dig the ground this spring. My husband also has a responsible job. So I have to do everything myself during weekends. But then the children and grandchildren come ... so I just hurry, hurry to give them what they need. I think the main problem is that it is only women who have to look after the family. I would immediately pay a student for help. But we cannot afford it financially, and ... I also do not know how people would look at it. You know, this is a village. Maybe in a city ... Family support? Hard to say. My husband is proud of the fact that his wife is a mayor. But to help me and to create better conditions for my work, no, it does not happen. Not that he does not help. I need help with many things in the office – driving, buying materials, arranging repairs, reconstructing. Yes, he helps with that. But I have to do it in such way that I pretend it is for a private, family purpose. If he discovers that it was for the office, he is angry.

The younger mayor of Ostrá Lúka has a more pragmatic and modern approach to the family duties although she also has to struggle with double-burden:

> I can only thank God that my husband understands and supports me. Being a mayor means that many people come to your home any time, on Saturday, Sunday, during holidays. The family is permanently disturbed. But as a mayor I am here for these people. A woman has a disadvantage that when she comes home, she is supposed to cook, to wash, to clean, all things which men usually don't do. If a male mayor is in the office till late, everything is ready when he comes home, his wife makes a dinner, cleans, all is done ... My solution was that I saved money for a dishwasher. I have had it for a year now; and it is an incredible help ... During the week I do not cook very often. It is mainly Saturday when I can clean, wash, cook properly. It is good that the family tolerates it. I cannot afford any paid assistance from my salary.

Everyday Life in a Rural Community: Problems and Challenges

During the process of regional reform and decentralisation in 2002–2004, municipalities were given broad responsibilities (local government; primary education; basic health care and care of elderly people and unemployed people; local infrastructure; and housing). This put a great deal of pressure on mayors who have not been prepared to cope with such a wide range of problems, mainly due to lack of experience, but also because of a lack of human and financial resources and capacities. In addition, problems of transition have had a worse impact in small and marginalized regions and villages than border regions and bigger cities, as has been pointed in several studies of postsocialism (e.g., Pine 1996, 2001; Buchowski 1997).

Both mayors of the studied villages emphasized that their work entailed a twenty-four hour day without let up. Because of the size of the villages and close personal relationships, people are used to asking the mayor for help if any problem emerges. The mayor is a community leader, an adviser, a psychologist, and a social worker, as well as a manager and an economist.

> There are two of us in the local government office: me and the accountant. Everything is my responsibility. Maintenance. I organize repairs, looking for the cheapest options for everything, every purchase, every repair. I provide supplies, I am a driver, I buy building materials, stationery as well as presents for our pensioners when they have birthdays … I have to do fundraising, prepare and manage projects. (Ostrá Lúka mayor).

One of the problems of the postsocialist era is unemployment. It is a relatively new phenomenon, which appeared with the transition to a market economy. The unemployment rate in Slovakia was high in the 1990s (up to 18.8 per cent), but has been slowly decreasing since 2000 (10.5 per cent in the first quarter of 2008). Unlike some other countries, unemployment in Slovakia does not show significant gender differences. The percentage of unemployed women has been similar, and in some years even lower than that of men. This proves that when writing about postsocialist countries, one should avoid generalizations. Verdery (1991) mentions as one of the features of the transition increased unemployment, disproportionally effecting women. Although the situation of women in postsocialist countries shows many similarities, there are also many differences deriving from the different stages of women's emancipation during the presocialist and socialist periods (e.g., women in interwar Czechoslovakia were present in all educational cycles and professions, which continued in socialist Czechoslovakia although influenced by communist ideology and propaganda).

In Ostrá Lúka there were twenty-three unemployed people in 2005, out of whom thirteen were women. In Veľká Lúka out of thirty-five unemployed people twelve were women. To combat unemployment, the mayors in Slovakia have a responsibility for helping unemployed citizens who cannot find a job by offering them work in the village beneficial to the public.

> We have to provide them [unemployed citizens] with work, materials, work tools, and we have to organize their work. It is all in the framework of the national programme, 'Motivation work'. This includes work for the benefit of the village such as cleaning, gardening, digging drains, etc. Each unemployed citizen who is involved in this work gets 1500 Sk monthly. (Ostrá Lúka mayor).

Although the number of unemployed women and men in both villages is similar, public opinion about them differs according to their gender. Unemployed women are generally more accepted than unemployed men. In this traditionally patriarchal society a man is still considered a breadwinner, while a woman is seen differently, usually as a significant contributor to the family economy, working in the garden, growing vegetables and breeding animals.

> I think that it is harder for men to be unemployed ... It has an impact on their psyche. I can see it here in our village. Women always find something to do at home. They can cook, clean, do gardening. Even if it does not bring in real money, they work all the time at home and produce 'material' values for the family. (Ostrá Lúka mayor).

There are various workshops, trainings and requalification courses organized for unemployed women in the region, mainly run by non-governmental organisations. NGO VOKA runs one of these projects, organizing meetings for women where they can talk about their problems and gain skills such as how to start their own business. Only one woman from Ostrá Lúka has been involved and she now works in the office of the local government. The mayors support these activities, but they are rather sceptical about whether the final effect is good. 'Not everyone can be a businesswoman', mayor Mirka comments.

Community Activism

Socialism suppressed motivation and disrupted most voluntary community activities for fear of an organized protest against the government. One of the tasks of the mayors is to support and build communal life in their villages again. The mayors try to motivate citizens to be more active, to participate in community activities, and to strengthen their identity through the organization of various sports and cultural events. Many of these activities are still based on traditional customs and annual ceremonies. Erecting maypoles for single girls during Whit Monday is considered a significant event and young people value it highly. In Ostrá Lúka an informal community of young men take responsibility for the event, while in Veľká Lúka it is organized by a very active group of firemen. During Easter all the boys and young men visit girls in their homes, following the old custom of watering female friends, neighbours and relatives, a custom not very popular with the women. On 24 June (St. John's Day) and also on the occasion of the anniversary of the Slovak national uprising on 29 August [5], young people, local football clubs and the fire brigades prepare a bonfire where families, neighbours, friends from the village and relatives 'from the town' meet and celebrate. At Christmas, a Christmas tree is raised in the middle of the village and the inhabitants meet by it at midnight on Christmas Eve and New Year.

In Ostrá Lúka a one-day festival called the 'Cultural Spring of Adela Ostrolúcka'[6] is organized every year.

> Our citizens identify with this event very much. Most of them are involved, either as participants (acting in drama performances or folklore ensembles) or helping

with organizational details. Some people like folklore and prepare a performance with a few songs and dances, others organize a theatre performance – both for adults and children, classical or modern. And they do it all themselves, including preparing costumes, scenery, and all, without asking for any money.

Partnerships and Cooperation with Other Partners

The mayors of the villages are active in cooperation with non-governmental organisations. They realize that the villages are too small to survive alone and without collaboration with other partners. Both villages are members of micro-regions that are supported by the Rural Parliament in Slovakia (*Vidiecky parlament* – VIPA) and VOKA – the Rural Agency for Community Activities. The objective of the Rural Parliament is to improve the quality of life in rural Slovakia by advocating good rural policies and encouraging experience and knowledge exchange among local developmental civic groups. VOKA is a community association aimed at the sustainable development of rural areas by educating and motivating local citizens, protecting local cultural heritage, and supporting rural small and medium entrepreneurs and rural leaders.

Ostrá Lúka is part of the micro-region of Adela, which comprises five villages. Veľká Lúka is a member of the micro-region of Pozdola Bystrice, which comprises seven villages. Through the joint efforts and activities of the micro-region associations it is easier to apply for funds from the European Union, mainly structural funds.

> It is not easy to get money from EU funds. You need to have technical projects ready and they are costly. That is why we joined the micro-region association and we slowly started our activities. We have not yet succeeded in getting a grant from the EU, but we are motivated and we work on it. We need to repair roads in the village, we have already prepared the technical project and want to try to apply for European structural funds. But in this system you first need to invest your own money and then it is reimbursed afterwards. And that is impossible in a small village. So we try as a micro-region – we will stand each other's surety with the village properties. (Ostrá Lúka mayor).

Ostrá Lúka's mayor is more active in a number of projects. The village took part in a VOKA project, 'Listening', which was aimed at improving communication among citizens and local government, listening to people and asking what they would like to change in their village. A group of volunteers from the village made a questionnaire and then two activists visited all the houses in the village. The mayor valued the improvement of mutual communication with the villagers, but reflected also on her previous experience:

> We did this project with VOKA and Catherine from the U.S. We used to do the same during socialism. It was called "pairs of canvassers or agitators". And now someone from abroad has to come and teach us what was forgotten (Ostrá Lúka mayor).

On the basis of the results of the 'Listening' project several proposals were implemented. The inhabitants themselves applied for small grants from VOKA and learnt about community activism, which disappeared during socialism, but has started to revive again. 'One group of inhabitants asked for support to clean a canal, another group took care of the lime trees. Others planted trees in a small park and built water-pipes leading to a sports ground. Several citizens wrote a brochure about the history of the village. We received approximately 14,000 Sk per project (350 EUR).'

One of VOKA's activities is looking for and supporting rural leaders, including female leaders. VOKA organizes regular meetings of female mayors with the aim of exchanging examples of good practice and educating community leaders. Together with the Rural Parliament they organize an annual competition, the 'Female Leader of the Year', as part of the World Day of Rural Women (15 October), which was agreed at the Beijing Women's Conference in 1995. In Slovakia, every October the 'Week of Rural Women' takes place. Exhibitions, conferences, workshops, competitions and informal meetings of rural women are organized that week throughout the whole countryside. The competition for the 'Female Leader of the Year' is aimed at motivating and encouraging female leaders. Several categories are open for nominations:

1. a woman-activist (for women active in NGOs, clubs, associations, etc.)
2. a woman–politician (for women in local politics – a mayor or member of the Rural Parliament)
3. a woman-devotee (for women who are not members of any organization, but are active in their village as individuals).

Although both mayors of the studied villages know about the event and follow it with great interest, neither they nor any other women from their villages have been actively involved in the competition.

The Urban-Rural Connection

Ostrá Lúka and Veľká Lúka both benefit from close proximity to the cities of Zvolen and Banská Bystrica. In recent decades several urban families have moved to and built new houses in the villages. This trend, of city inhabitants moving to nearby villages, is increasing rapidly all over Slovakia. Both districts, of Banská Bystrica and Zvolen, belong to the Slovak territories that show high suburbanization – a growing trend of moving from the town to the countryside (Piško 2005). Because of a low birth rate and higher population mobility, the population of big cities has been slowly dropping, while it has been increasing in the regions surrounding cities.

The mayor of Ostrá Lúka is very satisfied with this development. She has managed to involve new inhabitants in various activities and appreciates their contribution to the village.

We have six new houses here and more are going to be built. I was surprised how active all the newcomers have become. They are involved in the village life. They help. They are educated. The lawyer helps with his expertise for free. Then there is a telecommunication expert who always gives advice about PCs or telephones and he also takes pictures at every event we organize. Women help with receptions and cultural activities. And they have all made friends with local people, which is very good. They have a wider overview and intellect. We are more introverts here and maybe our thinking is limited and small as a result. Problems which we see as big ones, they can solve easily.

Conclusion

National and local-level data presented here reflect the changing nature of women's civil and political participation in Slovakia during the postsocialist era. Whilst during the socialist period women's political activities were organized from the top down and controlled by the ruling Communist Party, since 1989 women have been trying to find their own way in the civic and political arena. Although the number of women in national and municipal politics has been slowly increasing, there are still a lot of obstacles on the bumpy road to women's full and equal civic and political representation. Generally, the lower representation of women in politics in Slovakia results from:

1. cultural factors (gender roles in the family and society; and stereotypes rooted in history);
2. religion (regions as well as countries where Catholicism is dominant have lower women's representations than Protestant regions and countries[7]);
3. socioeconomic factors (social and economic consequences of the transition towards a market economy have put an enormous pressure on the lives of men and women in marginalized regions with no work opportunities, which has also had a negative impact on women's political participation);
4. the political and electoral system in the country (the absence of positive discrimination mechanisms such as quotas; an electoral system placing women in non-eligible positions).

Our ethnographic data gathered from two small rural communities demonstrates the everyday life of women in municipal politics. The main findings of the research are:

1. Local governments in small villages in Slovakia have a limited amount of financial and human resources, and therefore the position of a mayor in these municipalities is less attractive for men in terms of power and money. As a result, women are more successful in municipal elections in small localities.
2. The political affiliation of candidates for mayor plays an insignificant role in municipal elections. It is more the personality and the character of the candidate which is a decisive factor.

3. The motivation of women to become a mayor is based not on a desire to win power, but on providing a service for others, and on community work.

4. A significant factor in women's decision to run for mayor is the possibility of harmonizing family and work duties without a need to move and leave the family.

The view of the importance of women's representation in decision making at all levels is still lacking in postsocialist Slovakia. This lack increases as one moves from bigger towns to small villages, from younger people to older ones, from left-wing parties to right-wing parties, and from Western Slovakia to Eastern Slovakia. The high status of women in society, the high participation of women in public and economic life, and the increasing option of harmonizing family life and professional career, are arguably all features of developed democracies. Slovakia shows low indicators in most of these categories. Until it realizes the importance of gender awareness and gender mainstreaming at all levels of society, it can hardly be considered a strong and developed democracy. Gender equality is not a luxury as it is often described by male politicians. It is an everyday necessity and the only way forward.

Notes

1. This study uses data from the research project 'Enlargement, Gender and Governance: The Civic and Political Participation and Representation of Women in the EU Candidate Countries' (EU 5 Framework Programme Project, SERD 2003–00033), in which A. Bitušíková participated as a national coordinator for Slovakia and K. Koštialová as a project partner. The paper was written by A. Bitušíková, but most of the fieldwork and interviews were carried out by K. Koštialová.

2. For example, in the paper by Liszka, the author writes about the geo-historical and cultural region of Matyusfold in south-west Slovakia (the land of the fourteenth century petty monarch Matyas Csak). The term appeared in Hungarian literature in the sixteenth century, but has never been used by the Slovaks living in the region and it is not a term known and used in the Slovak ethnological literature.

3. Tomas Garrigue Masaryk was influenced by his wife Charlotte Garrigue who was an educated American conscious of women rights. Masaryk took her surname as his middle name.

4. IVO Project 'Potential of Active Participation of Women in Public Life, 2002, www.ivo.sk; accessed on 28 May 2005.

5. The Slovak national uprising (in 1944) was the biggest uprising against Nazism during the Second World War. Banská Bystrica was the centre of the uprising and a large number of people from neighbouring villages and districts were involved in the struggle through the partisan movement. Memories of the uprising remain alive, and every year on 29 August (the anniversary of the uprising) memorial activities are organized, including bonfires (known as partisan bonfires).

6. Adela Ostrolúcka, a daughter of the Ostrolúcky family, was a woman who became famous for her romantic and platonic love of Ľudovít Štúr (the Slovak national leader in the nineteenth century). Their love was not fulfilled and Adela died young after a serious illness.

7. www.feminet.sk; accessed 2.5.2002.

References

Arendas, Z. 2003. 'Identities in Change: Integration Strategies of Resettled Hungarians from Czechoslovakia to Hird (Southwestern Hungary)', in D. Torsello and M. Pappová (eds) *Social Networks in Movement*. Šamorín – Dunajská Streda: Forum Minority Research Institute and Lilium Aurum, pp.41–64.

Berňatová, M. et al. 2001. 'Public Perception of Local Government in Slovakia', in P. Swianiewicz (ed.) *Public Perception of Local Governments*. Budapest: OSI, Local Government and Public Service Reform Initiative, pp.224–76.

Bitušíková, A. 2000. 'Contrasting Symbols and Rituals: The Case of Slovakia', in T. Dekker, J. Helsloot and C. Wijers (eds), *Roots and Rituals. The Construction of Ethnic Identities*. Amsterdam: Het Spinhuis, pp.220–228.

――――. 2002. 'Slovakia: An Anthropolgical Perspective on Identity and Regional Reform', in J. Batt and K. Wolczuk (eds), *Region, State and Identity in Central and Eastern Europe*. London: Frank Cass, pp.41–64.

Buchowski, M. 1997. *Reluctant Capitalists: Class and Culture in a Local Community in Western Poland*. Berlin: Centre Marc Bloch.

Burawoy, M. and Verdery, K. (eds). 1999. *Uncertain Transition. Ethnographies of Change in the Postsocialist World*. Lanham, MD: Rowman and Littlefield.

Bútorová, Z. et al. 1999. 'Rodová problematika na Slovensku [Gender in Slovakia]', in G. Mesežnikov and M. Ivantyšin (eds), *Slovensko 1998–1999: Suhrnná správa o stave spolčcnosti*. Bratislava: IVO, pp.653–706.

Cotterill, P. 1992. 'Interviewing Women: Issues of Friendship, Vulnerability and Power', *Women's Studies International Forum* 15(5–6): 593–606.

Danglová, O. 2001. 'Rurálna komunita v transformácii [Rural Community in Transformation]', *Slovenský národopis* 49(3): 279–98.

Danter, I. 2003. 'Traditional Economic Life in the Northern Part of the Danube Lowland', in D. Torsello and M. Pappová (eds), *Social Networks in Movement*. Šamorín – Dunajská Streda: Minority Forum Research Institute and Lilium Aurum, pp.89–98.

Einhorn, B. 2003. Cinderella Goes to Market: Citizenship, Gender and Women's Movements in East Central Europe. London and New York: Verso.

Filadelfiová, J., Z. Bútorová and O. Gyárfášová. 2002. 'Ženy a muži v politike [Women and Men in Politics.', in M. Kollár and G. Mesežnikov (eds), *Slovensko 2002: Súhrnná správa o stave spoločnosti I*. Bratislava: IVO, pp.333–45.

Funk, N. and M. Mueller (eds). 1993. *Gender, Politics and Post-Communism: Reflections from Eastern Europe and the Former Soviet Union*. London: Routledge.

Gal, S. and G. Kligman. 2000. *The Politics of Gender after Socialism*. Princeton: Princeton University Press.

Gyárfášová, O. and K. Pafková. 2002. *Potenciál aktívnej účasti žien vo verejnom živote*. [Potential of Active Women's Participation in Public Life]. Bratislava: Institute of Public Affairs, www.ivo.sk.

Haukanes, H. (ed.) 2001. *Women after Communism: Ideal Images and Real Lives*. Bergen: University of Bergen.

Heitlinger, A. 1993. 'The Impact of the Transition from Communism on the Status of Women in the Czech and Slovak Republics', in N. Funk and M.

Mueller (eds), *Gender, Politics and Post-Communism*. London: Routledge, pp.95–108.

Kiczková, Z. and E. Farkašová. 1993. 'The Emancipation of Women: A Concept that Failed', in N. Funk and M. Mueller (eds), *Gender, Politics and Post-Communism*. London: Routledge, pp.84–94.

Krekovičová, E. 1999. 'Politika vo folklóre – folklór v politike [Politics in Folklore – Folklore in Politics]', *Slovenský národopis* 47(1): 5–18.

————. 2002. 'Identity a mýty novej štátnosti na Slovensku po roku 1993 [Identities and Myths of the New Statehood in Slovakia after 1993]'. *Slovenský národopis* 50(2): 147–70.

Lass, A. 1999. 'Portable Worlds: On the limits of replication in the Czech and Slovak Republics' in M. Burawoy and K. Verdery (eds), *Uncertain Transition. Ethnographies of Change in the Postsocialist World*. Lanham, MD: Rowman and Littlefield, pp.273–300.

Liszka, J. 2003. 'Between Cultural and Geographical Borders: Denomination of the Matyusfold Region', in D. Torsello and M. Pappová (eds), *Social Networks in Movement*. Šamorín – Dunajská Streda: Forum Minority Research Institute and Lilium Aurum, pp.155–64.

Pine, F. 1996. 'Redefining Women's Work in Rural Poland', in R. Abrahams (ed.) *After Socialism*. Oxford: Berghahn, pp.133–55.

————. 2001. 'Who Better than Your Mother? Some Problems with Gender Issues in Rural Poland', in H. Haukanes (ed.) *Women after Communism: Ideal Images and Real Lives*. Bergen: University of Bergen, pp.51–66.

Piško, M. 2005. 'Mestá sa vyľudnujú, okolitý vidiek ožíva [Cities are Getting Smaller, Nearby Countryside Is Reviving]', *SME*, 8 February, p.5.

Podoba, J. 1998. 'Rejecting Green Velvet: Transition, Environment and Nationalism in Slovakia', in S. Baker and P. Jehlička (eds), *Dilemmas of Transition: The Environment, Democracy and Economic Reform in East Central Europe*. London: Frank Cass, pp.129–44.

————. 2000. 'Nationalism as a Tool', in T. Dekker, J. Helsloot and C. Wijers (eds), *Roots and Rituals: The Construction of Ethnic Identities*. Amsterdam: Het Spinhuis, pp.315–27.

————. 2003. 'Kultúrne zaostávanie ako determinant sociálnych konfliktov transformačného obdobia [Cultural Lag as a Determinant of Social Conflicts in the Transformation Period]', *Slovenský národopis* 51(4): 447–67.

————. 2005. 'On the Periphery of a Periphery: Slovak Anthropology behind the Ideological
Veil' in C. Hann, M. Sárkány and P. Skalník (eds), *Studying Peoples in the People's Democracies. Socialist Era Anthropology in East-Central Europe*. Muenster: LIT Verlag, pp.245–71.

Regulska, J. and M. Roseman. 1998. 'What is Gender?' *Transitions – Changes in Post-Communist Societies* 5(1): 24–29.

Reinharz, S. 1992. *Feminist Methods in Social Research*. Oxford: Oxford University Press.

Šiklová, J. 1993. 'Are Women in Central and Eastern Europe Conservative?' in N. Funk and M. Mueller (eds), *Gender, Politics and Post-Communism*. New York: Routledge.

————. 1998. 'Men and Women United for a Higher Purpose', *Transitions – Changes in Post-Communist Societies* 5(1): 34–35.

Skalník, P. 1979. 'Modernization of the Slovak Peasantry: Two Carpathian Highland Communities', in B. Berdichewsky (ed.) *Anthropology and Social Change in Rural Areas*. The Hague: Mouton, pp.253–61.

————. 1986. 'Uneven Development in European Mountain Communities', *Dialectical Anthropology* 10(3): 215–28.

————. 1993. ,'Socialism is Dead and Very Much Alive in Slovakia: Political Inertia in a Tatra Village', in C. Hann (ed.) *Socialism: Ideals, Ideology and Social Practice*. London: Routledge, pp.218–26.

Štatistický úrad SR. 2001. *Sčítanie obyvateľov, domov a bytov v roku 2001* [Census 2001]. Bratislava: Štatistický úrad SR.

Štatistický úrad SR. 2002. *Voľby do orgánov samosprávy obcí 2002* [Municipal elections 2002]. http://www.statistics.sk/vs2002/sk/tab/tab1.htm; (accessed 6 May 2005).

Szarka, L. 2003. 'Border Region or Contact Zone: Ethnic and Ethno-Social Processes in Small Regions between the Hungarian-Slovak Language and State Border', in D. Torsello and M. Pappová (eds), *Social Networks in Movement*. Šamorín – Dunajská Streda: Forum Minority Research Institute and Lilium Aurum, pp.141–54.

Szep, A. 2003. 'Some Aspects of Roma Migration from Slovakia', in D. Torsello and M. Pappová (eds), *Social Networks in Movement*. Šamorín – Dunajská Streda: Forum Minority Research Institute and Lilium Aurum, pp.185–90.

Torsello, D. 2003. 'Managing Instability: Trust, Social Relations and the Strategic Use of Ideas and Practices in a Southern Slovakian Village', in D. Torsello and M. Pappová (eds), *Social Networks in Movement*. Šamorín – Dunajská Streda: Forum Minority Research Institute and Lilium Aurum, pp.65–88.

Torsello, D. and M. Pappová (eds). 2003. *Social Networks in Movement: Time, Interaction and Interethnic Spaces in Central Eastern Europe*. Šamorín – Dunajská Streda: Forum Minority Research Institute and Lilium Aurum.

Toth, K. 2003. 'A Village on the Ethnic Periphery: The Case of Dlhá nad Váhom, Southern Slovakia', in D. Torsello and M. Pappová (eds), *Social Networks in Movement*. Šamorín – Dunajská Streda: Forum Minority Research Institute and Lilium Aurum, pp.117–40.

Verdery, K. 1991. 'Theorising Socialism: A Prologue to the Transition', *American Ethnologist* 18(3): 419–39.

Weinerová, R. 2003. 'From East to West: The Roma Migration from Slovakia', in D. Torsello and M. Pappová (eds), *Social Networks in Movement*. Šamorín – Dunajská Streda: Forum Minority Research Institute and Lilium Aurum, pp.191–210.

Chapter 3

Property Relations, Class, and Labour in Rural Poland

Michał Buchowski

Property, privatization and reprivatization have undoubtedly become one of the most debated topics in the Central European postsocialist context. For politicians, changing property relations have been one of the landmarks of shifting the political-economic system from an authoritarian to democratic one, and bringing back the 'proper' ownership order has turned out to be the litmus test for those who claimed their entry into the Western sphere of politics. For neoliberals, private ownership has functioned as a cornerstone of the only feasible and efficient socio-economic system. For the local and international audience, the process of changing property relations has served as a sort of magical formula for transforming the deviant East into the appropriate West, for converting it from a communist mess into a capitalist regime, and for bringing it back on the correct track of civilized progress. For many local actors privatization has opened a space for quick and easy enrichment. Finally, the issue of ownership relations has grown to be one of the major topics of ethnographic investigations in Eastern and Central Europe. It seems that anthropologists have also been swayed by the dominant Western image that situates the cultural order in economics. In any case, from the blossoming literature on postsocialism one may gain an impression that privatization, modes of production, labour relations and other topics connected to economy have chiefly preoccupied experts in the field of study that is rather commonly associated with culture and society.[1] Conjoining this interest in economy with concentration on culture, one may perhaps claim that anthropologists have confirmed Marshall Sahlins's statement that in 'bourgeois society, material production is the dominant locus of symbolic production' (1976: 212). Below, I follow these steps by scrutinizing the Polish case, which, like any other case, is particular, but which in one major aspect is unique for the whole former communist bloc. Polish agriculture was never collectivized and this has had a corollary in the postsocialist transformation that, at least to my knowledge, has not as such been studied by Western anthropologists[2]. Rather, these have been mostly preoccupied with the radical consequences of de-collectivization, for example in Romania (Kideckel 1993; von Hirschhausen 1997; Verdery 1996, 1998, 2003), Bulgaria (Creed 1998; Kaneff 2004), Slovakia (Danglová 2003; Torsello 2003), Hungary (Lampland 1995; 2001), Russia (Humphrey 1998) or as a phenomenon seen in a more comparative overview (Kideckel 1995; Abrahams 1996; Maurel 1997; Leonard and Kaneff 2002; Hann et al. 2003; Verdery and Humphrey 2004), to mention merely European postcommunist countries. Of course, there are scholars preoccupied with the Polish rural communities (Conte 2001; Nagengast 1991, 2001; Pine 1994, 1998; Zbierski-Salameh 1999), but they have not directly addressed the issue of property relations. My case is grounded in the ethnography of a rural community that should illustrate social relations and the cultural order with much wider implications. Global changes, state policy and nationwide processes constitute a structural framework in which people at the grass-roots level operate, which they interpret within their own symbolic systems, and which they co-produce in everyday practice. I am interested in the way the order of things, particularly land, relates to the order of people and their identities, and how these two are related to and are legitimized by existing cultural values. Both the structural framework and also collective and individual practices exercised have historical underpinnings.

This chapter serves a dual purpose, informative and interpretative. With respect to the first, I would like to provide some data on the Polish privatization processes in agriculture. It will also provide a background for the second, in which I offer some anthropological insights into this process that go beyond statistics and the 'raw' data. I begin with an outline of the historical setting that has conditioned the direction of economic reforms after 1989 with regard to agriculture. Nationwide changes in property relations comprise a part of this story. Here, I restrict my interest in property relations to land ownership. Then, I present an extremely concise outline of the social history of the locality of Dziekanowice in the Wielkopolska region of Poland, as well as the scope and character of transformations in property relations there. Past socialist relationships have conspicuously affected current transformations in the property order and social hierarchy. In this way I would like to intertwine local and national perspectives that are obviously linked and can only be appropriately understood when studied in conjunction.

In what follows, I do not problematize the notion of 'property' itself since, as it turns out, a native notion of 'property' is close to the average Western, if not neoliberal, one. This standard notion is not only present in public discourse, but also shared by my interlocutors. In modern history, the issue of private property in land was a slogan of peasant movements; redistribution of land was the practice that at the inception of the 'progressive' system in the late 1940s helped the communist to win social support; and last but not least, individual farming on privately owned land functioned for decades as a symbol of resistance to the communist authorities striving to curtail private ownership not just in agriculture. In the postcommunist period the argument of 'natural', 'sacred' and 'untouchable' property rights claimed by various social groups, particularly interwar landlords, have been raised in conflicting debates about to whom a given kind of property belongs. Thus, the concept of the private ownership of land has been well entrenched in the consciousness of farmers and other collective actors in Poland and in many situations forges individual and group identities. The convergence of basic ideas about private property found in Central Europe (see Verdery 2004: 142, for Romania) with the commonly accepted Western one should not, however, prevent us from contextualizing it in the social milieu in which it functions. The latter is an outcome of diversified forces operating at the global, national, regional and local levels. Elucidation of this conjunction at the community level comprises the major aim of this chapter.

Historical Background

The privatization of services, industry, finance and agriculture is well advanced in Poland and in this respect it does not differ significantly from other countries in the region, especially those which have already joined the European Union. Privatization has taken various forms, ranging from the buyout of state companies by the single foreign or local investor to the selling off of company's shares via the stock market to collectives and individuals (including Employee Stock Ownership Plan).[3] It sounds like a paradox, however, that among postsocialist states the country that started regional changes, with global repercussions, called the 'transition from socialism to capitalism', remains unique in comparison with its neighbours with respect to reprivatization and, particularly, the reprivatization of land. According to the opponents of this process, it does not make sense in Poland to reprivatize land, because land was mostly kept private during the socialist period anyhow, and meeting reprivatization demands can harm fragile ownership relations in the countryside and endanger balancing the state budget. Moreover, giving land back to the interwar owners or their descendants is practically impossible, since postwar Poland was established as a 'new' country with radically changed borders.[4] As in any other political debate, arguments presented as 'objective reasons' that prevent reprivatization are, in fact, discursive arguments which are ironically at odds with a prevailing democratic and neoliberal devotion to the 'proper' and lawful rules of individual ownership.[5] These world-view discussions and (re-)privatization practices mirror, on the one hand, social relations associated with the property regime and, on the other, the political stands of various interest groups. Altogether, they exemplify how property relations are embedded in social relationships and cultural values (e.g. Hann 1998).

The successful transformation of land ownership is usually presented as a postcommunist breakthrough. However, as I mentioned, Poland, alongside the former Yugoslavia, does not fit the pattern. In Poland, property relations in the countryside evolved together with the transformation of socialism itself.[6] The current transition is just a drop in the ocean of history and it results in changes that are not revolutionary at all, especially when compared to the 'proletarian revolution' following the decree to nationalize land which was issued in 1944 and implemented soon thereafter.

Thus, the proportion of land owned privately and by the state fluctuated accordingly to the changing agricultural policies of the authorities. Under communism at least five periods can be distinguished:

(a) 1944–48: Characterized mainly by nationalization and redistribution of land to peasants, connected with the creation of state farms mostly in 'Regained (Western) Territories'. Following the 1944 'July Manifesto' promulgated by the 'government' installed by the Soviets, holdings in excess of 50 ha (100 ha in the western provinces, including Wielkopolska) were expropriated by a decree of 15 August 1944 (Roszkowski 1992: 133, 141). More than 13,000 land estates were thus confiscated by the State Land Property Office (*Państwowe Nieruchomości Ziemskie*) and largely redistributed to peasants (Kersten 1990: 147). As a result, a class of landed gentry was eliminated and this goal was later written into the constitution of 1952, which declared that the People's Republic 'contains, expels and eliminates social classes that live on the exploitation of workers and peasants'.

(b) 1949–56: Characterized mainly by attempts at collectivization. The number of cooperatives rose from 243 in 1949 to 9800 in 1955, but this process was relatively slow, since by 1956 only nine per cent of arable land was administered by cooperatives (Roszkowski 1992: 215).

(c) 1956–1970: Collectivized farms were largely disbanded and the area owned by the cooperatives diminished from 1.9 million hectares in 1955 to 260,000 hectares in 1957; at the same time, the proportion of privately owned farms rose from 78 per cent to 85 per cent (Roszkowski 1992: 250–251).

(d) 1970–1983: This period can be described as 'oppressive tolerance' (Gorlach and Seręga 1991) towards farmers during the so-called Gierek period.[7] In 1972, the policy of 'compulsory deliveries' was abandoned, but the leadership's deep belief in central planning reinforced collectivization in the guise of agricultural modernization. Ageing smallholders were strongly encouraged, under laws passed between 1974 and 1979, to cede their deeds to the state in return for a retirement pension otherwise refused to landowners: accepting this offer implied excluding one's children from the 'peasantry'. The State Land Fund (*Państwowy Fundusz Ziemi*) prohibited the sale of land to individual farmers. Consequently, between

1976 and 1980 alone, the proportion of arable land in private hands fell from 71 per cent to 68 per cent (Roszkowski 1992: 319, 340). However, this 'awkward class', considered by many communists as a 'ball and chain', proved to be more efficient than the state sector. Gierek's policy led to a drop of overall agricultural production by 8 per cent during the late 1970s and caused shortages of meat and other agricultural products. This penury was one of the major factors which sparked off the workers' strikes in 1980.

(e) 1983–1989: Only in 1983, during the extreme political crisis of martial law and under the pressure of the Polish Peasant Party, which was a formal ally of the Polish United Worker's Party (the communist party), was 'family farming' officially recognized as equal to 'socialist forms of agricultural production'. In order to increase food supplies the authorities supported the agricultural sector by cheap loans and by offering decent prices for agricultural products. Thanks to this relatively favourable policy, the proportion of arable land in private hands increased from 68 per cent to 76 per cent.

This concise review not only demonstrates that, in contrast to other Central European countries, agricultural land was largely privately owned in postwar Poland, but also shows how socialist agricultural policy as well as property rules and relations fluctuated. In 1990, at the end of socialist period, 76 per cent of agricultural land was private, 18.7 per cent of land was tilled by State Farms, 3.7 per cent was in the hands of co-operatives, and 1.6 per cent was in the possession of 'agricultural circles' (cf. Pilichowski 1994: 165–166; Maurel 1994: 99). This means that less than one quarter of a major agricultural means of production, i.e., land, could be classified as part of 'socialist agriculture'. Changes in property relations intertwined with communist policies towards agriculture were assisted by huge social shifts. First, as a result of rapid socialist industrialization, the proportion of people working in agriculture dropped steadily from 66 per cent in 1946 to 26.6 per cent by 1990 (*Rocznik* 1997: xxxv) – that makes on average a drop close to 1 per cent a year. However, the number of farms decreased only slightly whereas the birth rate in the countryside remained high and almost compensated for migration to towns. In the meantime, the town population increased almost threefold, from 8 million in 1946 to 23.6 million in 1990. In the countryside it dropped in total numbers only from 16.1 million to 14.6 million, while in percentage from 68.2 per cent to 38 per cent (Eberhardt 1993: 34). This means that it was the peasantry that provided the human resources for urbanization.

The purportedly systemic transformation of the 1990s has not solved the age-old 'peasant problem'. Today, farmers and agricultural workers still compose a quarter of Poland's population. Actually, the percentage of the population working in agriculture had already started to slow down in the 1980s, falling by 4 per cent over the course of the decade (from 30.6 per cent in 1980 to 26.6 per cent in 1990). Paradoxically, and contrary to the mystified image of the Great Transformation, this percentage stabilized during the 1990s and amounted to 26.8 per cent in 2002 in the common category of 'agriculture, hunting and forestry' while an estimated 16.1 per cent of the labour force worked on private farms alone (Rocznik 2004: 41). The number of farms, i.e., households with property holdings larger than one hectare, actually dropped from 2.138 million in 1990 to 1.850 million in 2003. Related to this trend is the steady increase in the average total farm area, 7.6 hectares in 1995 to 8.2 hectares in 2003 (Rocznik 2004: 457). Also, the number of farms larger than 15 hectares rose from 164,000 in 1995 to 183,000 in 2003, so they covered more than 44 per cent of agricultural land that year. These changes are in line with the 'modernization' policy of Polish and EU authorities whose aim is to reduce the number of farms to levels between 600,000 and 800,000. The above statistics indicate a steady but moderate decrease in the number of holdings, but this process is neither 'revolutionary' nor new, and it was initiated as long ago as the 1920s. As a consequence, even under 'capitalism reborn', small farmers still appear as an 'awkward class' that again has to be lessened and remains recalcitrant to 'rationalization'.

Neoliberal rationalization and the consolidation of land have been combined with the gradual privatization of state enterprises. On 1 January 1992, the Agricultural Property Agency of the State Treasury was created[8] and was recently renamed the Agricultural Real Estate Agency or *Agencja Nieruchomości Rolnych* (hereafter 'the Agency'). Its task has been to administer and restructure state-owned agricultural assets. Altogether, since 1992, the Agency has acquired 1,666 state enterprises comprising 332,000 apartments and hundreds of thousands of agricultural workers (even in official reports their number varies between 192,000 and 434,000) and 4.7 million hectares of land.[9]

The process of privatization proved to be much more complicated than many assumed. Disbanded state farms created reservoirs of jobless people. In the agricultural regions of Mazuria (former Eastern Prussia) and Western Pomerania, official unemployment rates oscillate between 25 and 30 per cent. Most uneducated people have been trapped in cages of worn-out concrete apartment blocs and structural unemployment. Despite official declarations by the Agency that it helps these people to adapt to the new context, they have mostly been granted early retirement or remain redundant; very few continue to work on 'restructured' farms either run by the Agency or leased to or owned by private entrepreneurs.

The Agency's activities are restricted by many factors. Legal regulations limit possible buyers to Polish citizens[10] who, especially among those involved in the agricultural sector, often lack money for investment. Due to competitive markets, not too many farmers are interested in the expansion of their farms. State-owned agricultural land is for the most part located in the regions where a 'hunger for land' does not exist (west, north-west and north-east Poland) since most lack the financial means to acquire it and the land is inaccessible to former state farm workers. In south-east, south and central Poland farmers who would like to expand their acreage cannot do so. The Agency itself is a huge public employer and, according to the logic of self-perpetuating bureaucracy, its 'human resources' are not interested in concluding its operation. The conundrum with respect to reprivatization of course works to the benefit of the Agency's employees. Although it is not a written law, in some regions land claimed by the prewar owners or their inheritors cannot be sold to anybody else without the claimant's official consent and an unofficial financial compensation.[11] All in all, at the end of 2004, after thirteen years of the Agency's existence, less then one third of the land has been sold (31.4 per cent, i.e., 1.479 million hectares) and most of it is leased (49.1 per cent, i.e., 2.311 million hectares). The remaining land has been disposed of differently (returned to owners, to the Church, to communities, to the State Forests Enterprise) or remains to be allocated (479,000 hectares). Anti-foreign sentiment and legislation is reflected in the minuscule proportion of land sold by the Agency to alien citizens (only 925 hectares) or leased to them (114,971 hectares).

Property Relations in Dziekanowice

Dziekanowice is a small village in Wielkopolska, a historical region and administrative province (*województwo*) called Greater Poland or Poznania in English and located in the Łubowo commune (*gmina*), about 35 km north-east of Poznań on the way to Gniezno, the capital of the district (*powiat*). Since the end of 1994, when I conducted fieldwork in Dziekanowice for six months, I have been doing regular intermittent research in the community every summer. This makes me acquainted with local life and keeps me updated with village affairs. I use a variety of ethnographic methods ranging from casual conversations with people, participation in friends' meetings, family celebrations, community gatherings, Commune Council meetings, and participant observation of everyday life and the functioning of the community. These materials are supported by data from historical archives, local public and self-government offices, as well as state administration offices. What attracted me first to Dziekanowice was the visible complexity of its social structure, comprised of all the major groups one can find in the Polish countryside. In a sense, it is a microcosm of rural Poland, although it cannot be completely representative, due to the fact that different parts of this country and its divergent populations have experienced idiosyncratic histories. By now it is not only the social mosaic that makes Dziekanowice an interesting object of study for me, but also my personal engagement in local relations and friendships resulting from years-long conversations and interactions. My involvement with Dziekanowiczans' lives reminds us of the common anthropological wisdom that 'research sites are not found, they are made' (Geertz 1995: 106).

However, there is another reason for choosing a village in Wielkopolska. The research sites of Western authors working on Poland are predominantly located in the southern and south-eastern parts of the country (with the exception of Zbierski-Salameh 1999), in the area of Małopolska, known also as Galicia, an area that was partitioned from Poland in the eighteenth century and comprised a part of Austria till 1918. Some characteristics of Małopolska – its fragmented land structure, the small size of farms, the relative impoverishment of country people living there (at least in the past) – make it perhaps more 'attractive' for fieldwork study, but by focusing solely on this region anthropologists have created, at least in Western academia, an impression that it is typical for the Polish countryside. My intention is to balance the picture that can be found in the writings of Pine, Hann, Nagengast, Conte and Dunn, even if the latter 'merely' studied an industrial plant linked to the agricultural sector. Historical accounts of the Polish peasantry conducted by Western scholars are also mostly preoccupied with the Austrian part of then still partitioned Poland (e.g. Stauter-Halsted 2001), and the same applies to the contemporary studies on symbolic aspects of peasant life (see Cooley 2005).

The region of Wielkopolska began to undergo capitalist transformation at the end of the nineteenth century under Prussian rule and, in contrast to Galicia, farms could not be divided into parts smaller than seventeen hectares. Land estates were commonplace and German *Junkers*, supported by the government in Berlin, became rivals for land with the long-settled Polish gentry. At that time, soil had a vital national quality. Prussian rule resulted in a land structure that still differentiates Wielkopolska's rural areas from other parts of the country to this day. Sizeable farms and former land estates, converted mostly into state farms under communism, alongside high productivity, have been among the most conspicuous features. Also during the socialist period, farmers were producers and often interested in keeping their farms for commercial production. The further commercialization of agriculture after 1989 has caused great interest in land in most parts of the region and, in contrast to territories transferred to Poland from Germany after 1945, rising rural entrepreneurs here compete for this scarce good.[12]

Several of these processes can be seen in Dziekanowice's history and ethnography. A village cadastre map from 1820, with corrections from 1835,[13] shows that three families present in the village today occupy more or less the same place as their nineteenth century ancestors. There are some hints that the first families established themselves in the village by 1780 and one of my informants claims that his family has resided in Dziekanowice for at least eight generations. Furthermore, according to parish registers, there are five other families which came to the village in the nineteenth century. A number of families took up residence in Dziekanowice in the first two decades of the twentieth century and several others since the interwar period. It was also at that time that some rural proletarians' families, still present in the community, today settled here. During the Second World War a lot of people were evicted from their farms and sent either to the German occupied part of Poland[14] or to Germany to work as forced labourers, but most returned home after 1945.

Existing records also show that farm ownership changed as a result of purchase, marriages and the continuing arrival of new settlers. However, despite these transfers, changes in state sovereignty and political systems, there is a continuity of settlement stretching over several decades and in some cases almost two centuries.[15] Peasants/farmers constitute the most durable social component since there was a large ebb and flow among the agricultural workers. The ownership of the largest estate in Dziekanowice[16] has had a complex history, having changed both in size and ownership. It was forcefully taken over by the Prussian state from the Roman-Catholic Church and during interwar period, besides the c.160 hectares that fell back into Church hands, the estate was owned by the Polish state and leased to a relatively rich, although not gentrified, family. In 1939, the family was evicted by the Nazis and a Baltic German (*Baltendeutscher*) from Estonia managed the manor and land. When Polish communists seized power, the estate shared the fate of many similar agricultural entities in the country. Immediately after the Second World War, the holding was distributed among fifteen rural working families whose farms ranged between 7 and 12 hectares. In the early fifties, together with some – although not all – long-established peasants' farms, it was collectivized, and then, after the 'October Thaw' of 1956,[17] decollectivized. At the end of 1950s the state farm was established. Its property consisted of the remaining local state property in Dziekanowice and its vicinity, including those lands partly confiscated from the Church, as well as the land of eleven beneficiaries of the Nationalization Act who relinquished their assets to the state almost for nothing. It functioned for the next quarter of a century. Only one person out of all those who gave up farming found employment in the new enterprise while the others left the village. In the 1960s farming was a difficult occupation and delivering compulsory allotments to the state was a demanding chore. Land ownership was no longer highly valued by all. Settling in towns or even joining state farms as a manual worker was regarded as a more comfortable life than farming. Nevertheless, four former rural proletarian families stayed on the land they received in 1945 and dwell there to this day. Radical socialist agricultural reforms left their mark in local property relations and converted a number of former rural workers into farmers.

By the end of 1980s the state farm enterprise in Dziekanowice tilled 379 hectares of land, of which 211 hectares were within the village itself. Of the latter, the Agency took over 212 hectares (including one hectare from the State Land Fund). However, of these only 25 hectares (11.8 per cent) have been sold. The biggest local beneficiary of the systemic transformation was the Roman Catholic Church to which 151 hectares (71.2 per cent of all land acquired by the Agency) were returned. 11 hectares (5.2 per cent) have been given to previous owners, 22 hectares are being leased (10.4 per cent) and 3 hectares managed by the Agency lay fallow.[18] This data is not very representative for the commune or region, not to mention the entire country. In Dziekanowice the proportion of Church property is exceptionally high and it mirrors the historical development of this locality that started in medieval times. Prussian confiscation and communist nationalization caused substantial reversals of fortune, but the latter turned out to be merely a whimsical episode. Nationwide, the state has given the Church close to 71,000 hectares which comprises only 1.5 per cent of the whole land overtaken by the Agency.[19] At the commune's borders, for example, the proportion of land returned to the Church amounts to 28.3 per cent. Farmers in Dziekanowice have therefore not had much opportunity for buying land. They can rent it from the local parish, which alone owns more than 100 hectares, or buy it in the surrounding area. By the end of 2001, very little of the land comprising the previous state farm in Dziekanowice had fallen into individual farmers' hands. This, in a drastic way, illustrates how scarce good land in this region is. In the communities where the majority of the population are farmers – in the Łubowo commune agriculture is a main source of income for 80 per cent of its inhabitants – farm size expansion is only possible by reducing the number of farms, by allowing some farms to swallow others. The concentration of farmers and their interest in land in Wielkopolska have made the price of land among the highest in the country: one hectare costs the equivalent of 2,000 euros.[20] This hunger for land shows that the value attributed to land is high among farmers in Dziekanowice and EU subsidies to agriculture calculated on the basis of acreage cultivated by a household has strengthened this tendency.

Nevertheless, private owners prevail in Dziekanowice. Coordinating the Agency and the Commune Office's data is difficult.[21] In any case, out of the c.879 hectares documented in the office register for the Dziekanowice area in 2001, farmers alone owned 611 hectares (68 per cent), other private proprietors 10 hectares (c.1 per cent), the commune 16 hectares (1.9 per cent), the Church 100 hectares (12 per cent) and the state, in the form of its legal subjects (e.g., the Museum of First Piasts of Lednica),[22] 61 hectares (7 per cent). The Agency itself, as the representative of the state, still possessed 90 hectares (10 per cent) that was mostly tilled by its commercial farm establishment in Łubowo, but apparently, in the last three years, it returned about ten hectares to the Church and sold some pieces into private hands.[23] One can therefore say that in 2001 public property (the state and the commune combined) comprised 19 per cent of Dziekanowice's land, while the rest was in private hands. Today this proportion is even more in favour of private owners. The dissolution of the state farm has also caused the emergence of a whole new group of 'owners'. Former state farm workers, altogether thirty families, were each given 0.05 hectare pieces of land for free (altogether 1.5 ha) which they used as garden plots during communism. Moreover, the apartments they live in were sold to them on very favourable terms. Their market value is not very high, although recently one family from the outside the village moved into the flat left by their deceased kin. Beyond farmers and former state farm workers, a group of rural settlers also live in Dziekanowice. Most of them either have worked for the Museum or in the non-agricultural enterprises in the vicinity. They often own small plots of land (between 0.18 and 0.89 hectares) and small houses. Recently, some of them have sold parts of their plots (13 parcels covering 4.3 hectares in total) to newcomers, representatives of liberal professions from the surrounding cities, who build new houses in the village. One among them is an Italian who married a Pole and runs a business in the immediate area.

That concludes my description of property relations in the tangible sense. The detailed account above is meant to provide evidence of several points. First, if we look at the development of property relations from the perspective of structures of the *long durée*, some important features become visible. Since the Prussian confiscation of Church property, four major players in the real estate market have been present: the state, the Church and private proprietors. Private proprietors can be further divided into peasants/ farmers and landowners, although this latter effectively disappeared after communist nationalization. However, one of the farmers in Dziekanowice has recently substantially increased the size of his enterprise and in 2001 he paid taxes on 236 hecatres of land. This estate is definitely not an average farm[24] and there are other farmers who are making efforts to increase their acreage. Second, the nationalization of big land estates carried out in 1945 left its mark on property relations and transformed some rural proletarians into small farmers. Nevertheless, in the case of Dziekanowice, the outcome of nationalization has been very limited and less then one in ten farms today are owned by the descendants of the beneficiaries of land reform who till only a small amount of the total village farmland. Third, the socialist state tried to dominate the stage, but it failed. An attempt to eliminate the Church as an important title holder (during the socialist period the authorities left the parish in Dziekanowice only ten hectares) turned out to be unsuccessful and today the Church, especially in this area around such an important religious centre as Gniezno,[25] is again a big landowner that mostly leases its agricultural land. Fourth, private ownership has for decades, if not ages, dominated property relations. It has been revitalized in the last fifteen years and went so far that even former agricultural workers were enfranchised with minuscule land plots and the apartments in which they live. Fifth, the concept of private property, strengthened recently by the neoliberal fixation on individual ownership, is not a new idea for the people in Dziekanowice. Especially for farmers, it simply confirms their 'natural' right to hold the land they till. Sixth, the state has accepted this philosophy and is gradually withdrawing from land ownership, although this process is not as rapid and as conspicuous as in other Central and Eastern European countries. It remained strong throughout the communist period, although it was not always ideologically accepted by the authorities (see my points above, about the stages of state policy). Today it is being implemented vigorously so that a fringe of hectare (0.05) of land has even been given to former state farm workers.

Land Ownership, Labour, and Identity

In the community of around 400 inhabitants four major social groups can be distinguished and this structure is still conspicuous after sixteen years of free market reforms and change in property relations. The position of these groups is not simply defined by individuals' relations to material goods, particularly land. It emerges from much more multidimensional analysis that takes into account Pierre Bourdieu's notions of power, knowledge, control of the means of production, forms of economic, symbolic and social capital, as well as subjective identity (see Buchowski 1997: 15–24). These social classes can be distinguished by looking at the everyday practices of people that have a certain relationship to the means of production: looking at marriage patterns, inheritance practices, and work ethos; comparing their education, modes of adaptation to structural changes; looking at changing lifestyles and political attitudes. Using these criteria, one can distinguish four social categories, which I have classified as farmers, village proletarians, agricultural workers and white collar workers.

Given our concern with property relations, farmers appear as the most significant group. Their families have often lived in the village for generations, and they strongly identify with village affairs and dominate public life. For example, post-war village leaders (*sołtys*) have always been farmers while the village representatives to the Commune Council are virtually all peasants. Their social status and identification is emphasized by their shared ethos of industriousness and appropriateness of behaviour in public and private life, their political views and, last but not least, ownership of land. For generations they owned land ranging in size and quality causing them to be perceived as a unified class although they can be divided into several factions. It is not easy to determine their actual farm size, since many farmers from Dziekanowice own or also rent land beyond its limits. In any case, 46 households registered there pay agricultural tax, *podatek rolny*. The size of land owned and taxed in Dziekanowice itself for individual farmers ranges between 0.11 hectares and 236 hectares. The size of farmland does not have to coincide with prosperity, although it has become a pattern that those rich in the past have become even richer today. Some have expanded their acreage significantly, while others have preferred to accomplish economic success by focusing on niche production.

Second, there are agricultural workers. In 1994 all employees of the former state farm were taken over by the Museum. In this way, the twenty men and women who were workers on the state farm switched to manual work for another state institution. At present, only four of them still work there while most have either retired or passed away. Some of their descendants have found permanent jobs at the Museum or are employed seasonally there. Privatization made these families owners of the flats they lived in and of their tiny garden plots in 1994. This enfranchisement has not changed their lives a lot, because under the new guise it perpetuates an old state of affairs and the market value of these assets is close to nil. They were also inactive at the moment when the possibility of forming a workers' company appeared in 1993. They preferred to be 'taken over' by the Museum. None of these people ever thought to buy land, for two combined reasons: lack of funds and lack of competence. Thus, they missed an opportunity to work on their own.

Third, there are members of the village proletariat who were not employees of the state farm, but worked in various companies in the vicinity and usually held some small pieces of land. Those who lived in the commune's apartments were also enfranchised for symbolic payment. Some seized the opportunity and sold parts of their land as parcels to new settlers who built houses on them. None among them acquired new land.

Fourth, there are white collar workers, who either work for the Museum or settled here in the recent past. They, even when they have been living in Dziekanowice for a quarter of a century, are considered outsiders. This is so not only because of their different social status, but also because they do not socialize with local people belonging to other groups. Taking property as the differentiating factor, white collar workers (or 'intelligentsia') should be divided into newcomers, who bought some parcels or houses, and those who do not strive to have any property since they reside in the Museum's apartments, which satisfies their needs. Among those first, thirteen families altogether, is the Italian who married a Pole and runs a business in the area.

At first sight Dziekanowice appears as a unified community that shares many cultural features, such as language, religion, basic education; it comprises a group of people using the same infrastructure, attending the same primary schools and church masses; it constitutes a collective adhering to the same nation and congregation. People also participate in similar public discourses, witness and exchange views about political debates and often watch the same TV programmes and mass events (among which the death of the 'Polish Pope' at the beginning of April 2005 was a spectacularly unifying, although ephemeral, experience). However, as I have indicated above and elsewhere (Buchowski1995, 2003) they are divided in many ways and by many qualities. Property is only one among various discriminating factors. Social relations generate divergent identities that surface in the least expected circumstances. For instance, everybody declares that love is decisive when people get married. However, it is not surprising that mutual love bonds partners practically always from the same social echelon. But social distinctions are not usually so easily perceptible. Behaviour reproduces patterns entrenched in culture and this explains why proletarians that have relied on the socialist state for years exploit the existing social security system today without hesitation. This raises objections by 'real peasants' (*prawdziwy gospodarz*, an indigenous term that means literally 'real landlord') for whom the attitudes of proletarians would not be appropriate. Such silent barriers are created by every fraction. White collar workers from the museum are considered 'relics' who do not really belong to the local community. They in turn consider proletarians 'aborigines' and uneducated 'simpletons'. Agricultural workers are perceived by the village proletarians and others as the lowest class, being deprived of moral values and a dignified ethos. Farmers typically perceive proletarians as 'lazy jerks'. For agricultural workers, farmers are hicks, *bambry*. From the point of view of mutual perceptions, Dziekanowice looks like an everlasting and slowly altering huge hall of mirrors.

Property seems to be the most tangible distinguishing factor, but it does not mean that it is decisive in establishing social hierarchy. White collar workers do not feel 'lower' in relation to even the most affluent farmers. Proletarians have no desire to buy land and become farmers. This attitude results from both cultural patterns and constraints already indicated: it is beyond their aptitude and financial possibilities. Most agricultural workers actually look down at farmers for their devotion to toil that does not pay adequate returns. Nevertheless, as Katherine Verdery writes: 'Property is about social relations. These include both relations among persons and the power relations in which people act' (1998: 180). Property thus serves as a window through which we can see local culture and society, especially since it is 'simultaneously a cultural system, a set of social relations, and an organization of power' (Verdery 2003: 19), or 'a relation among persons with respect to values' (2003: 172).

Even if farming is not considered the best mode of subsistence, possession of a piece of land is desired. If one considers the fact that even agricultural proletarians now officially also own land, there are virtually no families (with the exception of several white collar workers) totally landless in this community. Rural proletarians, both former state farm workers and village proletarians, value garden plots since they contribute to their often meagre incomes in the form of food products. In the case of the latter, who own larger plots, it can comprise a considerable contribution to their household budgets. Unemployed and retired persons spend time working there, and cultivating them is a subject of daily conversations among them. Vegetable and fruit raised on one's own plot are considered better than purchased ones.[26] Actually, most families tend to be self-sufficient in this respect and therefore making jars and preserves is not only a question of livelihood, but also of pride. One can say, paraphrasing Bronisław Malinowski, that these soil gardens have their magic. Gardens are an appreciated source of foodstuff that, by virtue of being natural and self-grown, improve the quality of life of their immediate consumers. The market or monetary value of these plots is not impressive. However, these gardens acquire additional value assigned to them by owners who cherish them as economic assets as well as culturally defined symbols of rural identity and, at least partial, independence.

For farmers, land assumes a much more complex meaning. In their eyes, it divides people into haves and have-nots and the size of plot owned counts. Being a farmer means being a holder of a piece of land that enables the family to survive and thrive. In their eyes land is indeed a synonym of the most important and tangible kind of property. A farmer is an owner (*właściciel*) who poses (*posiada*) land (*ziemię*). Farms smaller than seven to ten hectares are considered today to be merely a supplementary source of income. There is only one family owning so few hectares that is considered a fully-fledged farming family. It successfully specializes in commercial gardening and a large part of their now eight hectares of land is covered by greenhouses. A usual comment about smallholders is that 'phi, what do they have?!' ('*te, co oni tam mają?!*') Garden plots owned by village proletarians, particularly former state farm workers, are not seen as assets at all and therefore farmers view them as destitute and despised, simply *burki*.[27] Land is for farmers a traditional and major means of production. It is also a symbol of their wealth and a tool for keeping their independence. Working on the land creates their identity, a phenomenon that mysteriously bonds the mental with the material. Working properly, producing (visible) wealth, feeding family and educating children is a question of individual pride. A farmer is a master of his (rarely her) land and can show his skills to the others. In the community of growers settled in Dziekanowice over generations, land attains the additional meaning of having the quality of the patrimony, until very recently customarily inherited according to the ultimogeniture principle. Tilling forefathers' land (*ojcowizna*; *ojciec* means father) is a source of wealth, but also puts on the farmers an obligation towards this cross-generational community of kindred. In this perspective, a landholding has a sentimental value that stretches well beyond its market value. Farmers that do really badly – usually as a result of alcohol abuse – and sell their land, are very few and definitely disrespected. 'Why does he behave that way?', was a comment I heard about one of the farmers coming from a proletarian family that benefited from the land reform of the 1940s, from another man of similar family history but steady in his farming. As if bowing to this opinion, the person concerned committed suicide not long ago.

Value assigned to land by most farmers is thus socially and culturally imbued. The sentimental surplus attached to land goes beyond its market value and it is particularly significant for those who remember collectivization attempts. The political significance of their resistance is clearly remembered by the older, now outgoing generation. In some contexts it functioned as a factor that divided farmers themselves, and persons active in this project were openly scorned in conversations that I held a decade ago. At present, all former campaigners of collectivization are gone, so it is becoming a scarcely remembered episode of history for farmers operating today. For farmers, it has for long been extremely important that they owned land, that they have been on their own, autonomous and self-governed. Relentless sweat and toil have been unable to depress the intimate and elevating feeling that one's labour is not appropriated by somebody else, at least in a tangible, straightforward way. At the ideological level, neoliberal principles with respect to self-reliance and private ownership of agricultural land or means of production in fact coincided with those they have held 'forever'. However, the actual introduction of free-market principles and prioritizing private ownership has had several effects. One of these was that land started to acquire first and foremost an economic value. Its sentimental meaning started to wane, although it is still persistent. In the first half of the 1990s, price fluctuations made many farmers cautious and reluctant to invest. This was definitely a reverse side of the neoliberal coin that the majority of farmers abhorred. 'Wait and see' was their officially declared policy. However, there was a group of farmers who took the risk and invested both in land and in the specialization of production (note that risk is another notion important in the glossary of economic liberalism). Today, this group includes at least five farmers among whom two are visible and commonly recognized rural entrepreneurs, capital makers and job creators. One is the above-mentioned family of garden growers who produces vegetables, strawberries and flowers. At the peak of the season they employ more than thirty people from Dziekanowice and the surrounding area. The other one is the owner of a chicken farm that within last decade has grown in size from 35,000 to 120,000 broilers, and the area of land he tills covers now more than two hundred hectares. Beyond the commune borders he also currently rents c.1200 hectares. He employs several people, some of them from the village.

For both economic and symbolic reasons, land is a scarce good in Dziekanowice. In daily discourse at a grass-roots level its ownership appears as non-ideological, at least in the sense that it is expressed overtly at the nationwide level and perceived by the public. People have some abstract 'fears' against foreigners buying up 'Polish soil', but at the same time nobody objects to the right of the Italian man to have property in the community and he is fully accepted. ('He is a nice man who doesn't bother anybody. He attends mass each Sunday'). However, as mentioned above, land has its symbolic power in creating social distinctions. Economic power, individual aspirations and political control translate into property relations that are realized within the framework of existing possibilities. The distribution of property is necessarily a function of overall political organization. Power relations are implicated in it, and those who are richer can afford more and gain more thanks to their economic capital and influence, partly rooted in historically configured relations based on ownership titles. But by no means is this the only factor that shapes property relations. Local political relations can turn out to be equally important. There was a case of a bid for land in which, according to common opinion, 'connections' (*znajomości*) played a role. In 1994, a big piece of land from the previous state farm was taken over by the Museum that outbid, among others, the chicken-farm owner. The first bid resulted in an extraordinarily high price and was soon annulled. Another public bid was arranged in which the Museum bought the land for a 'reasonable' price. Regional politicians, both administrators and the Agency's managers, openly manipulated the tender in such a way that their plans with regard to the development of this cultural institution could be carried out. This kind of personal experience of social actors creates images about power relations related to property. For farmers this boils down to an age-old opinion that they, the ordinary people, can always be manoeuvred and overruled by the tricky and powerful authorities.

For most farmers, cultivating land is practically the only option for life available, although their adult children often work outside agriculture. 'Where should I go now?' (*'A gdzie ja teraz pójdę?'*) is a typical reaction to my question about leaving agriculture and starting something new. Despite constant complaints about production circumstances (and there were several reasons to complain; see Zbierski-Salameh 1999) this is their inherited livelihood and part of their personality. In the communist past the acreage allowed was limited, big farms discouraged and farm-size not so important for the person's status in the community. The free market and privatization policy opened fields (in both the literal and metaphoric sense) for competition and caused shifts in social relations. Land for farmers has not been definitely devalued, as has happened in some other postsocialist regions (cf. Verdery 2003). Those rich and resolute enough started to expand and this makes them distinct and proud. They not only work on their own, but some of them also perform managerial work. In economic terms this makes them not only direct and simultaneously independent producers, but persons appropriating part of the value of somebody else's labour, i.e. exploiters. The latter differentiates them from other farmers who only work on their own, and at the same time endangers relatively new relationships with several other community members.

The latter issue brings us to the problem of labour.[28] Rural entrepreneurs were able to enlarge their acreage and output, but it involves the employment of people from the community. In the recent past, all people in Dziekanowice worked physically either on their own farms or for the state enterprises, mainly the local state farm and the Museum. White collar workers were an exception with regard to the character of their trade, but they also belonged to a group of hired workers employed by the state in the same fashion as many manual workers. Today a group of entrepreneurs encounter new relationships with their fellow residents that have not in fact been seen in the Polish countryside since the Second World War. This new context raises several problems. Agricultural workers, *burki*, dislike working for *bambry*, farmers. Instead of working for the abstract state, people in the community now work for a tangible employer. Working for a real person that used to be on a par with them appears as degradation and runs counter to their image of equality. Work in state institutions is still highly valued: *'nie ma jak to państwowa robota'*, or, 'nothing compares to a state job'. However, the dissolution of the state farm has led to the shortage of state-sponsored jobs for village proletarians in the community and vicinity. The Museum, the major state institution in the commune, has limited possibilities of employment for local people. Competition for positions there is high. Most of those who cannot find a job there have to consider other options and now tens of them are left with no option but to work for the farmers, especially the two entrepreneurs already mentioned. In this straightforward way property relations translate into social relations that significantly affect the perception of individuals' and groups' statuses.

In the socialist past, private ownership existed, but it functioned alongside state property. This situation created two parallel worlds of people who worked physically and, although differentiated, were not dependant on each other (at least from the grass-roots perspective). This status quo reinforced a sense of equality among proletarians, particularly agricultural ones, who traditionally were perceived as 'the wretched of the Polish earth.' State employment was steady and appreciated by them. The appropriation of wealth and value from their work, as well as that of the farmers', was concealed. It was the state that regulated prices and wages, and channelled profits into its own pockets that it later redistributed in the name of 'social justice'. Appropriation was obscured, while what was promulgated was the generous reallocation of means. Such obscurity made the state an abstract employer and exploiter. It was perceptible at the local level merely in the form of agents (managers) hired by the state and regulated by a set of practices, in which ordinary people participated. Now this situation has changed radically. An owner, an employer and an appropriator, all in one, is visible and corporeal. Moreover, s/he comes from the same community. Entrenched egalitarianism results in a strong ideological resistance that makes proletarians reluctant to take up jobs at farms. They prefer all other alternatives, including unemployment with its meagre benefits. Forced to work for rural entrepreneurs, proletarians experience immediate inequality which they perceive as humiliation and participate in a hierarchical job relationship they sense as exploitation. Workers see that their labour contributes to the wealth of their neighbours, former equals in the local society. Individual identities in the community have been unsettled.

At the core of these transformations are changes in ownership relations prompted by neoliberal ideas of the 'naturalness' of private property accepted by the state authorities and elites. The new ownership regime has created a situation in which property has started to matter again significantly in shaping social hierarchies and dependencies. Property owned entails a social bearing proportional to its size and accepted market and symbolic value. This convergence of the value of an agricultural property and the social prestige associated with it fits images held by farmers for whom 'it is the way things should be'. It causes resistance on the part of those whom such a dominant view, promulgated by all advocates of the new order, puts in a subordinate and degrading position in the social hierarchy. Through the systematic withdrawal from the agricultural sector and the distribution of land to private economic actors, the state has also devolved responsibility towards many of its citizens. This point is appallingly valid with regard to the former state farm workers. Hundreds of thousands of them lost their jobs overnight and no real assistance, except unemployment benefits and early retirement, was offered to them and, as in many cases it has turned out, to their offspring. Former state farms are today considered as sites of emerging pockets of permanent poverty (cf. Tarkowska 1997). In Dziekanowice this was not exactly the case, because the Museum functioned as a 'social cushion' in the process of privatization of agriculture. Nevertheless, the disappearance of the state farm has coerced many to work for private owners to whom new possibilities of expansion and enrichment opened. In turn, this has created a spate of social conversion and cultural conundrums. Both identities, those imposed by others and self-identities, have changed. The identification process has been privatized. Individuals construct their personalities by relating to, or being related to, other members of the community. Furthermore, the central and moderating role of the state, represented locally by a state-run institution, has significantly diminished. One can also say that by pulling out from local property relations and affairs, the state also privatized social relations. Group identities and differences have been redefined according to diversifying prosperity based on private ownership. Rich, usually industrious, farmers are becoming even richer, while, devoid of property and safe state jobs, workers are becoming relatively poorer and dependant on the former. This dependency individualizes daily relationships. Employers prefer people who work diligently and in this way personal qualities determine an individual's success on the job market and in life. This, in consequence, leads to the commodification of labour through which people are gauged. During socialism such measurement was restricted to the farmers' ethos alone. Now it is becoming more universal, but at the same time privatized. It seems evident that seemingly tangible property relations have many intangible social and cultural consequences.

Notes

1   Of course, this does not mean that other topics have not been addressed by Western anthropologists in postsocialist countries. Nationalism, civil society and religion appear to be next on the research priority list. For a concise review of the anthropological research agenda in postsocialist countries, see Hann (2000).

2   As Chris Hann, in his introduction to the volume that summarizes the work done on postsocialist property relations in Eurasia by the group of scholars at the Max Planck Institute for Social Anthropology in Halle, writes: 'Regrettably, we have had no project on Poland, where mass collectivization was abandoned after a political crisis in 1956 and private family farming remained dominant. This is precisely what makes the Polish case so interesting' (2003: 17).

3   For a summary of the various forms of and the process of privatization in Poland, see Hunter and Ryan (2004). They distinguish seven different models of privatization of the state enterprises (ibid.: 929–933). Their article does not make any direct reference to the situation in the agricultural sector. For an anthropological account of the privatization processes in the industrial sector, see the brilliant work of Elizabeth Dunn (2004).

4   As one of the major 'winners' of the anti-German alliance (the fourth largest military force and with over six million victims) Polish borders were shifted westward by c.200–300 km and the country reduced in size by almost a quarter (from 388 to 312 thousands square km). Poland lost its eastern territories at the expense of the Soviet Union and was compensated with lands taken away from Germany. This has created a problem for people resettled from interwar eastern territories and who lost their property there. Despite international agreements they have still not been properly compensated for their losses until today. This makes their situation fundamentally different from Germans expelled from Central Europe.

5   'The neoliberal programme tends to construct in reality an economic system corresponding to the theoretical description, in other words a kind of logical machine, which presents itself as a chain of constraints impelling the economic agents' (Bourdieu 1998: 96). This project operates at three levels: at the international level, states 'adopt policies that enhance their positions' in the global markets; '[n]ationally, governments sell state-owned enterprises and cut their financial support, forcing them to compete for customers'; and at the level of an individual, 'the construction of selfhood draws less and less on waged work' (Colloredo-Mansfeld 2002: 114). Private ownership of land and other means of production, implicit in the second point, were acutely underscored in all postcommunist economic reforms programs directed by international agencies such as the World Bank and IMF as well as local pro-neoliberal ideologues and policy makers. As Humphrey and Verdery write: 'Property was the idiom used by international organizations, which made economic assistance conditional on changes in property rights; it was used as well by local and national politicians' (2004: 12). At some other point they notice that '[t]he increased legitimacy of "private property" is widely associated with the advance of capitalism in its various guises and with the spread of neoliberal discourse into new settings' (2004: 18).

6   A process of parcelling of land in Poland as well as in the region started already in the interwar period (see Roszkowski 1995, particularly Table 10, p. 131).

7   Edward Gierek was the First Secretary of the Polish United Workers' Party between December 1970 (after workers' strikes) and August 1980 (again, after workers' strikes and the rise of Solidarity).

8   Following legislative work initiated by the government, the parliament adopted on 19 October 1991 the Act on the Management of Agricultural Property of the State Treasury (complete text in the Journal of Laws, No.57, Item 299 with subsequent amendments). The Act entrusted restructuring and privatization in the state-run sector of agriculture to the Agricultural Property Agency of the State Treasury. The property entrusted to the Agency forms the Agricultural Property Stock (APS) of the State Treasury. Almost 80 per cent of APS land comes from liquidated state farms.

9   All data about the Agency and its activities comes from materials published by it. Most of them can be found on its website (see: *Agencja Nieruchomości Rolnych*; http://www. anr. gov.pl). See particularly links to 'Wyniki działalności': http://www.anr.gov.pl/pl/section/ wd. Accessed 15.05.2005.

10   Poland is the only country that entered the EU in May 2004 which negotiated a twelve-year moratorium that strictly restricts the free flow of capital with respect to the sale of land (in all other postsocialist countries the grace period will last for seven years). The discussion on land acquisition in Poland has been mired in nationalist arguments ('Germans will buy Polish soil in which our ancestors' blood is soaked … '). Let me outline my own reading of this allegedly patriotic problem. The lack of a reprivatisation bill reflects power relations between, on the one hand, a politically weak interest group of interwar landowners and their heirs, and, on the other hand, a strong lobby of agricultural entrepreneurs, many among them former members of the *nomenklatura* (i.e. former communist party activists), and rich farmers. The Agency leases and gradually sells land to the latter at relatively low prices. Expected price increases when the market opens in 2016 will quickly enrich new landowners. Thus, fears against foreigners coincide with a mystified economic interest of those who 'defend Polish soil'.

11 Currently the unofficial price for such a 'favour' is c.1,000 zlotys (250 euros) per hectare, which approximately comprises forty per cent of an average monthly salary in Poland. This is of course in addition to the official cost of any land on which there are legal claims (in Wielkopolska it is on average 7,000 zlotys per hectare).

12 About patterns in land structure in Poland see Głębocki 2000.

13 Landratura Gniezno 20. Measurements were done in 1820 by an individual by the name of Smul; copied in 1835 by Demmler.

14 When Germany and the Soviet Union divided Poland in 1939, Polish prewar territory occupied by the Nazis was divided into a part annexed by the Third Reich, which included Wielkopolska, then called Warthegau, Danzig-Eastern Pomerania, Upper Silesia, and the Suwałki District, and the occupied territory of 'Generalgouvernment', which included such cities as Warsaw, Cracow, Lublin, Radom and, after 1941, Lvov (cf. Conte and Essner 1995: 267).

15 It does not mean that this kind of continuity is universal in the region. For example, in neighbouring Lednogóra, in which a lot of German settlers used to live, a lot of people only arrived in the last fifty years.

16 The name of the village has religious and economic connotation that reveals what institution owned it in the past. In the Catholic Church a *Dziekan* (Dean) is a priest who heads the cathedral chapter, in this case the cathedral is in Gniezno. The ending -*wice* is very common in Polish topography.

17 The end of Stalinist period was marked in Poland by a workers' uprising in Poznań in June 1956, followed by political relaxation in October of that year, signified by a change of Party leadership headed by Władysław Gomułka who pronounced 'the Polish road to socialism'. The latter implied also the end of the policy of forced collectivization of agriculture.

18 These data were valid for 28 February 2005. I received them from the Poznań Branch of the Agricultural Real Estates Agency. Special thanks to Mr. Paweł Andrzejczak, head of the analysis department.

19 In 1989 Parliament (*Sejm*) accepted a bill thanks to which the Church was granted back confiscated rural lands. Besides, each newly established parish in the countryside has had a right to be granted fifteen hectares from the state. Together with a land the Church kept during the communist period, it now owns a hundred thousand hectares, which makes it the second largest landowner in the country, after the state treasury. The Church usually rents its land out to farmers or institutions (cf. Sowul and Katka 2005: 4).

20 Land price grows systematically and in Wielkopolska reached almost 4,000 euors by 2008. This fact alone somehow confirms my interpretation given in footnote 10.

21 All statistical data about Dzickanowice was gathered in the Commune's Office in Łubowo. I would like to thank the staff of this administrative centre, particularly commune's leader Mr. Andrzej Łozowski, for their help.

22 The Museum was established in the early 1970s and includes an archaeological section that preserves historical sites considered to be the cradle of the Polish Christian state, an open-air museum and the Lednica Landscape Reserve. The administration of the Museum is now located in the administrative building of the former state farm. It employs almost a hundred people (ethnographers, archaeologists, botanists, administrators, and blue collar workers working as wardens or manual workers, many of them preserving the landscape around the lake). During summer several local people are employed as seasonal workers guarding houses in the open-air museum. For more about the official activities of the Museum see Fryza (1992) and Kaszubkiewicz (1998).

23 These are my own calculations based on the data I received from the Commune Office in February 2001. Measurements are not always compatible with each other and depend on the purposes they are designed for. This does not mean that registers are imprecise, but statistical configurations may vary according to the purpose. Even the data I received from the Agency office in 2001 and 2005 are not congruent. I have to emphasize that nowadays both local people and local bureaucrats are unwilling to share knowledge and data about ownership relations. In the first case, it seems to be considered a private issue, while in the second the law protecting individuals' data is always kept in mind.

24 A legal regulation states that 'a person counts as an individual farmer if s/he owns or leases agricultural real estate of a combined acreage not exceeding 300 ha' However, the biggest individual landowner in Poland, Senator Henryk Stokłosa from Wielkopolska, owns 16,000 hectares (Sowul and Katka 2005: 4), which equals the acreage of six former average state farms (cf. Verdery 2003: 86, Table 2.2). I should probably add that now (i.e., in August 2008), Stokłosa is a former senator now facing trial for tax evasions.

25 This has been the region where Christianity was first accepted in the tenth century, the cradle of the Polish state. Since the year 1000 it has been the seat of the archbishop and of the primate of the Polish Roman Catholic Church.

26 This observation confirms attitudes also registered by Frances Pine 2001 and Andre Czegledy (2002).

27 *Burek* is a common name for dogs.

28 I have discussed this in detail elsewhere (cf. Buchowski 2004), so here I will refer only to questions relevant to my current concerns.

References

Abrahams, R. (ed.) 1996. *After Socialism: Land Reform and Social Change in Eastern Europe*. Oxford: Berghahn Books.

Bourdieu, P. 1998. 'Neo-liberalism, the Utopia [Becoming a Reality] of Unlimited Exploitation,' in *Acts of Resistance: Against the Tyranny of the Market*, New York: New Press, pp.94–105.

Buchowski, M. 1995. 'Chacun laboure comme il peut', *Etudes rurale* 138–140: 173–83.

———. 1997. *Reluctant Capitalists*. Berlin: Centre Marc Bloch.

———. 2003. 'Coming to Terms with Capitalism: An Example of a Rural Community in Poland', *Dialectical Anthropology* 27: 47–68.

———. 2004. 'Redefining Work in a Local Community in Poland: "Transformation" and Class, Culture, and Work', in A. Procoli (ed.) *Workers and Narratives of Survival in Europe: The Management of Precariousness at the End of Twentieth Century*. Albany: SUNY Press, pp.173–96.

Colloredo-Mansfeld, R. 2002. 'An Ethnography of Neoliberalism', *Current Anthropology* 43(1): 113–37.

Conte, E. 2001. 'Was the Peasantry of Zamojszczyzna a Creation of Socialism? Ethnic Cleansing and Land Reform in Southeastern Poland', in M. Buchowski, E. Conte and C. Nagengast (eds), *Poland Beyond Communism: 'Transition' in Critical Perspective*. Fribourg: Fribourg University Press, pp.93–123.

Conte E. and C. Essner. 1995. *La Quête de la race: Un Antropologie de nazisme*. Paris: Hachette.

Cooley, T. J. 2005. *Making Music in the Polish Tatras: Tourists, Ethnographers, and Mountain Musicians*. Indianapolis: Indiana University Press.

Creed, G. 1998. *Domesticating Revolution: From Socialist Reform to Ambivalent Transition in a Bulgarian Village*. University Park: Pennsylvania State University Press.

Czegledy, A. 2002. 'Urban Peasants in a Post-socialist World: Small Scale Agriculturalists in Hungary', in P. Leonard and D. Kaneff (eds), *Post-Socialist Peasant? Rural and Urban Constructions of Identity in Eastern*

Europe, East Asia and the Former Soviet Union. New York: Palgrave, pp.200–20.

Danglová, O. 2003. 'Decollectivization and Survival Strategies in a Post-socialist Co-operative Farm', *Anthropological Journal on European Cultures* 12: 31–56.

Dunn, E. 2004. *Privatizing Poland: Baby Food, Big Business, and the Remaking of Labor.* Ithaca: Cornell University Press.

Eberhardt, P. 1993. 'Depopulation Processes in the Rural Areas of East-Central Europe (1950–1990)', *East European Countryside* 0: 31–40.

Fryza, M. 1992. 'Muzeum Pierwszych Piastów na Lednicy', *Muzealnictwo* 34: 28–34.

Głębocki, B. 2000. 'Changes of the Agrarian Structure in the Polish Agriculture in the Years 1990–1996', in B. Głębocki (ed.) *Poland's Agrarian Structure in the Period of Political and Economic Transformation.* Poznań: Bogucki Wydawnictwo Naukowe, pp.9–74.

Geertz, C. 1995. *After the Fact: Two Countries, Four Decades, One Anthropologist.* Cambridge, MA: Harvard University Press.

Gorlach K. and Z. Seręga. 1991. *Chłopi we współczesnej Polsce: przedmiot czy podmiot procesów społecznych?* Kraków: Państwowe Wydawnictwo Naukowe.

Hann, C. 1998. 'Introduction: The Embeddedness of Property', in C. Hann (ed.) *Property Relations: Renewing the Anthropological Tradition.* Cambridge: Cambridge University Press, pp.1–47.

———. 2000. 'Introduction: Farewell to the Socialist "Other"', in C. Hann (ed.) *Postsocialism: Ideals, Ideologies and Practices in Eurasia.* London: Routledge, p.1–11.

———. 2003. 'Introduction: Decollectivization and the Moral Economy', in C. Hann et al. (eds), *The Postsocialist Agrarian Question: Property Relations and the Rural Condition.* Münster: LIT Verlag, pp.1–46.

Hann, C. et al. 2003. *The Postsocialist Agrarian Question: Property Relations and the Rural Condition.* Münster: LIT Verlag.

Humphrey, C. 1998. *Marx Went Away – But Karl Stayed Behind.* Ann Arbor: University of Michigan Press.

Humphrey, C. and K. Verdery. 2004. 'Introduction: Rasing Questions about Property', in K. Verdery and C. Humphrey (eds), *Property in Question: Value Transformation in Global Economy.* Oxford: Berg, pp.1–25.

Hunter, R. and L. Ryan. 2004. 'Privatization and Transformation in Poland: An Update', *The Polish Review* 49(3): 919–45.

Kaneff, D. 2004. *Who owns the Past? The Politics of Time in a 'Model' Bulgarian Village.* Oxford: Berghahn.

Kaszubkiewicz, A. 1998. 'Symbioza zespołu muzealnego z parkiem krajobrazowym na przykładzie Muzeum Pierwszych Piastów na Lednicy', *Ochrona Zabytków* 1: 47–50.

Kideckel, D. 1993. *The Solitude of Collectivism: Romanian Villagers to the Revolution and Beyond.* Ithaca: Cornell University Press.

Kideckel, D (ed.) 1995. *East European Communities: The Struggle to Balance in Turbulent Times.* Boulder, Colorado: Westview.

Kersten, K. 1990. *Narodziny systemu władzy.* Poznań: SAWW.

Lampland, M. 1995. *The Object of Labor: Commodification in Socialist Hungary.* Chicago: University of Chicago Press.

_____. 2001. 'The Advantage of Being Collectivized: Cooperative Farm Managers in the Postsocialist Economy', in: C. Hann (ed.) *Postsocialism: Ideals, Ideologies and Practices in Eurasia*. London: Routledge, pp.31–56.

Leonard, P. and D. Kaneff (eds), 2002. *Post-Socialist Peasant? Rural and Urban Constructions of Identity in Eastern Europe, East Asia and the Former Soviet Union*. New York: Palgrave.

Maurel, M.-C. 1994. *La Transition post-collectiviste: Mutations agraires en Europe centrale*. Paris: L'Harmattan.

Nagengast, C. 1991. *Reluctant Socialists, Rural Entrepreneurs: Class, Culture, and the Polish State*. Boulder: Westview.

_____. 2001. 'Post-peasants and Poverty', in: M. Buchowski, E. Conte and C. Nagengast (eds), *Poland beyond Communism: 'Transition' in Critical Perspective*. Fribourg: University Press, pp.183–207.

Pilichowski, A. 1994. 'Chłopi w persepktywie strukturalnego przystosowania', *Kultura i Społeczeństwo* 38(1): 163–73.

Pine, F. 1994. 'Privatisation in Post-socialist Poland: Peasant Women, Work, and the Restructuring of the Public Sphere', *Cambridge Anthropology* 17(3): 19–42.

_____. 1998. 'Dealing with Fragmentation: The Consequences of Privatisation for Rural Women in Central and Southern Poland', in: S. Bridger and F. Pine (eds), *Surviving Post-socialism: Local Strategies and Regional Responses in Post-socialist Eastern Europe and the Former Soviet Union*. London: Routledge, pp.106–123.

_____. 2001. 'From Production to Comsumption in Post-socialist Poland, in: M. Buchowski, E. Conte and C. Nagengast (eds), *Poland beyond Communism: 'Transition' in Critical Perspective*. Fribourg: University Press, pp.209–223.

Rocznik 1997. *Rocznik Statystyczny 1997*. Warszawa: Główny Urząd Statystyczny.

Rocznik 2004. *Rocznik Statystyczny 2004*. Warszawa: Główny Urząd Statystyczny.

Roszkowski, W. 1995. *Land Reforms in East Central Europe after World War One*. Warszawa: Institute of Political Studies – Polish Academy of Sciences.

_____. 1992. *Historia Polski 1918–1991*. 2nd edn. Warszawa: Wydawnictwo Naukowe PWN.

Sahlins, M. 1976. *Culture and Practical Reason*. Chicago: The University of Chicago Press.

Sowul, S. and K. Katka 2005. 'Księża zrabiają na Unii', *Gazeta Wyborcza* 75, March 31, p.4.

Stauter-Halstedt, K. 2001. *The Nation in the Village: The Genesis of Peasant National Identity in Austrian Poland, 1848–1914*. Ithaca: Cornell University Press.

Tarkowska, E. 1997. 'An Underclass without Ethnicity: The Poverty of Polish Women and Agricultural Laborers', in: R. Emigh and I. Szelényi (eds), *Poverty, Ethnicity, and Gender in Eastern Europe During the Market Transition*. Westport: Praeger, pp.83–122.

Torsello, D. 2003. *Trust, Property and Social Change in a Southern Slovakian Village*. Münster: Lit Verlag.

Verdery, K. 1996. *What Was Socialism, and What Comes Next?* Princeton: Princeton University Press.

————. 1998. 'Property and Power in Transylvania's Decollectivization', in C. Hann (ed.) *Property Relations: Renewing the Anthropological Tradition.* Cambridge: Cambridge University Press, pp.160–80.

————. 2003. *The Vanishing Hectare: Property and Value in Postsocialist Transylvania.* Ithaca: Cornell University Press.

————. 2004. 'The Obligations of Ownership', in: K. Verdery and C. Humphrey (eds), *Property in Question: Value Transformation and the Global Economy.* Oxford: Berg, pp.139–59.

Verdery, K. and C. Humphrey (eds), 2004. *Property in Question: Value Transformation and the Global Economy.* Oxford: Berg.

von Hirschhausen, B. 1997. *Les Nouvelles campagnes roumaines: Paradoxes d'un 'retour' paysan.* Paris: Belin.

Zbierski-Salameh, S. 1999. 'Polish Peasants in the "Valley of Transition": Responses to Postsocialist Reforms', in M. Burawoy and K. Verdery (eds.) *Uncertain Transition: Ethnographies of Change in the Post-socialist World.* Lanham: Rowman and Littlefield, pp.189–222.

Chapter 4

Migs and Cadres on the Move: Thoughts on the Mimetic Dimensions of Postsocialism

Hana Červinková

So what is this tickling at the heels to which Kafka's all too human ape would refer us all too apish humans to? I call it the mimetic faculty, the nature that culture uses to create second nature, the faculty to copy, imitate, make models, explore difference, yield into and become Other. The wonder of mimesis lies in the copy drawing on the character and power of the original, to the point whereby the representation may even assume that character and that power.

(Taussig 1993: xiii)

Foreword

In this chapter, I approach 'post-socialist transition' from the perspective of identity change, which that I see as the displacement of one particular form of mimetic faculty in favour of another. I focus on the institution of the Czech Air Force and its officers whose professional identity has been seriously challenged by the circumstances of large sociopolitical and institutional changes that accompany the 'transition' from socialism to democracy. The mimetic faculty which is at the basis of the professional identity of the Czech Air Force officers whom I interviewed is firmly tied to Soviet technology and Soviet-type military discipline. Following the sociopolitical reorientation of the Czech Republic from the East (membership of the Warsaw Pact) toward the West (membership of NATO), the Czech state apparatus of legitimate violence (the war machine) changes the original object to be mimicked from the Soviet to the Western type of military discipline and technology.

In this essay, I use ethnographic material, which I have collected during sixteen months of fieldwork (2001–2002) to comment on how this process of mimetic change happens on the level of individual Air Force officers who find themselves in the liminal (Gennep 1960; Turner 1966) space and time of the war machine in transition.

Stepping through the Looking Glass – Anthropology at Home?

While sociologists, psychologists or political scientists have traditionally paid attention to the military institution and created within their disciplines a specialized niche for its exploration, anthropologists have only recently put the military on their field's map of interests (Cohen 2001; Lutz 2002). My motivation for conducting ethnographic research in the Czech military was therefore not so much an effort to contribute to a body of ethnographic literature on the military or to join in a disciplinary canon on the subject. Rather, I hoped that by learning about the post-Soviet military institution, and post-Soviet military officers, would allow me to explore the postsocialist condition more generally. I was especially interested in learning how the postsocialist Czech state – one of the new NATO members – uses its institution of legitimate violence to affirm its new identity on the international stage, and how the military and its members cope with the resulting pressures to change and transform. I was also using my study of the military and its officers as an observation point from which I wanted to examine certain themes I found recurrent in my wider observations of postsocialist Czech national identity and state building. 'Transformation' or 'transition' was not only a central theme, but also the motivating force behind my choice of the military as the site of my ethnographic research. After the Czech Republic's accession to NATO in 1999, it was announced that the sweeping changes which had by then touched most state sectors, were also to be implemented in the military, an institution which had until then largely resisted change. I was thus driven to the field by the exemplary anthropological motivation of the awareness of upcoming and inevitable change to the institution and by the effort to capture the life of a culture threatened with disappearance.

Research in the military poses certain practical challenges, which might be at the root of its low popularity among anthropologists. The greatest problem is that of gaining access to your subjects, members of the military institution, who are bound by rules of professional secrecy. The military is a closed institution which does not readily allow intruders in its midst. Most social scientists who conduct research in the military therefore sooner or later become 'insiders' – employees of the military establishment. While I did not have such plans, I knew I needed to gain temporary employment within the military to be able to do ethnographic research. I should add that it took me two years of intensive contact-seeking and contact-making to eventually receive a sixteeen-month employment contract at a military research institute attached to the office of the Chief of the General Staff.

A rather interesting issue pertinent to the present volume, subtitled, 'Perspectives from home', is the fact that in order to be employed by the military institution, one usually needs to be a national of the country in whose military forces one wants to conduct research. My own case may be rather interesting: I am a Czech citizen, but I have lived for many years in the United States, where I studied anthropology. As a Czech national, a woman and an anthropologist educated in the United States, I was both an insider and an outsider to the culture which I was studying. I shared national identity and language with my ethnographic subjects. In most cases, however, our gender was opposite and so was our professional identity. Most importantly, however, in our experiences and our views of the world and the military's place in it, out positions were fundamentally different. Hence, while ostensibly an insider (as a Czech and a military employee) I remained an outsider (a woman anthropologist with a more than hesitant view of the military institution and the work of my subjects). While not an American spy, as some thought, I certainly felt like an intruder during most of the sixteen months of research when I lived and worked closely with my fellow nationals and members of the military. This poses, I believe, an interesting challenge to traditional views of what is inside and outside in anthropological research. Rather than a matter of national provenance or a geographic distance that divides the anthropologist from her ethnographic field, 'being at home' or 'not being at home' in anthropological research hinges on a complex interweaving of personal, professional, national, gender, race, class and other forms of identity that divide the researcher from her ethnographic subjects. My own experience shows that crossing the threshold of a home institution can be like stepping through the looking glass into a wholly different world.

Becoming a Military Researcher

Like most anthropological sojourns into unknown cultures, my ethnographic research in the Czech military, which lasted from February 2001 to May 2002, was an intense professional and personal experience. Even though I was a civilian in the military, many of the same military rules applied to me and the first six months on the job were quite difficult. The main pillar of my dissertation research proposal, which I defended before my doctoral committee at the New School for Social Research in New York, was a plan to interview officers about the changing demands of the military profession. But for the first five months on the job, I was not sure whether I would be even allowed to leave the premises of my office. Most of my work at the time consisted of translating and editing what my boss and other people wrote and meeting foreign military researchers and NATO representatives to whom I was presented as 'our Hanka who lived in America for 10 years' and who 'speaks such good English!' After months of being mentally and physically exhausted from endless commutes to my job, long work hours, and general exhaustion from employment in the military research establishment, I was beginning to lose hope that I would ever be able to accomplish my ethnographic ambitions. I realized, and was repeatedly reminded in case I forgot, that in order to go anywhere and talk to anybody, I needed to secure the order of the top military man – the Chief of the General Staff. I was told that this difficult task could only be achieved by writing a proposal for a project that would be completely indispensable to the military.

In the absence of access to literature on which I had previously so foolishly relied, and without the customary (and by the standard of military social science highly overrated) freedom anthropologists like to enjoy when they are conducting their fieldwork, I created a project over two days and nights in the office, based on media reports that at the time spoke of the upcoming exodus of Czech Air Force officers (Gazdík 2001a, 2001b, 2001c; Mácha 2001). I already knew how most newspaper reports about the Czech military were produced – through isolated phone calls between several higher-ranking officers and the three or four Czech reporters who were loosely interested in military and security issues – and so the question of whether the rumour was fact or fiction seemed particularly irrelevant. Based on these media accounts, which talked of the imminent depopulation of the Czech Air Force, I wrote a project proposal bursting with urgency. The reasons for such an exodus of qualified and indispensable officers must be investigated! I included a plan of action to deal with the problem through ethnographic research. My research, I said, would help the military leadership deal with this burning issue, crucial for military institutions in the twenty-first century. I did not forget to list the exact number of people I would interview, the length of each session and the methods of data processing. This proposal got me not only the necessary signature from the Chief of the General Staff, but also a grant from the Office of Naval Research of the United States Navy through its Human Factors program entitled *Attrition and Retention in the 21ˢᵗ Century.* I was free to go! Thanks to the grant, for which I was very grateful, I had funds for gas for my ancient Škoda car, a laptop computer on which I recorded interviews, and an order in my bag signed by the Chief of the General Staff, laminated for protection against frequent use.

For twelve months I lived and worked on several Air Force Bases in the Czech Republic, where I interviewed officers about their motivations and plans for staying or for leaving the Air Force. When I arrived at Base X, I had more than thirty interviews completed and transcribed, based on sessions with men who were planning to leave the military that year. After several months of interviewing at one base, I was now slightly frustrated by what I perceived was a sense of repetition – of hearing similar stories over and over again. Before going to the field I was told by my supervisor that the point when you feel like you are not learning anything new is usually a good indication that you should stop what you are doing and start with something else. I could not do that – for one thing, my project proposal to the United States Navy stated that I would complete 101 interviews – and I did not dare to mess about with numbers when it came to military research! More importantly, I felt strongly that there was significance to the repetition of stories. I realized that the monotonous content of the interviews was indistinguishable from their manner of deliverance – the resigned discourse of men leaving the military institution, saturated with disenchantment and melancholia. In the stories of these experienced officers, the decay and finally the termination of utilization of the old Russian fighter planes – Migs and Sus (popularly called *sučka*) – intermingled with ironic and self-deprecating observations testifying to the end of the good times for the people of the Czech Air Force and for the institution in general. Crucial to the men's stories was the narrators' acute awareness of a historical process of change which was bringing about their own obsolescence as soldiers. Their accounts of the decline of the military profession as they had known it and of the deterioration of the aging Soviet technology on which they had spent their lives flying and working, were simultaneously stories of their own inevitable displacement.

Professionalizing the War Machine: Forms of Displacement

The displacement of the military men and machines was an integral part of the process of military professionalization, which was instigated by the geopolitical changes following the end of socialism. It was largely from the interviews with the men who were leaving the Air Force that I came to see military professionalization itself as a highly paradoxical form of displacement – a movement of the military in the outward direction from the core of the state. But while this characteristic process of postsocialist modernity involves the removal of the military from the centre of state power through its depoliticization and voluntarization, it simultaneously entails a greater infiltration and dispersion of the very idea of the military in the minds and lives of the civilian public. The goal of military professionalization is the achievement of the harmonious and therefore uncontentious coexistence of the military with the democratic state and civil society. This is achieved by the externalization of the war machine to where it really belongs – outside the state apparatus (Deleuze and Guattari 1987) – to a less prominent location from where it can be more conveniently and without public participation or protest harnessed for the goals of the state and the transnational regime of military violence.

This general movement of the military in the outward direction is accomplished through a series of concrete measures, which involve multiple layers and forms of displacements. The one that became central to my fieldwork in the Czech Air Force had, like all things military, a name. It is usually called 'officer attrition'. Attrition normally denotes gradual deterioration, the slow death of an object. In the military terminology, 'attrition' as opposed to 'retention' denotes the termination of the employment contract between personnel and the military institution. Military scientists spend much time and tax payers' money looking for scientific ways to determine the appropriate levels of attrition, in order to prevent the deterioration and the death of the military institution (Rosen 1995; Stone 1998; Gibb 1888). [1] In my project for the Office of Naval Research and the Chief of the General Staff called, 'The Problems of Officer Retention in the Czech Air Force', I followed the calling of military science and promised the military leadership that I would use ethnographic methods to try and explain the reasons for the exodus of qualified people from the Czech Air Force.

Essentially, what I encountered in the results of my research was a highly predictable process of displacement initiated by a new military law and by concrete measures instituted by the state. The Czech Republic's new *Law on Professional Soldiers*[2] directly encouraged people to leave the military institution, determining substantial pensions based on the number of years spent in service. Moreover, unlike the previous law, which only loosely defined the relationship between rank, education and job position, the new code strictly determined this relationship, generally requiring a higher level of educational and a lower associated rank for a given job position than was customary before. At the same time, an official military decree gave promotional advantage to those people who passed special military English language exams. An associated ruling lowered the number of high ranking officers allowed to serve on the military bases outside the headquarters. The combination of these measures forced many officers with high ranks but low levels of education and no English language skills to leave the military. The new law thus set a new standard of 'the military professional' and the new 'professional military' – a modern, young, English speaking, internationally deployable, mobile and quantitatively small force.

While the standard explanation blames military downsizing on the advancements in technology and military strategy that require operation by fewer personnel than before, the case of postsocialist militaries reveals an additional factor, namely, the reorientation of NATO-member militaries from large forces intended to protect the nation state, to smaller militaries composed of highly specialized units capable of contributing to allied military operations. 'The new NATO,' said NATO's secretary general, 'is going to be about countries who [sic] do different things, and each of them well' (Richburg 2002). During the second Gulf War, the negligible importance of the actual numbers of soldiers and amount of technology needed to contribute to the allied operations was shown by the U.S. appreciation of Poland's loyalty in the American struggle against Saddam Hussein. Poland was praised by the United States for the combat participation of approximately 250 members of the Polish military in Iraq and awarded the administration of a large section of the country after the war. This American decision has caused a dilemma for the Polish state and its military, utterly unprepared for such a task and unable to finance the operation from its own resources. The grotesque effect of the situation whereby the former Soviet satellite is awarded the privilege of colonizing another country, for which it lacks means and motivation, was topped by the fact that due to insufficient finances, the American government had to co-finance the participation of the Polish contingent.

In the case of postsocialist militaries, the quantitative reductions of forces and their reorientation toward international deployment especially strongly affects the national air forces. In the Czech Republic, as well as in the other new postsocialist NATO-member states, the air force was considered the most expensive and difficult part of the military to modernize due to the cost of new technology and training (Szayna 2001). Moreover, the new logic of the political and military alliance of which the Czech Republic became a part did not encourage the new member countries to build up their air force, considered an ineffective investment limited to the defence of the national air space and not useful for deployment in allied operations. Despite international pressure, most postsocialist countries have attempted to save their national air force through modernization programs and extremely costly contracts for the purchase of new aircraft. During his visit to the Czech Republic in the spring of 2001, NATO Secretary General George Robertson (as well as other NATO leaders) was quite upset with the Czech government's decision to purchase new supersonic jets, JAS 39 Gripen, from a British/Swedish consortium. In his criticism, Robertson seconded Frank Kramer, Deputy Secretary of Defense of the United States, who had warned the Czech Republic in November 2000 against the purchase of new supersonic planes: 'Your military is too big, it is awkward, most officers are not educated, you do not have enough ammunition with which to shoot, enough fuel for your cars and planes. Those are the things in which you should invest!' The angry author of an article covering George Robertson's visit, which he entitled, "Jet Fighter for Švejk," laments: 'Three months later, the government did the exact opposite. As if to flout the "American hawks" the government decided to put out a tender for the acquisition of supersonic jet fighters!' (Spurný 2001) The conflict over the purchase of the planes finally escalated to the point where it seemed that their potential purchase would result in the suspension of Czech Republic's membership in NATO (Spurný 2002). Eventually, the country's financial difficulties caused by the disastrous floods of 2002 led the Czech government to use the two billion dollars set aside to buy the new Gripen combat aircraft for flood relief. In the absence of a Western-made replacement for their Soviet jet fighters, the last of which was to be grounded in 2004, the Czech Air Force was to be left without a single supersonic fighter plane. Jaroslav Tvrdík, the member of the social democratic government that for several years unsuccessfully advocated the purchase of the new aircraft before the Senate, resigned in

May 2003 in protest at budget reductions. The Ministry of Defence was then led by Miroslav Kostelka, who was not a party member, but like Tvrdík was a former officer who swapped his uniform for civilian clothes to become a leader of the defence sector. The new Minister of Defence presented a peculiar solution to the problems of the Air Force – to lease the protection of national air space from the Germans. He did not last long though. In 2003, he was succeeded by Karel Kühnl who later 'baptized' the fourteen brand new Gripen planes acquired in 2005.

Migs and Cadres on the Move – Mimetic Exodus

It is no wonder that my research among Czech Air Force officers satisfied one of the fundamental urges that bring anthropologists to the field: to study and record the life of cultures threatened with disappearance. But beyond the displacement of people and machines, ostensibly brought about and explained by the discourse and practices of military modernization and professionalization, a less tangible and infinitely more complicated dilemma of postsocialist modernity is reasserting itself with great insistence. In the liminal absence of secrecy which covers military power with a veil of seriousness, the excessively mimetic condition of the modernization process was revealed – cadres and technology from the Soviet era merging in their melancholic exodus.

The mimetic faculty, according to Walter Benjamin, is 'nothing other than a rudiment of the powerful compulsion in former times to become and behave like something else' (Benjamin 1978: 160). Mimesis, the faculty 'to copy, imitate, make models, explore difference, yield into and become Other', Michael Taussig claims (1993: xiii), testifies to the fundamentally sensuous nature of human thought. 'Like Adorno and Benjamin … my concern is to reinstate in and against the myth of Enlightenment, with its universal, context-free reason, not merely the resistance of the concrete particular to abstraction, but what I deem crucial to thought that moves and moves us – namely, its sensuousness, its mimecity' (Taussig 1993: 2). Both Benjamin and Taussig also indicate that the mimetic faculty as a fundamental aspect of human thought is strongly brought out by modernity. Together with the resurfacing of the primitive, and the juxtaposition of the very new with the very old, modernity 'both stimulates and is predicated upon mimetic modes of perception' (Buck-Morss 1991: 267). Initially through the optical perception of the camera and the movies, but now increasingly through the computer, the internet and television, the language of the human body 'combines thought with action, sensuousness with intellection' (Buck-Morss 1997, cited in Taussig 1993: 20), signalling the importance of mimesis for human thought.

The pilots' and the technicians' stories of attachment to the Soviet planes – which for them *were* the Air Force – were saturated with an abundance of sensuousness based on tactile knowing. Over the course of their careers, in the process of mimetic transference made possible by bodily contact, the men have merged with their machines and with the military institution itself. There is no doubt that the displacement of the Soviet machines, the displacement of the officers, and the displacement of the former military system, are connected through the logic of mimesis, whereby the original becomes indistinguishable from the copy. It seems, moreover, that what I encountered in the melancholic stories of the Czech Air Force officers, was a condition of mimetic excess, spilling out of control. After the supply of spare parts from the Soviet Union ceased, the old technology was slowly dying out, while new Western-made forms had not yet replaced it. Trapped in the moment of liminal uncertainty (Gennep 1960; Turner 1966), the Czech Air Force officers realized their own obsolescence had been brought about by postsocialist modernity, which required different forms of technology and corporeal knowledge that was not at their disposal. While visiting base X, this mimetic cause of the melancholic disposition of the Air Force officers who were the subject of my study of military attrition was revealed to me in an illuminating set of experiences.

Entering Base X: An Ethnographic Interlude

I was staying in barracks quite far from Base X, so I left very early – I could not be late. I did not mind getting up before sunrise, because I looked forward to the drive, which I knew would hold surprises for me. I avoided the highways. The roads were empty and I passed only a few slowly moving tractors going to the fields and buses collecting workers at countryside stops to take them to their jobs in towns. I preferred to drive off the main roads because that way I could watch the intriguing pace of life in the villages. I was especially fascinated by the regularity with which people went to work before sunrise and returned in the early afternoons to tend their beautiful gardens full of useful vegetables. While the inhabitants of Czech cities have largely adopted the capitalist work ethic, in the villages as well as in the military, the old work principles of the socialist period still reign – after coming home from their public jobs, men and women work even harder at their second shift, cultivating a family plot.

When I arrived at the base two hours later, I knew what to do. I had ten minutes till my scheduled appointment at 7.15 a.m. After I had parked my car, I called the Base Commander from a familiarly dilapidated gatehouse. While I waited, a teenage conscript whose tired eyes spilled apathy filled out my visitor's pass. As I watched him fill out my pass, unhurriedly dropping cigarette ashes on my ID, I felt confident that this would be a good day.

The Commander was already expecting me in his office. After an official welcome and after I showed him my research authorization and my previous report to the command, he asked the secretary to bring us coffee. The secretary asked me what coffee I wanted – Turkish or instant and whether I wanted milk or sugar. I asked for black Turkish coffee. The secretary did not ask the Commander. She knew exactly how he drank his coffee. We chatted informally with the Commander for about ten minutes during which time I laughed at his jokes and he in return seemed to accept my presence. He was a man with authority – commanding a base with thousands of employees – yet his manner was lenient, almost jovial. On the wall behind the commander was the Czech Armed Forces 2001 official calendar, which featured women in uniform (figure 4.1). I had seen the calendar on all the bases that I had visited and I had my own copy in Prague. Everybody had the calendar in the Czech military – before the beginning of the year the central military

Figure 4.1. The cover page of the official 2001 calendar of the Czech Armed Forces. Source: Photo Oldřich Jeřábek, Ministry of Defense of the Czech Republic, Prague, 2000.

publishing house distributed it to all the departments. The calendar bonded military employees together in the same manner accomplished by the special internal military phone system with receiver displays that identified callers from the outside world, enabling you to prepare for unpleasant questions from civilians and to treat them differently. As I was laughing at the Commander's jokes, I realized that his humour matched remarkably well the playfully pornographic rendering of female military officers in the calendar. Having mentioned strategic names of people we both knew in the Air Force and having thus clarified our mutual positions and networks, the Commander entrusted me to his subordinate who led me to the place where I was to meet the group of officers that I was planning to interview that day.

As we were silently walking through the base, passing dilapidated barracks and staff buildings, I was overcome by a sense of warm familiarity. When I first came to the Czech military, I wondered what NATO observers and official visitors thought when I saw them driving in the latest models of military jeeps through bases overgrown with grass or when I once accompanied a group of them to see the decades-old Russian Mig jet fighters helplessly stationed in the hangars. Most of these Western men built their careers at a time when the Czech Republic was on the other side of the Cold War divide as a member of the Warsaw Pact. I figured, therefore, they must have felt like victors inspecting a combat zone after a prolonged battle. The irony was that due to the vagaries of history, the former Warsaw Pact enemies were now NATO allies, and their military weakness was no longer of advantage to the victors. Now, after less than a year of studying the military, things that had at first shocked me made me feel at home. The decrepit buildings, overgrown grass, bored conscripts, gloomy officers in uniforms, diffident secretaries – they were all part of my world now. While walking through Base X, I realized that I was more shaken by the congenial beauty of the Bohemian countryside through which I drove to get here than by what my senses a few months ago had perceived as the desolate ruggedness of the military establishment. A week before I arrived at base X, I had met a friend in the centre of Prague, and I remember feeling quite traumatized by what I recognized as the city's dazzling beauty and optimism. I had been broken in, having mimetically merged with an institution that had at first shocked my eyes as an appalling remainder of Communist power.

After few minutes of walking from the Staff building where I had met the Commander, my escort and I arrived at an edifice located at the end of the row of barracks. Because of the sharp light outside, I could not see much of anything in the long dark cold hallway completely lined with old yellow and brown tiles. When we arrived at the hallway's end, my escort knocked on the door and left without a word. After some time, the door opened and I was let into another hallway. When my eyes got used to the darkness, I was first comforted by the familiar sight of pornographic posters of well-endowed blondes on the yellowed walls and cigarette smoke lazily hanging in the air.

I was in the right place, I thought, and lowered the computer bag from my shoulder. I then looked into the room to the left where, in torn armchairs and on a very old polyester couch, sat several men who were smoking cigarettes and sipping unidentified liquid from chipped mugs. Except for one, they were all dressed in old tracksuits wearing slippers. The man who opened the door turned out to be their superior, which I realized because he told the others: 'This is the young lady from the General Staff who has come to interview you, so be nice' (*Pánové, to je ta slečna z Generálního štábu co dělá průzkum, tak se chovejte slušně*). The men continued to sit and smoke, quite unimpressed by my presence. There was an awkward silence: none of us knew what to do next. I felt the acute absence of a female secretary who would be asked to bring me coffee, which would interrupt the uneasiness of the situation.

At the worst possible moment, as usual, I needed to use the bathroom. Into the general silence interrupted only by a radio on which popular Czech singer Lucie Bílá was singing her early hit, 'Love is love, when girls marry girls and boys marry boys' (*Láska je láska, když se holky ženěj s holkama a kluci s klukama*), I asked the commander of the group for directions to the toilet. He hesitated a little, but then showed me to the door back in the hallway. It is not that I was not ready for the dirty lavatory customarily found in this part of the world, with the reassuring sour smell of urine and no toilet paper. But this one was special. The bowl was caked with layers of excrement of various ages and sources. There was also urine on the floor and cigarette buts swimming in a half-empty dirty pickle jar on the miniature sink to the left of the toilet. Pornographic posters that I expertly judged to be the socialist Škoda Car company advertisements from the early 1980s were not missing from the walls. 'Láska je láska,' I thought, 'Love is love'. My natural instincts directed me to 'put my hands on my nipples and run' – as I was recommended to do on my second day on the job by a retired colonel employed in the same department within the military. But because I was desperate after four hours of driving and the coffee with the Commander, I did what I needed to do and for which toilets are made, and, slightly shaken by the experience, I returned to the room where I left my bag.

I set the computer on a dusty desk, which I cleaned with my sleeve and asked for coffee, which was eventually brought to me in a filthy mug. I walked out of the room and asked the group of smoking men for four volunteers whom I would interview in the course of the day, one at a time.

The Mimetic Life of Officer X

The man who came in the room first was in his fifties, rather good looking, slim, in a golf T-shirt and blue jeans. He was smiling at me as he entered the room and closed the door behind him. I liked him. He asked me how I was and I said that I thought I had had better days. He said he understood that, noting that I looked tired and pulled something out of his pocket. Then he extended his hand and opened it – on his palm was an exquisite head of garlic. He said he grew a lot of garlic in his garden and this one was fresh and he wanted to give it to me to make me feel better. He had a slightly perceptible Slovak accent – that was nothing surprising, at least one third of the people I have interviewed were former Slovaks who opted for Czech citizenship after Czechoslovakia divided into two separate states in 1993. After the Velvet Divorce, as the separation of the Czech and Slovak federation was called, former mates eventually became military opponents, since Slovakia was not admitted to NATO at the same time as the Czech Republic, Poland and Hungary, but only three years later. I asked him to sit down, and he did. He seemed in a great mood and kept smiling at me. This was a little disconcerting to me. I was not used to meeting happy people in my interviews with departing officers. I told him, like all others before and after him, that I was doing research, which was paid for by the U.S. Navy and the Czech Armed Forces and that I was interested in hearing about his career and why he was leaving the Air Force.

Officer X, as we shall call him, was a groundcrew member – a technician – and he had served in the air force for thirty-two years. He was married and had three children, all of whom were married – one of the two sons was an officer in the military. His wife was a teacher and all of their life together they had lived in the same two-bedroom apartment in a military bloc of prefabricated flats (*panelák*) in the nearby housing estate (*sídliště*) built in the 1950s for the officers' families. His salary was approximately 16,000 CZK (450 U.S. dollars) a month, only slightly more than mine.

When I asked him to tell me something about his motivations for joining the air force and to talk generally about his job, he smiled broadly and told me a passionate story of his love affair with planes. His story included the initial *falling in love* – when he first sat down in a Russian Mig during an air show as a teenager in the early 1960s; the *pursuit* – surviving through and graduating from military high school; the *frustration and setback* – when he did not pass the physical tests required for him to receive training as a pilot; the *consummation* – becoming a technician and spending almost thirty years in a beloved job in which, as he said, 'I was able to touch planes everyday, feeling like they touched me gently back right where my soul is.'

I asked him to tell me more about planes, which he did, smiling incessantly, his eyes shining with pure pleasure. In his account, his love of planes and the Air Force family was the main storyline for which the history of the Soviet occupation and then political change and NATO membership were little more than stage sets that switched between acts:

> You see, with planes, it is not like with cars. When something goes wrong with a car, you stop by the side of the road and repair it. But when something goes wrong with the plane, it falls down on the ground and it is gone. In almost thirty

years that I have been a technician, not a single plane that I prepared for flight had a mechanical failure. I have worked on three types of Migs and then Sus. Those I particularly loved. I have a beautiful miniature model at home and whenever I touch it, I feel warm all the way to my soul. The day when they recently took them out of operation was a terribly sad moment for me. Those planes could have lasted several more years. They never failed you. I remember that once one of the planes sucked in part of the cabin, the engine was bare, but it was still running till it stopped at the depot. Those Russian engines were great; they just kept going, completely reliable. You cannot compare that to this new Czech plane L-159 that they are bringing in now. The day that they put the Sus out of operation was one of the saddest days in my life. I thought that the best planes would stay, but the decisions were made at the top where other things than technical considerations mattered. It is such a shame that we do not have this great plane any more.

You probably don't think so when you look around and you are so young, but I think my job was beautiful and I loved it. I looked forward to coming to work every single day, because I loved planes and here I could touch them all day long. We used to be in contact with the pilots all the time as well. The pilot, the technician and the plane – we were all one. We were like a family. The pilot depended on the plane and the plane depended on the technician. When the Soviets brought the Sus for the first time, it was terribly exciting. We prepared the plane for the test pilot who took it for a ride and when he returned, and said that it all ran smoothly, there was such a great feeling that spread all over me. We had an excellent collaboration with the Soviets. When they came here, they brought all the technology with them and they showed us how to work on the planes. We could also understand each other – the languages are so similar, it is not like with English. We were real partners, not like now. I thought we would get new planes and we would work with the NATO guys on them, but they are nowhere to be seen. I thought that we would collaborate much more closely. I thought perhaps we would go and visit one of the Western bases, to exchange experience and learn something new. Or maybe, I thought, they would come here and look at what we are doing – but nothing …

You see, those were very different times before the change came; we were flying all the time, we worked all the time. Overtime was never paid; we were tired as dogs but happy because we worked. There were emergencies, we were on call twenty-four hours a day, and there were mock alarms – but you could never know they were mock, because the enemy was there. We worked weekends too … There were planes standing ready all the time … We were the attack force of the Warsaw Pact and that was what we were being prepared for. I know it was a different international situation – there was the enemy to the West and the friends were in the East and so you knew how things stood and why you exercised. Now, after the change, things are different – the discipline is gone. We used to have to walk in uniforms – people could see that you were a soldier. Now you don't have to wear a uniform and the discipline has gone down terribly. We don't have the enemy now, but we also do not have people who understand the military at the top. Now with the new young minister – Tvrdík – things might change, because he is a former military man and he seems to be taking the military seriously. But I remember Havel, how he mocked the military at first and then he turned around and thought we would not remember it. Or one of the first civilian Ministers of Defence after 1989 – I remember him on TV, showing the military shoeshine kit and ridiculing it. That really hurt me – how could someone like that make decisions about the air force?

And you ask me what changed? Everything changed – those times are gone now. There are no planes for me to work on – the old ones are gone and new ones are not about to arrive any time soon. I am leaving in few months – I never thought I would leave, I thought I would serve till retirement, but then this new law came and now I do not have enough education for my rank. I have already been asked to stay as a civilian, but as what – as a guard at the gatehouse? But I might consider staying if I could be a civilian groundcrew member. They have this new law, which they follow, but they are losing people they will not be able to replace – apparently they do not have enough ground crews. But I do not know if I will be offered the job. It means anyway, I will never wear the uniform again. It is so sad you know – what it came down to. I sit here in the office all day long, waiting for my time to go home and then soon, I might never come back. When they were taking those last planes to be put away, I cried … And you see, now I am crying too. I just never thought this would be the end – like this, here – waiting for the end. But this is the end and that is how I look at it. Fortunately, I have my garden.

He stopped talking, and I looked at him – his eyes were shining, there were tears in them. But then he gave me a broad smile and said:

You should see my garden, it is an unbelievable thing – I work on it now all the time. I have a lot of garlic, but many other things as well. I have these new roses coming this week, I cannot wait to go and plant them.

I looked at the garlic he gave to me and then at him. This man astounded me. It is not that he had said anything so different from what I had heard many times before when interviewing other officers on other military bases. The difference between them and Officer X was primarily the latter's astonishing lack of melancholia. Articulating the reason for his sadness – the loss of his beloved work with planes – he was able to mourn it as genuinely lost (Freud 1914). His mourning of the past signalled the lack of melancholic desire that refuses to acknowledge the missing object as forever gone. He cried about the planes and the dying Air Force, but only as a closed chapter in his life that he was able to externalize and displace onto a different object and activity – the planting of garlic and roses in his garden.

As I later found out, he was not alone in establishing the fetishizing connection between flying and gardening. While reading a contemporary history of the Czech Air Force, revealingly named *Displaced Wings (Zrušená křídla)*, I came across a photograph which showed a disabled Soviet jet fighter placed as a decoration among roses in the garden of a retired air force pilot who could not part with the plane after leaving the military (Figure

4.2). But later in my research I witnessed yet another and more absolute kind of mimetic merging of people and technology in the Air Force. On one of the elite Air Force base where I worked, the pilots arranged an intriguing exhibit. On one of the walls of their club room, they placed metal pieces of wrecked planes. Each piece of the plane on the wall carried the name of the pilot who died during the plane's crash. It would be difficult to imagine a more complete consummation of love through mimesis.

But perhaps the best example of the mimetic nature of the post-socialist moment in the Czech Air Force was an incident that occurred shortly after I had returned to the base, which was my primary fieldwork site. At the time, the base Commander was approached by American film-makers with an intriguing proposition. Another line of Soviet jet fighters, which were in fact the only fighter planes left on his base, were going out of operation. The American star and movie director Vin Diesel was making a film in the Czech Republic and insisted on having Russian jet fighters included in its final action scene. The Commander welcomed the proposition in exchange for English language laboratory equipment for his pilots.

For several weeks, the elite pilots of the base were trained under the instruction of American film-makers how to elegantly run towards their planes before take-off. Ironically enough, I saw the film, *XXX* (the actual name of the movie and its main protagonist), on the plane from the United States. In the theatre of violence which the movie essentially is, the Czech

Figure 4.2 Photograph of a disabled plane that Pavel Vaňous purchased from the Air Force and placed in his garden. Source: Photo P. Vaňous, in Lorenc and Rogl (2000).

landscape and Czech women serve as a backdrop to the battle between the American government and the Soviet mafia. Vin Diesel, the lover of extreme sports is XXX who is hired by the U.S. secret service to fight his Soviet counterparts on Czech territory. The final scene in which the planes fly over the Vltava River was filmed in the historic part of Prague. In an American action movie, the melancholic Czech pilots with whom I worked on a lonely country base fly their Soviet jets into the timeless space of the Hollywood silver screen. The filming took place on the last day when the Soviet jet fighters were in operation. 'At least we can now look at them whenever we want,' commented the pilots when I asked them how they felt about the film.

Conclusion

Pointing to the fetishizing tendencies of the mimetic urge, Michael Taussig claims: 'The wonder of mimesis lies in the copy drawing on the character and power of the original, to the point whereby the representation may even assume that character and that power' (Taussig 1993: xiii). In their current displacement from the military, the Czech Air Force officers have merged with the Soviet planes and the socialist Air Force – the technology, the people and the institution indistinguishable from each other in their melancholic disappearance. The connection between the officers who spent their careers in the socialist Air Force and the Soviet military technology on which they worked clearly surpassed the level of regular habitual attachment. As we have seen, the relationship resembles rather that of love and mutual dependence than a detached rapport of a human to an inanimate object. Over the years under socialism, the Soviet planes became animated by the officers' affection, drawing life from the men who invested their lives in their maintenance. Through this fetishizing process, the distinction between the human and the machine (the original and the copy) becomes mimetically blurred. It is not surprising, therefore, that their separation in the process of military transition produces a trauma, leaving the feeling of melancholia that has come to pervade the entire military establishment.

I have shown that viewing the institutional transformation of the Czech military through the prism of traumatic displacements of the objects of mimetic desire allows us to see the human dimension of the process of social change. My research in the Czech Air Force reveals the disturbing human dimension of the postsocialist military transformation, which could otherwise seem as a composite of dispassionate procedures of institutional alterations. This insight also supports the value of anthropological inquires into the nature of the complex process which we call postsocialism.

Notes

1. The military studies focused on attrition and retention usually identify determinants that are sure to affect military personnel retention, such as 'the family factor', pay and bonus, job content satisfaction and peer recognition, as well as different sets of psychological dispositions of individual soldiers. Through questionnaires and psychological tests, the researchers find the most likely factors causing attrition and through mathematical calculations they determine the probability of future levels of retention if each of the factors negatively affecting retention is eliminated.
2. The law was passed in 1999, being effective from November 2001. See Zákon č. 221/1999 Sb., o vojácích z povolání, www.army.cz. It was the first law on this issue since 1959, see Zákon č. 76/1959 Sb.

References

Benjamin, W. 1978. 'On the Mimetic Faculty', in *One-Way Street and Other Writings*. New York: Verso, pp.160–63.

Buck-Morss, S. 1991. *The Dialectics of Seeing: Walter Benjamin and the Arcades Project*. Cambridge, MA: MIT Press.

Cohen, D. 2001. *The War Come Home: Disabled Veterans in Britain and Germany 1913–1939*. Berkeley: University of California Press.

Deleuze, G. and F. Guattari. 1987. '1227: Treatise on Nomadology – The War Machine', in *A Thousand Plateaus: Capitalism and Schizophrenia*. Minneapolis: University of Minnesota Press, pp.351–423.

Freud, S. 1914–1916. 'Mourning and Melancholia', in *The Standard Edition of the Complete Psychological Works of Sigmund Freud, Vol.14*. Trans. and ed. J. Strachey, pp.239–58.

Gazdík, J. 2001a. 'Šedivý: Čekají nás mimořádné potíže: Krize armády, důstojníci chtějí do civilu', *Mladá fronta DNES*, March 22, p.3.

———. 2001b. 'Armáda se vylidňuje kvůli fámám a nejistotě', *Mladá fronta DNES*, March 24, p.4.

———. 2001c. 'Armádu deptají zastaralé stereotypy,' *Mladá fronta DNES*, March 27.

Gennep, A. van. 1960. *The Rites of Passage*. London: Routledge and Kegan Paul.

Gibb, G., T. Nontasak and D. Dolgin. 1988. 'Factors Affecting Career Retention Among Naval Aviators', *Journal of Business and Psychology* 2(4): 321–25.

Lorenc, M. and S. Rogl. 2000. *Zrušená křídla: Poznámky k československému a českému vojenskému letectvu v letech 1989 až 1994*. Olomouc: Votobia.

Lutz, C. 2002. *Homefront: A Military City and the American Twentieth Century*. Boston: Beacon Press.

Mácha, P. 2001. 'Mozky a stíhačky', *Aeronoviny,* November 4.

Richburg, K. 2002. 'Czechs Become Model for New NATO: "Niche" Expertise in Chemical Weapon Defense Compensates for Military Shortcomings', *The Washington Post*, November 3, p.A22.

Rosen, L. and D. Durand. 1995. 'The Family Factor and Retention Among Married Soldiers Deployed in Operation Desert Storm', *Military Psychology* 7(4): 221–34.

Spurný, J. 2001. 'Stíhačka pro Švejka,' *Respekt*, February 26, p.3.

———. 2002. 'Gripeny, nebo NATO: Vláda chce za každou cenu koupit zbytečné stroje.' *Respekt*, April 22–28.

Stone, B. et al. 1998. 'Air Force Pilot Retention: Evaluating the Results of Alternative Models', *Armed Forces and Society* 121–35.

Szayna, T. 2001. *NATO Enlargement 2000–2015: Determinants and Implications for Defense Planning and Shaping.* Santa Monica: RAND.

Taussig, M. 1993. *Mimesis and Alterity: A Particular History of the Senses.* New York: Routledge.

Turner, V. 1966. *The Ritual Process: Structure and Anti-Structure.* Ithaca: Cornell University Press.

Zákon č. 221/1999 Sb., o vojácích z povolání. www.army.cz

Zákon č. 76/1959 Sb., o vojácích z povolání.

Chapter 5

Diasporas Coming Home

Identity and Uncertainty of Transnational Returnees in Postcommunist Lithuania

Vytis Čiubrinskas

In the contemporary world of much increased interchange between *roots* and *routes,* as James Clifford puts it (Clifford 1997), patterns of migration do produce multiple diasporic identities of people who are 'in' but not entirely (or only) 'of ' the place they are in (Rushdie 1998). It is in particular visible in the West, where postcolonial and postcommunist immigrants are going through the challenges of acculturation. But it increasingly also happens in the East, where the same postcolonial and postcommunist migrant-producing societies of *uncertainty and freedom* are now experiencing the repatriation of their former expatriates and transnational migrants.

Lithuania is a good example of such a situation. It is a country from which, starting from 1860s onwards, there have been three waves of emigration to the West, mainly to the U.S. It twice became a nation state in the twentieth century, it survived communism, and it now struggles with its consequences[1]. Immediately after regaining independence in 1991, it saw increased attempts by the Lithuanian diaspora to come 'back home'. Expatriates of Lithuanian background in the U.S., ethnic tourists from America in search of their 'links', and other returnees or settlers, were faced with the Lithuanian reality. Their encounters with the local public sphere and private lifestyles are challenged by transitional dilemmas of the postcommunist practice of democracy and the national identity politics of the Lithuanian State.

Returnees from the West settle in Lithuania but in what kind of Lithuania, to what degree is it the Lithuania of their expectations? Are they migrants of nostalgia rather than returnees?

Our focus is on Lithuanian returnees and/or migrants from the West mostly the U.S. and Canada. We explore their accounts of the ongoing process of social and cultural accommodation after coming back to Lithuania. The different categories of returnees as well as different dimensions of return are discussed.

Currently there are only few hundred returnees in the country. In the autumn of 2005 a focus group interview was conducted with the representatives of different generations of returnees from the U.S., Canada, Australia and the U.K. Potential and actual returnees and settlers were observed and interviewed on the both sides of the Atlantic. Twenty-five interviews were conducted during the period of 2002 -2005 in the offices of various organizations, including the Lithuanians Returning Back to Homeland Centre in Vilnius and the 'American' Section of the Senior Citizen Retirement Home in Vilnius. The returnees and their offspring were studied alongside their interest groups and networks, revealing diversity in terms of generation, class, cultural background, occupation as well as their ethnic/national identity as defined by informants themselves.

The problems of the 'rerooting' and 'rehoming' of the transnational uprooted and displaced Lithuanian migrants are the focus of this chapter, together with a notion of 'transnational Lithuanianness' as a model of identity, transplanted to foreign soil and brought back by the Lithuanian transmigrants. The key questions to be answered are:

- what is brought (brought back) to Lithuania by the returnees in terms of knowledge, social capital and heritage?
- what are the shapes of identity among transmigrants in a transitional society? How are the identities brought (brought back) from the country of departure challenged?
- what are the patterns of emplacement after displacement in terms of home (homeland), occupation (mission and other social practices and networks), status and prestige?

Introduction

Some Key Terms for a Theoretical Framework

There is ample theoretical literature in the field of transnational migration which serves as a methodological background for analysis of the problems of intergration/segregation as well as acculturation/essentialization of 'foreign' people, coming into 'foreign' soil. In comparison, the literature focusing on returnees is much more sparse, a fact probably explained by the more recent emergence of the phenomenon of return migration. In terms of postsocialist return migration, there are a number of models of evaluation for the Western returnees, inherited from stereotypes of the Soviet era, of such Westerners as 'distant other', as 'imperialist arrogant millionaires', and these inform both the public and private reception of returnees.

I will outline here some of the key terms I will draw on to analyse the situation of the returning migrant.

'Transnationalism' means being in situations of transmigration, of border crossing and of transcending one or more nation states. As defined by Vertovec (1999), it is a type of consciousness or mode of cultural reproduction (cf. Al Ali and Koser 2002: 2). As a type of consciousness transnationalism involves transcendence of a single truth. The open-minded patterns of consciousness of Lithuanian repatriates contrast with the remnants of the 'captive mind' traced in the former nomenclature and in 'corrupted' ways of conduct faced by returnees. As a type of consciousness it encompasses a sense of identity based on a variety of experiences generated among contemporary transnational communities (Povrzanovic Frykman 2001: 16).

As a sense of identity, transnationalism means a variety of national loyalties and relocated patterns of nationality, and it is extremely important where nationality (as a discourse about and identification with nation) is accommodated; whether it takes place in the homeland, in a neighboring country, or in the further diaspora. It is obvious that in the case of a returned emmigrant we have to engage with transnational and thus displaced, and presumably transplanted, patterns of nationality. Such 'relocated' patterns of identity need to be addressed as being deterritorialized, or at least differently territorialized (Clifford 1997) and this is why they can be approached as *ethnic* patterns rather than belonging to the range of nationalities.

The shaping of identities depend on both 'identity politics' and the 'politics of identity'. The difference between these two was defined by Jonathan Hill and Thomas Wilson (2003: 2):

'Identity politics' is how culture and identity, variously perceived to be … articulated, [is] constructed, invented and commodified as the means to achieve political ends. In this sense … identity politics [is] discourse and action within public arenas of political and civil society … . '[P]olitics of identity' … refers more to issues of personal and group power, found within and across all social and political institutions and collectivities, where people sometimes choose, and sometimes are forced, to interact with each other in part on the basis of their shared, or divergent, notions of their identities. The politics of identity can take place in any social setting, and often best and first recognized in domains of the private, the subaltern, the subversive, where culture may be the best way or means to express one's loss or triumph.

Such a distinction is relevant to understand how Lithuanianness is 'managed' in contemporary Lithuania, and how it is conducted as a dominant discourse of 'identity politics' by locals, drawing on their advantage of 'local life experience', and as a 'politics of identity' shared by returnees, disadvantaged by the lack of 'local life experience'. Both models of identity imply the ascription of a certain social strategy and ideology, and are motivated and reinforced by 'symbolic capital' taken from the 'repository' (Castells 1997) of national or ethnic culture and heritage.

The category of 'home' or 'homeland' is one of the key elements of the nation's repository and is extremely important for the transnational Lithuanians. 'Home'('homeland'), as a category, could be defined in two ways: as a socially homogeneous and physically fixed space, or as a dynamic, transnational symbolic space. In the traditional connotation 'home' is a safe, secure, peaceful place linked to 'family', 'community' and 'homeland/nation' (Al Ali and Koser 2002). Homeland is the space in which 'the conduct, expectations, attitudes, feelings and reactions of others are predictable and in which one knows the rules of appropriate behavior' (Holy 1996:186). From another, transnational and dynamic perspective, the understanding of 'home' implies place, which undergoes displacement and uprootedness, and becomes crucial for belonging and identity 'work'. It applies mainly to political migrants/refugees, for whom the idea of 'home' becomes elevated to a degree of ideal place and resource for nostalgic feelings. Expatriates settled in diasporas retain a sense of belonging to the 'culture' associated with 'home'. But, at the same time, it appears inevitable that the expatriates turned into repatriates find the 'culture', along with the 'home' or 'homeland', as full of strange, unusual and alien elements: in the Lithuanian case, the lingering Soviet past, even more than a decade after the regime's collapse. If Lithuanian-born repatriates become easily frustrated by facing a 'homeland' so different from what they imagined it to be, this is not a case for second-generation returnees who feel free to shift from one shore of the Atlantic to the other. It is much easier for them to accept the postmodern transnational shaping of 'home' as a place where you realize yourself best and 'home is where you are'.

'Acculturation' is another important element implied by transnationalism as a mode of cultural (re)production. It involves the process of interaction and diffusion of cultural values and traditions between individuals or societies, resulting in the acquisition of new cultural characteristics, and, which is more important in our case, the cultural translation of 'national culture', 'heritage' and even 'morality'. For example, acculturated to the mainstream, American-born diaspora Lithuanians are 'practicing ethnicity' at ethnic festivals, displays of ethnic artifacts, sharing of ethnic meals, get-togethers in the ethnic clubs and maintenance of ethnic sites, for example Lithuanian Catholic graveyards (Čiubrinskas 2004). Such practices of Lithuanianness are far from essentialist and are rather focused on transnational and *bricoleur* ways of 'consuming' ethnicity/nationness through symbolically charged items from the repository of national/ethnic culture. They accommodate the repositioning of ethnicized culture into modern narratives and cultural commodities familiar to the mainstream, and actually adopt American cultural politics of cultural pluralism and multiculturalism. The latter gives legitimacy to the ethnic practices, such as ethnic education, as well as for many public events and open discourses on identity, memory and heritage (Čiubrinskas 2004).

Such a pattern of 'practicing Lithuanianness' fits well with the current national cultural politics which promotes the practice of 'Lithuanian ethnic culture' (a term which is used interchangeably with 'traditional Lithuanian culture') in postcommunist Lithuania. The way culture is locked in to a concept of ethnicity[2] makes it peculiarly compatible with the reacculturation of returnees. Folklore festivals of arts and crafts, not to mention the National Song Festival in Lithuania are beloved of second-generation returnees to most of whom dancing Lithuanian dances in Northern America were a part of becoming Lithuanian.

In the process of acculturation into mainstream society transmigrants are also encountering patterns of civic life which could be, and in the Lithuanian case definitely are, quite different from those they are used to. Here the returnee's practicing of Lithuanianness in cultural ways becomes challenged by the postcommunist Lithuanian bureaucrats and practitioners of public policy and confronted with local, again postcommunist, standards of social status and social prestige.

'Diaspora' is the last unavoidable theoretical term for dealing with transnationally shaped cultures. According to Clifford (1997: 251):

> Whatever their ideologies of purity, diasporic cultural forms can never, in practice, be exclusively nationalist. They are deployed in transnational networks built from multiple attachments, and they encode practices of accommodation with, as well as resistance to, host countries and their norms ... Diaspora discourse articulates, or bends together, both roots and routes to construct ... forms of community consciousness and solidarity that maintain identifications outside the national time/space in order to live inside, with a difference.

Despite Clifford's assurance of diaspora cultures not being exclusively nationalist, but rather transnationalist, it could be argued that the Lithuanian-American diaspora was, at least from the 1950s to1980s, nationalisistic and irredentist: aimed at nation regaining, reviving and rebuilding. However, Clifford is right that diaspora cultures are not national, but rather produce an alternative public sphere 'of living inside with a difference'. Both the recent wave of Lithuanian migrants to Chicago (Kuzmickaite 2003) and Lithuanian-American repatriates in Vilnius are 'living inside with a difference' by belonging to 'groups of their own'. Although Clifford points out that some articulations of purity and exclusivism come from diaspora populations, he stresses that diasporas have rarely founded nation states, except for Israel (Clifford 1997). The Lithuanian case as well as the Latvian and Estonian is comparable to Israel in terms of the imperative to 'regain what was lost because of the Soviet occupation'. Such a determination to regain the Lithuanian nation state meant, first of all, 'to be always ready for homecoming'. In contrast to Israel, where 'homecoming' to the regained place acted, in Clifford terms, as 'negation of diaspora' (Clifford 1997: 251), the Lithuanian 'homecoming' was different. Many were reluctant to return and also the return itself was debated if not denied at least by some diaspora organizations. These used to put forward arguments like: 'Look, the former communists just changed jackets and are back in power, so your return won't be welcome'. Similar phrases could be found throughout the Lithuanian-American media.

The Lithuanian Case

There is a need for more empirical data and ethnographies from urgent sites of repatriation. There are several case studies, from Latvia (Herloff Mortenson 1999), the Czech Republic (Nešpor 2002), Germany and Israel (Muntz and Ohliger 2003), and also from Ghana (Bruner 1998), which show that actual political and legislative changes in the postsocialist and postcolonial countries do not go smoothly. In particular, there are difficulties in terms of reestablishing the rights of offspring as well as of former citizens themselves, who fled or were taken from the country, to regain their status of 'fellow citizen', to say nothing of their encounters with the 'natives' in the job market (Herloff Mortensen 1999) or sharing of cultural heritage (Bruner 1998).

What are the challenges in the process of reemplacement of Lithuanian transmigrants in Lithuania? First of all, challenges are visible in the legislation of citizenship, a powerful tool for controlling access to public wealth. The postsocialist Lithuanian citizenship law[3] in particular well exemplifies the limitations of its applicability to returnees. But even more than the legal implications, the discourse of the law constitutes strong categorical and xenophobic divides between the locals and the returnees (Akstinaviciute 2005; Dauksas 2004). Despite the fact that both divided parties – returnees and locals – virtually share the same ethnic belonging and national loyalty to the Lithuanian Republic, there is always an intrinsic intra-ethnic encounter (Herloff Mortensen 1999). The dividing line is between those who return from outside (with a label 'must be foreigner') and those who can always be proud of the status of being hosts.

Secondly, all returnees undergo the challenge of being true Lithuanians in Lithuania after being true Lithuanians in America. The reconfiguration can be seen as a reinforcement of identity ('the return to the homeland made me a genuine Lithuanian') or as a hybridization (hyphenation) of their ethnic/ national identity. The latter is visible when returnees, Lithuanian in the U.S. or Canada, realise after repatriation, when all attraction and romance for Lithuania becomes lost, to what extent they are deeply American or Canadian and actually hybrid Lithuanian-Americans or Lithuanian-Canadians. Such pattern of hybridization are also shaped by the experience of double acculturation. First, in the late 1940s, when Lithuanian refuges became Lithuanian–Americans and second, in the 1990s when returnees back to the country were given the name of American–Lithuanians (*Amerikos lietuviai*). Both definitions signify hybrid and different identities. In the modes of manipulation of identity politics migrants evidence, there are profound differences according to whether this politics takes place in the diaspora or in the home country, whether with the support of official institutions or without it, and according to the social networks conducting, in Hill and Wilson's terms (2003), the politics of identity.

Thirdly, the social strategies of different groups of returnees make the picture of return diverse in terms of their different categorizations of home(land). Home is materialized as *place* instead of being an *idea* as it was in the diaspora (Kelly 1997). The same happens with the national culture and heritage, more virtual than real in the diaspora. In this case the issues of the *home(land)* and the *cultural heritage* become elevated, especially by returnees born in Lithuania, into the *place* of their mission and their duty to help the 'former communist country', as well as the core of their politics of identity.

Categories of Returnees and the Implications of Return
Lithuanian Transmigration: From Expatriates to Repatriates

In order to explore the returnee or migrant identity in a transitional and transmigrant society we have to deal first with the experience of displacement of the Lithuanian forced migrants, which group includes those political refuges and exiles who, at the end of the Second World War, fled from the Soviet-sponsored communist regime to the West, and became concentrated in the Displaced Persons camps in Germany. In the end of 1940s they were given the chance to move to the U.S., Canada, Britain, Australia and other countries. At least 30,000 of these Lithuanians from the Displaced Persons camps (DPs) settled in the U.S., of whom about 12,000–15,000 settled in Chicago (Kucas 1975).

My research in 2000–2005 has shown that it is not the offspring of labour migrants, hundreds of thousands of whom immigrated to the U.S. since 1860s, but these political émigrés and their offspring who constitute the major part of the returnees. These expatriates and their offspring, in the second and third generation, are the largest group of returnees and/or settlers in Lithuania, the majority coming from the U.S. and Canada and in much smaller numbers from Australia.

In terms of social capital this wave of migrants is different from earlier labour migrants. The former belong to the lower middle class and middle class, and most of them are professionals with a university education (Čiubrinskas 2005). Most, if not all, of them underwent ethnic 'Lithuanian' enculturation in their families and Saturday schools, and through the afforts of The Lithuanian American Community[4]. The Lithuanian American Community was and still is the major Lithuanian organization in the U.S., with its sections in each large city, and it also acts as an umbrella organization for almost all activities focused on retaining Lithuanian ethnicity and nationness.

Ethnicity framed in culture and/or culture locked in ethnicity, that is, somebody being a bearer of, say, the Lithuanian culture being supposed to be a Lithuanian national of Lithuanian ethnicity, is a phenomenon very well known and deeply engraved in Central-East European nationalism. Such a mindset was popular during the interwar period of the 1920s and 1930s and it was also a part of the enculturation the former DPs and their offspring had to undergo in the 1940s in Germany and later, even now, in the U.S. (Sidrys 1996; Saldukas 2002). It was inscribed in the Lithuanian Charter – the document adopted in 1949 by the Lithuanian refuges in DP camps in Germany for maintaining and retaining their loyalty to Lithuanianness. Such values as the Lithuanian language, Lithuanian family, and Lithuanian homeland were emphasized in particular, and the Charter itself was a mission-like statement for the refugees.

The ethnonationalist ideology which perpetrated *Lietuviskoji veikla* (Lithuanian activity) in the trans-Atlantic diaspora worked through a kind of prescribed identity enshrined first of all in the enculturation of refugees and their offspring. Lithuania for them became a mythical reference, an idea, not a country and place. Lietuviskoji veikla, as the Lithuanian activity and agency in diaspora was extremely 'retaining of Lithuanianness', oriented especially to the Lithuanian past, and carried by the devoted national intelligentsia. In its scale of devotion and upheaval it is comparable to the Sajudis (National Front) movement (cf. Vardys and Sedaitis 1997) in Lithuania, of the Singing Revolution period of the late 1980s and early 1990s. It was idealistic and public. It was an idealized version of Lithuanianness, based on the nation-state nationalism of the interwar period extremely well known to Central/East Europeans:

> Our parents were young when they left Lithuania. They were nurtured in the interwar spirit. Those times in Europe there was a nationalistic and national-socialistic spirit. It influenced the organizations of emigrants. It helped to keep Lithuanian culture; nurture the young generation, which more ore less could speak Lithuanian. That nationalism helped to keep the Lithuanian spirit. From this influence was created the idealized portrait of the interwar period. (Lithuanian-Canadian male, 35)

> We were escaping from [Soviet] occupation and it was such a sacred thing to retain the Lithuanianness (*lietuvybe*). Strictly to speak only Lithuanian in families and avoid integration ... it was like the protest against occupation. (Lithuanian-Canadian female, 75)

Such an idealistic nationalism was functional in diasporas and turned into devoted work for the own country in terms of charity and different political and civic campaigns to help occupied Lithuania. Consequently almost any Lithuanian expatriate had to be ready to become repatriated one day. Before his/her eventual repatriation back to Lithuania he/she normally had to be involved in 'Lithuanian activity' (lietuviskoji veikla).

The Obligation to Return

The commitment to Lithuanian culture and heritage of the DP generation migrant is made explicit by being already inscribed in the motivation of their return to their 'mother' country. This was the generation of immigrants which themselves had been the bearers of some sort of missionary role of conduct. The 'obligation of return' was a central imperative of Lithuanian activities throughout the Lithuanian diasporas after the Second World War. It was inscribed in the enculturation model used in the families of DPs. It was implied if not imposed for the second and even third generation of American born Lithuanian-Americans.

> In my family my parents didn't allow us to watch TV. While at home we had to speak only Lithuanian. Each word pronounced in English was fined with ten cents fine. There was always talk about Lithuania, how it needed to be helped to be liberated and that we would obviously return to it right after it became free. (American-born male, 51)

As sociological research conducted among American-born Lithuanian-Americans has shown, the 'obligation to return' is a far from constant imperative. It changes depending on the time and generation. Even certainty about the return, not to talk about the actual practice of returning, decreases sharply from the 1950s to the present (Cernius 2005: 149):

> In 1957 the majority of the respondents stated that if Lithuania were independent they would return there. In 1973–4 the respondents divided evenly between those who would return home and those choosing the United States as their permanent home. Today (2002) most of them, if not all, are staying in the USA. This is because of many reasons: the US feels like home, the children and grandchildren, relatives and friends are here; medical care is better. Today the respondents are about sixty-two to sixty-three years old. One goes to Lithuania for a visit or makes it possible for the grandchildren to visit there.

Nevertheless, as it was mentioned, the imperative of the 'obligation to return' was materialized by the dominance of DP emigres among the Westerners of Lithuanian background who came to settle in Lithuania over the past fifteen years. Lithuanians of the other ethnic groups, even of major ones, those Poles or Germans who left the country in the late 1940s and early 1950s during the Soviet forced 'repatriation' campaigns, or those Jews who were allowed to emigrate to Israel in the 1970s and 1980s, are generally not repatriating, neither themselves nor their children, except for a few German-Lithuanians. This implies that the ethnonationalist Lithuanian patriotism of the DP generation plays an outstanding role among the commitments of expatriates and is an important motive for repatriation. The general features of the returnee-repatriate category are: belonging to (either themselves or their parents) the DP wave of migration, with a strong Lithuanian self-identity, fluent speaking of the language, and following ethnic endogamy marriage rules. All such cases show that these returnees-repatriates have followed the prescriptions of how not to lose their Lithuanianness, built from ethnicity plus culture, which is inscribed in the Lithuanian Charter.

Rational Choice to Return

The decision to move back to Lithuania is not only influenced not by 'irrational' motives like the 'obligation to return', or 'nostalgia for homeland', as we will see in the following section. There is also a rational choice here, for example: 'Getting retirement pensions from the West makes financial life better here'. This in particular applies to the old generation of returnees:

> It is expensive to get medical treatment for my wife in USA but it is cheap and good enough here. Labor is cheap here. (Male returnee from the U.S., 85)

> I decided to come here after my husband got cancer. I thought it would be too difficult for me to take care of him alone. Then I persuaded my husband to go to Lithuania. We had savings and here we will have a better life. We receive retirement pensions from America. (Lithuanian-born female returnee from the U.S., 90)

Returnees also choose to rely on the Lithuanian standard of living, which especially in terms of prices for goods and services compares favorably with the one left behind:

> You know its too expensive there [in the U.S.], you know its impossible even if you take the train to go to the theatre with a discount it's one hundred dollars. (Male Lithuanian-American)

Among the returnees the number of those who are middle aged is small. Why is it only retired and young people return or come to the country to live? Why people either before their career or after, but those in the middle period of life? My informants spoke out explicitly about that:

> The middle-age group ... well, they are professionals or have good jobs and positions. For those who have ten years to work till retirement it would be financially unrewarding to leave everything. If he just quit the work in the firm were he is a specialist ... he will come here and ... what will he do? (Male, 80, Lithuanian-Australian)

> Only young people, those who haven't started their career, and older ones, who have ended it, can come to Lithuania. It is natural that others don't, because of

career steps. It is difficult to move your family, children and to start life from the beginning. It is natural that there are not many middle-age people. Speaking straightforwardly, those who have already made a good life there, it is difficult to change it. (U.S.-born male, 30s, who worked for Landsbergis government in 1991)

Differently from an older generation who, with a few exceptions, belong themselves to the repatriate-returnees category, the younger generation came over also basically idealistically motivated 'to help Lithuania', but there was less missionary passion in it. It was rather a rational and cognitive interest in familiarizing themselves with a country known before mainly from their family stories and Saturday school readings. A significant part of the foreign-born younger generation identify themselves not as belonging to returnees but rather to newcomers (*atvaziavusieji*) who came to Lithuania and moved here as temporary inhabitants (*laikinai gyvenantys*).

Only a few of them happen to have visited the country several times before they moved here. Most of the younger generation of returnees/newcomers are sceptical or ignorant of the older generation's 'brain washing' imposition of their own opinions on how to help Lithuania. They do come (not return) and live for several years in the country doing businesses here. Newcomers' explanations as to why they are neither repatriates, nor returnees, although having Lithuanian, and possibly other, backgrounds, is that they never went left the country. So they say they are not *returning to* but rather *entering* Lithuania. Most of them are not sure about 'staying in the country forever'. They emphasize that they do not have long-term future plans. The reason they came is rational choice – usually private business or a work position, and also the natural beauty and quietness of Lithuania.

The Dimension of Home(land) and Nostalgia in Transmigrant Identity

The key point of reference of the transmigrant identity construction and reconstruction process is the role of home and homeland. This applies both to those who 'left home' and to those who are 'coming back home'. The dimension of 'home' covers the particular way of belonging to a certain place. As Mary Kelly points out, the identity of transmigrants is dependent on 'whether homelands are constructed as a place or as an idea' (Kelly 2000: 65). This social construction is partially determined by when and how individuals or their ancestors emigrated as well as when and how they are coming back.

The issue of coming back 'home' or returning to the ancestral place can be understood as a process of rerooting or 'rehoming' of transmigrants. The most popular returnees' answers to the question, why am I here, are based on *nostalgia* for birthplace, motherland and roots.

This is my part ... to say ... this is my birthplace [and] relatives ... Here language, birthplace ... can't change this. (Lithuanian-American female, 80, of mixed marriage)

Love of motherland, yes, I feel I just want to live in Lithuania. I didn't flee Lithuania, I didn't neglect it and that's why I want to live here. There is a feeling called nostalgia. (Lithuanian-Australian male, 80)

My roots, patrimonial ties, relatives are here, I was alone there. (Lithuanian-American female)

Lithuania is the home of my parents, where the roots of my grandparents and forefathers are. The language of this country is the same I speak, and it is the spirit of the culture, which I embrace also, which I got from my parents. Those things mostly hold me here. (Lithuanian-American female, 45)

The most popular explanation given among retired Lithuanian-Americans living in the Gerontology Center in Vilnius was simply: 'I don't know, I only feel it, my roots are here'. In addition, most cited the 'clean air and nature'.

The concept of home is first of all shaped by the ultimate belonging to a particular domicile – a locality – where 'we', the Lithuanians, are located. This locus of identity implies an understanding of the locale as homeland or 'home'. Such an emplacement of identity involves the shaping of identity in primordial terms and draws on a notion of a sedentary, permanent, many-generational residency in one country, the historical habitat of a particular nation. Thus, in the eyes of local Lithuanians, any nonresident Lithuanians, including returning migrants, are perceived as having, in Herlof-Mortensen's terms, 'lost the sense of the land', which is a substantial repository of Lithuanianness.

The traditional connotation of 'home' as a 'certain place where I belong' is challenged by the tension of double loyalty, both to the country of departure and to the country of return. The period of the last fifteen years of Lithuania's independence shows how returnees' loyalty towards Lithuania as home has changed. The issue of housing, the actual buying of a new house, is of central importance for all returnees. It was true even of those repatriate-returnees who returned to the country during perestroika, with a missionary motivation 'to help the motherland', and were engaged in the work of the National Front (Sajudis) and in the parliament during President Vytautas Landsbergis's term of office (1990–1992). Idealism, related to the *idea of home* shaped as an ancestry myth, the spirit of fathers and forefathers, became reconstructed by the actual practice of settling in a place, *placing home* in Lithuania. But even after returnees started to accommodate themselves fully by purchasing an apartment, house, or land and getting along well with their relatives in the country of return, they didn't experience a proportional change in their double loyalty. Not to talk about those who are more recent newcomers to Lithuania and whose double loyalty is evident. According to one informant, an expatriate old man who came from Australia and who has lived in Vilnius for the last five years: 'Lithuania is motherland/fatherland, home is Australia'. Certainly the reference to home(land) is very different among the foreign born second or third DP generation newcomers: 'Canada is my home but I like being here. I'll perhaps stay for another five years' (Lithuanian-Canadian young man, who came to Lithuania in 1999).

If new housing becomes home as a 'place', then, to a certain extent, it changes the home left in the country of departure into an 'idea'. Such a situation creates another kind of double loyalty; being in Lithuania but not entirely (or only) of it. Lithuania becomes more real but not entirely real. It is a direct consequence of the diasporic community's life. Being a people with historical roots and destinies outside the host nation, diasporic communities are *not here*. Diasporic cultures mediate in 'lived tension, the experience of separation and entanglement, of living here and remembering/ desiring another place'(Clifford 1994: 310–311). Home(land) secures its status of imaginary subject. It becomes *hyphenated* and seasonal, and many returnees possess two homes and stay season by season in one land or another. More often, homes in Lithuania are used for summer and vacation periods for younger and senior generations. Homes in America or elsewhere are used for the same purpose by the older generation of returnees who can afford to travel.

Missionary Identity: Standards of Lithuanianness Brought by the Returnees

Before becoming returnees, the older generation of refugees went through the challenges of acculturation in the countries that gave them refuge after 1945. Upon returning to Lithuania they feel they have become 'experts on the retention of Lithuanianess'. Such an 'expert' position is based on knowledge of the 'free world' and the codes of conduct elaborated in the diaspora community life as a ready-made formula of 'how to be Lithuanian in the free democratic world'.

Diaspora Lithuanians followed the openly ethnonationalist rules of Lithuanian enculturation enunciated in the principal imperative of the Lithuanian Charter: 'a Lithuanian is always a Lithuanian'. This dictum, in the end of 1980s and beginning of 1990s, for example, was used in the U.S. to confront the newly arrived Lithuanian immigrants from the former communist bloc. They were said to be marked by a 'lack of culture' and 'contaminated' by being exposed to the communist way. Postcommunist immigrants were met by 'culture experts' – diaspora Lithuanians, who acted as 'gatekeepers' (cf. Corra and Willer 2002) or advisers, both in approaching general American society as well as getting into the ethnic community (Kuzmickaite 2003; Čiubrinskas 2004).

Lithuanian transmigrants living in diasporas, particularly in the U.S., put a great deal of effort into ensuring that their ethnicity was, in Reginald Byron's words, furnished with a culture and a history (Byron 1999). Lithuanian ethnicity was not only shared as an ancestry myth, as a common heritage and a social memory, it was seen as Lithuanian 'national' culture. The DP generation, in particular, assumed a *nationalist mission* to contribute to Lithuanian culture by devoting their private lives to a range of Lithuanian cultural projects and practices such as the completion and publication in Boston in the 1970s of a thirty-six volume universal encyclopaedia in the native language (Kucas 1975). The Lithuanian-American intelligentsia took on the responsibility to instruct the younger generation and to reproduce their culture in ethnic schools, organizations, and churches.

The diaspora was busy not only with the retention, but even more so, with a new standardization of Lithuanian culture. A codified overview of Lithuanian culture and heritage was used in the textbooks for the ethnic schools. Pre-Second World War Lithuanian textbooks, to say nothing of the Soviet texts, were treated either as useless in the New World or 'wrong' politically. A good example of culture codification is the Lithuanian-American textbook by Danute Brazyte-Bindokiene, *Lithuanian Customs and Traditions*, designed for the world Lithuanian youth to learn about their nation's traditions (Brazyte-Bindokiene 1989:10) and to be used in ethnic classes as a textbook. Like other essentialist projects and practices of this kind, the textbook poses a question: what is the core of nationness? It implies another question, a question of purity versus contamination, authenticity versus borrowing. These distinctions were of particular importance to the diasporic intelligentsia, as it secured its right to design and standardize 'proper Lithuanian culture' and to manipulate it in identity politics.

In Lithuania itself, during the initial period of its reestablishment after regaining independence, public representations of Lithuanian culture were also dominated by the Lithuanian ethnic culture models. This was particularly explicit in public and private discourses about 'true' Lithuanian identity, while a network of 'ethnic culture' institutions mushroomed in the country. Thus, the diaspora-made, ethnonationalist model of 'proper Lithuanian culture', brought back to Lithuania, fitted well the process of national reidentification, and the returnees, especially during the Singing Revolution period,[5] felt their mission was being achieved and their expertise accomodated.

Large charitable donations, including IT equipment, books, consumer goods and financial assets, were arranged and brought to Lithuania by the returnees, and these were extremely significant in the late 1980s and the beginning of 1990s, just before, during and immediately after the Singing Revolution. Another good example of 'missionary' work for Lithuania was the reestablishment of the University in Kaunas, the second largest city in the country, in 1989. With the support of the Lithuanian diaspora in the U.S. and Canada, the Vytautas Magnus University was reopened as a modern

Western university, becoming a prime example of the postcolonialist-style export of Western standards. The first two university presidents were Lithuanian-Americans. They established a system along the North American model with a strong 'Anglo-Saxon' bias, an emphasis on English, a friendly attitude to foreign faculties, and a flexible system designed to accommodate visiting faculty staff. Some faculty from the diaspora came to stay and devote themselves to the implementation of Western academic standards (Vastokas 2005).

Sympathy for the needs of postsoviet Lithuanians among the diaspora is particularly rooted in the U.S. Lithuanian diaspora intellectual group 'Santara-Sviesa'. With the broad-minded attitude inscribed in its logo: 'open face to Lithuania', Santara-Sviesa was opposed by the radical wing of the diaspora who refused any possibility of public cooperation with Soviet Lithuania, despite their proclaimed 'enlightened campaigns for spreading information about democracy and the free world' (Dapkute 2001). It was, and still is, the case for Santara-Sviesa members like the current President of Lithuania and his wife, Valdas and Alma Adamkus, to be strongly motivated and devoted to helping the country and its people.

Before making their decision to move (or move back) to Lithuania, most members of the diaspora made several visits to the country.

For the first time I came to Lithuania as a tourist, in 1988. I stayed longer in 1992. Just came here to work in the parliament [Auksciausioji Taryba]. I was working in the Secretariat of Landsbergis, later in the Department of Information. I stayed here by accident. I didn't have plans to come here, and to stay. I just wanted to do some work and then go back to continue my studies in the U.S ... . I came here because of my overwhelming idealism; I wanted to help [Lithuania] somehow. Soon I understood that my help is not needed. I understood I just have to work. That's it ... . I have started to work here and invested my time. So, as it is going well, it pays to work here, if it doesn't, than, maybe, I would live somewhere else. (Lithuanian-American male, 30)

Returnees Contested in the Public Sphere: Labels and Stereotypes

Despite the returnees' most common self-image of being faithful to their patriotic mission, the local image of the returnee is different and controversial (Vastokas 1993; Sidrys 1996). In the returnees' personal encounters with 'locals' in the public sphere, particularly in their competition for social statuses and positions, differences arise in terms of their right and authority to represent Lithuanianness. This compares with the data from Latvia collected by Herloff-Mortensen:

[Returnees] occupy important positions in different ministries, newspapers and so on, where they have a lot of contact with foreigners. They explain Latvia, they do translations, and they are advisors. Basically they are the transmission belt in the middle between Latvia and the West. Most local Latvians don't understand how to do that, they don't understand the West. (Herloff-Mortensen 1999)

In such cases, returnees, especially professionals, are accepted as experts, but at the same time they are constantly challenged, both publicly, by local preconceptions about foreigners coming from the West, and privately, in James Scott's terminology, by exercising the weapons of the weak, 'hidden transcripts' (Scott 1985, 1990). Labels and stereotypes of 'Westerners moved to the East' are based on the schema of *them* – as 'prosperous and successful enough to do what they want' – and of *us* – as 'having unique local experience'.

Rich Uncles from America

The stereotype about a 'rich uncle from America' was already coined in nineteenth-century Lithuania, a country producing numbers of emigrants to the New World. The label has survived and has merged with the Soviet epithet of 'arrogant millionaire from the imperialist world'. This attitude to returnees from the West and, especially, from the United States, is firmly rooted in the postcommunist mental map. One of my informants, when asked if he faced any expressions of disapproval on this account, answered: 'I never faced any censure openly and personally, but some implications about being rich were felt. Here local people regard foreigners [from the West] as rich uncles who are available to be milked, but nowadays people here have started to become rich themselves'. Another informant mentioned jealousy as a common attitude towards the rapid advance of a returnee. Compared with locals, returnees are assumed to be wealthier: 'I think that negative attitude is because we came with money and can afford more. I don't think that Lithuanians should be jealous so much, as we had to work hard too'.

What Can a Yankee Like You Tell Us?

Other labels and stereotypes of 'Westerners moved East' are based on locals, 'us', encountering newcomers, 'them', where 'us' stands for 'having unique local life experience' and 'them' for a lack of it.

> What do you know about us, they say, you are American, you can't understand anything ... But this is my land, my home, my nation, past and present. My parents brought me up; I'm one hundred percent Lithuanian, not fifty fifty. That is why it is painful when somebody points a finger at me and says: 'You are American'... . When Adamkus (the Lithuanian-American President of Lithuania) does something good in politics, they say 'hey, our little Lithuanian', but when he does something which doesn't suit one group or another, you can hear: 'Hey, look, an American, he doesn't understand anything about Lithuania'. (Lithuanian-American male, in his 50s, former MP in Lithuania)

Peculiarities in local experience, derived from Soviet modes of behavior, include 'in groups' (or 'groups of their own'), clientelism, nepotism, *blat* (the economy of favors), and bribery. Returnees react to such behaviour with protest. One returnee, coming into a hospital, immediately announced loudly: 'Be aware, I won't bribe anybody here'.

Social Uncertainty: Acculturation Challenges

Lack of local social knowledge is tightly connected with social uncertainty, different levels of which returnees must undergo. Many of them become puzzled about the ambivalent situation they experience in terms of resocialisation and acculturation. There are two opinions about the need for acculturation. The first claims that there is no need for acculturation, as returnees belong to Lithuanian culture as ethnics and patriots. This position is shared by repatriate intelligentsia, 'rooted and devoted to the roots'. They claim that they 'have never been away, but always "were" in Lithuania' and in their 'deeds for retention of Lithuanianness' they are comparable to the local dissidents and those deported to Siberia.

The second position states that there is a need for acculturation or, rather, resocialisation, because the returnees have to integrate into a postcommunist society. Either argument describes a situation of uncertainty, something very familiar to transmigrants, who already faced it once, during their first acculturation in their host society. The need for a 'second' acculturation or reacculturation is clearly evident because not a single returnee can avoid the uncertainty brought about by changes in the social fabric.

The new social status and prestige of the returnee is different from the one left in the host countries. The direction of change of status differs from group to group but generally it is higher: nearly all of the returnees belong to the economic and intellectual elite of the country, which includes prominent businessmen, writers, artists, university professors and politicians. However, it is still the case that the most productive period of life of the older generation of returnees was spent abroad.

> The most productive part of my life was there. It was already routine, friends, membership in clubs. You had a name there and now you have to start everything. Of course, not from the beginning, but the system and many more things are different in Lithuania. (Older Lithuanian-American male)

Due to lower living standards in Lithuania, most returnees can afford higher quality goods and services here compared with the country they left. Despite that, they experience social uncertainty. The most sensitive issue is citizenship.

Citizenship

The issue of citizenship is crucial for many potential returnees. Many, after deciding to return, changed their minds because they could not have dual citizenship. According to Lithuanian Citizenship laws from 1990 to 1995, dual citizenship was impossible: it was necessary to renounce the citizenship of any other country when applying for Lithuanian citizenship. The most serious consequence of this step would be the loss of retirement pension from the host country.

> Many friends of mine were determined to return from Australia, but all of that [immigration law] blocked up and they gave up the matter of return. They said, it's better we stay here, because if our being born in Lithuania is ignored, if we can't buy property, can't obtain citizenship, what we will do there? (Older Lithunian-Australian male)

> The question of obtaining citizenship is not only complicated bureaucratically, but also an extremely acute issue for returnees. It was impossible for many returnees or potential returnees to understand why they were denied citizenship if they were eligible on both normally accepted grounds: born in the country and being ethnic Lithuanians. Many became so indignant that they are now reluctant to have any contact with Lithuania. (Lithuanian-Canadian female, 60)

Even after the exceptional dual citizenship law was implemented in 1995, the dividing line was still visible between those who had no doubts and eagerly sought Lithuanian citizenship, and those who looked back and had second thoughts, especially those returnees who were related to strategic institutions in their host countries.

> I didn't want to get dual citizenship. If I had to come back to the U.S. and work there in government institutions such a citizenship would be noticed. I'm not hung up on those things; it is only little bit of paper, it doesn't make me a better or worse Lithuanian… . Nobody [in the U.S.] would pay attention if I had dual citizenship. But in spheres like defence, or foreign policy, there can't be double loyalty. (Lithuanian-American male, 45, who worked in President Landsbergis's office as a consultant).

Corruption, *Blat* and Bureaucracy

Corruption is an extremely sensitive issue in the returnees' discourses. The remnants of Soviet-style bureaucracy, bribing, and, in particular the phenomenon of *blat*, well described by Ledeneva (1998) as an economy of favours, is an enigma to returnees who face it in everyday life activities, from running errands to obtaining civil documents.

We didn't imagine such dishonesty: the authorities can steal, and if you need some business to be worked out, here comes *blat*. Give money, and your need will be worked out faster. We did paperwork for the house ownership, it was so much walking there and here. In the bureaucracy in Lithuania [of the interwar period] it was never like this. (Lithuanian-American male, 90)

I wanted to get my own postbox in the Vilnius Central Post Office in 1996. I went to the vice-director and she told me that there were no boxes available. I gave her money and told her to share the sum with the head of the office. In a week, when I came back, I was asked about my 'long disappearance' … the box had been waiting for several days and only the paperwork needed to be done. (Lithuanian-Australian male, 80)

Bureaucracy … I didn't have a Lithuanian passport, only the old one, of the Smetona [interwar] period, so I was sent to bring my birth certificate, to get this and that, so it took three months to obtain the passport. You can't get a telephone line without a passport. Later, my wife had to get her [passport], and again … After that I had to pass the driving test. I drove for fifty years in America and had no accident … Here I had to pass the test. (Lithuanian-American male, 89, who lives in the Vilnius Gerontology Centre)

The examples could be continued, but even these are enough to demonstrate the clearly visible arenas for social uncertainty encountered by the Lithuanian returnees. The problems of acculturation of returnees into postcommunist Lithuanian society are widely discussed in the Lithuanian diaspora media and the negative examples are used fuel the motivation not to return. There is a mistrust or an 'imagined mistrust' of Lithuania, which keeps thousands of diaspora Lithuanians from returning despite Lithuania's membership in NATO and the EU.

Conclusion

In delineating a portrait of the 'migrants of nostalgia' in postcommunist Lithuania we notice that they are a very small fraction of the total global Lithuanian diaspora, which numbers about one million emigrants. The majority of returnees are repatriates from the West, former political émigrés from the end of the Second World War and their offspring, second and third generation foreign-born Lithuanians.

Governed by a formula of 'how to be a Lithuanian in the free world', inscribed in the Lithuanian Charter of 1949, as well as encultured by ethnic institutions in the diaspora, they brought a *missionary identity* to Lithuania. Their standard of nationness included both the 'obligation to return' and 'to be of use' to Lithuania. From one point of view their professional skills, knowledge of civic participation, and moral qualities, are all shared in different niches of society including parliament and the presidency. From another angle, it is clear that the diaspora idealists, by becoming 'missionaries', were keen to implement their own Lithuanian culture-codifying standards in a country 'devastated by communism'. Such enshrined ethnonationalism fitted well into mainstream Lithuanian cultural politics intent on promoting Lithuanian ethnic culture and heritage.

Smaller in number is that category of returnees who came by making a 'rational choice'. These have an interest in familiarizing themselves with the 'transitional' country and its people. The patterns of successful acculturation and emplacement of such returnees bespeak their excellence as professionals and experts and also covers the process of extending their loyalty towards Lithuania as their home. In buying their own housing, returnees are materializing the 'obligation to return home' but at the same time their homes in their original host country become themselves 'idealized'. 'Home' becomes hybrid and interchangeably used as both an idea and a place.

The process of acculturation of the returnees is challenged by local postcommunist expressions of xenophobia, labelling and stigmatizing of foreigners. Even those returnees who claim that while physically living in the diaspora, they have 'never been away, but always (at least culturally), in Lithuania' are labeled as 'Americans'. In general, returnees are puzzled by the sense that they are in a familiar culture but in a strange, sometimes incomprehensible society of social uncertainty with Soviet remnants of corruption and bureaucracy. The issue of citizenship has been perhaps the most significant factor in reducing the number of returnees to a trickle: even the change in citizenship law in 2002[6] has not erased the indignity of being alienated in their 'home', and has given an excuse 'not to return' to many potential returnees.

Notes

1   From the thirteenth century, and especially after being united with Poland in the sixteenth century, Lithuania was one of the major European powers until the end of eighteenth century. It lost its independence to Russia in the wake of the partition of the Poland-Lithuania Commonwealth. Lithuania became an independent republic in 1918, but was occupied by the Soviet Union in 1940. Occupied by Nazi Germany in 1941, it again was reoccupied by the Soviet Union in 1944 and became the Lithuanian Soviet Socialist Republic, a member state of the USSR. After half a century, it regained its independence in 1989–1991(Vardys and Sedaitis 1997).

2   Postsoviet Lithuania is to be understood as a nation state where its ethnic majority is seen vis-a-vis other ethnic minorities and where the term 'ethnic culture' is understood, first of all, as the ethnic culture of the Lithuanian majority. There is a parliamentary commission within the Lithuanian Parliament, the Council for the Protection of Ethnic Culture (Etnines Kulturos Globos Taryba). Its mission is 'to insure guardianship of national ethnic identity and state protection of [Lithuanian] ethnic culture'(http://www3.lrs.lt). In public discourses, the term 'ethnic culture' is used quite often as a substitute or synonym for Lithuanian [national] culture.

3   The post-socialist Lithuanian citizenship legislation in particular well exemplifies the limitations of its applicability to many potential returnees by application of ethnic criterion

for the Lithuanian citizenship applicants. As it is well described by Darius Dauksas (2006), who proves that the specification and the question of "émigré" became central right after the Law on Citizenship of the Republic of Lithuania was adopted after re-establishment of Independence in 1990. Later amendment of 1994 introduced the definition of "person of Lithuanian origin". In 2002 it was changed into "person of Lithuanian descent". All these editions eventually led to make an exception – double citizenship only for persons of Lithuanian descent, i.e. on ethnic aspect of belonging (Dauksas 2006: 75–76).

4   The Lithuanian American Community, Inc. was established in the U.S. in 1952, with the primary goal of maintaining Lithuanian culture and heritage outside the borders of Lithuania and seeking independence for Lithuania. The Lithuanian American Community is part of the World Lithuanian Community, conceived and launched in Hanau Displaced Persons' Camp in Germany, in 1946 (Saldukas 2001).

5   Gorbachev's program of social and political reforms (perestroika), was enthusiastically supported by the Lithuanians as well as the Latvians and Estonians. Led by intellectuals, the Lithuanian Reform Movement, Sajudis (National Front), was founded in mid 1988. It declared a program of democratic and national rights, and achieved nationwide popularity. Pressed by Sajudis, the Soviet Lithuania Supreme Council passed constitutional amendments on the supremacy of Lithuanian laws over Soviet legislation, annulled the 1940 incorporation of Lithuania into the USSR, legalized a multi-party system, and adopted a number of other important decisions. In 1989, on 23 August, fifty years after the Molotov-Ribbentrop pact that preceded the Nazi-Soviet occupation of the Baltic countries, the Baltic Road, a human chain of joined hands from Vilnius to Tallinn via Riga was organized by the National Fronts of all three countries. It was the beginning of the Singing Revolution in the Baltic Countries, an idea that crystallized out of the ancient tradition of utilizing songs as an expression of passive resistance to oppression and repression. Another Baltic pattern, well known since the end of the nineteenth century, is the singing of the masses during the National Folk Song Festivals.

In 1990, Sajudis-backed candidates won the elections to the Lithuanian Supreme Soviet and declared restitution of Lithuanian independence. There followed a period of Soviet economic and military threat and aggression until the eventual collapse of the USSR in 1991. The Lithuanians protested against Soviet actions in public gatherings and the singing of folk songs. In January 1991 Soviet armed forces seized the Lithuanian National Publishing House, National Radio and TV. Tanks attacked the Vilnius TV Tower. Fourteen were killed, seven hundred injured, of the thousands who were gathered around the TV Tower, unarmed and singing. Despite the military attacks the Lithuanian Parliament continued to work day and night, surrounded by thousands of supporters who were firing fires and singing (Vardys and Sedaitis 1997).

6   In 2002 the amendment of the Law of Citizenship encompassed the exceptional principle of dual citizenship but only to the persons of "Lithuanian descent". To obtain citizenship a person had to present a set of record where his Lithuanian descent was proven. Such management of citizenship was its ethnification and bureaucratization (Dauksas 2006). Even the amendment of *dual citizenship* itself after four years in 2006 was explained as anti-constitutional by the Constitutional Court and lost its power.

References

Akstinaviciute, I. 2005. 'Lietuviu diaspora ir Lietuva', M.A. dissertation. Kaunas, Lithuania: Department of Sociology, Vytautas Magnus University.

Al Ali, N. and K. Koser. 2002. 'Transnationalism, International Migration and Home', in N. Al Ali and K. Khalid (eds), *New Approaches to Migration? Transnational Communities and the Transformation of Home*. London: Routledge, pp.1–14.

Brazyte-Bindokiene, D. 1989. *Lithuanian Customs and Traditions*. Chicago: Lithuanian World Community.

Bruner, E. 1996. 'Tourism in Ghana: The Representation of Slavery and the Return of the Black Diaspora', *American Anthropologist* 98(2): 290–304.

Byron, R. 1999. *Irish American*. Oxford: Oxford University Press.

Castells, M. 1997. *The Power of Identity*. Oxford: Blackwell.

Cernius, V. 2005. 'The Acculturation of Lithuanian Immigrants Who Arrived in the United States After World War II', in D. Kuiziniene (ed.) *Beginnings and Ends of Emigration: Life without Borders in the Contemporary World*. Vilnius: Versus Aureus, pp.123–56.

Čiubrinskas, V. 2004. 'Transnational Identity and Heritage: Lithuania Imagined, Constructed and Contested', in U. Kockel and M. Nic Craith (eds). *Communicating Cultures*. Münster: LIT Verlag, pp.42–66.

———. 2005. 'Lithuanian Transnationalism: Constructed, Imagined and Contested Identity of Lithuanian Americans', in D. Kuiziniene (ed.) *Beginnings and Ends of Emigration: Life without Borders in the Contemporary World*. The Lithuanian Emigration Institute, Vilnius: Versus Aureus, pp.33–50.

Clifford, J. 1994. 'Diasporas', *Cultural Anthropology* 9(3): 302–38.

———. 1997. *Routes. Travel and Translation in the Late Twentieth Century*. Cambridge, MA: Harvard University Press.

Corra, M. and D. Willer. 2002. 'The Gatekeeper', *Sociological Theory* 20(2): 180–207.

Dapkute, D. 2001. 'Lietuviu iseivijos santykiu su okupuota Lietuva dinamika 20 a. 6–9 Desimtmeciais', *Istorija* 47(2001): 34–47.

Dauksas, D. 2004. 'The Transmission of Ethnicity, Family and State: A Lithuanian Perspective', Unpublished manuscript. Vilnius: Department of Ethnology, Lithuanian Institute of History.

———. 2006. 'Defining Belonging: Citizenship as a form of Ethnic Inclusion and exclusion. The Case from Post-soviet Lithuania', *Acta Historica Universitatis Klaipedensis: Studia Anthropologica* 13(2): 71–80.

Herloff Mortensen, M.-A. 1999. 'The Latvian Thing: Narratives of Place and Identity among Local and Diasporic Latvians', M.A. dissertation. Copenhagen: Institute of Anthropology, University of Copenhagen.

Hill, J. and T. Wilson. 2003. 'Identity Politics and Politics of Identity', *Identities: Global Studies in Culture and Power* 10: 1–8.

Holy, L. 1996. *The Little Czech and The Great Czech Nation: National Identity and the Post-Communist Social Transformation*. Cambridge: Cambridge University Press.

Kelly, M. 2000. 'Ethnic Pilgrimages: People of Lithuanian Descent in Lithuania', *Sociological Spectrum* 20: 65–91.

Kucas, A. 1975. *Lithuanians in America*. Boston: Encyclopedia Lituanica Press.

Kuzmickaite, D. 2003. *Between Two Worlds: Recent Lithuanian Immigrants in Chicago (1988– 2000)*. Vilnius: Versus Aureus.

Ledeneva, A. 1998. *Russia's Economy of Favours: Blat, Networking and Informal Exchange*. Cambridge: Cambridge University Press.

Muntz, R. and R. Ohliger. 2003. *Diasporas and Ethnic Migrants: Germany, Israel and Post-Soviet Successor States in Contemporary Perspective*. London: Frank Cass.

Nešpor, Z. 2002. 'The Disappointed and Disgruntled: A Study of the Return in the 1990s of Czech Emigrants from the Communist Era', *Czech Sociological Review* 38(6): 789–808.

Povrzanovic Frykman, M. (ed.) 2001. 'Challenges of Belonging in Diaspora and Exile', in M. Povrzanovic Frykman (ed.) *Beyond Integration: Challenges of Belonging in Diaspora and Exile*. Lund: Nordic Academic Press, pp.11–40.

Rushdie, S. 1998. 'Imaginary Homelands', in G. Marshall, (ed.) *Dictionary of Sociology*. Oxford: Oxford University Press, p.295.

Saldukas, L. 2002. *Lithuanian Diaspora*. Vilnius: Vaga.

Scott, J. 1985. *Weapons of the Weak: Everyday Forms of Peasant Resistance*. New Haven, CT: Yale University Press.

———. 1990. *Domination and the Arts of Resistance: Hidden Transcripts*. New Haven, CT: Yale University Press.

Sidrys, R. 1996. 'Lithuanians on Lithuanian Americans', *Observer* 1(2): 4–9.

Vardys, S. and J. Sedaitis. 1997. *Lithuania: The Rebel Nation*. Boulder, CO: Westview.

Vastokas, R. 1993. 'Lietuvos ir iseivijos sankryza', *Europos Lietuvis* 32(47): 1–4.

———. 2005. 'From Glasnost to NATO: Retired and Restless in a Post-Soviet State', *Trent University Newsletters* 2: 14–16.

Vertovec, S. and R. Cohen (eds), 1999. *Migration, Diaspora and Transnationalism*. Cheltenham: Edward Elgar Publishing.

Chapter 6

A Rainbow Flag against the Krakow Dragon: Polish Responses to the Gay and Lesbian Movement

Grażyna Kubica

Introduction

On 1 May 2004 Poland entered the European Union.[1] In Krakow, the last day of April was marked by a festive celebration: at midnight thousands of Krakovians carrying EU flags gathered at the Main Marketplace (the biggest square in Europe) to listen to Beethoven's Ninth Symphony splendidly performed by the local philharmonic orchestra and choir. The whole city appeared to be united in common joy (maybe because the 'eurosceptics' stayed at home). At the same time preparations for another spectacle were in full swing. It was intended for a limited audience and, as some believed, concerned marginal problems. But it turned out that the performance was of interest (or disgust) to a much larger audience than that involved in the rehearsal.

The theatrical metaphor reflects the character of the events that accompanied the 'Festival of Culture for Tolerance', which was initiated by students belonging to an association called the Campaign Against Homophobia. One act of the 'drama' took place at the Jagiellonian University: a conference on homosexuality organized by the Institute of Sociology, where I am based. Our Rector's reluctant attitude, together with a political witch-hunt launched by the media and right-wing organizations, made me feel morally obliged to take part in the enterprise and to collect ethnographic data about it. Helped by a small group of students[2] I recorded several hours of videotape during the main events which we later analysed in class. I also interviewed the organizers and their adversaries; I recorded media coverage and took part in other relevant events. Currently, I am editing a documentary film about the event, which presents a parallel narrative to the present chapter.

The metaphor used above is not merely a rhetorical device but also reflects my methodological stance. The present study is a kind of processual analysis of social phenomena, which assumes changeability and cultural heterogeneity. Its aim is to describe and interpret. My stance is close to postmodern performative ethnography, especially to its assumption that each cultural 'performance' is unique and each 'actor' is creative (Fabian 1992). My study is an attempt to sketch the entire arena in which the conflict took place.

Polish scientific literature contains some works about gays and lesbians (for example: Kochanowski 2004; Majka-Rostek 2002), and there are numerous studies about the Polish Catholic Church (e.g. Borowik 2002; Załęcki 2001), but there is nothing on a new right-wing movements or football fans. I want to present both sides of the conflict, giving them a chance to air their views. But at the same time my position is an example of critical anthropology, which tries to fight against the negative phenomena it describes (see Marcus 1999). [3]

My paper comprises of three sections: an account of the most important events; a presentation of the main actors' ideas and experiences; and the theoretically crucial contexts against the background of which I will venture some interpretations with the help of literature from anthropological, sociological, gender, queer and cultural studies.

An Account of Events

In autumn 2003, Tomasz, one of the leaders of the Krakovian branch of the Campaign Against Homophobia and a student of journalism, suggested organizing a festival of gay and lesbian culture, following the example of such events in the West which he had come across during a vacation spent abroad.[4] At first it was to be a small-scale event for a student audience only, with a conference on homosexuality, a film presentation, an exhibition and a picnic with a concert. Various organizational difficulties resulting from the reluctant attitude of many people, however, led the Campaign's leaders to take a more public stand, and they proposed a march through town. They took their request to the municipality for official approval. Their proposed date, Saturday 8 May, 2004, was changed to Sunday 9 May, due to some sporting event taking place on the Saturday.

In mid April the official website of the 'Festival of Culture for Tolerance' appeared: 'During four days in May we want to show society that LGBT [Lesbians, Gays, Bisexual, Transsexual] people constitute a valuable and creative part of Polish society' and to discuss 'the place and role of LGBT people in Poland'.[4] The patrons of the event were: the Government

Plenipotentiary for Equal Status of Women and Men, together with the Institute of Sociology, Jagiellonian University. A poster was prepared with information about a planned series of events (Wawel castle against rainbow flag colours: see Figure 6.1).

On the morning of 19 April, the Rector of the Jagiellonian University was invited to the Roman Catholic Archbishopric, and we can only guess that the Archbishop expressed his disapproval of the University's involvement in the planned event. Later that day the Rector called the Dean of the Faculty of Philosophy and the Directors of the Institute of Sociology. He accused the vice-director who was helping organize the conference, of transgressing her authority by illegally using the University logo. Only then one could learn that the Rector is the logo's legal owner. On the same day the University coat of arms was removed from the website. Another problem was with

Figure 6.1 A poster of the Festival 'Culture for Tolerance'.

the date of the march, because Sunday 9 May happened to be the Feast of St Stanislaw, when a traditional procession made its way from the Wawel Cathedral to Skałka Church. The Municipality suggested that date without taking into consideration the religious procession which did not require official permission. But the result was that the Campaign was accused of religious provocation. They immediately changed the date again, to Friday 7 May.

But on 20 April the *Gazeta Wyborcza*, a liberal newspaper, ran an article entitled 'Rendezvous on Wawel Hill' claiming that: 'When participants of the St Stanislaw's procession will be praying at the Wawel cathedral, a gathering of gays and lesbians will be coming to an end at the bottom of the hill. It is not a provocation, it is a coincidence – the organizers of the manifestations are assuring'; however, 'the University authorities dissociate themselves from the gathering' (Kula 2004). The article was accompanied by an illustration showing two processions: one with a cross and another one with rainbow flags separated by a screen running along the middle of a street.

The witch-hunt increased in intensity. The same day councillors of the Catholic party, the League of Polish Families (Liga Polskich Rodzin, or LPR), addressed the Mayor and the Rector in a letter stating that behind the event was 'a rebellious ideology, threatening social order' and 'a promotion of deviant attitudes'. There was a petition campaign to 'protest against the planned march of homosexuals'. The Catholic Campaign of Krakovian Archdioceses raised its objection against 'the event that has nothing to do with culture' in 'Krakow, a town of men of knowledge, a town of Saints, a town of the Pope and a World Centre of God's Mercy, a town of so many priceless national mementoes'. The Father Piotr Skarga Association of Christian Culture distributed 280,000 leaflets by mail: 'Say No to the promotion of homosexualism in Krakow'. The monumental Wawel Cathedral was on the top of the leaflet and colorful drag queens at the bottom. The leaflet contained an appeal for people to say the rosary for the sin of sodomy and to send protests to the Mayor and the Rector[5]. The Archbishop made a special statement: 'Moral disapproval of homosexual behavior is not intolerance, on the contrary, it is a sign of caring for the people'. The nationalist All-Polish Youth announced a counter-campaign: 'Let's kick homosexualism out of Krakow'. Football fans were using the internet to team up, planning to beat up queers. The regional parliament pressed the mayor and the Rector to prevent 'the demonstration of homosexuals'. There were only four councillors against this, all of the postcommunist Democratic Left Alliance (Sojusz Lewicy Demokratycznej, or SLD). There was also an interpellation of the nationalist party, Law and Justice (Prawo i Sprawiedliwość), in the Polish parliament to the Government Plenipotentiary for Equal Status of Women and Men: 'Why does the Government support an event organized by homosexuals, a manifestation against good taste and public morality, offending Polish society and the Church?' The Plenipotentiary answered that the support resulted from the mission of defending human rights and protecting against discrimination[6].

She also wrote to the Mayor asking him not to give in to 'aggressive groups opposing the Days of Tolerance'. Leaders of the Campaign sent information concerning crimes ranging from incitement to hatred by the League of Polish Families and the All-Polish Youth to the prosecutor's office. They also organized a petition campaign, arguing that 'one of the most splendid achievements of European culture is respect for different ideas and attitudes', and managed to get the support of both Krakovian Nobel prizewinning poets: Czesław Miłosz and Wisława Szymborska, together with many other distinguished artists and academics. A few columnists wrote sympathetic articles. A Swedish-Polish Campaign activist organized an international supporting campaign. Hundreds of emails were sent to the Mayor and the Rector, many foreign journalists came, among them a Swedish film-maker, who collected material for a documentary (Voxerbrant 2004).

The route of the march was eventually agreed upon by the Municipality: it was to proceed along the Planty boulevard, a park surrounding the medieval centre of Krakow that today is a pedestrian area (not requiring special permission). The conference on 'Homosexuality – a public or private matter?' took place on the May 6 in a small room of the new campus of the University far from the centre of Krakow (where the Rector ordered it moved). It was officially opened by the Vice-Dean of the Faculty of Philosophy, the vice-Director of the Institute of Sociology and a representative of the Government Plenipotentiary for Equal Status of Women and Men. Several papers were delivered (by both academics and students), among them: 'Homosexual Identity Development'; 'From the Theory of Deviation to Queer Theory'; 'Everyday Life of Homosexual Couples'; 'Love between Women in the Middle East'; 'The Public Image of Homosexuals in Poland' (see Slany et al 2005). TV reporters and other journalists attended, a rare occurrence for academic conferences. There were also many regular participants, some of whom had to stay outside. The atmosphere of serious debate prevailed, but participants also experienced some political tension. Despite the Rector's fears, the conference was not disturbed.

On the morning of May 7, representatives of the Campaign and the International Lesbian & Gay Cultural Network layed flowers before the Wall of Executions in the Auschwitz-Birkenau Concentration Camp. Later that day a senator, and the author of a proposed bill about partner relationships, delivered a lecture, 'Laws Concerning Sexual Minorities in a Democratic Society'.

The March for Tolerance was planned to start at 4.30 P.M. in front of Collegium Novum (the main building of the University), but groups of people had gathered there in advance with numerous representatives of the media. Campaign participants were to gather close to a big Campaign banner, a leader informed everyone through a loudspeaker. One could recognize several MPs (from the postcommunist Democratic Left Alliance only), and the placards of Young Social Democrats, Greens, anarchists, anticlericals, and feminist organizations. Campaign participants carried rainbow flags, EU flags and many banners proclaiming, for instance: 'Yes to tolerance', 'Legalism, Pluralism, Equality', 'I am a Lesbian, I am a Human Being, I am a Pole'. Activists distributed leaflets and stickers saying 'Freedom, Equality, Tolerance'. Spontaneous discussions broke out. Journalists interviewed people; so did we, anthropologists. [7] Here are some statements:

> We support those people who are weakened by parts of society. We think that they have the right to express their ideas. (A young couple)

> [I came here] to protest against that rabble of deviants and lesbians. It is a scandal. Krakow is a European city! Where is the Dean? Where is Parliament? Where is the University Council? If only to tolerate it in front of the University! (An elderly lady)

> People, who are not able to adjust to some norms, try to impose their views on normal society in a very aggressive way. (A young biker)

> I think that they should march easily, and this should not disturb anybody. (An older man)

> It can not take place in Krakow. In such a city, royal ... And before such a Feast Day of Stanislaw, to boot! And on the first Friday (of the month)! [8] There is a Christian church every two steps. Such a rabble! (Two middle aged women)

The march started to move along the Planty and then eggs and vulgar epithets started to be hurled by young men with close-cropped hair and elderly people: 'Perverts!', 'Chuck them out to Berlin!" Policemen tried to limit this aggressive behavior. On both sides of the march two lines of spectators formed: casual passers by and excited rubberneckers. Many people photographed the march. Participants chanted: 'Come with us, gays and lesbians!', 'Tolerance, tolerance!'. Everybody in the march smiled and felt a communal joyfulness. There were approximately 1,500 people actively taking part in the event (the organizers had only planned for two hundred). (See Figure 6.2).

On the approaches to the Barbican, the march stopped for a while at the request of the police, because there were groups of counter-demonstrators further along the route. Later the march changed direction and went along the streets of the medieval centre and down Grodzka street leading to Wawel Hill. The mouth of the street, close to the Katyń Cross, [9] was again obstructed by an aggressive crowd. The participants in the procession managed to get further by passing through an open-air coffee bar. Then both parties took positions: counter-demonstrators at the foot of the Wawel Hill and on the road leading up to the castle (many of them sitting on the pavement), and the march participants stretched out around. Police tried to separate the two crowds and were helped by an anti-riot squad with dogs. (See Figure 6.3)

Figure 6.2 The last part of the March for Tolerance walking along Grodzka Street approaching Wawel Hill. The banners read: 'Campaign against homophobia'; 'Yes for tolerance'; 'Love your neighbour'; 'I have a phobia on homophobia'. Photo by Julia Heller.

Figure 6.3 Participants of the March protecting themselves with umbrellas against stones and eggs thrown by counter-demonstrators from the road leading to the Wawel Castle. Photo by Grażyna Kubica.

The All-Polish Youth's adherents carried banners with: 'The Wawel Dragon[10] was straight'; 'Our streets – your hospitals'; 'Homosexuals of the world, cure yourselves!'; 'Stop Homosexuality'. Football fans blew their whistles deafeningly and shouted: 'Feminists, dykes, queers – all Poland laughs at you!'; 'Police you too are the queers' friends!'; and simply: 'Fuck off, fuck off!" or 'Perverts, perverts!'. The skinheads added: 'Gas the queers!', 'Labour-camps for lesbians!'. Stones, bottles and eggs were thrown down towards the march participants, who opened their umbrellas to protect themselves and tried to shout down the opponents with their own slogans: 'Tolerance for Krakow!'; 'Do you know what it means?". (See Figure 6.4).

This test of strength lasted for a while. The leader of Polish Campaign said then, in front of a TVN camera: 'We can see the state of our democracy today. What we hear – fascist slogans – shows us how long the way before us is. How many festivals like this one are needed?' Finally police managed to persuade the organizers of the march to end it and asked them to disperse.

Participants started to sneak away. Some of them, individually or in groups, headed back towards the Main Marketplace, the heart of the town. On their way they were followed by aggressive opponents. Some managed to escape, but some were threatened with direct attacks and rescued only by police intervention. Counter-demonstrators attacked the policemen and vandalized metal barriers prepared for the next day's sporting event. The riots lasted for another half an hour.

I managed to avoid danger because, immediately after the march was dispersed, I went home to record the media reporting. TVN presented live coverage from the Main Marketplace in a catastrophic tone. The main item on TVP1 News was wholly devoted to the death of a Polish journalist in Iraq and had nothing on the march. The night edition only had a minute

Figure 6.4 Counter-demonstrators blocked by the police. The banner reads: 'Wawel dragon was strait'. Photo by Grażyna Kubica.

report of the riots at the Main Marketplace caused by the football fans. The following day, the local TVP3 channel broadcast a longer and more detailed account of the events with comments by different people. Newspapers presented the events according to their political profile: the right-wing press reluctantly, the liberal press in a more nuanced fashion, and the Catholic *Nasz Dziennik* not at all.

The festival went on, and on Saturday there was a film presentation, a poetry recital and a panel discussion. It was chaired by a colleague from the Institute of Sociology, with the participation of a representative of the Government Plenipotentiary and a cultural attaché of the Swedish Embassy. The voice of this last, as is typical for Western activists, was sympathetic, but also patronizing.

On Sunday 9 May, as every year, undisturbed, the St Stanislaw procession from Wawel Cathedral to Skałka Church took place. There were almost 100,000 faithful. The preacher in his sermon alluded to the recent events as 'a shameless provocation, humiliating the city of a hundred churches with its sanctities: Wawel, Skałka and a sanctuary of God's Mercy at the head' (cited in Skowrońska 2004). He did not mean the violent counter-demonstration but the march itself.

Another 'Festival of Culture for Tolerance' was planned for April 2005. However, the organizers decided to cancel the march, not because of the problems of the previous year but because of the mourning for Pope John Paul II. The decision was not unanimous and the Lesbian Gay Bisexual and Transexual Foundation asked the Mayor for permission to go ahead with the march, but did not succeed for procedural reasons. The next ones took place in 2006, 2007 and 2008; there was an increased police presence and the marches passed off relatively peacefully despite many opponents.

The issue of rights for gays and lesbians, and more generally the issue of homosexuality, has become very popular in Poland. Demonstrations similar to the Krakow one continue to be organized (many without official approval); TV debates carry on; the issue is used in a political context.

ACTORS

Campaign against Homophobia

At first glance the main actors seem to be the organizers of the festival, that is, members of the Krakow branch of the Campaign Against Homophobia. The association was created in 2001 by 'a group of gays and lesbians, who would no longer tolerate humiliation in the name of "values" or in the name of ignorance by those who refuse homosexuals the right to normality'.[11] Their most spectacular project 'Let them see us', in spring 2003, showed images of thirty gay and lesbian couples holding each other's hands.[12] The photographs were displayed in galleries and on billboards in several Polish cities. This was meant to accustom ordinary people to the real presence of gays and lesbians in everyday life, but it became a Polish Stonewall (Gruszczyńska 2004; Leszkowicz 2004).[13] In Krakow the project was confined by the Mayor to the city outskirts.

The Krakovian branch of the Campaign consists of several students (of sociology, journalism, philology) of both sexes, a majority of whom do not come from Krakow. They are all united by their common situation and activities but also by mutual respect and bonds of friendship. Some of them are interested more in self-help activities, and others in wider political actions (like the Festival). The group to them is an important support structure, especially when their own families do not serve as such.

Their experience of organizing the festival made them realize the political character of their work, even if they had not considered it so before they started. The very decision about organizing the march resulted from the difficulties they experienced with getting the festival off the ground (for example, with finding a place for the exhibition), and expressed a felt need to enter the public sphere to manifest their presence. The whole affair also had positive effects: they acquired some organizational skills, an awareness of legal aspects, fund-raising abilities and media literacy. Their academic knowledge (for example, of press law) helped them handle some problems. On the other hand, not all of them had 'come out' so they could not appear on television; public activity carried a grave risk to their private life: familial and social. But the main outcome of the event for them was to realize just how powerfully nationalist and religious ideology is in Poland. Ida put it metaphorically: 'We were just a group of children riding a small bike and suddenly a tank came out' (Voxerbrant 2004). To counter this, they searched for support among authoritive figures, such as the Nobel prizewinning authors. They discussed among themselves whom they should approach. The choice of people was not based on their sexual orientation, but rather their liberal and pluralistic attitudes to public matters.

The Campaign activists had never experienced any homophobic attacks before, the march exposed them to such behavior. For Marcin it was a shock when he heard people shouting 'Gas the queers' at him. Samuel talked about the physical threat he faced: 'When hooligans and skins ran into the Marketplace and chased me, I was trembling, after all you are not followed by people who would like to kill you every day' (Voxerbrant 2004). Ida summarized the situation with a meaningful phrase: 'I was too angry to be scared', and later an American lesbian poet wrote a poem about it, which she recited the following day at the festival.

Earlier, in the build-up to the march, the activists had also gathered valuable experience. Tomasz, who had been repeatedly asked in interviews: 'What does it mean to be a gay in Poland?', finally rebelled, addressing a journalist: 'What does it mean to be a heterosexual white woman? My identity consists of many things and my sexual orientation is not the most important'.

Ida stressed the positive emotions during the festival, where a certain climate of openness prevailed:

[It was as if we were in] some greenhouse [conservatory], where the temperature was more favourable, where everything could be said openly without hesitation … . People started to take the floor, for many it was the first such experience in their lives. [There were many] very intense, accumulated experiences of participation in such events without the sense of fear and without the sense of inappropriateness.

The Institute of Sociology

The second group involved as actors in this drama consisted of students and academics of the Institute of Sociology. This was not a homogenous assembly. It could be divided into those who supported the idea of the festival, the march and the conference, those who opposed and those who did not expressed their opinions. The supporters were participants in a newly established area of study, 'Sociocultural gender identity', under the leadership of the vice-director of the institute together with another colleague. A broader group of scholars, mostly women, cooperated with them.

My participation in the march was to show support for gay and lesbian demands for respect and space in the public sphere. I also encouraged my teenage daughter to take part in the event (she helped me with the filming). For both of us it was an important experience, and a sign of our political stance, but we also shared some sense of communal joy among the participants. Yet for me it was not an entirely new experience. The events reminded me very much of the Solidarność demonstrations in the 1980s. Then it was the power of community and sense of moral right that balanced the threat of being arrested or beaten up by the militia. This time the threat was perhaps less severe and caused by hooligans (who in the previous case had joined us against the militia). The call to 'Come with us, gays and lesbians!' echoed the 'Come with us!' of the eighties, directed towards passive bystanders.

A sociology lecturer involved in the new sociocultural gender identity program, stressed the meaning of the whole affair of the festival to the University with a sad statement about the lack of democracy, the fossilization of its structures and the need for a debate about all these problems. This has, however, not been taken up.

There were only a few active opponents to the involvement of the Institute of Sociology in the conference. A Ph.D. student, supported by his professor, addressed the Director with a letter exhibiting indignation at the Institute's involvement, and asked why it was not agreed in consultation with the Institute's Council and staff. The young man also published an article entitled 'On Strife against Homophobia' in the right-wing daily *Rzeczpospolita*, where he argued: 'If you accept homosexuality as a sexual orientation possessing equal rights, other restrictions will be impossible to keep' (Czarnik 2004). He wrote from the Catholic position but did not formulate this clearly. He maintained that the proposed conference (in fact it took place a day before) would present only one point of view, but in fact he did not attempt to present his ideas at the event, choosing rather to write to a nationwide newspaper.

Another sub-group consisted of those sociology students who took an active part in the march. The Swedish film-maker recorded the following exchange from some of these (Voxerbrant 2004a):

> We are sociology students at the Jagiellonian. Our Institute actively supports the march and the whole event.
> *Are you proud of it?*
> Yes. We are ashamed of those who can not behave and are aggressive, they present Krakow in such a [bad] light. But, as you can see, there are a lot of young people who think differently

For these girls the norm was pluralistic tolerance.

Among the demonstrators there were also students taking my course, 'Gender in Contemporary Anthropological Research'. I took the opportunity of the festival to discuss the problem of the presence of gays and lesbians in Polish society with my students. They were in fact obliged to take part in the march and carry out participant observation. Later students were to describe their personal experiences. As one of them said:

> It rouses great emotions in me, the fact that there were so many people who share the same ideas. I had the impression that despite not knowing each other we created a community. The most striking was the contrast between the atmosphere inside the march and outside it. People inside were smiling at each other, I felt as if I were among friends. Awfully striking was the sight of those who protested, hurling invectives. For the first time I met hatred which was expressed directly, directly at me. For the first time skinheads wanted to attack me. But I am very glad I was there.

Representatives of several other organizations took an active part in the march: Greens, anarchists, anticlericals, Young Social Democrats, the Helsinki Foundation, Amnesty International. There were also several leftist MPs, and the representative of the Government Plenipotentiary. I could also recognize people from the *Tygodnik Powszechny* (the only liberal Catholic paper); an intellectual and Holocaust survivor; the Director of the Festival of Jewish Culture; journalists of a leftist weekly *Polityka* and the liberal *Gazeta Wyborcza*.

This community was nicely described by my colleague as 'a kind of Noah's ark of oddities, which only those who don't have much to lose get into'.

The Father Piotr Skarga Association of Christian Culture

How did the other side of the barricade present itself? It was also very diverse. First appeared the Father Piotr Skarga Association of Christian Culture (its patron being a leading figure of Polish counter-reformation). They released thousands of leaflets opposing 'the promotion of homosexualism in Krakow'. The Association is a non-profit organization which is described as ultra Catholic. It is financed by the donations of the faithful, whose patriotic, religious feelings and relationship to the Virgin Mary are appealed to: 'If we are not faithful to the covenant with the Virgin Mary, our Motherland will be exposed to the risk of falling into the precipice of immorality, narcotics, television, corruption' (quoted in Kula and Sidorowicz 2005). The Association is publicly visible only because of its protests: for instance, in 2000 against the film *Dogma*; in 2001 against parliamentary candidates advocating abortion (illegal in Poland after 1990); in 2005 against burying the Nobel Prizewinner, Czesław Miłosz in a national necropolis at the Skałka Church (because he was a 'Lithuanian' and a 'communist'). The most spectacular was the action against 'the promotion of homosexuality in Krakow' in May 2004, but they were also responsible for a poster campaign, 'Stop Homosexual Depravity', in December 2005. The website of the Association is devoted to a large extent to the fight with the 'homosexual revolution', and many of their commentaries and book reviews deal with the theme.[14] I recognized (and recorded) leaders of the Association at the beginning of the Campaign march, both in front of the Collegium Novum, and also later, at the foot of the Wawel Castle. They also participated in all the other 'anti homosexual' events.

The All-Polish Youth

The All-Polish Youth was the second important group in the anti-festival action. This is a nationalist organization, whose interwar predecessors developed fascist tendencies. In their 'Declaration of Ideas' we can read that, 'The Nation is the most important worldly value. First, after God, service is deserved by our own nation'. The Roman Catholic Church is very important for them because it 'creates and strengthens Polish national identity'. The organization is at war with doctrines of 'lawlessness, liberalism, tolerationalism and relativism', and its goal is 'to build a Catholic state of the Polish nation'.[15] It was the All-Polish Youth who organized the counter-demonstration at the Katyń Cross. They can be seen in our films together with their banners, the texts of which I cited earlier.

In December 2004 one of the students attending my course, 'Anthropology of Cultural Pluralism', suggested a meeting with the All-Polish Youth to discuss the March for Tolerance. Four representatives came from their Academic Group. The meeting proved that indeed nationalist ideology together with Catholicism is the main reference point for the All-Polish Youth. They said that they were fighting with 'different pathologies' (like drug addiction or juvenile delinquency), and therefore they opposed the 'promotion of homosexualism', which was an illness, and homosexual behaviour, which was evil and sinful (like pedophilia or zoophilia). They told us how they prepared themselves for the event, how they invented slogans to be rather funny, appropriate for the 'occasion', as they called it. One of the members said they had been against throwing stones and eggs, and that therefore they had sat down on the pavement to stop the escalations. Another one, a girl, was shocked by the shout of somebody from the march: 'Throw a grenade on a tray!'[16] (it was probably some militant anticlerical), and 'Queen Jadwiga was a lesbian'. The third one mentioned the presence of a 'fake priest' among the homosexuals and felt hurt by this (it was in fact a Protestant pastor, see below). They estimated that there were 150 of their colleagues present.

The discussion between the two groups showed that they each adopt two different viewpoints. One of my students summarized it: 'I am interested in the good of and the rights of an individual (for instance the right to love), while you look from an overall perspective and impose this on others'. The All-Polish Youth activist agreed: 'We are convinced that our nation is the overriding value'.

Football Fans

The next group of counter-demonstrators consisted of football fans of the two, usually feuding, Krakow football clubs: Wisła and Cracovia. Another student of mine interviewed a supporter of the latter (before the events) (Bujak 2003):

> I have been following Stripes [Cracovia] for about seven years. I remember when I went to a game with my mates from our housing estate for the first time. It was incredible, the atmosphere, flags, scarves, singing, everything. After the game we went through the city, one big party, we were singing, people got out of our way. Later [we headed] to the bus, [where] people panicked too. And that omnipresent police, we were following each other, [there were] shambles, shouts, emotions, [there was] adrenaline. And thus I got involved.

The group is not homogenous, the most visible are 'hit-squad' members (like the ones cited above), but the majority are less violent. For all of them, however, such values as honour, respect and brotherhood are of the greatest importance.

In my film a large group of fans can to be recognized. They wear hooded sweatshirts of specific brands (Lonsdale, Hooligan, Pittbull). During the counter-demonstration at the foot of the Wawel hill they adapted many of their stadium practices to the situation. For instance, a chant: 'Feminists, dykes, queers – all Poland is laughing at you' is a version of an anti-Wisła slogan: 'All Poland is laughing, the Polish champions are gays'. 'Fuck off, fuck off' is shouted when a player of an opposite club goes out of the field or towards the police. Shouts are accompanied by gestures to strengthen their rhetorical power. The same with loud whistling. All these devices were used to try and to dominate the opponents. Similarly, gaining the flag of the opponents and burning it in front of them is a means to humiliate them.[17]

On the internet forum of Cracovia fans it was possible to find reports of the counter-demonstrators, for example:[18]

> From Wisła there were 40–50 people, from Cracovia about 20. It is curious that Wisła and Cracovia were fighting side by side against queers.

> We managed to stop that affair, and we met a leading queer (the one with a loud speaker) on Wiślna [street], he scrambled off to a shop, and had it not been for the police and television approaching, he would have been leading a march of the disabled next year.

> It is good that there were courageous people in Krakow who opposed the demonstration, and homage to those who were there yesterday.

But what was really surprising was the presence of at least one fan of Cracovia among those in the March for Tolerance:

> Yes, I walked in this march together with, as you call them, queers; I walked despite my hundred per cent heterosexuality, and together with me there walked one and a half thousand people. I met a lot of heterosexual friends, many male-female couples holding each other's hands, many politicians, artists, journalists. It was not a lesbian-gay manifestation, it was a demonstration against intolerance, hatred, as shown by most of you here.

Thus, even if football fans were the most visible they were not the majority of the opposing party, and not all fans were of one opinion.

Among the counter-demonstrators one could also detect several skinheads (who wear bovver boots and camouflage trousers), a man in a T-shirt with NZS printed on it (Independent Student Association), and another one in a sweatshirt printed with the name of Burzum, a heavy-metal band drawing on pre-Christian Scandinavian mythology, as popularized in Slavonic pagan subculture.

The Roman Catholic Church

Despite the fact that the Roman Catholic Church, as an institution, was not actively present on the march, it was instrumental on other occasions: putting pressure on the Rector; making public statements of discontent; and articulating a condemnation of the festival at the St Stanislaw procession, all cited above. During the march only a brown-frocked monk (a Benedictine), appeared from time to time and made the sign of the cross. The impression could have been that he was blessing the participants and had a rather sympathetic attitude towards them. However, the opposite was true. We managed to record a short interview with him. He was an American (speaking very good Polish) and he was not blessing but performing an exorcism. He said that there could be no tolerance of evil, and that if Jesus had lived on earth now, he would have been on the side of what was natural.

Even the most liberal hierarchs condemned the march. Perhaps the only clergyman who did not do so in public and whose attitude was rather positive was a Jesuit known for his broad interests. At the Forum of Deep Democracy organized a month after the events, he said he was surprised by the escalation of aggression:

> We have to consider how to speak to each other without throwing stones. The choice of the date of the march was very unfortunate, because it was received as a provocation. The world is very diverse, the Church's mission is to judge, but after Vaticanum Secundum the Church is more temperate. Certainty does not always result in evangelical behaviour. The Church is a very inclusive concept, I do not share the opinions of some hierarchs and I am not outside the Church.

In fact he is no longer a priest. He decided to leave the Church after being banned from making public statements (for reasons unrelated to the Festival of Tolerance).

Catholic priests were present at the march, but they were all incognito. A Latvian pastor of the Free Reformed Church said that during the event he was approached by some young men who, seeing his clerical collar, told him that they were Catholic priests and asked him to demonstrate also in their name and gave him a stole[19]. He put it on and marched in it (Voxerbrant 2004). One of my students at the march was accompanied by a man who told her he was a Catholic priest and gay, and wanted to support the idea of tolerance for homosexuals, but he was there anonymously.

The attitude of ordinary Catholics was not very favourable to the events. They seemed to see the festival and especially the march as a provocation by homosexuals who deliberately wanted to offend people's religious feelings. They did not accept the explanation that it was unintentional that the date originally chosen for the march coincided with the St Stanislaw procession. It was taken for granted that everybody in Krakow knows when the procession takes place (because everybody is a Catholic). It was also stressed that Krakow, as a 'city of a hundred churches' and a holy place for all Poles, was especially unsuitable for such an event.

This group was not, however, completely unanimous. There were also Catholics among the sociology students who supported the festival and took an active part in the conference. One of them, Piotr, told me that it was not easy for him to combine his academic interest in homosexuality with his Catholic faith, but he finally managed to adopt a stance that his religious beliefs were his private matter and should not interfere with what he did as a student.

The State

The state was another important actor in the events. The organizers of the festival were strongly supported by the Government Plenipotentiary for Equal Status of Women and Men. She gave some financial and moral assistance, which she saw as related to her professional mission to defend human rights, as she put it in answering a parliamentary question on the matter. The government was then composed of the postcommunist party SLD (Democratic Left Alliance) and the post-Solidarity Labour Union, whose leader was the Plenipotentiary.

The Mayor of Krakow, who was supported by the SLD, was another important figure. His policy towards the Campaign was not unambiguous, probably due to fear of the 'conservative citizens of Krakow'. The regional parliament, dominated by right-wing parties, opposed the festival and put pressure on the Mayor to ban the march. In trying to ensure his citizens' freedom of assembly, he risked his position, with rightist councillors calling for his dismissal. The most curious stance was taken by the liberal PO (the Civic Platform) who condemned the march to win right-wing voters. They chose the occasion to adopt a new defining position: that the PO is liberal in economy and conservative in customs. In Poland political wings are defined primarily by their relation to the Church and tradition.

Police guarded the legal demonstration, but its forces, only one hundred people at the beginning, proved to be too small to break the counter-demonstration. Even a special squad did not help. When police officers realized they could not bring the situation under control, they suggested the organizers terminate the march.

But to some extend state bureaucracy was responsible for the whole affair with the date of the march. It was because of the special position of the Catholic Church, who was not obliged to inform Municipality about religious events like processions.[20]

The Media

I would also like to mention the media at the end of this list of actors because of their active role in the events. Commentaries, obviously, depended on the paper's political profile; however, the leading titles pretended to be objective and sometimes published opinions supporting the festival. The most notable element, regardless of the paper's political profile, was the dubious quality of journalism. From the very beginning all dailies presented the event as a provocation. Even the liberal *Gazeta Wyborcza* published an article, cited above, under the very characteristic title: 'Rendez-vous at Wawel Hill', accompanied by an illustration presenting two processions divided by a screen. A right-wing journalist wrote in *Rzeczpospolita*: 'This event, as others of the kind, has all the hallmarks of a provocation against traditional symbols and cultural attitudes. As can be seen, tolerance does not apply to the majority who believes in [these traditions]' (Wildstein 2004).

Moreover, before the festival, newspapers illustrated their reports with photographs of Love Parades in Berlin and other such events showing drag queens or men wearing make-up. They did not call the event by the official name, The March for Tolerance, but a 'gay and lesbian parade' or a 'march of the homosexuals': for example, 'The march of the homosexuals splits Krakow' (*Gazeta Wyborcza* 5 May 2004), or 'Krakovians do not want a vulgar parade' (*Nasz Dziennik* 6 May 2004). On the other hand, televisions did not devote much time to the march itself but focused on the riots afterwards.

This is the typical technique of producing 'news', that is, information solely to attract the interest of the readers. Such a commercial approach pigeonholed the event with a ready-made cliché with which the actual event had little in common. This was easily observable by the march participants and organizers because they had firsthand access to the original information. Thus, as Ida explained:

> It was tabloid journalism. It was the media who escalated everything. They asked questions like: 'You are provocative, aren't you?'; 'You are anti-Catholic, aren't you?'; 'Is there going to be a riot at the march?' And it was like that for three weeks … . We were portrayed as wanting to do God knows what. And on the St Stanislaw holiday to boot! That we simply wanted to let loose some naked men with feathers in their asses.

Tomasz stressed the ignorance of journalists, to whom he had to explain basic information about gay and lesbian movements. 'They certainly did not do their homework', he said.

The other party too had reservations. The fans of Cracovia complained that newspapers wrote about 'skins' only and did not take into account that such a haircut is not necessarily a marker of a political stance.

The journalist of *Gazeta Wyborcza*, earlier quoted as the writer of the first article on the event said: 'No newspapers, at least the important ones, wrote about the Campaign Against Homophobia or about the festival, unjustly. They only portrayed dominant Polish feelings and the extent of division in opinions' (Voxerbrant 2004). Thus, in her view, the media does not report on events but on people's opinions. They strengthen prejudices and stereotypes, creating a non-existant reality. This could also be observed at the TVP3 debate about the march in which two parties participated: the organizers and opposing politicians, together with 'citizens of Krakow', among whom the supporters of the march were not given a voice at all.

The only medium that was open and useful to the organizers of the festival was the internet: only there could they present their arguments and use it as a means to put pressure on their opponents (e.g., on the Rector, whose email box had been blocked by letters of protest); only there could sympathetic reports be published (see Harley 2004); only there could unrestrained discussions take place (unrestrained also by manners and orthography). The internet was also used by the other side: on the Cracovia website forum there is a theme called 'Kick a queer's ...' that has been alive since that May of 2004 and contains about 1,600 posts.

CONTEXTS

Homosexuality

I would like to start with the matter which is most important here – the way of understanding homosexuality. Under communism, gays and lesbians were invisible in Poland. Steven Seidman's thesis that the 'power of the state was mobilized to keep homosexuals socially invisible and publicly scandalized' (Seidman 2004: 247) was even more true in the case of the communist state. But here there was also another factor: homosexuals were pressed to collaborate with secret police, who threatened them with divulgence of their sexual orientation to the public. Democratic changes only really began after 1989, when gay and lesbian organizations could finally start their activities legally, although Monika Baer has discussed some first tentative attempts date in the eighties (Baer 2004).

The Campaign Against Homophobia's activity is a very good example of the affirmative politics of identity, which emerged in the West in the sixties and seventies, with the spirit of pride and rebellion of the Blacks' and Women's movements (Seidman 2004: 246). In Poland the homosexuals could not base their actions on other emancipatory movements, since they were practically invisible. The Krakovian Campaign activists, similarly to their Western counterparts earlier, built their gay and lesbian identity around such experiences as living in secret, the necessity of pretending to be somebody else, the difficulty of coming out, the manifold oppression; but also their opposition to all these. In the West some divisions in such emancipatory movements quickly appeared: between men and women, but also between assimilationists and separatists. In the Polish case there is a version of the latter: between those who are active and want some changes in Polish society and the passive majority, who accept the situation and are afraid of changes. Ida put it as follows (Voxerbrant 2004):

> Polish homosexuals live hidden and in fear. Our organization, however, wants our presence recognized in society, that we are here, we are normal and we will stay, and never be sent back to the closet! On the other hand we are sending a signal to gays and lesbians: you are visible and get used to it. It is the end of

lenience, the end of hiding in the closet. I do not agree to hide myself, to hide my love, who I am.

Tomasz reported the reactions of other gays and lesbians to the Campaign: 'Because of your political or personal ambitions, you are exposing us to be devoured. We have to live with this. And we have put so much effort into hiding.'

As we know from the works of Michel Foucault (1978) and Jeffrey Weeks (2000) the meaning, social organization and history of sexuality are deeply social. Weeks observed also, that gay activists refer to the 'naturalness' of a homosexual identity to justify the idea of its normality, and to argue that therefore homosexuals deserve respect and equal rights. This activity has had some effects – seeing homosexuality as a stigma (abnormal and unnatural) has become less common (Weeks 2000). This political naturalizing of homosexuality is also to be seen among Polish activists. Essentialization is a common feature of many different social movements. June Nash observes that 'it is particularly prevalent among new cohorts of activists in the early stages of mobilization, as they use what some consider to be essentializing language to unite distinct groups among common elements of group consciousness' (Nash 2005: 11).

Despite the differences in their approaches all gay and lesbian theoreticians until the eighties grasped homosexuality as a minority experience based on a homogenous and common homosexual identity, some of them phrased it in 'ethnic' terms (Seidman 2004: 253). Gays and lesbians were bound by the desire for the same sex and the sense of social discrimination that resulted from that (Mizielińska 2004: 158). In Polish conditions this tendency is still to be found, especially in the very name 'the business', seen as that which differentiate 'us' (gays and lesbians) from 'them' (the straight), positively valorizing the first, and negatively the second. Ida experienced the negative effects of such essentializing. As a person describing herself as bisexual, she is often charged either with 'treason' or 'not owning up' to homosexuality. Queer theory explains this unfavourable attitude towards bisexuals as a fear of blurring clear-cut divisions and a need to maintain comprehensible categories and definitions (see Mizielińska 2004: 166).

But to imply that the Polish gay and lesbian movement inhabits the stage their Western counterparts occupied in the seventies would be a crude oversimplification. The Campaign's ideology and activity proves that together with their work to spur on gays and lesbians, they are also utilizing queer theory by demanding the right to voice their ideas and access to the public sphere. My observations are, though, that these claims were not present in the Campaign's idea of the festival from the very beginning, but rather resulted from their experience of and disagreement with the homophobic environment. Ida's statement cited above can be taken as a variation of the famous: 'We are Here, We are Queer, Get Used to It'[21].

As far as other active participants of Krakovian events outside of 'the business' are concerned, that is members of the Institute of Sociology, we were, I think, more concerned with the dominant majority's tendency to monopolize the public sphere and to limit the minority's rights. But we certainly had an operational definition of homosexuality. It was essentializingly understood as a biologically-determined sexual orientation, that can not be modified by a person or blamed on them (in contrast to Catholic ideas of curing or 'promoting' it). We saw homosexuality as natural and normal, and homosexuals as rightful citizens entitled to their dissimilarity.

The opinions of the opposition could be grouped into several themes. First, that homosexuality is and should remain a private matter. Szymon Czarnik (2004) wrote in *Rzeczpospolita*:

> Personally I have nothing against concerts, performances and vernissages carried on in private clubs or pubs by artists who think it fit to share the information about their sexual preferences with the public. But I think it highly improper to organize a public demonstration to this effect, when intimate matters are exposed on posters and broadcast by loudspeakers.

Our interlocutors said the same more bluntly: 'We are tolerant when they do it in bed, not on a street. Sex is not to be engaged in on the Planty', or simply: 'Queers, go home!'. It was also in fact the opinion of the homosexual majority, who opposed public events like the march. The Campaign tried to fight with this internalized homophobia.

The second theme was to see homosexuality as an illness, a deviation, an abnormality. This was expressed by football fans shouting: 'Deviants, deviants', or more subtly by the All-Polish Youth's banner slogans: 'Our streets, your hospitals' (we possess public space, you should be sent to hospitals), or 'Homosexuals of the world, cure yourselves'.

Finally, homosexuality was seen as evil. The American monk cited above said: 'It is not sinful to be a homosexual, but to practice [is evil]. Zero tolerance for evil. To follow one's drive in homosexual practices is a sin' (Voxerbrant 2004a).

Steven Seidman points out that speaking not about homosexuality but about homosexual behaviour was characteristic of the ideas of the nineteenth century. On the other hand, seeing gays and lesbians as sexual deviants is a result of a scientific and biomedical discourse (Seidman 2004: 245). In fact the Catholic Church's dissociating the person from the practice is, paradoxically, very close to the contemporary queer theory.

Nevertheless I am afraid none of the above definitions could explain the span and high level of social emotions that the March for Tolerance evoked in Krakow (and not only there) on those spring days of 2004. In my opinion only queer theory can help us in this respect. Eve Kosofsky Sedgwick in her *Epistemology of the Closet*, writes, that homosexuality is not a matter of a social minority and its rights, integrity, or equality, but a matter that challenges the whole society by influencing the cultural order (Sedgwick Kosofsky 1990: 1). Indeed, the March for Tolerance disturbed the balance of the 'heteronormative grid' (see Bunzl 2005: 226–7). That is the reason why the reactions were so intense.

Matti Bunzl, in his paper, 'A Queer Reading of Austrian (Homo) sexualities', describes an event that was, like the March for Tolerance, a temporal disturbance of the heteronormative grid. In fact, the grid is constantly threatened with disintegration and therefore generates homophobic acts of performative heterosexuality. Homosexuality is indispensable as the constitutive Other (Bunzl 2005: 223). Bunzl points out (as was also visible in Krakow), that homosexuality in Austria was seen primarily as a private matter; and came to the conclusion that 'heterosexuality signifies and performs itself as a public event, thereby legitimizing the hetero/homo binary in terms of the dichotomy of public/ private' (Bunzl 2005: 224). Indeed the counter-demonstrators could not stand homosexuals marching in public.

Gender

Gender is another dimension which is important in understanding Krakovian events. My observation of them allows me to formulate some generalizations. The idea of the Festival of Tolerance (the associated march and the conference) was actively supported primarily by women, while men were mainly among the most spectacular opponents. And again, some of those men who supported the idea of the Festival felt the need to conspicuously stress their heterosexuality at the same time. For instance a journalist, Adam Szostkiewicz, marched putting his arm around his wife's neck. The football fan who took part in the event pointed out his 'hundred per cent heterosexuality' (in capital letters).

The anti-gay coalition consisted of several types of organizations: Catholic (The Skarga Association), nationalistic (the All-Polish Youth) and sporting (football fans). The common feature of them is the almost solely male membership (although there are some women entering the All-Polish Youth nowadays, they do not play an important role there).

Studies of masculinity derived from feminism can be helpful in interpreting the phenomenon, especially the work of Elisabeth Badinter, *XY: on Masculine Identity*, and the works of Robert Connell. I adopt here the constructivist approach to masculinity which is seen not as an essence but an ideology substantiating male dominance. Badinter argues that, because of the ideology, man constantly has to prove that he is not a woman, a child, or a homosexual. A 'patriarchal' man vents his fears in aggression, in misogyny and homophobia (Badinter 1992). Counter-demonstrators shouted: 'Feminists, gays, lesbians, all Poland laughs at you'. By ridiculing they create a distance from groups that threaten the patriarchal structure.

Nancy Chodorow has pointed out that male identity is more negative, stresses diversification, distance to others and rejection of emotional ties (Chodorow 1978). Gary Alan Fine's research on boys' gangs (groups of football fans are a variety of them) proved that they are not formed as a result of some group instinct but because of the need to break with the familial culture of women and to create a masculine culture. Due to the lack of a father who could be a positive model of masculinity, young people unite under the leadership of an older, stronger and cleverer leader (see Badinter 1992).

The aggressive attitude of hooligans towards homosexuals in Krakow can be interpreted also as an attack against the Other, and thus the expression of common values and a reassurance of their own heterosexuality. This masculinity is realized in aggression against the Other who tries to enter the public sphere on equal footing to the 'dominant'. It is hegemonic masculinity that sets the hierarchy. Pierre Bourdieu pointed out that among Kabyles to be a man is to right away have the position of power (Bourdieu 2001).

We have also to note the social significance of 'violence as an experience of solidarity' (Verkaaik 2003: 21). In Krakow we could see this solidarity among normally feuding clubs' fans (stressed by one of them, cited above); among hooligans and the All-Poland Youth' members, who thanked the fans in their report of the events; and generally among all those counter-demonstrators united in shouting at the foot of Wawel, as is clearly visible on our films.

But there are also other types of masculinity. Badinter observes that various political movements, like ecologists, pacifists, and human-rights activists, condemn traditional 'male' values like war, rivalry and domination, preferring 'female' ones like life, sympathy, and forgiveness. Thus, it is not surprising that representatives of all those movements were present at the march. This gender explanation is perhaps as important as a political one.

Robert Connell, in his book *Masculinities*, as the title suggests, stresses the plural nature of masculinity, but 'to recognize diversity in masculinities is not enough. We must also recognize the relations between the different kinds of masculinity: relations of alliance, dominance and subordination' (Connell 1995: 37). In the case I am analyzing we can see such an alliance. Football fans represent a masculinity based on physical violence, but they do not have a high position in the hierarchy of power and prestige. The All-Polish Youth' members are also quite aggressive but use more subtle methods. They have been quite marginalized politically, but now they have some MPs. They are still not high in any hierarchies. Similarly with representatives of the Skarga Association, who are quite active and visible but not very important. They all occupy a rather low position in the hierarchy of power and prestige, but they also can be characterized by their fighting spirit and pugnancy (they often use war rhetoric). They could be called 'contemporary warriors'. They display stereotypically hegemonic behaviours that are typical for masculinity, and therefore they 'may still claim much of the respect and status of hegemonic men' (Connell 1995: 37). By contrast, women and gays are situated at the very bottom of the hierarchy, because hegemonic masculinity is indissolubly bound to heterosexuality. Gays entering the public sphere threatened the hierarchy and the very concept of dominant masculinity. Thus it had to meet opposition. We can also see in the Krakovian events how (dominant) masculinity is in fact unstable and fluid, and how it gains coherence in the context of action and conflict.

Nationalism

A thorough observer of the March for Tolerance could easily grasp the nationalistic dimension of the event. The most striking evidence was that demonstrators were carrying mainly EU flags while their opponents were carrying only Polish ones.

The problem of relations between homosexuality and nationalism has been studied for some time. Kathryn Conrad (2001: 125) stresses that any category of identity is harmful to the national one, but:

> homosexuality in particular threatens the stability of the narrative of Nation: the very instability and specific historical contingency of the definition of homosexuality makes the category more fluid than most, and thus brings into question the fixity and coherence of all identity categories.

On the other hand the gender dimension of nation is also important. Joanne Nagel points out that in traditional models of nationalism a woman is identified with passivity and needs male protection. A warrior fights to defend a nation embodied as woman. She is to remain the moral guardian of the nation (Nagel 1998). Thus within the very idea of a nation there is a condition of heterosexuality and gender complementarity built in. But sexes are not equivalent. Jarrod Hayes finds that nationalism usually marginalizes women and persecutes sexual dissidents (Hayes 2000: 11).

Badinter observes that the crisis of masculinity in the eighteenth century was phrased in nationalistic terms: the feminization of men was equated with national treason, and a traditional masculinity with patriotism (Badinter 1992). These were the arguments used by the representatives of the All-Polish Youth: 'We know that the point is to feminize a nation in order to manipulate it easily'.

Gill Shepherd has argued that 'the more fertility and sexuality are seen as personal property in any society, the less opprobrium will be attached to homosexuality', and, conversely, 'the more the individual's sexuality and fertility are the property of others, the more those particular rights are slighted by homosexuality, and the more they are cheated of children who might have come from a conventional fertile union' (Shepherd 1987: 267). In this respect it is enough to mention that the first legal debate that took place in Poland after democratic change in 1989 concerned banning abortion.

Tim Edensor states that the universal manner of defining membership in a nation consists in pointing out what is perceived as 'key' similarities and differences (Edensor 2002). In the Polish case it is a slogan 'a Pole – a Catholic' (and, taken for granted, a heterosexual). Catholicism was always a marker of nationality and a way to rule out Others. The most important others were Jews, until the Second World War, and later, communists. The All-Polish Youth' slogans were derived from a deep symbolic reservoir of exclusions. For example: 'Our streets, your hospitals' refers to a reputedly Jewish saying: 'Your streets, our buildings' (this is your town but our property). The skinheads shouted: 'Gas the queers', 'Hitler on you', and these Nazi shouts were the most powerful rhetorically. On the other hand, the slogan 'Homosexuals of the world cure yourselves!' refers to the communist 'Workers of the world unite!'; the same with: 'Red rabble', shouted by hooligans.

The Krakovian events serve as a good example of a 'complicated geography of national identity' (Edensor 2002). I am focusing here only on a nation's 'holy sites'. Undoubtedly Wawel Hill, with the Cathedral, the Royal Castle, and the cave of a legendary dragon, is such a place for Poles. However, symbolic meanings of this 'holy site' may be different. The poster of the 'Festival of Culture for Tolerance' shows the silhouette of Wawel on the background of a rainbow of colours. The message would be: we are queering Wawel during the event, when Krakow will be dominated by the emancipatory movement of gays and lesbians. The opponents also used Wawel in their leaflet, 'Say No to homosexual promotion in Krakow', but it was organized differently: the photograph of the majestic cathedral on the top, and 'vulgar' drag queens at the bottom. The point was to juxtapose the two: Polish nationality and global queering.

Again, the counter-demonstration itself may be seen as protecting the 'national sanctuary' against a 'hostile campaign'. It was a spectacle of the defense of the city, as it was against Tartar invasion in the Middle Ages. Just after the March for Tolerance, the All-Polish Youth website run a report under the meaningful title: 'Wawel Dragon defended'. One can see in the event a kind of 'performance' (in Judith Butler's sense), that is, intentional and deliberate enacting (Butler 1993). It was a national spectacle, an active (re)creation of a nation performed by nationalists. One of the banners read: 'Wawel dragon was strait', which can be understood: our tradition, history, even our legendary monsters are heterosexual. It is also necessary to note the ironic potential of the slogan.

The football fans' subculture adopts a specific concept of space (Gullianotti and Amstrong 2002; Feixa and Juris 2000), which was also observable during Krakovian events. A Cracovia fan called others to react to 'deviants' entering their 'beloved City', what he saw as an insult.[22]

But the nationalistic, exclusive concept of the Polish nation is not the only available. There is also another one – inclusive and based on citizenship, cultural rights of minorities, the secularism of the state, and so on. This notion is characteristic of the coalition supporting the march. Wawel is for them a symbol of a Polish state guarding its citizens' rights.

The interpretation of Krakovian events may be aided by the differentiation made by Don Handelman between the cultural world of ritual, and subsequent world of spectacle (in Herzfeld 2001: 259):

> The practice of ritual is integral to cultural worlds that are organized holistically, worlds in which 'religion' constitutes the whole through comprehensive, taxonomic classification of the cosmos, and from which the organizing premises of moral and social order derive.

This is the world many Polish Catholics are still living in. A sociologist of religion, Irena Borowik, diagnosed the Polish Catholic Church during this time of transition as incorporating the methods and styles of the past: 'Messianism, Ritualism, ease of social engineering and turning against the state'. It treats itself as an infallible institution and has no awareness of multicultural society. It does not use the language of democracy but that of struggle (Borowik 2002: 250). A very characteristic example of the 'cultural world of ritual' the Church inhabits was the St Stanislaw procession, with over a hundred thousand faithful, that took place two days after the march and during which the march was described as 'shameless provocation'.

The March for Tolerance, and the riots at the end of it, might be described as spectacles. Don Handelman formulates these as 'public masks of the bureaucratic ethos' (Handelman 1990). Even if the Krakovian events were quite dramatic and noisy they were also bureaucratically planned and designed, all requirements were met, one demonstration was legal and the other one illegal. And in fact the biggest affair (the first official date of the march) was the effect of a bureaucratic decision but the blame was put on the organizers.

Globalization

Another important context that should be stressed is globalization. A Polish sociologist, Bohdan Jałowiecki (2005: 117), enlists three types of identity that are evoked by global influences: these are the identity of mimicry, of resistance, and of protest. He uses the two groups I am dealing with here as examples of the latter. He writes:

> The identity of protest consists in searching for and/or confirmation of identity by various types of more or less spectacular manifestations, which is in fact a goal on its own. One of the many examples of this type of behaviour are parades of sexual minorities, which want to confirm in that way an otherwise obvious fact of their social existence.

The author does not explain why they want to confirm the 'obvious fact'. The second group he distinguishes is 'youth gathered around football clubs'. Another type – the identity of resistance – 'above all consists in manifesting anti-modernistic attitudes and cherishing traditional values'. The examples given here are religious fundamentalism and nationalism (Jałowiecki 2005: 117). The All-Polish Youth and the Skarga Association could be placed in this group.

I am afraid, however, that the problem is more complex and needs more thorough inspection. On one hand we certainly have to deal with the globalization of the gay and lesbian movement. For instance, Tomasz came up with the idea of the festival when he was on vacation abroad and learned about similar events. The international connections of the Swedish-Polish activist were used to put pressure on the Rector and the Mayor of Krakow. The Campaign activists carried the EU flags at the march, because Poland's accession also brought hopes for improving the gay and lesbian situation. Although the Campaign Against Homophobia is a Polish organization, it takes part in the International Lesbian & Gay Association and thus its members participate in the international lesbian, gay, bisexual and transexual community through conferences and workshops. There are also Polish branches of other international associations. But it is still, I am afraid, far from 'global queerhood'. What we have here is rather an attempt to adopt organizational forms that proved suitable elsewhere to Polish conditions. The result is the mixture of globalism and localism, a kind of hybrid form: an essentializing and 'solemn' discourse of an 'ethnic' group, that tries to present to the public gays and lesbians as 'decent and the same as others', together with queer practices of ironizing and demanding equal rights.

Dennis Altman proposed a concept of 'global queering' in which he presented the influence of three main processes of globalization on sexuality (Altman 2001). Economic changes cause its further commoditization (in advertising and prostitution). Political reality determines which forms of sexual behavior are acceptable. 'Cultural changes mean that certain ideas about behaviour and identity are widely dispersed, so that new ways of understanding oneself become available that often conflict bitterly with traditional mores' (Altman 1999: 563). Krakovian events were indeed a bitter conflict.

Other authors stress the diffusion of activist strategies from the West, with some anti-nationalism and pacifism, as well as referring to the demands of human rights guaranteed under international treaties as the means to overcome almost universal marginalization (see Binnie 2004: 39). The case of the Campaign shows this globalizing effect very well. There is, however, the other side of the coin: 'global queerhood meets global homophobia'. Joanna Mizielińska analyses the problem in a Polish context, referring to other students elsewhere. Lisa Guggan has described the homophobic practices of the new right, that perceives the human rights demands of gay and lesbian organizations as the promotion of homosexuality and a request for special rights. Cindy Patton points out that the new right does not speak about concrete persons but about 'homosexual lobby' who manipulate different institutions, and especially the media. The author found also that the strategy of 'rhetoric reversal' is used, in which the majority presents itself as an endangered minority (see Mizielińska 2005: 127–8). Constance Sullivan-Blum in her research concerning Christian fundamentalists observed that homosexuality became for them the 'icon of modernity' (Kulick in press). In Krakow we could witness all these strategies. The Skarga Association raised an alarm about the 'promotion of homosexuality' all over the town. Their website is good example of an obsession with 'iconic' homosexuality. The All-Polish Youth called myself and a group of sociology students a 'homosexual lobby' in their report of our meeting with them.[23] Hierarchs of the Roman Catholic Church often present themselves as a smothered minority (Załęcki 2001) and this was also the case in Krakow.

Joanna Mizielińska writes that in the Polish case 'we deal with a homophobic backlash that precedes any form of real queer visibility' and refers to Zygmunt Bauman, who points out that an advance reaction to threats coming from outside is one of the features of globalization (Mizielińska 2005: 127). Again, Krakovian events are a very good example: during our discussion with the All-Polish Youth it become clear that they did not react to the demands of the Campaign but to the state of affairs some Western movements have achieved, for example the right of gays to adopt children (Polish organizations do not even dare to mention it). The media certainly play a special role in this geographical shift of backlash. And it is despite their political orientation. As I stated earlier, there is a common and frequent practice of using photographs from elsewhere and foreign names to illustrate local events. The practice causes readers (or viewers) to adopt a monstrous and decontextualized vision of the world, but also of their local Others. And the audience's opposition is not to be surprised at.

Don Kulick stresses that the very emergence of gay and lesbian movements in many countries 'corresponded with increasingly overt hatred towards gay men and lesbians' (Kulick in press). One of our Krakovian interlocutors at the March for Tolerance said the 'people now will dislike them even more'.

Final Remarks

My analysis leads to several conclusions. One of them is about the condition of Polish civil society. It has become clear that the social activity that in the West was launched by the Afro-Americans and Women's movements, in Poland has been evoked by gay and lesbian emancipatory activity. This is perhaps because of the lack of visible ethnic minorities (the main minority, Polish Jews, died in the Holocaust or having fled) and the minuteness of the feminist movement, which has been ridiculed and discredited even before it was able to establish properly. Thus gays and lesbians (or rather their organizations) are thus the dominant social activists attempting to break up the homogeneity of Polish nationalism. And it is not true that the very names – the March for Tolerance (in Krakow), the Parade of Equality (in Warsaw) or the March of Equality (in Poznan) – were meant to blur the 'sexual' character of the events, as formulated by Mizielińska, but on the contrary, they were because the events were indeed about tolerance and equality for all those excluded and marginalized. The breaking of homogeneity is indispensable for civil society to develop and in the Polish situation it is extremely difficult due to the cultural and political importance of the Roman Catholic Church. Ernest Gellner pointed out in his *Conditions of Liberty* that civil society can not be based on 'a single faith' and its institutionalization calls for 'a high level admission that truth was no one's monopoly' (Gellner 1994: 96). The Polish example confirms the insight of the thesis. The holistic religious-nationalist ideology fills the whole 'state-scape' leaving no room for any Others. And their humble manifestation of existence is perceived by the holistic nationalists as crude provocation. Thus, we can speak about the beginning of Western-type civil society only now. But it does not mean that Poles did not have anything of that kind before. We did have well established civil society (Solidarność being the best example) but it was within the nationalist Catholic idiom, not outside of it (cf. Hann 1996; Buchowski 1996).

One has also to remember that after 1989 Poland (and other Eastern European countries) underwent multiple changes of political, economical and cultural character which is often called the period of transition. If we add the simultaneous impact of globalization, we can only imagine the cognitive 'bigos' Poles have been expose to for the last several years.[24] This cognitive mixture has made some Poles entrenched in their position of traditional nationalist Catholicism (that proved to be such a very fruitful tactic to oppose communism), and some others, on the contrary, enclined to launch emancipatory policies, that could benefit from the experience of their Western counterparts adopted to the local conditions. The two parties met at the foot of Wawel Hill. The hope is that just as bigos is more digestible when reheated several times, so, with the passage of time, gays and lesbians will be more accepted by most Poles in the public sphere, something to which sociological pools bear witness.[25] Then people will learn that they do not have to 'like' the queers, they only have to respect them.

On the other hand, Western observers (some anthropologists included) should abandon orientalizing way of seeing East Europeans as their backward counterparts, who are on the stage the West occupied in the sixties. Even if the thesis is true as far as economic development is concerned, it is certainly not that simple with culture. The cultural world we are living in nowadays in Poland is premodern, modern and postmodern at the same time. As, I hope, my paper has sketched convincingly enough.

Notes

1. Another version of this chapter was published in Polish in *Studia Socjologiczne*, 2006, vol. 4, p. 69–107. I would like to thank Beata Kowalska, Ewa Kopczyńska, Marcin Lubaś and Ida Łukawska for their comments and Natalia Błaszczyk, Krystyna Cech and Petr Skalnik for correcting my English.
2. My co-workers were: Joanna Reinelt, Piotr Prokopowicz, Anna Dobranowska, Rafał Rudzki, Krzysztof Grzebyk, and also my daughter, Julia Heller.
3. I would like to note that I consider my position of a "native anthropologist" as favourable for my project, since I am a Pole enough to understand national symbols and everyday context easily, but I am also a Silesian and I come from a Lutheran family what furnishes me with the sound anthropological distance towards the mainstream Polish-Catholic culture.
4. I gathered information for this account from interviews with the Campaign's activists and from: *www.tolerancja.gej.net; www.rownystatus.gov.pl*. Accessed between 15 April 2004 – 30 September 2005.
5. As a citizen of Krakow I received such a leaflet with my mail. Other information in this paragraph were gathered either by direct observation or through media. The media coverage was to be found also on www.toleranga.gej.net (accessed between 15 April 2004 and 30 September 2005).
6. See *www.tolerancja.gej.net* (accessed between 15 April 2004 and 30 September 2005).
7. All citations that are not followed by bibliographical notes come from my film or other field material.
8. The first Friday of a month is a day to commemorate Christ's death. Catholics should confess their sins and take holy communion.
9. Katyń [now in Ukraine] is the site of the assassination of 4 400 Polish Army officers, prisoners of the Soviet Red Army in 1940. The Soviets denied committing the crime and Polish authorities under communism supported that version.
10. Krakovian Wawel dragon was a legendary bloodthirsty monster which lived in a cave under the Wawel hill and was killed by a trick of a young shoemaker.
11. See the Campaign Against Homophobia website, *www.kampania.org.pl* (accessed between 18 April 2004 and 30 September 2005).
12. See *http://niechnaszzobacza.queers.pl*; accessed date 15 April 2004 – 10 October 2008.
13. The Stonewall Inn was a gay club in New York where in 1969 riots started opposing discrimination. The site is a symbolic beginning of an international gay and lesbian liberation movement (Leszkowicz 2004: 86).
14. See *www.piotrskarga.pl*: accessed date 30 September 2005.
15. See www.wszechpolacy.pl: accessed date 30 September 2005.
16. This refers to a practice of collecting money on a tray during Catholic services.
17. I am very grateful to Jakub Bujak for familiarizing me with the football fans subculture in Krakow.
18. See *www.cracovia.krakow.pl/forum*: accessed 8 May 2004.
19. A stole – a liturgical vestment, a kind of shawl used during a Holy Mass.
20 This also concerns other churches, but they are so marginal that practically invisible in public sphere (at least in Krakow).
21. "We are Here We are Queer. Get Used to It" – the popular slogan of the Queer Nation, an organisation founded in 1990 in the USA as a response to escalation of anti-gay and lesbian violence and prejudice. Queer Nation is known for the militant protest style of their actions and starting the successful process of reclaiming the word 'queer' previously used only in pejorative sense.
22. See *www.cracovia.krakow.pl*: acccessed 8 May 2004.
23. See *www.ma.wszechpolacy.pl*: accessed .10 January 2005.
24. Bigos is a delicious Polish dish consisting of sauerkraut, different kinds of fried meat and sausages, mushrooms, prunes and other ingredients all cooked together

25. A poll agency, CBOS, states that the acceptance of gays and lesbians' rights to public manifestation increased in 2005 from twenty per cent in July to thirty-three per cent in December. The last poll was done after the Poznan March of Equality had been banned and the illegal demonstration was brutally broken up by police. The acceptance of gays and lesbians in the public sphere increase with: personal acquaintance with a homosexual person, younger age, higher education and level of income, and weaker religiosity (CBOS 2005a, b).

References

Altman, D. 1999. 'Globalization, political economy and HIV/AIDS'. *Theory and Society* 22 (4):559–84.

──────. 2001. *Global Sex.* Chicago: University of Chicago Press.

Badinter, E. 1992. *XY: L'identité masculine.* Paris: Odile Jacob.

Baer, M. 2004. '"Let Them Hear Us": Queering Postsocialist Poland',.*European Association of Social Anthropologists Conference*, 8–12 September. Vienna.

Binnie, J. 2004. *The Globalization of Sexuality.* London: Sage.

Borowik, I. 2002. 'The Roman Catholic Church in the Process of Democratic Transformation: The Case of Poland', *Social Compass* 49(2): 239–51.

Bourdieu. P. 2001. *Masculine Domination.* Cambridge: Polity Press.

Buchowski, M. 1996. 'The Shifting Meanings of Civic and Civil Society in Poland', in C. Hann and E. Dunn (eds), *Civil Society: Challenging Western Models.* London: Routledge.

Bujak, J. 2003. 'An Interview with a Fan of "Cracovia"'. Unpublished Seminar Paper. Author's archive.

Bunzl, M. 2005. 'Outing as Performance/Outing as Resistance: A Queer Reading of Austrian (Homo)Sexualities', in J. Robertson (ed.) *Same-Sex Cultures and Sexualities: An Anthropological Reader.* Malden, MA: Blackwell, pp.212–31.

Butler, J. 1993. *Bodies that Matter: The Discursive Limits of Sex.* London: Routledge.

CBOS. 2005a. *Akceptacja praw dla gejów i lesbijek i społeczny dystans wobec nich.* Komunikat z badań (research report).

──────. 2005b. *Prawo do publicznych manifestacji gejów i lesbijek.* Komunikat z badań (research report).

Chodorow, N. 1978. *The Reproduction of Mothering: Psychoanalysis and the Sociology of Gender.* Berkeley: University of California Press.

Connel, R.W. 1995. *Masculinities.* Berkeley: University of California Press.

Conrad, K. 2001. 'Queer Treasons: Homosexuality and Irish National Identity', *Cultural Studies* 15(1): 124–37.

Czarnik, S. 2004. 'O zmaganiach z homofobią', *Rzeczpospolita* 7 May 2004.

Edensor, T. 2002. *National Identity, Popular Culture and Everyday Life.* Oxford: Berg.

Fabian, J. 1983. *Time and the Other: How Anthropology Makes its Object.* New York: Columbia University Press.

Feixa C. and J.S. Juris. 2000. 'Football Cultures', *Social Anthropology* 8(2): 203–08.

Foucault, M. 1978. *The History of Sexuality. An Introduction.* New York: Pantheon Books.

Gellner, E. 1994. *Conditions of Liberty: Civil Society and its Rivals.* London: Hamish Hamilton.

Giulianotti, R. and G. Armstrong. 2002. 'Avenues of Contestation: Football Hooligans Running and Ruling Urban Spaces', *Social Anthropology* 10(2): 211–38.

Gruszczyńska, A. 2004. 'Kraków, europejskie miasto homofobów', in Z. Sypniewski and B. Warkocki (eds), *Homofobia po polsku*. Warszawa: Sic!, pp.77–84.

Handelman, D. 1990. *Models and Mirrors: Towards an Anthropology of Public Events*. Cambridge: Cambridge University Press.

Hann, C. 1996. 'Introduction', in C. Hann and E. Dunn (eds), *Civil Society: Challenging Western Models*. London: Routledge, pp.1–26.

Harley, A. 2004. 'Polish LGBT Group in Craków Seeks Our Help to End Discrimination', *www.ukgaynews.org.uk/Archive/2004042501.htm* (accessed between 25 April 2004 and 8 October 2008).

Hayes, J. 2000. *Queer Nations: Marginal Sexualities in the Maghreb*. Chicago: University of Chicago Press.

Herzfeld, M. 2001. *Anthropology: Theoretical Practice in Culture and Society*. Oxford: Blackwell.

Jałowiecki, B. 2005. 'Globalizacja, lokalność, tożsamość', in: W. Wesołowski and J. Włodarek (eds), *Kręgi integracji i rodzaje tożsamości. Polska, Europa, świat*.Warszawa: Scholar, pp.111–20.

Kochanowski, J. 2004. *Fantazmat zróżnicowany. Socjologiczne studium przemian tożsamości gejów*. Kraków: Universitas.

Kula, M. 2004. 'Randes-vous na Wawelu', *Gazeta Wyborcza* 20 April 2004.

Kula, M. and J. Sidorowicz. 2005. 'Między Bogiem a księgowym', *Gazeta Wyborcza* 11 March 2005.

Kulick, D. forthcoming, 'Introduction: Can There Be an Anthropology of Homophobia?' in D. Kulick (ed.) *The Anthropology of Homophobia*.

Leszkowicz, P. 2004. 'Przełamując hetero-matrix. Wojna seksualna w Polsce i kryzys praw człowieka', in Z. Sypniewski and B. Warkocki (eds), *Homofobia po polsku*. Warszawa: Sic!, pp.85–112.

Majka-Rostek, D. 2002. *Mniejszość kulturowa w warunkach pluralizacji. Socjologiczna analiza sytuacji homoseksualistów polskich*. Wrocław: Wydawnictwo Uniwersytetu Wrocławskiego.

Marcus, G.E. (ed.) 1999. *Critical Anthropology Now: Unexpected Contexts, Shifting Constituencies, Changing Agendas*. Santa Fe, NM: School of American Research Press.

Mizielińska, J. 2004. *(De)konstrukcje kobiecości: Podmiot feminizmu a problem wykluczenia*, Warszawa: Słowo/obraz/terytoria.

———. 2005. 'Poland Meets Queer Theory, in K. Slany, B. Kowalska and M. Śmietana (eds), *Homoseksualizm: Perspektywa interdyscyplinarna,*. Kraków: Nomos, pp.111–30.

Nagel, J. 1998. 'Masculinity and Nationalism: Gender and Sexuality in the Making of Nations', *Ethnic and Racial Studies* 21(3): 242–69.

Nash, J. 2005. 'Introduction: Social Movements and Global Processes', in J. Nash (ed.) *Social Movements: An Anthropological Reader*. Malden, MA: Blackwell, pp.1–26.

Sedgwick Kosofsky, E. 1990. *The Epistemology of the Closet*. Berkeley: University of California Press.

Seidman, S. 2004. *Contested Knowledge: Social Theory Today*, 3rd ed. Malden, MA: Blackwell.

Shepherd, G. 1987. 'Rank, Gender, and Homosexuality: Mombasa as a Key to Understanding Sexual Options', in P. Caplan (ed.) *The Cultural Construction of Sexuality*. London: Tavistock, pp.240–70.

Skowrońska, M. 2004. 'Mocni w trudnych czasach', *Gazeta Wyborcza*, 10 May.

Slany, K., B. Kowalska and M. Śmietana (eds). 2005. *Homoseksualizm: Perspektywa interdyscyplinarna*. Kraków: Nomos.

Verkaaik, O. 2003. 'Fun and Violence. Ethnocide and the Effervescence of Collective Aggression', *Social Anthropology* 11(1): 3–22.

Voxerbrant, D. 2004. *Tolerancja! Who Would Have Thought Tolerance Could Be So Controversial*. Documentary Film, Blackraw Productions.

————. 2004a. Raw material to the above.

Weeks, J. 2000. Making Sexual History, Cambridge: Polity Press.

Wildstein. B. 2004. 'Żałosna duma', *Rzeczpospolita*, 21 April.

Załęcki, P. 2001. *Między triumfalizmem a poczuciem zagrożenia. Kościół rzymskokatolicki w Polsce współczesnej w oczach swych przedstawicieli*. Kraków: Nomos.

Websites:

www.tolerancja.gej.net
www.kampania.org.pl
http://niechnaszobacza.queers.pl
www.piotrskarga.pl
www.wszechpolacy.pl
www.cracovia.krakow.pl
www.ma.wszechpolacy.pl
www.rownystatus.gov.pl

Chapter 7

Olivia's Story: Capitalism and Rabbit Farming in Hungary

László Kürti

Not all aspects of capitalism are pleasant. Not every capitalist investment produces positive results, and not all foreign plants are managed productively. Studies on capitalist penetration in Latin America, Asia and Africa suggest that native agricultural systems and labour relations are turned upside down and local economies rapidly collapse as foreign investments bring negative results to families struggling to make ends meet. European areas recently entering into the vortex of full-scale capitalist production display similar results: indeed, some global firms exploit local workers by relocating to areas of cheap labour, while others leave native producers in debt, leading analysts to conclude that few such industries might be considered successful in the long run.

Some, however, do manage to succeed. This chapter offers a look at capitalist development in postsocialist Hungary, a country that joined the European Union in 2004, having earlier established capitalist firms and production during the late socialist phase from 1989 to the present. By focusing on a single community — Lajosmizse — in central Hungary,[1] while at the same time considering the fate of a Swiss meat packing plant, I argue that some capitalist firms have been influential in restructuring local labour relations by introducing Western modes of production, work ethics, and regulations. This ethnography means to be, at one and the same time, a call for studies presenting a balanced picture of social change and a more committed view of local life that understands socio-economic transformation as a long-term process in communities whose citizens are read as active and conscious agents in charge of their own lives.

I realize that 'capitalism in Hungary' might be considered a somewhat pretentious title for such an essay. Some might argue that there is no real capitalism in Hungarian society, while others might argue that there is, in fact, too much capitalism; others still claim that the more things change, the more they remain the same. The polemics of such debates may well be justified, and I acknowledge fully the terms of these debates. There is, however, an equally powerful counter- argument I wish to propose, one predicated on the assumption that state socialism, as the primary ideological justification for the economic, political and cultural control of society, is no more. In its place, a particular version of capitalism has been implemented as a political-ideological system based on two interrelated constitutive elements: the first is a reconstitution and rearrangement of the link between social groups and power occasioned by the demise of state socialism; the second refers to new political, economic and social institutions that have emerged over the past eighteen years. To the degree that such theorization is possible, I seek to broaden the perspectives adopted in edited volumes on East-Central European societies which heavily accent the political or economic and gloss over cultural matters, highlighting as they do faults in the system, prevailing inequalities and the social schisms created by these new (in Hungary at least), postsocialistic capitalist developments. One such view is to isolate social processes determining the outcome of future events, moralities and justice, as in one scholar's proposition regarding a potential scenario for Hungary in the wake of the changes after 1990. Focusing on land privatization, Vasary has argued that in Hungarian society:

> a sharper differentiation will likely develop between an emerging agrarian bourgeoisie and a landless rural proletariat. To a large extent newly acquired lands are likely to be combined with existing small plots, but also we can expect the development of small agrarian associations, interest groups of various sports, and even independent modern farms in the Western European sense. (1995: 20)

Such an argument might not in fact work for an anthropologist remaining in a single locality for a short period, extrapolating future developments both at the national and local levels, even though some of these predictions may approximate to actual events. For no matter how much they may empathize with their subjects, scholars and anthropologists would do well to offer more contemporary-based observation rather than forecasting future social developments.

In order to better understand the present situation in Hungary, it is necessary to focus however briefly on the era of the Velvet Revolution and its sequels. The period between 1988 and 1994 is credited with laying the foundation to the changes that provides the basis for my analysis which suggests that, for Hungary during the years in question, the term 'transition' is a useful but by no means exclusive concept applicable to the era (Kim and Zacek 1992; Bugaric 2008, Bunce 1995; Nafus, 2006; Seleny 2006). Anthropologists have hardly been at the forefront of what is called 'transitological' literature; in their view, these transitological aspects of societal change were anchored in the difficulties observed at the local level (Müller 2007, Wolfe 2000). Communities facing dire consequences of economic transformation are clearly a central concern for observer and observed alike, and anthropologists have long championed the defence of local populations in their particular struggles.

But, we must ask, how much of this rapid and fundamental shift in production, ownership or employment following the collapse of the planned economy should be translated into long-term consequences in the service of theorizing societies and their economic transformation? Here, in my view, lies the heart of the problem: for anthropologists visiting a particular society at a crucial moment in time do see prevailing forces operating at both the local and national levels. By collecting information from their informants, they construct their theories about the observed phenomena, relying on what they have experienced in the moment. Consequently, more often than not, the entire postsocialist phase has been characterized negatively as a homogeneous global process, as if similar problems did not exist in Western Europe, North America or elsewhere where fundamental economic or social change occur.

The dominant pattern of a doomsday scenario offered by foreign scholars, including anthropologists, has been replicated in particular, for example, with regard to agricultural transformation, changes in the ownership of firms, and the re-privatisation of land after the disbanding of state agricultural enterprises. Today, few farmers in Hungary would care to engage in lengthy discussion about these matters with researchers, or perhaps would do so only in passing out of nostalgia for the good old days and the mayhem that followed. Many rural dwellers are rather cynical about this 'transformation' (*rendszerváltás*), calling it instead 'mode formation' (*módszerváltás*) in reference to the new modes through which former Communist leaders succeeded in capitalizing on their expertise and resources to acquire wealth and power. Making sense of this kind of local moralizing is inevitable for anthropologists; yet at the same time it means walking a tightrope. For just as theorizing socialism, as Verdery (1991) puts it, seems an exercise in futility (Wolfe 2000: 204–5), so, too, projects that cater to shorthand summarizing of postsocialist trajectories, based on brief investigation of a single community without considering the larger picture of local economies' operations within the national and international contexts, are doomed to failure.

In contrast to such views, and as an indigenous anthropologist, I am concerned with Hungary and the nature of change occurring over the past few years. In particular, I describe how locals in one community have experienced cataclysmic political and economic changes while managing to cope with difficulties. Thus, the main focus of my study is on the relations between various groups and national as well as transnational institutions during the period generally referred to as the postsocialist phase. More specifically, I am concerned to make social change intelligible by relating it to institutional and economic contexts in which it develops and occurs. To that end, I look at how a foreign industrial venture restructured local agro-industry and labour processes, an area of concern for scholars with an interest in flows of global capital and current forms of the international division of labour (Ortiz 2002).

It is a given that not everything is negative and not all aspects of the transformation from state socialism to market economy have dire consequences for citizens in former Eastern bloc countries. In Bulgaria, for instance, while the population at large may suffer significant consequences, women fared far better than men in the wake of the new tourist industry, and their prospects for finding adequate employment were successfully negotiated (Ghodsee 2005). A similar process was initiated in the region of my study where successful 'village tourism' developed and continues to flourish today (Kürti 2000b).

I wish to emphasize that in some cases there are phenomena that may be still characterized as inchoate or rudimentary in the economic, political and cultural life of Hungary but, as my case study of the rural economic recovery suggests, there are positive aspects of this development that warrant adequate discussion, analysis and evaluation. I would agree with Rudolf Tőkés and George Schöpflin – scholars who viewed the early phase of transformation with a healthy dose of scepticism – that Hungarian society in the midst of transformation has built both on the achievements of the 1990s and on those from the existing state socialist phase (Tőkés 1996; Schöpflin 1995).[2] In the following, I argue for the importance of a combination of a longer-term understanding and a worm's-eye view to comprehend such transformation at the local level.

Post-postsocialism I: A Country Transformed

The last years of the twentieth century in Hungary witnessed enormous changes that may be divided into three periods. The first, between 1988 and 1989, occurred when the state socialist system – originally created with the help of Moscow following the Second World War and lasting almost intact for forty years – collapsed. This was followed by an equally important second phase, until 1994, when a new constitution was drawn up, the privatization of former state enterprises was carried out and multi-party politics was laying firm foundations for the creation of Western-style democracies not only in Hungary but throughout the former Soviet bloc. The final period of social change began in the mid-1990s, when the patterns of the early 1990s were either followed with renewed vigour or, depending on the particular government in power, gave way to other types of economic, political and cultural schemes. These few years in the history of a society, a state or a nation are, to be sure, but an instant, especially when compared to historical transformations such as the shift from feudalism to capitalism. The momentous importance of these years and the impact of their concomitant changes in lifestyle and values are matters to be assessed here through a specific case-study, that of Lajosmizse, a rural community of 10,000 inhabitants which lies sixty-eight kilometres south-east of Budapest, Hungary's capital. This study, I propose, bears witness to the powerful effect of those changes on the lives of Hungarian citizens since the collapse of state socialism. That the country in the beginning of the twenty-first century is no longer the same as the country of the 1990s or, for that matter, of the 1980s, must be addressed in specific detail from information gathered at the local level and from intimate knowledge of informants' lives. We know a great deal about the contributing factors to the demise of state socialism and the emergence of the democratic capitalist system from a host of scholars both from within Hungary and from the west (Hann 1996; Kovács 1996; Lampland 2002). There are, however, few insightful essays describing exactly what changed, how those changes took place, and who the main players were, both initiating them and suffering their consequences (see, for example, Hollós 2001; Sárkány 2005; Vasary 1995).[3] While global historical treatises and macro analyses may convey some sense of the factors contributing to the creation of the new, non-socialist, capitalist and democratic Hungary at both the national and the local level since 1990, a more focused and detailed assessment is in order.

There is undeniably a tension between the invented images of unalloyed progress and the everyday realities of life, just as there are points of tension between the lifestyles of the country's new elites and those of the have-nots. Through the turbulent years between 1988 and 1990, Hungary managed to preserve its size and national unity during a period that saw other major states – Czechoslovakia, Yugoslavia, the Soviet Union – collapse or break apart. While the country's size – 10,000 square kilometres, or almost one percent of Europe's territory – has remained stable, Hungary in the early 1990s found itself in a changed international geospace. In 1989, Hungary bordered five states (Austria, Czechoslovakia, the USSR, Romania, and Yugoslavia), whereas by 1995 Hungarian foreign policy dealt with two additional neighbours (Croatia and Slovenia) as well as a divided Czechoslovakia, along with rearranged political processes in its former neighbouring states. It is clear that Hungary now finds itself at the crossroads of an entirely new and unknown geopolitical situation.

In retrospect, certain developments can be seen to mark these enormous changes. Along with the unfavourable, downward trend in population, the transformation of politics, industry, agriculture and white-collar employment were the major catalysts determining the new economic profile of Hungary in the 1990s (Halpern and Wyplosz 1998; Stark and Bruszt 1998). Despite many difficulties, the Hungarian economy experienced two years of growth, in 1994 and 1997, with a 3 and 3.8 per cent increase in GDP respectively, a trend that continued throughout the late 1990s. While the country's foreign debt continued to increase from $20 billion in 1987 to $24.5 billion in 1993, by the end of 2005 this amounted to an astronomical 55 billion USD.[4] Paralleling this, savings deposits multiplied from 1.2 billion

Hungarian forints (HUF) in 1993 to 600 billion HUF in 2005.[5] Nonetheless, citizens continued to experience doubt with regard to the value of their currency as well as their banking system, voicing misgivings about the upcoming introduction of the Euro in 2012. But this is only part of the larger picture, especially in view of the fact that, after changes in the law in 1996, Hungarians were able to invest in the West, buy properties outside their own country, and deposit savings in Western banks. It becomes obvious that the country's new upper and middle classes enjoy a degree of wealth similar to that of many Western Europeans. It is also true that, in line with the EU requirement, the rate of inflation was halved from 6.4 per cent in 2004 to 3.5 per cent by the end of 2005, a figure slightly higher between 2007–2008.

One of the prime movers behind Hungary's industrial transformation was the creation of East-West joint venture companies, a legal framework introduced by the socialist government in 1972, but it was only in 1988 (with Act IX on Economic Associations) that Western companies could fully participate in Hungary's economy.[6] While in 1989 alone, over 1,800 joint ventures were registered, by 1993 the figures stood at 19,000. At the close of the 1990s there were some 30,000 such ventures, a figure that approximates to current numbers. Most of the companies with foreign interests were and continue to be located in Budapest and its environs (with 14,560 firms); 6,713 more are in the western part of the country, while the eastern part of the country benefits from 4,857 joint venture companies (Kereszty 1998: 304), a trend that reveals the degree to which foreign investment contributed to Hungary's economic restructuring. The following simple calculations (given in millions US$) reveal the steady contribution of foreign investors to Hungarian development between 1991 and 1997:

1991	1992	1993	1994	1995	1996	1997
1,614	1,911	2,481	1,320	4,570	2,040	2,107

Thus, between 1990 and 1997, the total foreign investment in Hungary is estimated at almost $17 billion, just slightly less than that invested in the Austrian economy. After 2000, however, this trend started to decline as local markets were inundated and foreign investors sought opportunities for locating their firms elsewhere.

Together with these investments, the founding of the State Privatization and Property Agency (Állami Privatizációs és Vagyonügynökség), instrumental in overseeing privatization of Hungarian state firms, and the creation of the Budapest Stock Exchange, were the most important actions that placed the Hungarian economy on the track toward free market reform. In 1990, the State Property Agency controlled 1,859 state enterprises; by 1998 this number had shrunk to less than 500, a number that by 2002 had fallen to below 300, as more companies underwent privatization.[7]

Throughout all this, Hungary's agriculture – especially animal breeding – has fared much worse than its industrial or banking sectors. One indicator of the difficulties of agricultural transformation was the large number of agrarian demonstrations in the late 1990s and early 2000. What took place in Hungary in the 1990s to warrant such turmoil? This major transformation had four components: the disassembling of state farms, land restitution, the privatization of farming, and the rearrangement of agricultural trade. In 1988, only 93,000 hectares of agricultural land were in private hands; by 1994, when land restitution and privatization were completed following the 1992 law on privatization, over 5 million hectares had been transferred to private owners with only 26 large state farms of 'strategic importance' (stock breeding, viniculture, etc.) remaining in state hands.[8] As ownership of land changed, so too did agriculture as an activity (Harcsa 1994; Romány 2005). Even so, land allocation resulted in small properties for most farmers: by 2000, a total of 907,154 miniature estates had been created with sizes of 10 hectares or less. The new large landholdings – those between 500 and 10,000 hectares – has numbered about 2800 (Glatz 2005: 16).

With such a major transfer of agricultural land, production methods were put into effect that sent shockwaves throughout the entire society. Suddenly, more than two million Hungarians became landowners, although not actually agricultural producers: more than 50 per cent were female headed households and retired citizens. This strange ownership situation added to the havoc created by the continual devaluation of the Hungarian currency throughout the first half of the 1990s. Along with a lack of expertise and updated equipment, land parcelled out in small, discontinuous family plots and – especially problematic – the loss of former East European markets, led to disarray in the agricultural sector.

The creation of a new, primarily private and small-scale farming system in the 1990s also resulted in a major realignment of the social structure. The drastic decrease in the number of those actively employed in agriculture followed the general patterns in Europe: while in 1970, 1.2 million people worked in (then socialist) agriculture, by 1988 their number was only 911,000, which further decreased to 460,000 by the mid-1990s. However, this downward trend did not cease. By 1996, when most land was in private hands owned by local farmers' cooperatives or families, those working full-time in agriculture amounted to only 302,000.[9] This loss of almost a million people from agriculture over twenty-five years constituted perhaps one of the most serious transformations in the Hungarian economy at the end of the twentieth century. Many who left agriculture – together with those leaving both heavy and light industries – joined the ranks of the unskilled in the service industries and especially the unemployed living in rural poverty and uncertainty. In the late 1990s (especially in 1997 and 1998) there were national strikes by farmers, who burnt wheat, blocked roads and demanded that the new minister of agriculture and rural development (the peasant party's own candidate József Torgyán) make immediate concessions to Hungary's farming community. Although concessions were quick to arrive, it became clear that agriculture would remain a heavily subsidized part of the economy for years to come. Moreover, as the country became integrated fully into European, and in fact global, agro-industrial trade, agriculture had to undergo more reorganization: price and quality controls affecting both the products and the producers were refined.

Signs of this political-economic transformation and the oft-uttered 'economic miracle' – the antithesis of the former 'goulash communist' situation – were visible in other areas as well, a turnabout facilitated no doubt by the almost 100 million Euro provided by the EU's PHARE program since 1990.[10] With the almost complete collapse of heavy industry (steel and mining have been almost eliminated completely), and the rise of new economic players in high-tech, food and service industries, tourism is perhaps one of the most visible signs of globalized industry being concretized in a national setting. Tourism – especially the growing area of village tourism (*falusi turizmus*), sports tourism, niche health spas, wine and culinary events, hunting and national cultural programs – provides about 300,000 jobs throughout Hungary. This industry alone achieved an income of $2.9 billion in 1997 and $3.4 billion in 1999, equal to an average of 9 per cent of GDP.[11]

Post-postsocialism II: A Community Transformed

It is impossible to spend time in Hungary without noticing visible signs of change, both in terms of its healthy developments and its obvious strains. The town of Lajosmizse will serve here as a community that vibrantly illustrates these changes. Situated along the major M5 highway connecting Budapest and Kecskemét, it is only a forty-five minute drive from Budapest. Originally an agricultural community, Lajosmizse is a town of 11,668 people in the northernmost tip of Bács-Kiskun county.[12] Although strictly agrarian, Lajosmizse has not been considered a traditional or proper peasant community by ethnographers, folklorists and other scholars, a fact that is connected to its brief history, having being incorporated only in 1877. The original settlers arrived from the city of Jászberény, a town barely 70 kilometres away. The proud Jász (Jazygian) farmers received the empty grazing fields of Lajos, Mizse and Bene in 1745 after Maria Theresa re-sold it to Hungarians for a handsome sum.[13] The town's Catholic residents slowly divided up the land and began farming, animal husbandry and forestry activities.[14] By the mid nineteenth century residents in increasing numbers decided to move to their farmsteads, giving up their residency in Jászberény altogether. The town and its 'prairie' (*puszta*) residents ended up in a vicious battle over the almost 20,000 hectares of land with the latter being victorious in the end. The new township of Lajosmizse soon became a model to follow: arriving entrepreneurs raised geese, turkey and sheep for the market towns of Kecskemét, Cegléd and Nagykőrös. At the same time, pioneer farmers domesticated the sand dunes by creating numerous vegetable farms and fruit orchards.

By 1920, after the new political system was established on the ruins of the Austro-Hungarian monarchy, Lajosmizse's population had grown to 12,000 with many new arrivals from the neighbouring successor states. Inter-war Hungary was not called the country of 'three million beggars' without good reason. The countryside was devastated as the result of the First World war and the subsequent land-tenure system. The agricultural system changed notably as a few families (Mizsey, Bartal, Geréby, K. Kovács, Tarnay, Ricsováry, Kláber) were able to buy up large shares of properties from families who went bankrupt and could not afford to pay off bank loans.[15] The programs of Miklós Horthy (Hungary's ruler between 1920–1944) and his governments were unable to satisfy the hunger for land, capital and technology. The majority of farmers of Lajosmizse – like their counterparts elsewhere in the country – remained poor and destitute, relying on their few animals and smallholdings (hence their name as 'smallholders', *kisgazda*), which eventually gave rise to a populist political ideology as well as to agrarian demonstrations and unrest (Kürti 2001).

Following the Second World War, land was nationalized and peasants forced to give up their estates and thus their means of survival. Families labelled rich peasants – the Russian word *kulak* was used for them – faced severe punishment and often internment elsewhere. Many from Lajosmizse and the neighbouring community of Ladánybene ended up for months in the agricultural work camp of Hortobágy, an arid and barren region in the eastern part of the country. When they returned, they found empty homes and no land to cultivate. The returnees, as well as those who remained, were all forced into collective state farms, institutions well known from classic ethnographic descriptions in the 1960s and 1970s.

Under Stalinism and socialism, the workers of the sandy soil (often called the 'golden sand', *aranyhomok*) worked under the same ideology to help the fight against erosion, soil depletion and chronic water shortage in order to meet the desired socialist production targets. These, however, were rarely met and cooperative workers slowly opted for household production on their small plots, rarely over one hectare, as the economic 'miracle' of existing state socialism – following the directives of the New Economic Mechanism of 1968 to combat its shortages (Csikós-Nagy 1987: 32–35) – offered more opportunities for families to invest in different small-scale vegetable and fruit growing as well as animal farming.

As the town's residents witnessed major investment in a few small industrial plants (machine tooling, printing and a hydrogeological shop), during the last two decades of the socialist phase their future was sealed. Agricultural enterprises were increasingly left to their own devices to deal with shortcomings and face the hardships of production, trade and development matters. As a result, some agricultural enterprises invested in highly specialised fruit production (sour cherry, apple, apricot), while others opted for standardized pig, cattle and poultry farming. Both experiments appeared to be excellent choices, but that appearance was short-lived, for it soon turned out that state agricultural cooperatives – like many others in Hungary and elsewhere in the socialist bloc – were not successful, since most relied on important state and county subsidies in order to maintain production and meet targets. As the small industrial plants generated more profit, young and old, men and women were eager to leave agriculture and seek employment in local industry. Meanwhile, all – both those who remained in agriculture and those who worked in industry – remained true to their rural lifestyle, working on family plots and raising animals after completing their paid labour. This kind of 'double life' was not unknown in other communities in Hungary and indeed was hailed as a successful variant of 'goulash communism' that indicated the degree to which the state itself cooperated in allowing its citizens a greater degree of freedom. Thus was a somewhat distorted balance achieved: on the one hand, the locals found employment, and, on the other, an opportunity to remain faithful to their prior agricultural identities. Politics, economics and social life, or so it seemed, were ably organized and monitored from above by the government, the Communist Party and its extended arm, the local bureaucracy.

This form of 'goulash communism', so often disputed in both national and foreign sources, meant that by the late 1980s Hungarian farmers were in a position to reap the benefits of both the socialist and the private economy (*magángazdaság*).[16] By that time, some five million people (half of Hungary's population) were in one way or another involved with the 'private' or 'second economy' whose most pertinent sector was agricultural activity (Kovách 1985: 123).[17] In Lajosmizse, keeping cows for milk – milk bought by state farms in order to meet their own targets – was one such manifestation of the economy, while another extended to poultry farming, with geese, chicken and turkey being the most attractive commodities. Similarly, for most families, pig farming remained a primary activity, with pigs sold to state farms as well as to locals at market. A few farms ventured into raising fur-bearing animals (silver fox, nutria), snails, rabbits for meat, and angora for pelts.[18] The construction of a rabbitry was a favoured pastime of those working in industry and the tertiary sector because of the minimal amount of work required to feed and care for the animals. Following a national trend, about half of the industrial and white-collar workers commuting to work from Lajosmizse were engaged in some kind of poultry, pig and rabbit farming – primarily for home use – in addition to their main occupation. In the inner part of town, animal farming was limited to chickens and hens, although farms were equipped to sustain larger animals (pigs, cows) as well as diverse livestock. Sheep and goat herding – formerly so prestigious – has nearly ceased to exist as a specialization, and only a handful of families are willing to invest in this type of animal farming.[19]

Against this historical backdrop, how do we get to the heart of the matter of ascertaining whether such a local community is either experiencing a downward turn or prospering? Apart from informants' narratives, we can consider statistics with regard to income and expenditure that provide some solid ground for assessing the state of the local political economy. By far the largest source of income for the town is generated from business (*iparűzési adó*) and vehicle taxes (*gépjárműadó*). In 2004 and 2005, of the roughly 6 million total income for each year, roughly 1 million was collected in local taxes (an additional 1 million income represents the percentage of personal income tax that local communities receive from the government).[20] Although this sum may not appear substantial at first glance, for a town of this size it is a significant amount that reveals the ability of local government to rely increasingly on local businesses and producers.

In view of the foregoing, it would not be unreasonable to suggest that Lajosmizse is (by Hungarian standards) a fairly wealthy and prosperous agro-industrial business community,[21] notwithstanding the fact that it is difficult to determine the level of prosperity with any accuracy. Nonetheless, certain indicators suggest that daily life and the local landscape have altered dramatically since 1990. On the street where I live, for instance, the number of cars passing by has increased tenfold over the past ten years. I remember standing on the corner with a neighbour for half an hour during the mid 1980s and being able to converse with him while taking a good look at every car that passed by; only five appeared. Today, in two minutes the same number of vehicles pass by without arousing denizens' interest. I sought confirmation of my assumption from two acquaintances, both of whom operate a car repair shop, by inquiring about the comparative status of their respective businesses now and fifteen years ago. Both admitted (happily) that the number of passenger cars has multiplied, while commenting (regretfully) that today some fifteen car repair shops compete for business, compared to five previously. In 2005, then, the total number of vehicles amounts to 3,900, or approximately one car per household.

Another approach to signalling progress, apart from relying on informants' anecdotes and impressions offered to researchers at a given moment, is to calculate the number of dwelling units (both apartments and family homes) built in the last few years.[22] This reveals a slight increase from 119 in 2002 to 133 in 2004, a meagre rise that offers a useful perspective on the financial situation of the town's inhabitants. Similarly, the number of individual entrepreneurs (*vállalkozó*) licensed in town grew to 519 by 2005, or approximately 5 per cent of the total population. The number of businesses has not altered substantially: in 2002 there were 273 and two years later 279.[23] These figures might be seen to reveal a healthy atmosphere as far as economy, trade and services are concerned. Indeed, nearby villagers comment that Lajosmizse has become a prosperous business town with a visible and energetic entrepreneurial spirit. In two years three major supermarkets (Penny, Plus, Szil-Coop), a spring-water bottling company (Magyar Viz Kft) and several family farms have begun operation. Not all, however, have engaged in business activity by choice, and indeed some were forced into such activity by lack of viable alternatives.

Obviously, this optimistic picture would not be complete if in contrast to these figures the less benign aspects of past developments were to remain hidden from view. In the town's environs, as in the whole of Bács-Kiskun county, the number of traditional households has dwindled considerably since the late 1980s (Kiss 2004). Known as the 'farm' (*tanya*), this rural institution has almost entirely disappeared in certain regions. Prior to 1970, 60 per cent of Lajosmizse's population lived outside the town centre on more or less traditional farms, tending small plots and raising a few animals, while after 1990, less than 30 per cent lived in this way. Recently built farms are the result of families who remain faithful to their former lifestyle by attempting to manage the family business, and by the new entrepreneurs – chicken farms, feed companies – who have little concern for peasants' work methods or an agrarian way of life.

In Lajosmizse as elsewhere in Hungary, a political time-bomb was ticking and, in 1989, it exploded in full force as the Hungarian Socialist Workers' Party increasingly conceded to emerging alternative political forces, finally surrendering to total defeat. With the emergence of a multi-party democratic system, state enterprises (including agricultural cooperatives and state farms) were disbanded and an immense quantity of formerly state-owned land was reprivatized, some of which was returned to its original owners, from whom the state had requisitioned it away after the Second World War, while other parcels were auctioned off to those possessing restitution vouchers (*kárpótlási jegy*).[24]

What occurred in Lajosmizse also took place throughout Hungary: jubilant citizens – though some less so than others – ended up with sizable land holdings, many never having had any experience in farming or animal husbandry. Families rushed to buy what they could not afford, producing what need not have been produced and believing what ought not to have been believed: that is to say, that agricultural production was to be their domain, and they were poised to enjoy a new beginning of limitless opportunity for profit. The re-privatisation process was cataclysmic, causing many farmers to be soon indebted to banks as the result of inexpert farming techniques, which included purchasing greatly overpriced farm machinery. These losses were also attributable to increasing national as well as European-manipulated marketing strategies. By the late 1990s, major farmers' strikes tolled the death knell for traditional farming. Governments of various ideological persuasions (socialist as well as right-wing populist) grappled with this pressure cooker as the EU demanded specific quality goods at certain prices, while Hungarian agricultural production was not yet in a position to meet the requirements.

As many former farmers moved into the centre of town to work, new social problems accumulated. One result of this shift was that the new labourers were the first to lose their jobs when state industries collapsed, meaning that they were among the most destitute sector, adding to the numbers of the unemployed and the poor. This can be seen from the number of people needing health, social and monetary assistance: while their ranks have increased slightly over the past ten years, those requiring medical and health subsidies (*közgyógyellátás*) have increased considerably.[25] Similarly, the number of citizens receiving social security benefits (*rendszeres szociális segély*) rose at an alarming rate from a few dozen to hundreds during the 1990s, only to stabilize in 2002 at 209, a figure that remained unchanged for the next two years. The elderly, the unemployed and the Roma (according to 2002 statistics, about 10 per cent of the total population) are all part of this category.

In Lajosmizse, most found it difficult to use the resources and know-how of family farming as a successful basis for a switch to agribusiness. Most small-scale family farms – with a few cows, poultry and fruit and vegetable gardens – were only able to produce for home consumption with a minimal surplus for the local market. Many inhabitants became farmers by force of circumstances (*kényszerparaszt*) as the countryside failed to offer alternative jobs or investment opportunities. Whereas before 1990 many families operated milk production for central milk collection stations, today all but a handful of families depend on selling milk to one or two privately owned milk collectors.

The local government has not been able to thwart attacks on family farming as it, too, was forced to contend with budgetary constrains and crises in self-management. Most rural communities in Hungary have a similar profile, and tales of poverty throughout the countryside make the rounds in academic circles as well as in local and national media. Together with hundreds of its counterparts, Lajosmizse entered a new era with troubling questions and a dubious future ahead. Many farmers express the concern that they must play multiple roles, or 'stand on many legs', in order to survive (*több lábon álló gazdálkodás*) and are hence reluctant to embark upon the more profitable but risky business of specialization.

There is, however, another story, one that enables the present study to be undertaken at this time. No one foresaw what was to occur when the current economic zeitgeist brought in its wake new entrepreneurial activity to reshape agriculture in the region,[26] for a combination of local and transnational developments have offered Lajosmizse and its inhabitants a second chance. Situated between Budapest and Kecskemét, a major city eighteen kilometres to the south-west, Lajosmizse received a boost when a major highway connecting the two cities was opened in the early 1990s, immediately helping to re-route a transport system that until then had placed a heavy burden on locals, with thousands of lorries, buses and passenger cars spewing out carcinogens. The new M5 highway also opened up possibilities for industrial development as investors realized the importance of new and easier transportation as well as the proximity afforded by a new four-lane thoroughfare placing Budapest only a forty-five-minute ride away.

Another side of this story of rejuvenation has to do with emerging new businesses that relocated to or sprang up around Lajosmizse. As small state industries were privatized, most workers lost their jobs, but a few managers were in a position to buy the plants offered for sale. Some of these business opportunities – the machine-tool shop NUSPL, for example – began a second life, securing markets abroad. This development was the basis for the success of another company (FOLPLAST) which produces plastic goods for the EU. The Official Governmental Printing House, whose activity is restricted to government contracts, is another element of this story, providing secure employment for many. An additional major agro-industrial venture placing Lajosmizse at the centre of capitalism concerns the establishment of Olivia, a Swiss rabbit farm and slaughterhouse.

Here Comes Olivia: Rabbits and Rabbit Farming

In Lajosmizse, the making of a rabbit farming industry has exercised considerable influence in restructuring local labour. Olivia is a fully Swiss-owned rabbit-meat factory whose parent company (Delimpex) is based in Switzerland. The company's presence in the town signals both the beginning of capitalist production for the market, and the end of state-owned and controlled labour relations and factory bargaining plans concerning target dates, quotas and work regulations so prominent under state socialism (Kürti 2002). In 1991, a Swiss entrepreneur requested a permit to build a rabbit slaughterhouse on the outskirts of Lajosmizse, which was gladly accepted by the town council. In a few months, the plant was completed, with all the technology and know-how imported from abroad. In order to secure trained management, the owner sent in a top Swiss manager to Lajosmizse, who subsequently relocated to Hungary; in addition, several young volunteers with higher education were offered the opportunity to spend several months in Switzerland to study marketing and rabbit farming. Soon Olivia became the talk of the town as production increased and workers received bonuses in cash as well as rabbit meat.[27] The company's intrusion into Hungary was obviously not a matter of chance and followed an initial survey of potential host countries (Poland, Romania and Slovakia) and a careful planning strategy. Its final decision was facilitated by the realization that Hungarian state industries had collapsed or were on the verge of dismantling. These included a variety of food and agribusinesses (flour milling, sugar beet production, food processing, etc.) whose fate particularly affected the countryside. Hungarian family-style rabbit farming was experiencing a similar downturn in 1989–90 as the state withdrew subsidies, resulting in a downward spiral in rabbit meat output.

Rabbits have been known to be an element in the human diet since time immemorial. These herbivores are bred for their meat as well as their fur, while other recently recognised byproducts include rabbit manure –

a high nutrient content soil for gardeners and flower lovers – and brains, the latter a sought after material for pharmaceuticals.[28] Rabbits are shy, timid animals living in burrows in their natural habitat. While hunting or snaring wild rabbit was a favoured pastime of sportsmen and laymen alike, today only those with special permits are allowed to hunt. Because both wild and domesticated rabbits are extremely prolific reproducers, they are associated with fertility: Easter eggs – another symbol of fecundity – are linked not with chickens but with rabbits in children's folklore. In contrast, another study could analyze why in some countries rabbit is a favoured dish on the dinner table while elsewhere it is viewed merely as a pest.[29] In France, a rabbit science (*cunicologie*) has developed that includes breeding, farming and cooking. In Australia, however, until 1987 rabbit farming was prohibited because of the pest status of wild rabbits.[30] While rabbit farming, mostly of the backyard type, has been known for centuries, the end of the twentieth century saw commercial rabbit farming reach industrial heights with a hundred thousand metric tons of rabbit meat consumed worldwide. Today particular breeds are favoured by farmers while other hybrids are used in major scientific research programs as test animals.[31] Rabbit meat is light, highly nutritious, low in fat and cholesterol, and rich in proteins, vitamins and minerals, qualities that are not necessarily shared by other meats. In favour of rabbit farming, it is suggested that, unlike other large animals, rabbits do not compete with humans for food, water or space, and the numerous byproducts (brains, blood, fur, manure) make rabbit farming more efficient and profitable than any other animal farming: in opposition, animal rights activists have been vocal opponents of contemporary rabbit farming and view all breeding and farming techniques as inhumane.[32]

Rabbit farming was not unknown in Hungary under state socialism and even in the interwar years. It took place, however, on a small scale, primarily of the kind known as backyard rabbit farming with genetically mixed breeds. This meant that families raised rabbits – about 5–10 per family is sufficient – in makeshift cages for local consumption and for the central meat market that in turn exported them overseas. The state supported this activity by offering good prices for healthy rabbits and incentives to families interested in backyard farming. Feed was mostly natural: as locals referred to it 'from the available grains and greens'. Families used rabbit farming not as a 'get rich quick' scheme but to add to their income from this state-supported activity.

Hungary achieved minor celebrity status in Europe as one of the countries known to offer excellent quality live rabbits as well as carcasses.[33] From the early 1970s, the country exported over 14,000 metric tons of rabbit meat, a figure that grew to 44,000 metric tons by 1984 (KSH 1983, 1989). In addition to meat rabbit, in 1986 Hungary was the number one producer in the world of angora wool (187 metric tons). In the same year Hungary was second only to Malta in producing over four kilos of rabbit meat per capita (Lukefahr and Cheeke 1991), a figure that changed immediately after 1990, indeed so radically so that while Malta remained atop the chart (producing more than 8 kilos per person per year in 1998) Hungary no longer remained among the top five producers. The following table indicates the EU countries that, since the late 1990s, received Hungarian rabbit meat (in percentage terms):

Country	1996	1997	1998	1999	2000	2001	2002	2003
Italy	71	65	60	62	56	45,9	52	43
Switzerland	20	24	25	26	31	42	26	27
Germany	4	3	5	5	8	8	16	19
France	0.3	0.3	0.5	0.8	0.8	0.1	1.0	4
Belgium	3.8	5	4	3.5	1.3	1.8	3.4	4.6
The Netherlands	0.1	1.0	0.9	0.7	-	-	-	0.4
(rest in various countries)								

With the collapse of centrally monitored farming and distribution in 1990, a completely new rabbit farming industry had to be developed. In what ways, then, did farming techniques and distribution change? In 1993, the Hungarian National Rabbit Production Board (NRPB, *Nyúl Terméktanács*) was established, an agency required by law to oversee the whole rabbit industry in the country.[34] Under the new incentives of the NRPB, angora wool production ceased completely to function as an industry. While previously, backyard rabbit farming was the rule, producing 90 per cent of rabbits, today 75 per cent are raised on large farms. The largest slaughterhouses are foreign-owned: the Swiss-owned Olivia, as well as an Italian company, while others are located in the southern and western parts of the country: Bácska Agroindustrial Rt in Baja, Rabbit Line Kft in Környe, and others in in Baj. Since the mid 1990s, production at these slaughterhouses was as follows:

The number of rabbits (in millions) raised by the four major companies.
Sources: Bleyer and Szendrő (1999), Kling (2004).

	1998	1999	2000	2001	2002	2003
Lajosmizse	65	83	92	92	92	90
Baja	60	48	55	40	76	80
Baj	35	45	40	54	35	15
Környe	13	13	11	-	-	7

Together with the Olivia's own rabbitry, local farmers in the region produce Hungary's major share of rabbit meat, all of which is for foreign consumption, in Switzerland, Italy, Germany and France. In 1990, Hungarian rabbit farming earned the country $53 million, but by 1998 this was down to $23 million, a figure that has remained the same since (Bleyer and Szendrő 1999: 2; Kling 2004: 1).

As can be discerned from these figures, rabbit farming is not a major source of income affecting the state budget. What, then, might explain the focus on the rabbit meat industry to the extent that FAO issued a memorandum in order to provide a justification for increased rabbit farming worldwide (FAO 2001)? To be sure, international organisations have long been campaigning for rabbit farming as a possibility to alleviate food shortages especially in underdeveloped countries. Since the mid 1980s, world rabbit production has reached 1.3 million metric tons per annum. Cameroon, Tunisia, Morocco, Ghana, Gambia, and Egypt in Africa; Papua New Guinea, India, China and Australia in Asia; and Mexico, Brazil and Barbados are all rabbit meat-producing countries where the 1990s saw an unprecedented rise in both production and consumption (FAO 2001; Lukefahr and Cheeke 1990). The only exception perhaps is China, by far the single largest producer of rabbits in the world: angora rabbits are raised for fur but consumption of rabbit meat remains insignificant.

According to data from P. Magdelaine (2003), on average about 700,000 metric tons of rabbit meat is produced in Europe per annum. Italy alone produces more than 300,000 metric tons a year; France, meanwhile, produces half that amount and Spain somewhat less. All the other countries put together produce less than Spain alone.

The short gestation period and great fertility and fecundity (early growth, maturity and large number of offspring) of rabbits mean they offer a distinct advantage over other livestock animals (cattle, sheep, goats, pigs). A female rabbit, or doe, will reach maturity in 16 weeks, males (bucks) in only 20 weeks. Does and bucks are kept in separate cages and only put together for the time of mating. A doe gives birth to 7 or 8, and sometimes more, offspring, with a typical doe producing 7 to 9 litters per year if kept in a healthy condition; from these, 40 to 50 kittens survive to be fattened.[35] The gestation period is roughly 30 days but does are mated within the first week after giving birth (they are fertile after 24 hours). In mating techniques, family and industrial farms differ as the latter prefer to inseminate does as soon as possible to produce the largest number of offspring possible. After 12 to 13 weeks, during which they are fattened, rabbits gain up to 3 kilos of weight and are ready to be sold and slaughtered. Prices vary according to the market and the type of restaurant offering rabbit specialties. Rabbit meat can reach 6€ per kilo at certain markets; rabbit farmers in Hungary, however, only receive 1.5 euros per kilo at the slaughterhouse (2005 prices).[36] Rabbits can be purchased at the local livestock animal market but they are often highly priced bucks and does and rarely smaller ones for the kitchen table.

What did the Swiss company Olivia introduce in Lajosmizse, and how did its presence influence local culture and economy? It is rare for a foreign company to engage in construction and labour-related issues other than those which strictly concern its daily business. However, Olivia took a different approach,[37] realizing that scientifically monitored and effective large-scale rabbit production must be implemented to be profitable. In this way, Olivia embarked upon a bumpy road: it had to teach farmers how to feed, care for and keep animals. From the type of cages to the specific, high-nutrient content feed used, farmers had to learn new techniques and modes of breeding and selecting animals. What soon became obvious is that 'hobby farming' was far from efficient and farmers were given lessons and DIY materials. In a few years a small number of successful backyard farms emerged with ten to twenty does per farm. Such small-scale businesses seemed highly lucrative at first: cages were cheap or locally available, feed was mostly greens, and Olivia bought live rabbits at a good price. Several families decided to invest to a greater extent than previously, often giving up other activities such as farming poultry or vegetables in greenhouses. With Olivia in business two kinds of social groups were created: the first comprises those families who breed and raise rabbits either as a full or part-time occupation; the second is made up of those employed by Olivia in various jobs. There is no exchange between the two, for Olivia employees are salaried workers, while farmers are only paid when they sell rabbits to Olivia. Many farmers are disillusioned agricultural entrepreneurs who have been experimenting with various kinds of agriculture production that includes rabbit cultivation. Many, however, are inexperienced with rabbit or any other kind of animal farming: the more successful had been in prior contact with family type rabbitries. A farmer summarized the situation in this way: 'When I was a child we had rabbits and my family almost always prepared rabbit for our   dinner   table. So I knew something about rabbits before. Anybody who is ready to start large-scale farming should know rabbits well for they are extremely delicate animals to deal with'. A distinguishing feature that sets apart rabbit farmers from workers at Olivia is that of consumption: while farmers prepare rabbit meat for the family's dinner table, workers at the factory rarely, if ever, eat rabbit. Men engaged in rabbit farming – for without exception they are all men – also pride themselves on being adept at preparing various stews, baked rabbit legs and sautéed rabbit liver. In a household, I have rarely seen women killing and skinning rabbits; without question it is always a man's job.

With so many advantages, at first full and part-time farmers were eager to start making rabbit cages or hutches. A few bought ready-made cages but since most were short of cash nearly all opted for the DIY business of making cages. Rabbits are kept in small cages of 60 by 70 centimeters in size and rarely over 40 centimeters in height. Construction of different cages was necessary for does, bucks, and fryings (rabbits fattened after separation from the doe). Does with a litter need different size cages with feeders and water jars of various shapes and sizes; the cage had to be of a certain kind to allow waste to be expelled and letting a gentle but adequate breeze circulate to eliminate the ammonia emanating from rabbit manure. This process had to be learned by both old and new entrepreneurs ready to enter into the new challenge of rabbit farming. Farmers – and not only rabbit farmers – are under constant pressure to keep to the reproductive cycles of animals, timetables set by the buyers, outbreak of diseases and, more complicated still, to have an eye on market prices for feed, grain and pellets. Sick animals must be immediately separated or put down so as not to infect healthy ones.

As soon as Olivia began operation, management realized that one of its most serious challenges was to enable workers – especially the poor and women – to commute to work. The solution was simple: the company helped build a cycle path connecting the centre of town and its northern part (Felsőlajos, now almost a fully separate community) to the area where the plant is located. By contributing to construction, Olivia was not necessarily concerned with nature tourism. The cycle path allowed workers without cars to commute to work on their bikes. One worker expresses this development as follows: 'It was hard for me to find a job elsewhere because I do not have a car. But now, with the cycle path, it takes me about twenty to twenty-five minutes to go to work on my bike'. To this a foreman present at the interview added: 'I too use my bike whenever I can. It provides the cheapest transportation to work, but it is also a good exercise'. Interpretations by locals may differ, but understanding the usage and the function of the path was similar in other people's comments.

The completion of the cycle path was hailed by many residents as a real achievement in a town suffocating from heavy lorry and car traffic.[38] For Olivia this was an inexpensive solution, although at first it failed to yield adequate results in view of the constantly fluctuating workforce. Since workers had to commute from nearby settlements – namely Csemő and Ladánybene, two smaller communities, each roughly ten kilometres away – the management purchased two secondhand buses which enabled easy transportation of workers to and from the plant. This meant that the area of labour catchment around the town soon expanded as some workers opted for the higher wages available at Olivia, and by providing free transportation for commuting workers from the nearby communities the shortage of labour was quickly resolved. By restructuring the labour market, management was able to insure that absenteeism and lateness of shifts, two areas that had contributed to a chronic lack of work ethics under socialism, were kept to a minimum.

It should be noted, however, that working at Olivia is neither easy nor sumptuous. Women experience particular difficulty with shop floor work because of the newness of the industry and the uniqueness of production techniques. At the production belt men and women handling rabbit carcasses must stand during the entire shift, unusually demanding work resulting in complaints about the monotony of the job and the stench. To solve these issues, the factory has been equipped with an adequate air conditioning and filtering system even though the temperature must be kept low. The regularity of the entry of lorries carrying rabbits to the slaughterhouse and the actual speed of the conveyor belt means that labourers must work at a specific pace. Those who smoke, which includes most workers, are allowed to take short cigarette breaks, permitted only outside the building.

In establishing a factory in Hungary, Olivia has invested not only in agriculture and animal farming but also influenced the division of labour as well as employment practices at the local level. The two areas mentioned (monotony and the gruesome sight and stench of rabbit carcasses) are the main reasons why during the first few years Olivia had a difficult time in retaining its workforce. Most men on the shop-floor left because of the monotony of production and, especially, due to the lack of opportunity for promotion to a higher rank within the factory system; meanwhile, women left because of the unpleasant task of cutting, skinning and dissecting carcasses. By the mid to late 1990s, secure employment in and around Lajosmizse grew scarce as locals continued to lose jobs as a result of factory and plant closures, in particular in Nagykőrös, where large food processing plants and a canning factory closed down. Olivia, however, managed to keep a smaller and stable workforce, and the management established a new labour contract along with the introduction of a higher wage package for workers. By so doing the work force at the beginning of this century has become stabilized and gender balanced. Women who managed to retain their shop floor employment at Olivia turned out to be the real winners in this capitalist milieu, gaining as they did a secure standard of living.[39]

Figure 7.1 Construction work on the Olivia plant. Photo by László Kürti.

However, it would be incorrect – and unfair to locals who view the company with suspicion – to present Olivia's past fifteen years as untarnished. After its initial years of success, from the mid to late 1990s, a number of officials suddenly left Olivia, one of whom was the Swiss executive who had managed the factory since its inception but who eventually crossed swords with its owner. Another was a local woman in her mid thirties who departed after almost ten years. Had she remained, her story would have figured as one of several success stories of local women: having been hired at the beginning of

Figure 7.2 Work at the conveyor belt, Olivia, 2000. Photo by László Kürti.

her career, she gradually managed to advance in the hierarchy and was sent several times to Switzerland to study marketing, distribution and quality control. By her own admission, her salary was quite high by local standards, and she was well respected even by her Swiss colleagues. After ten years, however, she no longer considered her position to be challenging, and saw no further opportunity for advancement.

The situation of blue- and white-collar workers at the Olivia plant may be one thing, but that of local farmers is quite another, for few enjoyed the benefits of Olivia's restructuring and the completion of its own rabbitry. During its first ten years, Olivia's management provided technology, expertise and loans to prospective farmers who were offered special training courses in the farming of new genetic breeds of rabbits in addition to those already reared in Hungary. Many learned the importance of following breeding cycles with care, realizing that some breeds to which they had grown accustomed were less productive than others. Feeding techniques were also altered in order to maintain the high quality controls set by Olivia. Natural feed, often not available or in short supply, was offered to farmers in addition to artificial or pelleted feed (*táp*).[40] Similarly, the management was also keen to introduce farmers to the new sheds, cages and wire-mesh technology more adequate for rabbit farming. Hungarian backyard rabbitries were and continue to be small wooden structures, the argument being that rabbits should avoid the weight loss concomitant in free-range methods. In contrast, the new technology – based on 'happy rabbitry', an idea emanating from concerned Western animal rights activists – relies on spacious wire-mesh cages.[41] A 'happy rabbitry' is well ventilated and rationally divided to provide ample space for placing grains, water and greens separately from the sleeping corner at the opposite end of the cage. Farmers were also instructed in awareness of rabbits' habit of constant chewing, leading to the practice of equipping cages with a chewing board (*rágódeszka*) or piece of hanging branch; some farmers also use a rounded branch to encourage 'play'. While the utility of these farming devices may be debatable, many EU regulations now include such techniques. One farmer's amusing anecdote is telling:

> After I finished my new cages and I showed them to Olivia's manager he was flabbergasted. He immediately wanted to connect my rabbitry to an internet site so anybody could see how well my rabbits live. No shit, I said to myself, I do not even have an internet myself but my rabbits should have it? This was just too much for me, so I declined the offer.

The implementation of an entirely new production technology, to be sure, brings its own difficulties: locals must be convinced that rabbit farming is a profitable business if one undertakes it seriously with the will and stamina to make it work. Olivia's leadership devised two kinds of added incentives for farmers to interest them in the project: loans for starting anew, or reconstructing old rabbit sheds; and cash rewards for those producing extremely high quality, healthy animals. Initially, loans were interest-free, a great surprise to many farmers who had previously had to contend with opposition from banks when requesting loans, even ones at a high interest rate. Olivia's owner knew well that once farmers had invested their time, energy and finances in building a rabbitry, purchasing twenty to thirty does for breeding would eventually produce offspring and an acceptable profit. When the time came to bring the fattened animals to the slaughterhouse, a percentage of the loan was deducted from the payment. Thus farmers – always short of cash – no longer had to borrow or spend their own savings, and instead accepted a lower sale price in exchange.

All farmers engaged in rabbit farming are small producers (*kistermelő*) who build two or three sheds on their property for the ten to thirty does they keep. This process obviously cannot compete with larger farms with hundreds of does, nor the large factory-like atmosphere of Olivia with tens of thousands of does. Farmers understandably feel disadvantaged by this imbalance in many ways, most importantly due to the sheer size of large farms which undermines their bargaining position. The price of rabbits is always established by the buyer, in this case Olivia, who also require farmers to adhere to strict standards and quality control. Another disadvantage is that, after 1990, all farmers' interest groups and associations had to begin anew; many existed only on paper. This leads to a situation in which farmers feel that no one is on their side. As one complains:

> I am both a small producer (*kistermelő*) and a traditional farmer (*őstermelő*).[42] I have my permits to keep rabbits but nobody really cares about what happens to me when I have difficulties. When my animals die of sickness, or when the price of feed goes up, or when I have to sell my rabbits below the price, nobody gives a damn. I am totally on my own. We do not have a union, or an association. This is a really lonely profession.

Figure 7.3 Rabbit feast organised by Olivia, 1995. Photo by László Kürti.

This last sentence is all too true with respect to Hungarian animal husbandry. Rabbit farmers especially fall into this category because they have not yet fully realized the benefits of active union membership (Virág 1996). Apart from a few vocal advocacy groups, farmers' participation in both local and regional politics has yet to be effected: even the task force on rural policy has acknowledged that this lack is a primary element preventing effective cooperation among farmers (Glatz 2005).

There are, however, other reasons why rabbit farmers are unlike other animal keepers. Most farmers are extremely wary of strangers and friends who might wish to visit their rabbitry. Their fears are twofold: first, that of disease or infection; and second, that their hard-learned, secret techniques of breeding, feeding and keeping will be copied by others. A farmer in his forties explains:

> I designed the sheds and the cages, I mix my own feed, and – believe it or not – I make a special tea for my rabbits that helps their immune system. I put various fruits and greens in it and give it to them to drink once a day. This is why they are healthy and their fur so smooth and shiny. They are happy too.

To be sure, the year 2004 was an extremely difficult one: several government projects were cut, forcing small family farms to downsize or sell off most of their does. Previous aid had provided for the special health control of animals brought to the slaughterhouse, a task now billed to farmers at each handover of animals. Another form of assistance had helped farmers dispose of unused byproducts of animals, while the state also assisted in the maintenance of a healthy pool of does by providing cash incentives for selecting high-quality does and bucks. These sums were nearly halved in 2004. At the same time, price fluctuations in live rabbit markets were a constant source of conflict between farmers and Olivia. For these reasons, few farmers are currently willing to invest in full-time rabbit farming. In the region, only thirty to forty families sell rabbits to Olivia as a full-time agricultural business.

It is worth noting that Olivia's owner perceived other problems that required immediate attention such as the dwindling number of family farms and the rather haphazard shipments of rabbits to the slaughterhouse. Farmers, especially those who had recently entered the business of rabbit farming, were unable to maintain the tight deadlines and the stringent health codes set by the firm. Often, production cycles remained elusive because of the lack of shipments as well as the inadequate number (or quality) of live animals. To meet this challenge, and to maintain its standing, Olivia imported a hybrid (the Hy-Plus 19, first cross-bred by the French Grimaud Frères in 1984). The inclusion of this hybrid, in contrast to family farmers who use various cross-breeds by utilizing the Pannon White, is attributable to the success of does in maintaining a fairly steady number of healthy offspring. Many local farmers, nonetheless, have been quite wary of 'foreign imports', preferring as they do better-known breeds. In the words of one such farmer: 'We are all in the same business. But the companies and those monitoring our imports should pay more attention to breeds that are dearer to us. Even though the Pannon White is not a [Hungarian breed], it is our rabbit and we should pay subsidies to farmers who breed them instead of foreign breeds'.[43]

Breeds aside, both managers at Olivia and individual farmers agree that rabbit farming in the twenty-first century emphasizes quality, numbers and weights. Similarly, they see rabbit farming as a secure industry without the added difficulties that poultry, cattle and pig farming have recently experienced. Olivia's owner decided to venture into poultry farming in Jászberény with disastrous results. The company, called Corona Poultry, went into bankruptcy in 2003, leaving farmers in distress when their shipments were unpaid or when they were left with tens of thousand of chickens without buyers.[44] In stark contrast, Olivia has established itself as the single giant among rabbit meat exporters in the central part of Hungary, offering assistance, breeds and inexpensive feed to prospective farmers. It is, in the words of one farmer, a 'cut-throat game out there' because all farmers and slaughterhouses must produce better quality meat, larger but not fatty carcasses, and obtain a larger market share by increasing output over previous years. This is why both large farms and individual farmers cooperate with the medical and academic spheres in utilizing the latest research. As a company official assures, the success of the Hy-Plus 19 hybrid is based on simple mathematics: the number of kittens per birth (9) and the number of rabbits reaching maturity (8.5). Weights are important because, with this special hybrid, one doe produces 56 offspring weighing a total of 137 kilos per year, figures that are considered by the industry as an exceptionally successful production output. Obviously, some farmers have been successful in producing an even larger number of kittens and a more substantial average weight. These experiments, however, soon proved unrealistic, even fatal. One farmer tells his story with sadness:

> I started with several does giving birth to a much higher number [of young] than they could actually raise and many of the offspring did not reach maturity. At the same time, these does were soon useless for another mating. Then I experimented with a special feed (using lots of corn) but it turned out that Oliva did not buy the rabbits if they were too fat. They set the limit at 3 kilos maximum.

Seeing the difficulties farmers faced, Olivia invested in a plan that has facilitated its elevation into the first rank of rabbit breeding in Hungary: in 1999 it set up its own rabbitry in Lajosmizse and Ócsa (for 20,000 does), a town about thirty kilometres north, an investment worth almost 400,000€. In addition, to offset price increases, it concluded that it would build its own feed production facility in Dabas. In so doing, it resolved many issues. In relative proximity to the slaughterhouse, tens of thousands of does of equal quality and breed provide enough offspring. This is why Olivia now is able to ship 4,000 to 5,000 metric tons of rabbit meat per annum, which includes the individual farmers' contribution as well as its own 40,000 does producing 850,000 fryers.[45] Another development was also necessary: that of the disposal of an enormous quantity of manure. An ingenious plan was devised: in 2000 the company set up its own organic-manure plant and began to market it to those farmers involved with organic gardening.[46] A question arises: by building its own rabbit feed company and rabbitry, has Olivia disempowered and impoverished individual farmers? The answer is difficult to ascertain, yet it would seem that farmers are increasingly at the mercy of price and quality controls set by this transnational company.

As a consequence of Olivia building its own rabbitry, many farmers realized that their position had weakened considerably. The fact that the company no longer relied solely upon them created a complicated but not unmanageable system in which local farmers had to abide by target dates, quality controls and health standards. As the only rabbit buyer in the area, Olivia was in an advantageous position: not only could it set the price per kilo for rabbits but it could also decide which rabbits to purchase. This situation has made Hungarian farmers uneasy, and some families have withdrawn from the business altogether while others are aware that their bargaining position has been weakened. One farmer who quit rabbit farming had this to say: 'When I realised that Olivia would not buy my rabbits anymore at the same price I had to calculate my investment versus the profit. It worked out that I was barely breaking even so I decided to sell all my does to a friend'. Olivia's owner and the managers see the business's present situation as secure and reliable. While the company is modest by comparison to other foreign or multinational companies operating in Hungary, the owner is confident that it has advantages other, larger industries do not have. First of all, Olivia is able to maintain a steady flow of rabbits at regular intervals. This means that it can work with a stable network of farmers who are reliable and can provide the necessary amount and quality of rabbits needed to maintain the company's position. Secondly, the company need not be concerned about jeopardizing its share of the national (as well as international) market, all the more so as Olivia's owner has established another rabbit slaughterhouse in China. With such a strong market share, it is highly unlikely that another company would construct a competing rabbit meat industry in Hungary in the near future. The most important requirement for the Hungarian experiment is to maintain the standards subscribed to by the industry and provide fresh, first-class rabbit meat to consumers in Italy, France and Switzerland. As far as the local situation is concerned, Olivia has achieved what no other company has thus far been able to manage: it has been successful in infiltrating the local economy with little harm (if any) and no environmental damage. Further, it imported a work ethic and value system that locals associate with European-ness and therefore with quality. All in all, the management is confident that the presence of Olivia is beneficial to the local economy and society. The owner, too, agrees. Here is an example of one worker from the shop floor:

I had been out of work for two to three years in the mid 1990s as the result of my company going bankrupt. When the possibility came for me to work at the Olivia [factory] I said to myself 'Why should I do this?' but then I realised either I pack up and take my entire family elsewhere or I take this job. I did and I have been working at Olivia since then. I am not sorry for that. I have a secure job now and I learned about the food industry.

The owner of the plant sees his presence as follows:

Olivia's profit is only one aspect of our business and a small one at that. The most important thing is the entire operation of the company in Hungary. In this the company is at the top, but the smallest segment below are the suppliers, and all the way at the bottom – these are the widest base – the farmers themselves. If we do our job right – that is if we can produce and sell our quality goods – than the company prospers and workers are happy. This is a solid pyramid built on local production.

It can be argued, as some farmers have done, that by relying on its own animals and feed plants Olivia no longer needs Hungarian farmers. There is clearly a danger in this, as nearly 70 per cent of the rabbits shipped to the slaughterhouse come from Olivia's own rabbitry. But the counter-argument is equally sound: only those farmers manage to stay in business who are ready to meet quality control and tight schedules by adopting to newer technologies of both breeding and production. Farmers who have been relying on five to ten does are clearly at a disadvantage, and may lose their importance in the future. In contrast, those who keep forty to fifty or more does can expect, if not a huge, then at least a small and steady profit at fairly regular intervals. From recent changes it is obvious that rabbit farming in Lajosmizse and its immediate environs has been enormously transformed. To engage in full-time rabbit farming, families today – like others in various kinds of animal husbandry – need substantial capital, resources and expertise in order to remain in business. As one farmer puts it: 'It is after all a capitalistic economy where profit makes the world go around. This business is not a joke, we are not working with Bugs Bunny here'.

Conclusions

What can be learned from the above with regard to understanding changes in one community in light of national and transnational political economic transformations? It is clear that since 1990 Lajosmizse as a rural community has undergone a massive change in that it was elevated to the status of a town in 1993, in the wake of which new industrial development completely revolutionized work, agriculture and the rural-urban divide. The latter, long the hallmark of agricultural and industrial studies (Buchowski 1997, Kearney 1996), seems to be gradually disappearing as new industries cater to different classes of workers, producers and consumers that no longer operate in isolation without regard to the outside world. This process is visible not only in Hungary but elsewhere too where distant and fairly isolated rural communities are being transformed and different aspects of the economy developed locally' (Procoli 2004). Industrialized minimally under state socialism, Lajosmizse was a small community where development came to a sudden halt in 1989/90. With the establishment of a foreign meat processing company, inhabitants quickly learned industrial production methods, labour relations and work ethics that had been previously unknown to them. What was originally an agricultural town suddenly became both industrialized and somewhat urbanized as the result of the plant opening in 1991, the former because it welcomed in a new industry to replace those that had been closed and dismantled, the latter because transportation, communication and management styles added new dimensions to outdated modes of industrial production and labour relations. The connection between Olivia and its Swiss parent company by internet was at first awe-inspiring; eventually, other businesses joined in. In this way, Olivia has produced healthy and manageable competition among local industries and businesses. It successfully created a modern rabbit farming industry from a backyard family farming system that was not standardised, and was wrought with difficulty from pressured market prices, irregular feed distribution and a constant fear of animal diseases capable of decimating a family's entire rabbit population.

Is there a success story embedded within the Olivia narrative? One might be tempted to respond both in the affirmative and the negative. It is clear that foreign plants and capital investment do offer fertile ground for capitalist development, if only of a particular kind (cf. Szelenyi 2008). Apart from the fact that such plants can provide an excellent laboratory for scholars to study economic change at the local level, through the story of Olivia introduced here, it can be seen that during the initial capitalist phase in the countryside the most successful companies were in one way or another all connected to the food industry. For example, Homesweets (Házisweets) is a successful middle-size confectionery establishment run entirely by a husband and wife team, both of whom left their teaching positions in order to start a family business. Another family operates a well-known pasta factory and others involved with plastic production plants (Gajdácsi Flakon, Mizse Plast and FOLPLAST) owned and managed by local families. Several families practise poultry farming (Mizse Táp, Mizse Csibe); one family from Budapest moved to Lajosmizse to establish perhaps one of the most technologically advanced chicken farms in Hungary with EU funding. Meanwhile, another company (Mizsevad) has specialized in pheasants, longhorn cattle (*szürkemarha*) and wild boar, both for the food industry and for hunting associations eager to obtain such animals for sport. In addition, several local farms manage successful geese breeding with tens of thousands of well-fed birds shipped to local and foreign markets.

This list of the new entrepreneurs is far from complete, as many families also raise cattle, pigs, goats, and turkeys, all somewhat traditional practices for Hungarian village communities yet currently undertaken with more up to date technologies and in compliance with EU specifications. There are also farms specializing in village tourism, or its offshoot farm tourism (*tanyaturizmus*) where horse breeding on a small scale is both a hobby and a manageable local enterprise. A few households carry out beekeeping, an interesting occupation with its own logic and unique way of life (bees are kept on a traditional seasonal travel cycle, following the blooming of flowers on a north-south axis throughout the country). These examples demonstrate that animal farming and food production of various kinds has become a specialized agro-industrial business in Lajosmizse and its environs (Kürti 2006).

These diverse and novel techniques of animal husbandry lead us to ponder the reasons why rabbit farming might indeed prove to be such an enterprising and interesting endeavour. Scholars studying local level societal transformation are accustomed to looking at primary groups, whether they be the family, village community or a special group. Individual lives are often viewed in binaries of homogeneity versus heterogeneity or value differences juxtaposed to other differences that frame subjects in a more or less coherent fashion for a special readership. In contrast, setting out to view a community that is at the same time neither and both of the above is indeed challenging.

First and foremost, through the farmers' way of life, and thanks to backyard animal husbandry, the case of Olivia straddles agriculture and the meat industry. It cannot be said to be, strictly speaking, agribusiness, yet it is fundamentally connected to the economic and ecological niche of the countryside. Nor is it merely another industrialized meat packaging business, like a poultry plant or fish canning factory, located far away from the source of the packaged meat. Olivia's case is unique because it is not a multinational company but a strictly Swiss firm presenting an approach unparalleled by multinational companies located in Eastern Europe. It is a company controlled and managed by a single individual who is responsible for overseeing the entirety of production. Olivia may thus be considered a 'multilocal' company, connecting various countries in an intricately woven web of economic interests: the Hungarian firm looks nothing like its counterpart in the Far East, but its management and the internationalization of its product connect Switzerland, Hungary and China in a global product-related network.

What makes Olivia worth analysing is that it has been built entirely from foreign capital and expertise on Hungarian soil through careful preliminary planning and market research. It has not only brought technological advancement and a new concept of food processing to Hungary but it has also successfully managed to influence industry, agriculture and labour relations. While failing at poultry farming, in its continual development in rabbit farming the company has also paid particular attention to environmental, health and safety regulations. When Hungarian agriculture experienced great insecurity and the fluctuation of prices and products, workers at the plant were spared. Similarly, when Hungarian farmers took to the streets to protest over quotas, prices and the cutting of governmental subsidies, rabbit farmers and workers were absent from the demonstrations. Seeing the grain-burning farmers at the beginning of 2004, one rabbit farmer commented: 'Well, this is something you will not see us doing. The only thing we could burn is rabbit feed but that is too expensive to go up in smoke. We feed our rabbits instead'.

In conclusion, it is important to note that rabbit farming is only one segment of the local economy and not a very large one at that. Yet, if there is something to be learned from Olivia's story, it is that there is a precedent for foreign intrusion into the local market with care and attention rather than exploitation or destruction. While the meat processing plant is a small-scale operation – small in terms of both initial investment and profit compared to global multinational giants such as Volkswagen, Audi, IBM, Sony, Suzuki, Tesco or Nestlé – it has implemented an environmentally conscious plant with little or no damage to an already fragile ecosystem. Two essential constituents were time and speed: Olivia appeared at the right moment with the right idea to start something new out of the ashes of the former state farming collectives. It produced a positive ripple effect on the local labour market by offering work to job seekers, assisting dwindling family farms and offering something new to farming techniques such as organic farming. Moreover, it carefully managed to touch upon local politics not by attempting to overhaul or influence by force but, on the contrary, by entering only into those areas where it was most needed (for example, by providing infrastructure in the shape of a cycle path).

With all the difficulties it experienced, the company has been conducting its business appropriately in the postsocialist milieu in Hungary, for it has managed to stay in (profitable) business for eighteen years. While other industries have closed and left behind a gold rush-like atmosphere of fast and easy profits, the company expanded substantially by building another plant in China and two breeding farms in the vicinity and completely rebuilt its central slaughterhouse in 2007–2008 in Lajosmizse. To put the question boldly: if this is not success, then what is? This seems especially apt in view of the fact that 2005–2007 were unusually difficult years for farmers both in Hungary and elsewhere in Europe.[47] Finally, the Swiss firm has introduced a new gene pool to Hungarian traditional rabbit farming together with novel techniques of hygiene, quality control and safety, as well as contributing to culinary culture. This last point is the single most important aspect Olivia's incomplete success in Hungary: citizens still prefer to eat pork rather than healthier rabbit meat! After all, not all capitalist development can be an unmitigated success story ...

Notes

1. Fieldwork in Lajosmizse has been carried out continuously since the early 1990s when I started my research into the town's and my own family's history (Kürti 2000a) and when the first companies were visited and farmers interviewed. I would like to thank here Olivia's owner and managers, all of whom have been extremely kind in offering assistance. In particular I am indebted to Meinrad A. Odermatt and Attila Kele. Local farmers who offered advice and valuable information on rabbit farming are numerous but I will keep the promise I made to them and not disclose their identities. Several, however, have consented, and therefore I can thank them publicly: Béla Bojtos and Ferenc Fakan, both proud rabbit farmers. I owe a particular debt to Catherine Portuges, András Szigeti and Béla Szabó for particularly helpful comments and editorial assistance.

2. Tőkés's remarks on the difference between transition and transformation are apt here: 'The difference between transition and transformation is not one of labels, but one of perspectives. From a political-institutional viewpoint there has been a by-now-completed transition between communism and democracy. From the perspective of economic and social change there has been, as part of Hungary's "long wave" of overall modernization, significant transformation from a traditional to a modern society' (1996: 439).

3. Hungarian ethnographers have theorized these issues in Cseri, Kósa and Bereczki (2000).

4. The Hungarian National Bank reported that the country's total foreign debt to have reached 30 to 35 per cent of GDP, or about 55.8 billion, by the end of 2005, a figure previously unsurpassed. However, a more realistic figure is attained by the net sum of 24.8 billion which includes 12.5 billion owed by the private sector and 12.3 billion owed by the state, see "Növekvő adósság, kisebb hiány," *Népszabadság*, 31 December 2005, p.11. At the same time, foreign investment has reached 2.8 billion Euro in 2005 (ibid).

5. According to figures released by the Hungarian National Bank, only cash and savings deposits were well over 2,000 billion Hungarian forints and the hard-currency accounts reached 560 billion forints in 1998; see *Népszabadság*, 24 August 1998, p.12. On the contrary, the debt of social security benefit (*társadalombiztosítás*) was inherited from the socialist era: in 1990 it was 23 billion forints, a figure increased tenfold to 230 billion by 1997; see *Magyar Nemzet*, 27 August 1998, p.2.

6. Exactly what took place may be convincingly analysed by viewing the data discussed in 1991 by western firms in KPMG et al. (1991).

7. Aside from privatizing former state companies, one of the most important steps in disassembling the monolithic state economy came in 1987/88 when the state banking business was split into independent commercial banks (such as the Magyar Hitel Bank, Kereskedelmi Bank and Postabank). This introduced Hungary to capital and financial services of the Western kind. Today, more than 300 financial institutions, including 42 bank chains, serve Hungarian and foreign customers; within Hungary proper, the Hungarian state National Bank for Savings (OTP), however, continues to be one of the largest and strongest of them all.

8. One such model case is that of the Bábolna agricultural state farm. It turned out, however, that by 1998 it had accumulated millions of dollars of debt that resulted in the dismissal of its chief executive; see 'Balsiker Bábolnán' [Misfortune in Bábolna], *Magyar Nemzet*, 15August 1998, p.13; and its recent 'recovery' in 'Bábolna: Magyar hagyomány és európai környezet' [Hungarian tradition and European environment in Bábolna], *Magyar Nemzet*, 14 June 2000, p.11–14.

9. Statistics are calculated from the *Magyar Statisztikai Zsebkönyv 1988* (Budapest: KSH, 1989: 28), and in more detail in Kereszty (1998: 307).

10. Between 1990 and 1996, Hungary received 683 million for various infrastructural projects. Between 1997 and 1999, an additional 325 million was received, giving an average of 100 million annually during the 1990s.

11. These data are provided by the official Magyar Turizmus Rt., 'A turizmus helyzete a világban és Magyarországon' [The state of tourism in the world and in Hungary], *Turista Magazin*, 109, 1998, p.7.

12. Before 1950, after the Communist Party came to power, the old county administrative system was abolished. Between 1877 and 1950, Lajosmizse belonged to Pest–Pilis–Solt–Kiskun county with Alsódabas being the district seat. The population of the town has not changed considerably since the beginning of the twentieth century, when it reached 11,000.

13. I have described the town's past in more detail in several studies: Benedek and Kürti (2004), and Kürti (2003a, 2003b, 2004a, 2004b). The *jász-jazygian* connection is due to a thirteenth century invasion by a Turkic-speaking Cumanian and an Osset-speaking Jasz tribal federation. The area settled by the former is called Kiskunság (Cumania Minor) and Nagykunság (Cumania Major) and the latter is referred to as Jászság (Jazygia) in Hungarian history. Historically Lajosmizse belongs to the northern periphery of the Kiskunság region. What further complicates the picture is that in 1745 farmers from Jászság received the town from the Habsburg court in the buy-back option known as the Redemption. Thus, Lajosmizse past includes the history of both that of Kiskunság and Jászság.

14. Here the religious denomination matters as the original settlers from Jászberény were almost one hundred per cent Catholic. According to an old saying, the preferred marriage rule was *guba gubához, suba subához* (literally 'short fur-coat to short one, long fur-coat to long one', meaning that like should marry like). This meant that Roman Catholics should marry Catholics with similar wealth. Protestants and Jewish settlers began to arrive in the late nineteenth century and soon established their parishes and they, too, followed this rule to some extent.

15. Not all families managed to remain successful in business. The Kláber winery and distillery went into receivership in the early 1920s and never managed to recover until it was nationalized in 1945. Similar stories can be written about other well-to-do farms such as the Tarnay and the Sebők. Others, such as the K. Kovács, Mizsey and Ricsováry, however, flourished and were prime examples of capitalistic entrepreneurial success stories.

16. It is worth mentioning here the fact that, for example, Hungarian farmers were only allowed to buy trucks and tractors after the 1980 ministerial decree but – and this characterizes socialist planning strategy as well – could not exceed the allocated quota for the use of heavy machinery.

17. Interestingly, from 1970 to 1989, the number of full-time agricultural workers decreased substantially from 1,245,000 to 887,000 (Central Statistical Office figures). Thus, the argument that the introduction of a capitalist market economy after 1990 began to undermine agriculture needs to be seen in this light.

18. This picture of local animal farming would not be complete without mentioning those families which breed homing pigeons, dogs or horses. These sidelines concern only a few families and are thus not a considerable source of economic wealth to those involved. Only men who own pigeons are part of a breeders' association. In the late 1990s, ostrich farming was introduced in Hungary but aside from a few bold attempts most ostrich farms went bankrupt in a few months.

19. To give an indication of how much has changed in a little more than 100 years, it will suffice to recall the staggering number of livestock herded in the town's pasture: during the 1850s, one shepherd was responsible for a flock of 1,746, while another herder looked after 1,596 beef cattle. According to a medical report from 1872, in the Lajosmizse area the town of Jászladány (which owned part of the pasture under discussion) had 514 oxen and 1,367 cows in addition to the 2,479 cattle owned by individual farmers. This large-scale pastoral economy was quite normal for that time in the area: the town of Jászapáti owned Kocsér, a grassland about 30 kilometres away from Lajosmizse, and used it solely as a grazing ground. In 1842, altogether 3,000 cattle, 1,219 horses, 7,000 sheep and 500 pigs were kept from March to December on the pastureland. Data for these nineteenth century figures are from Rusvay (2003: 223) and Kürti (2004b).

20. It is no secret that local governments in Hungary are embattled with business owners and entrepreneurs over taxes. In Lajosmizse alone, altogether 500 cases were registered in 2004 where the local government had to press charges and forcibly collect taxes: see the minutes of Lajosmizse Város Önkormányzatának Polgármesteri Hivatalának beszámolója a 2002–2004. években végzett munkájáról, jövpkép felvázolása 2006–ra, 7886/2005 (Report of the Mayor's Office of Lajosmizse's Government for 2002–2004, and prospects for 2006), p.26, Lajosmizse, Local Government Archives.

21. Another figure that adds a considerably new dimension to the complicated picture of prosperity versus poverty in Hungary has to do with the number of mobile (cell) phone subscriptions. According to a national figure released by the Central Statistical Office, the number of cell phone owners has risen above nine million while, at the same time, regular telephone line subscribers are decreasing considerably: see *Magyar Nemzet*, 12 December 2005, p.13. This means that almost ninety percent of Hungary's population now owns a mobile phone.

22. Data is ascertained from the actual number of building permits given out: see Lajosmizse Város Önkormányzatának Polgármesteri Hivatalának beszámolója a 2002–2004. években végzett munkájáról, jövőkép felvázolása 2006–ra, 7886/2005 (Report of the Mayor's Office of Lajosmizse's Government for 2002–2004, and prospects for 2006), p.24, Lajosmizse, Local Government Archives.

23. Figures are provided by the Lajosmizse Város Önkormányzatának Polgármesteri Hivatalának beszámolója a 2002–2004. években végzett munkájáról, jövőkép felvázolása 2006–ra, 7886/2005 (Report of the Mayor's Office of Lajosmizse's Government for 2002–2004, and prospects for 2006), Lajosmizse, Local Government Archives.

24. This process and its consequences are well documented in excellent studies, such as Kovács (1996).

25. In 2002, 378 people were allocated governmental medical subsidies; by the first half of 2005 this number grew to 795. Lajosmizse Város Önkormányzatának Polgármesteri Hivatalának beszámolója a 2002–2004. években végzett munkájáról, jövőkép felvázolása 2006–ra, 7886/2005 (Report of the Mayor's Office of Lajosmizse's Government for 2002–2004, and prospects for 2006), Lajosmizse, Local Government Archives. One reason for this rise has to do with an aging population across the country.

26. Novák (2004) describes similar development in Nagykőrös, a city about 30 kilometres away.

27. Receiving gifts is a special issue discussed also by Dunn (2004: 87–91) with regard to Polish industrial culture. Olivia's gift-rabbits did not last long: the management realized that most workers were not interested in the culinary aspect of rabbit meat and offered the meat to friends and relatives. By the early 2000s, this kind of gift-giving ceased to exist.

28. In addition, rabbits' feet are sold at souvenir shops as good-luck charms, but this practice lies beyond the scope of our concern in this study.

29. In Italy, peasants raised rabbits as a 'subversive strategy' against fascist agricultural policies (Krause 2005: 600–1).

30. See 'Meat rabbit farming – an introduction', by CSIRO Crusader Rabbit webpage www.csiro.au/crusader.

31. Some of the favoured pure breeds are the Californian, New Zealand White, Flemish Giant, but more often than not hybrids are utilized in commercial breeding programs. The new preferred hybrids are: Zika, Hyla, Hycole, Hyplus, Solaf. In Hungary, the so-called Pannon White has been at the centre of immense research interest at the Kaposvár University of Veterinary Medicine. Farmers also use the Pannon White but prefer cross-bred or composite lines because they can combine strength, fecundity and meat quality.

32. There is a slight distinction between animal rights groups who oppose rabbit fur production and those who are against the inhumane farming techniques of animals including rabbits. For their perspectives please visit their website http://www.veggies.org.uk and that of the Coalition to Abolish Fur Trade (CAFT) www.caft.org.uk.

33. It is important to emphasize the difference: until the late 1970s, live animals were favoured – obviously for health reasons and also because of the lack of adequate freezing trucks – but after that carcasses came into fashion. There is also a difference when the slaughterhouse sells the whole carcass (either with or without the head), or caters only to certain demands by offering the best parts of the animals to wholesalers (the back and the legs). Most of the carcasses and parts are actually not frozen but refrigerated, and only a small percentage is actually transported as 'frozen foods'.

34. See the Nyúl Terméktanács Alapszabály (Charter of the National Rabbit Production Board), voted by the general assembly of 1994, and the Szervezeti és Működési Szabályzat (Organizational and Structural Regulation) of 1996.

35. In general, rabbits are extremely sensitive and stress-prone animals. In particular, they can be extremely fragile during gestation and kindling when adequate ventilation and temperature is a must. Stories can often be heard from farmers that a certain infection or disease wiped out almost their entire farm. Pasteurella (a bacterial infection), coccidia (a parasite), myxomatosis and calicivirus (both viral infections) are the main causes of diseases and extremely feared by rabbit farmers who often disallow visitors to rabbitries by calling attention to diseases.

36. Rabbit prices initially were established not in the Hungarian national currency (forints, or HUF) but according to the exchange rate of the HUF to the Swiss franc. Farmers received different amounts, according to summer and winter exchange rates, the latter being more advantageous for them because of the higher prices. Olivia, however, soon realized this and began introducing similar pricing during the two seasons. In 2005, rabbit prices barely reached 1.5 per kilo.

37. The introduction of the German angora breed together with the government's scientific program of breeding rabbits in India also revolutionized rabbit farming in the mid 1980s (see Phull and Phull 2003).

38. The use of the local road by trucks and lorries only changed in 2002 when the socialist government bought most of the shares from the AKA company and became the major share holders of the M5 highway – and made it affordable to citizens by offering a highway toll pass at a reasonable price.

39. This too may be part of the contradictory aspects of a globalized economy (Gille and Ó'Riain, 2002: 280).

40. The word *táp* in Hungarian has negative connotations, referring to any kind of animal feed that is not natural. The expression *tápos csirke* ('artificially-fed chicken') is a slur used for an unhealthy animal (or human). However, it should be noted that among rabbit farmers there is a distinction between feed made of ground corn, sunflower and wheat, and regular feed which includes hormones and steroid-like substances to increase body size and weight. Rabbits fed with the latter are immediately spotted by ecologically minded farmers who remark about the fatness and enormous size of the animals.

41. Raised wire cages are preferred because they provide better ventilation (the built up ammonia can be harmful to both farmers and animals) and droppings are kept at a safe distance from the animals and easily disposed of. Cages for does giving birth and those with a litter are somewhat different from the regular cages for fattening rabbits which include anywhere between 4 and 6 animals per cage.

42. The term 'traditional farmer' has to do with the law defining agricultural activity performed locally on the basis of one's own plot, equipment or know-how. This was meant to secure certain state funds and assistance to local farmers involved with small-scale family farming.

43. The concept Hungaricum refers to those animals and products that are considered as special to Hungarian history, culture and agriculture and form part of a wider subsidized state program including production, marketing and promotion. A few of these are the wines of Tokaj and the Bull's Blood of Eger, goose livers, paprika, horses (Nonius, Gidran), dogs (vizsla, puli, pumi, komondor), and other less known products and animals. Some rabbit farmers claim that the Pannon White should also be considered a Hungaricum.

44. The collapse of Corona Poultry Company in Jászberény made headlines in national newspapers in 2003 when 151 workers were laid off. In addition, almost 2 million was left unpaid to poultry farmers in the central and northern part of the country. As the case ended up in court, news circulated about the unreliability and the loss in profits of poultry farming, a warning that came to full realization in 2005 with the deadly chicken epidemic that caused the near collapse of the entire industry. The case became headline in the national daily, *Népszabadság*, on 28 March and 17 July 2003.

45. Figures on actual production quotas are fairly difficult to establish thanks to the company's policy of not disclosing data considered 'company secrets'. However, certain figures are available from indirect sources such as www.biotechnology.hu, www.agronaplo.hu, and other market-related scholarly and governmental publications.

46. Solid rabbit manure is heated to 57–68 degree Celsius for three weeks and allowed to decompose for another month and a half before it can be utilised as high-mineral-content gardening soil.

47. See the interview with the president of the National Association of Hungarian Farmers' Groups (MAGOSZ), István Jakab, who criticized the government for failing to support agriculture adequately in 2005. In the same interview, state secretary for agriculture, András Pásztohy, argued that agriculture in Hungary is a developing and stable part of the economy. He underlined his comment by pointing to the export capacity of Hungarian agriculture in comparison to other countries who had recently joined the EU and which are mostly importers of agricultural goods. 'Lendület és visszaesés', *Népszabadság*, 31 December 2005, p.11. Like many issues in Hungary, these, too, seem to have a governmental and an oppositional faction.

References

Benedek, G. and L. Kürti. 2004. *Bene, Lajos és Mizse oklevelei, történeti dokumentumai 1385–1877.* Kecskemét: Katona József Múzeum.

Bleyer, F. and Zs. Szendrő. 1999. 'A nyúltenyésztés helyzete Magyarországon'. 11. Nyúltenyésztési Tudományos Nap, Kaposvári Egyetem, Állattudományi Kar, Kisállattenyésztési Tanszék, Kaposvár, www.kaposvar.pate.hu.

Buchowski, M. 1997. *Reluctant capitalists. Class and culture in a local community in western Poland.* Berlin: Centre Marc Bloch.

Bugaric, B. 2008. 'Populism, liberal democracy, and the rule of law in Central and Eastern Europe.' *Communist and Post-Communist Studies* 41/2: 191–203

Bunce, V. 1995. 'Should Transitologists Be Grounded?' *Slavic Review* 54(1): 111–27.

Cseri, M., L. Kósa T. Bereczki (eds). 2000. *Paraszti múlt és jelen az ezredfordulón.* Szentendre: Magyar Néprajzi Társaság.

Csikós-Nagy, B. 1987. *Szocializmus, piac, gazdaság.* Budapest: Kossuth.

Dunn, E. 2004. *Privatizing Poland: Baby Food, Big Business, and the Remaking of Labor.* Ithaca, NY: Cornell University Press.

FAO. 2001. 'FAO Recognizes the Increasingly Important Role of Rabbit Breeding: Global Rabbit Production Exceeds 1 million Tonnes'. Press Release 01/57, United Nations Food and Agriculture Organisation, Rome. 28 September 2001.

Ghodsee, K. 2005. *The Red Riviera: Gender, Tourism and Postsocialism on the Black Sea.* Durham, NC: Duke University Press.

Gille, Zs. and S.Ó Riain. 2002. 'Global ethnography'. *Annual Review of Sociology* 28: 271–95.

Glatz, F. 2005 'A vidék közhaszna', *Ezredforduló* 3: 3–31.

Halpern, L. and C. Wyplosz, (eds), 1998. *Hungary: Towards a Market Economy*. Cambridge: Cambridge University Press.

Hann, C. 1996. 'Land Tenure and Citizenship in Tázlár', in R. Abrahams (ed.) *After Socialism: Land Reform and Social Change in Eastern Europe*. Oxford: Berghahn Books, pp.23–50.

Harcsa, I. 1994. 'Magántermelés a mezőgazdaságban', *A falu* 9: 61–67.

Hollós, M. 2001. *Scandal in a Small Town. Understanding Modern Hungary through the Stories of Three Families*. Armonk, NY: M.E. Sharpe.

Kearney, M. 1996. *Reconceptualizing the Peasantry. Anthropology in Global Perspective*. Boulder, CO: Westview.

Kereszty, A. (ed.) 1998. *Tények könyve: Régiók* [Book of Facts: Regions]. Budapest: Greger-Belacroix.

Kim, I. and J. Zacek (eds). 1992. *Reform and Transformation in Communist Systems*. New York: Paragon House.

Kiss, A. 2004. 'A kiskunsági tanyák a XXI. század küszöbén', in C. Bálint and A. Kiss (eds), *Tanyai kaleidoszkóp*. Kecskemét: Alföldi Tudományos Intézet, pp.19–63.

Kling, J. 2004. 'A Magyarországi nyúlágazat helyzete, az EU csatlakozás várható hatásai és új kihívásai. 15. Nyúltenyésztési Tudományos Nap, Kaposvári Egyetem, Állattudományi Kar, Kisállattenyésztési Tanszék, Kaposvár, www.kaposvar.pate.hu.

Kovách, I. 1985. 'A társadalom rétegződése és a mezőgazdasági kistermelés', in A. Bőhm (ed.) *Munka, gazdaság, társadalom*. Budapest: Magyar Szociológiai Társaság, pp.123–46.

Kovács, K. 1996. 'The Transition in Hungarian Agriculture 1990–1993: General Tendencies, Background Factors and the Case of the "Golden Age"', in R. Abrahams (ed.) *After Socialism: Land Reform and Social Change in Eastern Europe*. Oxford: Berghahn Books, pp.51–84.

KPMG et al. (eds). 1991. *Doing Business in Hungary: CBI Initiative Eastern Europe*. London: Kogan Page.

Krause, E. 2005. 'Encounters with the "Peasant": Memory Work, Masculinity, and Low Fertility in Italy', *American Ethnologist* 32(4): 593–617.

KSH. 1983. *Magyar Statisztikai Zsebkönyv*. Budapest: Központi Statisztikai Hivatal.

———— 1989. *Magyar Statisztikai Zsebkönyv*. Budapest: Központi Statisztikai Hivatal.

Kürti, L. 2000a. 'The Socialist Circus: Secrets, Lies, and Autobiographical Family Narratives', in R. Breckner, D. Kalekin-Fishman and I. Miethe (eds), *Biographies and the Division of Europe: Experience, Action, and Change on the 'Eastern Side'*. Opladen: Leske–Budrich, pp.283–302.

———— 2000b. 'A puszta felfedezésétől a puszta eladásáig: Az alföldi-tanyasi turizmus és az esszencializmus problémája', in F. Zoltán and S. Zsolt (eds), *Turizmus és kommunikáció*, Budapest: Néprajzi Múzeum, pp.112–28.

———— 2001. *The Remote Borderland: Transylvania in the Hungarian Imagination*. Albany: State University of New York Press.

———— 2002. *Youth and the State in Hungary: Capitalism, Communism and Class*. London: Pluto Press.

———— 2003a. 'Határperek és határkonfliktusok Lajos, Mizse és Bene történelmében', *Évkönyv Bács-Kiskun Megye Múltjából* 18: 249–64.

———— 2003b. 'Jászberény csárdái. Adatok a pusztai csárdák 18. századi történetéhez', *Zounuk* 18: 49–94.

_____ 2004a. 'A Kiskunság és a Felső-Kiskunság: betelepülés, tájtörténet, és regionalizmus', in D. Bárth and J. Laczkó (eds). *Halmok és havasok.* *Tanulmányok a hatvan esztendős Bárth János tiszteletére,* Kecskemét: Bács-Kiskun Megyei Önkormányzat Múzeumi Szervezete, pp.153–80.

_____ 2004b 'A jászok pusztai állattartása a Felső-Kiskunságban a 18–19 században', *Zounuk* 19: 47–92.

_____ 2006. *Ladánybenei évszázadok.* Ladánybene: Községi Önkormányzat.

Lampland, M. 2002. 'The Advantages of Being Collectivized: Cooperative Farm Managers in the Postsocialist Economy', in C. Hann (ed.) *Postsocialism.* London: Routledge, pp.31–56.

Lukefahr, S. and P. Cheeke. 1991. 'Rabbit Project Development Strategies in Subsistence Farming Systems', *World Animal Review,* 68(3): 60–70.

Magdelaine, P. 2003. 'Economie et avenir des filieres avicoles et cunicoles.' INRA Prod. Anim. vol. 15. no. 5: 349–56.

Müller, B. 2007. *Disenchantment with market economics. East Germans and Western capitalism.* New York – Oxford: Berghahn Books.

Nafus, D. 2006. 'Post-socialism and Notions of Context in St Petersburg', *Journal of the Royal Anthropological Institute* 12(4): 607–24.

Novák, F.L. 2004. 'Nagykőrös tanyavilága – közelről', in G. Pócs (ed.) *Falvak, földek, földművesek,* Budapest: Agroinform, pp.129–36.

Ortiz, S. 2002. 'Laboring in the Factories and in the Fields', *Annual Review of Anthropology* 31: 395–417.

Phull, A. and R. Phull. 2003. *Rabbit Farming and Its Economics.* Lucknow: International Book.

Procoli, A. (ed.) 2004. *Workers and Narratives of Survival in Europe.* Albany: State University of New York Press.

Romány, P. 2005. 'Földbirtok-politika és földtulajdon Magyarországon', *Magyar Tudomány* 1: 94–102.

Rusvay, L. 2003. *Jászapáti története.* Jászapáti: Jászapátiak Baráti Egyesülete.

Sárkány, M. 2005. 'Restudy of Varsány. Entrepreneurs and Property in Rural Hungary after 1989', in P. Skalnik (ed.) *Anthropology of Europe: Teaching and Research.* Prague: Set-out, pp.143–52.

Schöpflin, G. 1995. 'Post-communism: A Profile', *Javnost* 2(1): 63–74.

Seleny, A. 2006. *The Political Economy of State–Society Relations in Hungary and Poland.* Cambridge: Cambridge University Press.

Stark, D. and L. Bruszt. 1998. *Postsocialist Pathways: Transforming Politics and Property in East Central Europe.* Cambridge: Cambridge University Press.

Szelenyi, I., 2008. 'Making capitalism withouth capitalists: Revisited." International Political Anthropology vol. 1. no. 1: 139–148.

Tőkés, R. 1996. *Hungary's Negotiated Revolution: Economic Reform, Social Change and Political Succession.* Cambridge: Cambridge University Press.

Vasary, I. 1995. 'Labyrinths of Freedom: An Agricultural Community in Post-socialist Hungary', in D. Kideckel (ed.) *East European Communities: The Struggle for Balance in Turbulent Times,* Boulder, CO: Westview, pp.9–24.

Verdery, K. 1991. 'Theorizing Socialism: A Prologue to the "Transition"', *American Ethnologist* 18(3): 419–39.

Virág, G. 1996. 'A nyúlhústermelés jelenlegi helyzete', *Kistermelők Lapja* vol. 11. p. 20.

Wolfe, T. 2000. 'The Anthropology of Eastern Europe', *Annual Review of Anthropology* 29: 195–241.

Chapter 8

Punk Anthropology: From a Study of a Local Slovene Alternative Rock Scene towards Partisan Scholarship

Rajko Muršič

It is a festival which has already been held for ten years by KUD Zid na meji [The Wall at the Border Cultural Association]. For the last four years the festival has been organized in Trate, a place on the (non)border with Austria. In the place that has become, together with the group CZD – Centre for Dehumanization, a legend of Slovene rock creativity. What was going on in the youth club (in Trate), in connection with the group CZD, has been described in many monographs. Let's list the most important: *Trate of Your and Our Youth, CZD – Ethnological Description of the Rock Group, CZD –I Saw Them In a Dream*. Their author is Dr Rajko Muršič. The festival will be held in the place with the highest number of deserted historical buildings per capita in Slovenia. The entrance hall of one of the most beautifully preserved castles, which until recently housed the Hrastovec-Trate Psychiatric Institution, will be the site of this year's Mladi na meji [Youth on the Border] festival. Trate is the historical epicentre of the rock movement in north-eastern Slovenia. Back in 1978, what is nowadays recognized in Slovenia as the north-eastern Slovenian underground rock scene was started there.

—From the announcement of the Mladi na meji ['Youth on the Border'] festival, 2005, sent by mail to the press.

There are some remarkable similarities in the production, reproduction and star-system between popular culture, especially popular music, and academia. If the criteria of success in popular music are record sales, attendance at concerts and the broadcasting and mentioning of hits in the media and daily life, the criteria of success in academia are monograph sales, attendance at lectures and quotations from papers. When we use the famous Web of Science (SSCI or A&HCI), we may see the similarities between music charts and lists of quotations or between inventories of recordings and bibliographies. Moreover, the vast majority of academic and popular music products are produced in the West. More precisely: both are typically made and released or published in English-speaking countries.

With some distant reference to the old communist slogan of 'cultural imperialism' (even if wrapped in the cloth of post-modernism) and more recent discussions of cunning imperial reason (Bourdieu and Wacquant 1999), I will try to use results of my studies of the local alternative musical scene in north-east Slovenia to critically examine my own position as an experimental musician and a peripheral scholar. Being only a part of my scholarly interests, the local alternative music scene in the northern Slovenske gorice region initially attracted me with its music and a commitment to punk rock among the founding members of the group CZD (Centre for Dehumanisation). At the beginning, in the late seventies and eighties, their position was an alternative one. In a way, it has remained alternative ever since, although, at least musically speaking, CZD are doing many things which are far from alternative. My own study of the group and the local scene was initially an attempt to pay tribute to them. Despite the fact that the term 'alternative' nowadays has no deeper meaning attached to it, I will try to employ it, not only metaphorically, in order to discuss my own scholarly position in the light of recently expressed criticisms of what we can describe as 'epistemological imperialism' in 'mainstream' anthropology.

Therefore, whatever I will say about punk rock may – and should – be applied (not only metaphorically, but in my case perhaps metonymically) to anthropology. Concerning the predominant principle of pop discourse in both, 'punk anthropology' might become a true alternative to 'mainstream anthropology'. If this volume is a contribution to the search for alternatives from Central and Eastern Europe, I can only hope that ethnography of 'the alternative' in Slovenia might provide some different views on overall European anthropology.

Back in 1993, a founding member of the punk band CZD (Center za dehumanizacijo), Dušan Hedl, asked me to write a short portrait of the group for a record that was going to be released on their tenth anniversary a year later. I did it, but it eventually grew to the size of a monograph (Muršič 1995a). Ever since then, popular music has been my predominant research topic in cultural anthropology. Although I can no longer afford to follow it as much as I used to (especially its non-commercial, experimental and alternative streams), I still try to keep abreast of it as much as possible. Perhaps the main reason for this inclination is that during the socialist era popular music was never 'just music'. At least for some people I socialized with during the late 1970s and early 1980s, it was a much-desired island of freedom and creativity (see Cutler 1985; Opekar 1994; Muršič 1995a; Szemere 2001; Steinholt 2004; cf. Ramet 1994). And, at least in its oppositional, experimental, underground and alternative forms, it has remained so ever since.

Things changed dramatically with the fall of socialism, but despite the fact that underground and alternative bands in Central and Eastern Europe were deeply affected by the overall political and social change with the definitive triumph of market economy, and in many ways lost their appeal or even became marginalized (see, e.g., Szemere 2001; Steinholt 2004), structurally speaking their aesthetic position has not changed much. Although there was no MTV in the 1970s, there were products of pop culture present – or at least desired and consumed – everywhere in Western Europe and to some extent even in the Soviet bloc countries, from disco music to Hollywood 'happy-ending' films, fashion, cars and glitter. No matter if it was consumed in medicinal doses, the fruits of popular culture were consumed in the relatively autarchic socialist countries. In the early 1990s this medicine turned into a feast. The idea that Eastern European rock music was inherently political, pregnant with anti-totalitarian messages (cf. Ramet 1994) was a misconception for outsiders who did not experience the very basic need to party in a 'totalitarian' environment (see, e.g., Luković 1989; Tomc 1989; Garofalo 1992; Žikić 1999; Mirković 2004; Steinholt 2004: Barber-Kersovan 2005). What made rock music so special was its confrontation with the aesthetically dominant state-approved, commercial, mainstream pop music.[1] This delineation survived socialism to a certain extent.

The collapse of socialism had many different consequences. Therefore, the ambiguous term postsocialism carries many different meanings. Among them are wars in former Yugoslavia, riots and chaos in Romania and Albania, bloodshed in Lithuania, war between Armenia and Azerbaijan, war in Chechnya, conflicts in Macedonia and – as the part of the same collapse of socialism – the invisible wars in Africa as well as, in a way and to some extent, the wars in Afghanistan and Iraq (socialist parties were in power in both countries). On the other hand, we are inclined to believe that postsocialism brought new perspectives to the issues of human rights and freedoms. However, their limitations were soon exposed with the destruction of the welfare state and with the privatization and commercialization of the media. If we understand postsocialism as the transformation that occurred after the Velvet Revolution, postsocialism should predominately denote privatization, denationalization and new forms of subjugation caused by the final and eternal victory of liberal capitalism and consumerism.

Limiting my enquiry into postsocialist transformation to the situation in former Yugoslavia, I will use the example of the group CZD to show that for the common people it was more or less a case of falling out of the frying pan into the fire. For a couple of years, Yugoslav rock disappeared, with no performances or media coverage. Because of the violent dissolution of Yugoslavia, mainstream international rock groups were too afraid to enter Slovenia, and for a while the country experienced complete isolation. The wars in former Yugoslavia dramatically affected people's lives, including my own. It seemed that everything would have to be started again from scratch. The group CZD lost their rehearsal space in Sladki vrh and their concert venue in Trate. The situation was very complex. Nobody knew for sure what the future would bring.

Social Amnesia and Individual Habitus

To cope with the complexity of uncertain transformation from 'the end of socialism' to 'not quite capitalism', I will apply two concepts in trying to describe the manifold experience of individual continuity and social ruptures in time on the one hand, as well as social continuity and individual ruptures on the other. The first usable concept is the notion of 'social amnesia', willingly forgotten history and its surrogates, as applied to psychoanalysis and psychology by Russell Jacoby (1981). The second concept is the well-known notion of habitus as developed in the works of Pierre Bourdieu (1977, 2002).

Starting with the latter, it can be seen that drastic historical shifts in politics, economy and technology can leave some very stubborn habits of daily life virtually untouched. But younger people somehow anticipate social reality, although they are not yet fully socially integrated and are – typically – without clear notions of the recent past. They are pushed to live in the inherited present without knowing the recent past.[2] Younger people, for example, born at the time of the fall of socialism, do not have the slightest idea about it. Today's teenagers do not learn much about it in school and information about the socialist past in the media is far from reliable. However, they can easily behave as if they had socialism 'in their veins'. It is a matter of habitus, the system of orchestrated improvisations without a director, a system of dispositions which can be transferred only through practice without the application of any rationalized knowledge (Bourdieu 1977: 72–95).

There seems to be a paradox here. We are at the same time facing a historical memory embedded in 'flesh and blood', practical knowledge in the form of habitus – a structured structure which is at the same time a structuring structure – and social amnesia, a loss of knowledge and memory with superficial (pop) surrogates. Both form the essential condition for any successful restructuring of society. The result is ideological double talk which is an unassailable part of the 'transition': no matter what the new democratic authorities conceive in implementing structural reforms, it is never successful, because the remains of socialism are too strong. On the other hand, with the fall of socialism, the political situation in the West changed as well. The European left is still completely disoriented because it doesn't have anything better to offer than decayed socialism. Neoliberalism and the liberal democratic 'end of history' (Fukuyama 1992) are imposed as the sole and eternal alternatives.

Paradoxically, deep historical changes and ruptures in social reality may even be seen as preconditions for the stability and persistence of habitus in periods of the *longue durée*. It is this which received the paradoxical name 'New Europe' after the Vilnius declaration, when Central and Eastern European members of the EU gave support to American intervention in Iraq. Was this 'New Europe' an invention or was it created with former socialist subjugation to another centre?

Popular music might offer instructive examples in answering such questions. During the last decade, Central and Eastern European pop music became more and more successful, creating a kind of new 'Euro pop'. Modernized Central and Eastern European pop has become very attractive and has proved successful at the benign or degenerated Eurovision Song Contest. On the other hand, in all former socialist countries, domestic popular music production has come under control of multinational record companies and their national or regional branches. Although it seemed that alternative music would be forced either to commercialize or disappear (see, e.g., Szemere 2001), it has survived in the margins.

There was no essential difference between the alternative music circuits in former socialist and capitalist countries. The only difference was perhaps the political inclinations of the actors, being more leftist in the West (e.g., anarchist punk, Chris Cutler and Recommended Records or Robert Wyatt) and apolitical, liberal or even conservative in the East (e.g., The Plastic People of the Universe in Czechoslovakia or Akvarium in the Soviet Union). Nowadays there is no essential difference between these scenes. Although in decline, they still express counter-cultural inclinations, especially long-lasting punk and hardcore, metal, noise and improvised scenes.

The essential stance of followers of Minor Threat (later Fugazi) and Dischord Records in Washington DC, U.S.A., or among those of Crass and, later, Chumbawumba in Great Britain in the 1980s, was built around musical creativity that comprised an entire attitude towards living. It comprised the so-called straight edge attitude (no meat, no drugs, and no violence) and anarchist criticism of the dominant society. A similar attitude and experience was later incorporated into new movements and dance party scenes, especially in Great Britain (McKay 1998) and other English-speaking countries (on Australia, see St John 2001). This perspective and attitude 'from the bottom' is a common social experience of modernity and cannot be dependent on the political distinction between totalitarianism and democracy, not only considering the similarities in responses to rightist totalitarianism (e.g., in Argentinean *Rock Nacional*; see Vila 1992) or the responses of the Czech underground to leftist totalitarianism (see Opekar 1994). In general, subjugated people use music as a response to oppression (Lipsitz 1994; Keil and Feld 1994). In the case of the postsocialist ruptures in Central and Eastern Europe, it may seem that things became worse for the alternative or underground music scene. You may get similar complaints from the members of the once admired and later forgotten underground groups of Central and Eastern European countries (Opekar 1994; Szemere 2001; Steinholt 2004). However, their postsocialist marginal social position does not affect their integral art which is still embedded in their alternative credo.

I will present this double history of ruptures and permanent social change in the 'dominant society' as opposed to the unchanging sphere of creativity within the fluid living world with some examples from the history of the group CZD since 1984 and its predecessors since 1978. The group itself – and the artistic and local cultural scene that emerged around it – is not deliberately alternative. It has been perceived as such since their very beginning by the (mainly alternative) media and by the audience. The members of the group adopted an alternative stance in their early years and produced some of their long-lasting peaces of music in 1985 and 1986. Only three years later the group 'betrayed' its alternative credo with the release of its first EP *Izdaja* (a pun meaning both 'edition' and 'betrayal') for the Slovene Socialist Youth Association at a time when the organization took the decision to organize itself as a party. The Association was later transformed into the Liberal Democratic Party, which ruled Slovenia for almost twelve years. The video for *Izdaja* was played on national TV. But despite their constant efforts, CZD have failed to enter Slovenian mainstream popular music. On the contrary: the group is still one of the most important hubs of alternative culture in Slovenia, attracting a new and very young audience.

Let me mention a few of the more recent achievements of the group. The video for the song 'Nimam dnara' ('I'm Broke') reached the top of the national television chart *Video spotnice* in February/March 2004, and stayed there for a couple of weeks. In September 2004, they played at the European punk 'conference' in Kassel, Germany. In May 2003 the group was invited to play at the opening ceremony in Graz during its tenure as the European City Of Culture. In 2006 and 2007 they were touring again in Germany and Austria. Two members of the bend have established the a capella group Punkapella with two singers from New York, and were planning to release a CD.[3] Sadly to add, in 2008 the group was almost non existent: the drummer left the band in December 2007. Since then, the remaining members of the band had some acoustic shows, but at my knowledge they have not performed in public for more than half a year.

I have written about CZD and the local punk scene in the Slovenske gorice region extensively in both Slovene (Muršič 1995a, 2000a; CZD & Muršič 1999) and English (Muršič 1995b, 1995c, 1998, 1999, 2000b, 2003). CZD formed in 1984, though the founding members of the group had started to play punk rock in the villages of Slovenske gorice back in 1978, forming Masakr (Massacre) and Butli (The Doodles) in 1979 and 1980, and Džumbus (The Jumble) in 1982. In 1979 the later initial members of CZD participated in the establishment of a local youth and rock club in Trate which became famous in Slovenia in the mid 1980s. They used the club as a rehearsal space and as a concert venue.

By the late 1980s CZD had become one of the most important Slovene punk and underground bands. Combining a rude punk rock sound with experimental noise, industrial and electronic sounds, the group received an award in 1987 as one of the most promising new rock groups in Slovenia. After releasing two audio cassettes, they released their first EP *Izdaja* in 1989. A year later they moved to the city of Maribor, but soon lost their rehearsal space in a bomb shelter when the armed conflicts started that marked the beginning of Slovenia's secession from Yugoslavia. In 1991 they recorded an anti-war song, 'Hanging Paradise', for which they made a video. Two years later, the group lost another rehearsal space in another public venue, the former cinema hall in Sladki vrh. The club in Trate was finally lost in 1994 when the building was returned to its pre-Second World War owner; fourteen years later, however, the building is still deserted!

The only solution the lead singer of the group Dušan Hedl saw to the problem was to buy a small property at the edge of the village of Ceršak, and in 1996 they solved their rehearsal space problems forever. On a very small scale, with very small investment, they gradually rebuilt the house and created a rehearsal space and small concert venue, opened a club and an exhibition gallery, equipped a recording studio, and built an office for the newly established private non-profit organization Subkulturni azil (Subcultural Asylum) and the cultural association Zid na meji (The Wall at the Border). This private development soon became one of the most vivid epicentres of local culture.

Yugoslav self-management socialism allowed small-scale private and public initiatives. Therefore, the first independent record was released in 1973 and some small semi-private record labels were established in the 1980s. The group CZD established their independent record label, Front Rock, in 1986, while two years later the publishing house Frontier was formed, both under the official framework of the local independently established youth organization. After 1991, the transformation of these organizations was rather easy, being incorporated into Subkulturni azil. With the organization of the Mladi na meji (Youth on the Border) festival and the internationally significant punk rock event No Border Jam, the new centre of alternative culture could be seen to have successfully adapted the former local alternative music scene to the new capitalist reality. Despite the fact that Subkulturni azil is mostly without substantial funds, the units of the organization are extremely productive. Meanwhile, some younger people have become active in the scene and it seems they will push it further and help it survive current changes.

After 1991, when socialist rule ended and new independent states were established in the ruins of the former Yugoslav federation, we were all confronted with dramatic historical changes and shifts. With the 'New Constitution' of 1974, which effectively made the federation more similar to a confederation, Yugoslavia became a decentralized state, and its own path to socialism had gradually introduced many elements of a market economy. Its borders were open and people travelled abroad. In popular music, massive production of commercial records developed, located in the republican centres. However, despite the official non-existence of censorship, the country was effectively ruled by the Communist Party, which suppressed any threats to socialism.

During the 1980s, various new social movements appeared and developed in Slovenia, ranging from pacifist to anti-homophobic, and including open political struggles for the freedom of speech, the abolition of the death penalty, and campaigns against the so-called verbal abuse code. By and large, these activities stemmed from the trial of an alleged punk rock group called Četrti Rajh (The Fourth Reich). In late 1981, four members of the group were accused of 'Nazi' propaganda, and the 'Nazi punk affair' mobilized civil society. The determined reaction of the leading punk activists in mobilization of the scene and concerned intellectuals was successful. They reacted with public appeals, letters to newspapers, public discussions, etc. If they were not raised their voice in public, the scene would be too weak to survive. We can read the following claim by the leading conservative Slovene intellectual, philosopher Tine Hribar, from the present-day perspective:

> At the end of 1977, Slovene intellectuals observed the emergence of Pankrti [the first Slovene punk band] from a distance. Especially those who now consider themselves as intelligentsia have never shortened their view from a distance. However, some dissidents ... knew even then, and with present knowledge I can only confirm it, that Pankrti with their first blows left the door open to the space of a new liberty. (Hribar 2002: 6, author's translation).

The 'critical mass' of punk (Žižek 2004: 39) nudged Yugoslav society into carrying out reforms which bore fruits in late 1988 and early 1989 with the decision to gradually introduce political pluralism and through the establishment of new political parties in the Socialist Republic of Slovenia. The elections in 1990 brought the anti-communist coalition Demos to power. After the short armed conflict with the Yugoslav People's Army in June/July 1991, everything in Slovenia changed.

The most important shift for popular music in Slovenia was a sudden break with the very dynamic popular music scene in former Yugoslavia, especially in Croatia, Bosnia-Hercegovina and Serbia. Established connections were suddenly broken and bands could no longer tour around the whole of Yugoslavia. For a couple of months – some of theme even for years – groups from former Yugoslavia did not perform in Slovenia. With the exception of groups from northern Croatia, the exchange of music was almost impossible until the end of the wars in Croatia and Bosnia-Hercegovina in 1996. Even then it took another few years to re-establish some connections, and to this day things are not the same as before 1991. Only in the past few years have the youth from former Yugoslav republics begun to attend some festivals or events, perhaps the most important of which is the internationally well-known Exit festival in Novi Sad (see Bizjak et al. 2005).

It is important to stress that since the late 1950s, when the authorities recognized jazz and pop as an important part of popular entertainment,

Yugoslav popular music production – in contrast to other former socialist countries – has been a part of commercial (free market) production. It was indeed a radical shift, because in the 1940s jazz was denounced as corrupt capitalist music and was suppressed, especially in its more attractive modern dance forms like boogie-woogie (see Tomc 1989). In the 1960s, the Yugoslav music industry started to blossom. Record companies were established in the republican capitals and popular music achieved very high sales: the biggest hit records sold several hundred thousand copies, which was a remarkable level for a country with a population of around 20 million (see Luković 1989).

In the 1970s rock music became an integral part of mainstream culture in Yugoslavia, especially with the famously successful band Bijelo Dugme, which sold several hundred thousand copies of its first three albums. In the late 1970s, strong local punk scenes appeared and developed in Ljubljana, Pula, Rijeka and Zagreb, and soon afterwards in Belgrade and Sarajevo. However, in Slovenia punk became much more than merely music: it became a way of expressing something 'alternative', an escape from (mild) totalitarianism and a social scene which helped in the development of a powerful (and vocal) civil society. There is agreement among various Slovenian intellectuals about the importance of punk in the creation of the socialist political opposition and the development of civil society, moves which contributed to to the democratization processes of the 1980s (see, e.g., Mastnak 1994; Tomc 1994; Hribar 2002; Žižek 2004; cf. Carmichael and Gow 2001), but there is not much agreement on what happened afterwards. What is important is that punks had established their own scene exactly along the boundary which sharply separated their own and the previous generations' musical preferences. But it was not only music that was at stake. It was the public sphere that they were entering, albeit with a radical difference from mainstream society. They were not confronting 'totalitarian' socialism per se, but the 'old guard', without offering any alternative political programme, except to reject state power and to advocate human rights. The rupture in symbolic expression and comprehension from the mainstream seemed too radical to disappear even with the establishement of the new, 'democratic' political regime. Did it essentially change after the fall of the socialist regime? Yes and no. I will present some examples of the permanent confrontation between – to adopt Victor Turner's (1974) terms – the alternative 'anti-structure' (not only punk) and 'structure' during the postsocialist period and try to make some more general comments on the present-day situation.

Alternatives in the Period of Privatization, Denationalization and Neoliberal Capitalism

It is true that consumerism and the commercialization of daily life were among the first results of the postsocialist transition. However, consumerism was nothing new: it had already arrived in former Yugoslavia in the 1960s.

A lot of ink was spilled in analysing and criticizing consumerism during the socialist period. The loss of the organized youth movement was more drastic. The socialist youth organization had established a network of local youth clubs and centres, but suddenly, after 1991, they came under threat. Many of these disappeared, though many new ones were established under the auspices of the newly-established Urad za mladino (Youth Office) as well, supported by local branches of the national student organisation. Contrary to expectations, after eighteen years there are at least as many operating youth cultural centres as before 1991, although only a few of them have been successful in getting permanent financial support for their activities. Among them are the two largest youth cultural centres in Slovenia, one in Koper and another in Maribor.

The centre in Koper is perhaps the most radical and deserves more attention. Since the late 1980s, the centre has been led by the legendary Slovenian singer Marko Brecelj. He started his music career singing gospel in a high school quartet in the late 1960s. In 1974/75 he made perhaps the single most important recording in Slovenian popular music, the album *Cocktail*, a collection of brilliant songs, recorded with acoustic guitar and later arranged with the accompaniment of a big band. Subsequently, he joined the most important Slovene (and Yugoslav) underground rock group, Buldožer (Bulldozer), with which he made three records. Since 1980, when he left the group, he has radicalized his music and written quite a few more excellent songs. He still performs in alternative venues. Brecelj is something of an exception by making a career transition from mainstream (*Cocktail* was a huge hit and played extensively on national radio) via underground rock to alternative. Nowadays, in his late fifties, he organizes concerts of the most interesting and innovative punk, heavy metal and experimental groups from Slovenia and abroad.[4] Though usually presented in the media as a political clown, he is among the few individuals over 50 in Slovenia who didn't make any compromise with mainstream and are still fighting for 'liberated territories', as he describes 'his' Youth Cultural Centre in Koper and other clubs and centres around Slovenia, including squats. A couple of year ago he launched a campaign (*Dodogovor*, i.e. 'to-agreement') to unite various NGOs in negotiations with the state and governmental agencies to achieve financial stability and assure programme independence from the local authorities and the market economy.[5] Moreover, he was responsible for a very provocative campaign in Koper, silencing the church bells as a symbolic protest against the 'pollution' of the public sphere by the aggressive Catholic Church under the leadership of Slovenian former Archbishop Franc Rode.

Similar clubs, local organisations, pubs and venues are emerging, disappearing and re-emerging all around Slovenia, for example in Tolmin, Metlika, Krško, Brežice, Celje, Murska Sobota, Ormož, Škofja Loka, to name but a few. Their development after 1991 was unpredictably successful. Some venues were occupied by squatters and became the most vivid sites of alternative cultural activity in Slovenia. These include Metelkova mesto (Metelkova City) in Ljubljana, Pekarna (The Bakery) in Maribor, Stari bazen (The Old Swimming Pool) in Kranj, houses in Železniki (which were demolished by unknown hands), and Bajta (The Cottage) near Trate (which was actually squatted with the permission of the owner).

These places and venues are a continuation of what was going on in the 1970s and 1980s (see Bibič 2003). At the same time they are trying to transcend the limitations of 'the alternative' with organization of classical concerts, plays, films and video productions, etc. Metelkova City is extremely successful in these activities, although it is at the same time under constant threat of being demolished or closed by the government. The Metelkova story begins in 1991, when some former Yugoslav People's Army barracks were emptied. As the Slovenian Army did not want to use barracks in the centres of towns anymore, they remained empty. For quite a long time it was not clear whether they would become the property of the Ministry of Defence or local municipalities. Meanwhile, investors started to design projects for attractive new commercial housing developments. In 1992 the so-called Mreža za Metelkovo (Metelkova Network) was established, claiming the need to occupy the barracks on Metelkova Street for its activities. At first it seemed that the city authorities would allow it. However, before an agreement was reached, in late 1993, an unknown investor started to demolish the buildings. The reaction of younger activists from the Network – one of the leaders was my late colleague Borut Brumen – was immediate: during the night they occupied the place and saved what was left to preserve. Since then, they have successfully renovated and rebuilt some parts of the complex. There are several small concert venues (Gala Hala, Channel Zero, Gromki, Menza) plus some art galleries and studios. In the complex, the largest building of the former prison was reconstructed, becoming a popular youth hostel called Celica (The Cell). Furthermore, with the help of international volunteers, the people in Metelkova have raised some new buildings, among which is the Mala šola (The Small School). Being considered an illegally built structure, it was meant to be demolished in June 2005. The reaction of the people from Metelkova and the concerned public was very strong, and they were successful in delaying the demolition ordered by the inspectors from the Ministry of the Environment and Spatial Planning. For a couple of months, a permanent cultural festival has been held at Mala šola, but it was, finally destroyed. However, its mission survived in other occupied places.[6] As a matter of fact, the left-wing city government in a way supports Metelkova City, and they made possible continued electricity and water supplies. Although the legal status of the complex is still at issue, it seems that the complex may be declared a work of art, which in part it is.

Metelkova City is definitely one of the most important cultural centres in Slovenia, not only regarding 'alternative' culture. It is an epicentre of many different activities, from concerts to art exhibitions, theatre productions, public lectures, conferences and other activities. It is a definite continuation of what was happening on the alternative scene during the socialist period. But it is under permanent threat from the authorities and may be closed any day, especially if the rightist authorities decide to put an end to this miracle.

Seen from below, from the position of 'alternative' culture, it seems that nothing essentially new or different has occurred. Under socialism you could (mis)use the socialist infrastructure and framework in order to establish your own 'free territories'. Today you have two options: either to activate a private initiative or to try other verified and unverified ways of making dreams possible. These initiatives and organizations are not absolutely independent in the sense that they do not apply for any kind of government funds. On the contrary: though being libertarian, they are applying for different funds, both national and European, but they do so to give themselves a degree of autonomy. Having presented the example of the squatted 'free territory' on Metelkova Street, I now go back to the story of CZD who found an opportunity to create their own 'free territory' on the private property of their leading member.

CZD as a Self-determining Institution and the Screaming Metonym

In February 2005, CZD performed a live concert for the national television show *Sobotna noč* (Saturday Night). Two founding members of the group, now in their late forties and early fifties, and two younger members in their late twenties and early thirties, started with full-force punk. After some forty minutes of playing both old and new examples of their brand of powerful punk rock, they announced the last tune and said their goodbyes to the audience. However, after a short pause, they returned to the stage and announced another group, an a capella CZD. They then performed several vocal songs and concluded their performance with four recent numbers: 'Kri' ('Blood'), 'Kupi gnoja' (another pun: 'Heaps of Shit', 'Dunghills' or 'Purchase Crap'), 'Nimam dnara' ('I'm Broke') and 'Express Yourself'. These last four songs could not better illustrate the liminality of the final stages of the Central and Eastern European postsocialist transition. This was not their rational intention and the group has never been overwhelmingly political. But somehow they managed to express what I, as a scholar, was not able to express easily when asked to comment on postsocialism. CZD sang the following:

'Kri':   Blood has streamed / most madly
'Kupi gnoja':   heaps heaps heaps heaps / heaps of shit
                    heaps heaps heaps heaps / heaps of shit
'Nimam dnara':   As we have come / We shall be gone / With no money
                    I'm broke / I know why / I know why
                    I know why / I am broke / I am broke[7]

The last song, 'Express Yourself', was textually (with its repeated refrain of 'express yourself'), visually (and acoustically) the most effective of the four: it is one of CZD's few songs in English, and it was sung a capella with tape over the mouths of the accompanying singers. It was a combination of bodily expression and mumbling noise that made the performance extremely effective. The essential message was: after the bloodshed you buy shit, if you are not broke, but in any case you are being interpellated by the forces of neoliberal capitalism, symbolized by a slogan in English language. It may be the position of counter-cultural punks, 'alternatives' speaking from the margins of society, but symbolically, interpellation into the brave new postsocialist 'English' world is both a necessity and an impossibility. It is a paradox: you can and you should express yourself, but you will have to pay for it. If you are broke, you can only scream, and yet you are mute, muzzled.

I must admit that I use this example as a visual and acoustic expression of what I experience as an Eastern European anthropologist. I can taste the patronizing breath of my colleagues saying 'Express Yourself' and at the same time notice that what they get from me is only a murmur. If you are to express yourself, you should express yourself according to the rules, otherwise your expressions are incomprehensible. But it is not only a problem of patronizing (post)imperial anthropology (postimperial in the European sense, where continental empires dictated the limits of 'expression' among their subjugated 'subjects', otherwise we should read the term as (post)colonial). It is, more especially, the permanent habitual background of Western economic and political experts, entrepreneurs, media and even sports experts, and NGOs and their attitude towards Eastern Europe in general, speaking with a silent smile on the face: 'We shall civilize you by giving you assistance to express yourself'. Such a generous stance is not far away from the one derived from the West's view of the Balkans, be it that of travellers', journalists' or politicians' (see Jezernik 2004). If an Eastern European expresses themselves according to 'the rules', they are no longer an Eastern European. However, even successfully playing 'according to the rules', they cannot pretend not to be an Eastern European, for it is, in the eyes of the West, an inalienable part of their inherited essence. On the other hand, if Eastern Europeans do not successfully express themselves, they merely confirm the stereotype of themselves as backward and hopeless. Whatever an Eastern Europeans does, the interpellation process will make them even more of an 'Easterner' than before, just as liberal economic reforms will make poor people poorer and rich people richer. The gap will not disappear at all.

Before I conclude my ethnographic interpretation, let me stress another very important point. To avoid any misunderstanding of my scholarly position, I must explain that I take my daily life, especially my past involvement in the local alternative music scene and media, as well as a lasting appreciation of the anarchistic punk DIY stance, as a permanent ethnography.It is ethnography that transcends the limits of ethnographies 'there and then', or 'here and then', but is literally liberated 'do-it-yourself' ethnography, adjusted to ongoing fluctuations in space and time. And, most importantly, taking your daily life as ethnography (following Rihtman-Auguštin 2001) does not prevent to make any other 'proper' ethnography 'anywhere and anytime'. In scholarship, it brings a necessary different view.[8] The essential characteristic of this position is to reject the mainstream, be it popular music, fashion, politics or cultural imperialism. This is perhaps the reason why I often see my own position as a scholar in double opposition to both international hegemonic scholarship, with its postimperial or postcolonial connotations, and the domestic (post?)nationalist one. After all, this might be a response to the observation that cultural imperialism – or, for that matter, hegemony – 'never imposes itself better than when it is served by progressive intellectuals' (Bourdieu and Wacquant 1999: 51).

Leftist punk rock proved itself to be an efficient starting point in confronting both cultural imperialism and nationalism. Music should not be considered as merely textual or symbolic activity, although it is inherently symbolic (see Tagg 1987). If it is symbolic, its aim is to mediate between presymbolic experience, involving embodiment understood phenomenologically (following Csordas 1990), and symbolic spheres, but also between the Real and the Imaginary in the Lacanian sense (see Lacan 1996), both being in a way the consequence of entering into the symbolic. Moreover, it provides a very basic human experience (see Blacking 1995) of individuality and collectivity in radically different ways and aspects, it mediates between the self and others, and it mediates between the past and the present. Music provides people with a way to cope with rapid and radical cultural changes. In its specific non-discursive way it expresses sublime foundations of sociality and communicates this among individuals. Plato wrote in a famous passage that novelties in music are dangerous, for they may endanger the social order (Plato 1976: 424d – 424e). It is music that makes facing consequentially emerging cultural complexities possible, but on the other hand it mediates between social spaces and transfers complexities into simplified formulas of seemingly unchanging traditions. Furthermore, it links up upcoming and ongoing experience with nostalgia for a never experienced recent and distant past. This is the reason why music can be used in so many different ways (cf. Merriam 1964) and why it is important to take it seriously both as a social operator and as a multilayered social text. After all, it is a site of social interaction. Just like other symbolic forms and practices, music both identifies and differentiates simultaneously. Its power lies in linking the past with the present and at the same time differentiating the present society through the cultivation of taste (Bourdieu 1984).

In the village of Trate every consecutive generation of youth was socialized in/with different music. However, each consecutive generation of village youth was itself internally differentiated along issues of taste. Music ethnography in the village Trate and surrounding countryside is congruent with Bourdieu's (1984) macro-observations of French society. The microcosm of Trate and northern Slovenske gorice reflects the social differentiation of the entire complex society. Every generation inherits past social structures from its forerunners, but it always has to shape its inherited social space anew. The past structures they inherit are passing social facts. Nevertheless, the past always lies as a nightmare in the minds of living people, as Marx (1979: 452) reminded us long ago, as long as we do not recognize the difference between past and present in the present (Bloch 1989).

Concluding Interpellation: Express Yourself!

Social amnesia is a tool of social engineering. While youth nowadays easily go into and move out of new and old youth cultural formations (the term subculture is no longer usable; cf. Muggleton and Weinzierl 2004; Bennett and Kahn-Harris 2004), they reject the heroic attitudes of historic youth formations. Something similar has happened in scholarship: there are no more heroes in postmodern scholarship. I do not take the examples from my fieldwork as mere illustrations of the points that I am trying to develop: if I take myself seriously, I have to take these examples as metonyms. In the same way that my scholarly works in Slovene have affected the development of CZD and the scene around it, the group's music has affected my scholarly position. It is simply impossible to deny that we, as ethnographers, somehow affect the field we study and that various situations we experience in the field affect us.

No matter if, at least for some Central and Eastern European countries, the transition period was concluded upon joining the European Union, at least some of us are still deeply embedded in the turmoil of history. Karl Popper (1991) was right by warning that we can not predict the social future, but I am afraid that we as scholars in the humanities and social sciences are still too blind to be able to look at social reality in the twilight, when Minerva's owl is supposed to fly and finally see what the day has brought. I see the above described permanently partisan 'punk anthropology' as a possible solution to the most essential epistemological dilemma we are facing: what can we say about the present if we cannot say anything more substantial than to produce myriad of interpretations of the past. And what can we make of the present if we are able to express only obscure hints about the future? The answer might be in the urgent reassessment of the legacy of structuralism, in escaping the fallacies and paradoxes of time, but this is another story to be written back in the future.

Notes

1 See Steinholt (2004) for the Soviet Union, and Luković (1989) for Yugoslavia.
2 See the ethnography of Russian postsocialist youth in Markowitz (2000), and the historical ethnography of Csepel working-class youth in Kürti (2002).

3   See CZD's blog at http://www.vecer.si/blog/czd. Unfortunately, the recordings they made in New York were destroyed when the studio in New York burned down.
4   See the website http://www.dpzn.org/.
5   See the website http://www.dodogovor.org.
6   See the website http://www.metelkova.org/indexe.htm.
7   Lyrics by CZD; their approved translations can be found online at http://www.ljudmila.org/subkulturni-azil/czd/Aindex.html.
8   In this regard, I follow the late Croatian ethnologist Dunja Rihtman-Auguštin, to whom I owe a great deal. See Rihtman-Auguštin (1995, 2001).

References

Barber-Kersovan, A. 2005. *Vom 'Punk-Frühling' zum 'Slowenischen Frühling': Der Beitrag des slowenischen Punk zur Demonatage des sozialistischen Wertesystems.* Hamburg: Krämer.

Bennett, A. and K. Kahn-Harris (ed.) 2004. *After Subculture: Critical Studies in Contemporary Youth Culture.* New York: Palgrave.

Bibič, B. 2003. *Hrup z Metelkove: Tranzicije prostorov in kulture v Ljubljani.* [Noise from Metelkova: Transitions of Spaces and Culture in Ljubljana.] Ljubljana: Mirovni inštitut.

Bizjak, A. et al. (eds). 2005. *Petrovardinsko pleme: Raziskovanje fenomena Festivala EXIT/Petrovaradinsko pleme: Istraživanje fenomena Festivala EXIT/ Petrovaradin Tribe: Reflections of the Phenomenon of the EXIT Music Festival.* Ljubljana: KUD Pozitiv.

Blacking, J. 1995. *Music, Culture, and Experience: Selected Papers of John Blacking.* R. Byron (ed.) Chicago: University of Chicago Press.

Bloch, M. 1989. *Ritual, History and Power: Selected Papers in Anthropology.* London: Athlone.

Bourdieu, P. 1977. *Outline of a Theory of Practice.* Cambridge,: Cambridge University Press.

―――― 1984. *Distinction: A Social Critique of the Judgement of Taste.* London: Routledge.

―――― 2002[1980]. *Praktični čut* [Le sens pratique], trans. J.K. Štrajn. Ljubljana: Studia humanitatis.

Bourdieu, P. and L. Wacquant. 1999. 'On the Cunning of Imperialist Reason', *Theory, Culture and Society* 16(1): 41–58.

Carmichael, C. and J. Gow. 2001. *Slovenia and the Slovenes: A Small State and the New Europe.* London: Hurst.

Csordas, T. 1990. 'Embodiment as a Paradigm for Anthropology,' *Ethos* 18: 5–47.

Cutler, C. 1985. *Files under Popular.* London: November Books.

CZD and R. Muršič. 1999. *V sen sem jih videl.* [In a Dream I Saw Them.] Pesnica: Frontier.

Fukuyama, F. 1992. *The End of History and the Last Man.* London: Penguin.

Garofalo, R. (ed.) 1992. *Rockin' the Boat: Mass Music and Mass Movements.* Boston: South End Press.

Hribar, T. 2002. 'Pankrti, tovariši in drugi' [Pankrti, Comrades and Others], in P. Lovšin, P. Mlakar and I. Vidmar (eds), *Punk je bil prej: 25 let punka pod Slovenci* [Punk Came First: 25 Years of Punk under the Slovenes]. Ljubljana: Cankarjeva založba and Ropot, pp.5–7.

Jacoby, R. 1981[1975]. *Družbena amnezija: Kritika sodobne psihologije od Adlerja do Lainga* [Social Amnesia: A Critique of Contemporary Psychology from Adler to Laing], trans. J.Š. Riha. Ljubljana: Cankarjeva založba.

Jezernik, B. 2004. *Wild Europe: The Balkans in the Gaze of Western Travellers.* London: Saqui and The Bosnian Institute.

Keil, C. and S. Feld (eds). 1994. *Music Grooves: Essays and Dialogues.* Chicago: University of Chicago Press.

Kürti, L. 2002. *Youth and the State in Hungary: Capitalism, Communism and Class.* London: Pluto.

Lacan, J. 1996. *Štirje temeljni koncepti psihoanalize* [Four Basic Concepts in Psychoanalysis]. Ljubljana: Analecta.

Lipsitz, G. 1994. *Dangerous Crossroads: Popular Music, Postmodernism and the Poetics of Place.* London: Verso.

Luković, P. 1989. *Bolja prošlost: Prizori iz muzičkog života Jugoslavije 1940–1989* [Better Past: Scenes from Musical Life in Yugoslavia 1940–1989]. Beograd: Mladost.

McKay, G. (ed.) 1998. *DiY Culture: Party and Protest in Nineties Britain.* London: Verso.

Markowitz, F. 2000. *Coming of Age in Post-Soviet Russia.* Urbana: University of Illinois Press.

Marx, K. 1979[1852]. 'Osemnajsti brumaire Ludvika Bonaparta' [The Eighteenth Brumaire of Louis Bonaparte], in K. Marx and F. Engels, *Izbrana dela* [Selected Works], vol. 3. Ljubljana: Cankarjeva založba, pp.445–574.

Mastnak, T. 1994. 'From Social Movements to National Sovereignty', in J. Benderly and E. Kraft (eds), *Independent Slovenia: Origins, Movements, Prospects.* London: Macmillan, pp. 93–111.

Merriam, A. 1964. *The Anthropology of Music.* Chicago: Northwestern University Press.

Mirković, I. 2004. *Sretno dijete* [Lucky Kid]. Zaprešić: Fraktura.

Muggleton, D. and R. Weinzierl (eds). 2004. *The Post-subcultures Reader.* Oxford: Berg.

Muršič, R. 1995a. *Center za dehumanizacijo: etnološki oris rock skupine* [Centre for Dehumanization: An Ethnological Description of a Rock Group]. Pesnica: Frontier.

_____ 1995b. 'Punks in the Village: The Rock Group CZD (Center for Dehumanisation) between Villages on the Border, Slovenian Dominant Culture and Popular World Culture', *Folia Ethnologica* 8: 55–66.

_____ 1995c. 'The Creative Game of Believing and Misunderstanding: An Anthropological Field Research of Punk Rock in two Slovenian Villages', *Etnolog* 5: 269–81.

_____ 1998. 'Autochthonisation of Rock Music in Rural Slovenia', in T. Mitsui (ed.) *Popular Music: Intercultural Interpretations.* Kanazawa: Graduate Program in Music, Kanazawa University, pp.281–88.

_____ 1999. 'The Rock Scene in the Village of Trate and the Ethno-Pop Show "Marjanca" in the Town of Maribor: On the Complexity of Musical Identifications', in B. Jezernik (ed.) *Urban Symbolism and Rituals: Proceedings of the International Symposium Organised by the IUAES Commission on Urban Anthropology, Ljubljana, June 23–25, 1997.* Ljubljana: Filozofska fakulteta, pp.221–32.

_____ 2000a. *Trate vaše in naše mladosti: Zgodba o mladinskem in rock klubu* [Trate: The Story of a Rock Club], 2 vols. Ceršak: Subkulturni azil.

_____ 2000b. 'Transference and Invention: Punk in the Slovene Village of Trate', *East European Meetings in Ethnomusicology* 7: 113–26.

_____ 2002. 'Local Feedback: Slovene Popular Music between the Global Market and Local Consumption', *Beiträge zur Popularmusikforschung* 29/30: 125–48.

_____ 2003. 'Destinies of the Post-War Colonists in the Village of Trate: Unintended Phenomena in the Appropriation of Public Spaces', in D. Torsello and M. Pappová (eds), *Social Networks in Movement: Time, Interaction and Interethnic Spaces in Central Eastern Europe*. Šamorín and Dunajská Streda: Forum Minority Research Institute, pp.99–113.

Opekar, A. (ed.) 1994. *Central European Popular Music.* Prague: Czech Branch of IASPM, Institute of Musicology, Academy of Sciences of the Czech Republic.

Plato. 1976. *Država* [Polythea], trans. A. Sovre. Ljubljana: DZS.

Popper, K. 1991[1957]. *The Poverty of Historicism.* London: Routledge.

Ramet, S.P. (ed.) 1994. *Rocking the State: Rock Music and Politics in Eastern Europe and Russia.* Boulder, CO: Westview.

Rihtman-Auguštin, D. 1995. 'Victims and Heroes: Between Ethnic Values and Construction of Identity', *Ethnologia Europea* 25: 61–67.

_____ 2001. *Etnologija i etnomit* [Ethnology and Ethnomyth]. Zagreb: Naklada Publica.

St John, G. 2001. 'Alternative Cultural Heterotopia and the Liminoid Body: Beyond Turner at ConFest', *Australian Journal of Anthropology* 12(1): 47–66.

Steinholt, Y.B. 2004. *Rock in the Reservation: Songs from the Leningrad Rock Club 1981–86.* Bergen: University of Bergen

Szemere, A. 2001. *Up from the Underground: The Culture of Rock Music in Postsocialist Hungary.* University Park: Pennsylvania State University Press.

Tagg, P. 1987. 'Musicology and the Semiotics of Popular Music', *Semiotica* 66(1–3): 279–98.

Tomc, G. 1989. *Druga Slovenija: Zgodovina mladinskih gibanj na Slovenskem v 20. stoletju* [The Other Slovenia: A History of Youth Movements in Slovenia in the 20th Century]. Ljubljana: UK ZSMS (Krt 54).

_____ 1994. 'The Politics of Punk', in J. Benderly and E. Kraft (eds), *Independent Slovenia: Origins, Movements, Prospects.* London: Macmillan, pp.113–34.

Turner, V. 1974. *The Ritual Process: Structure and Anti-Structure.* Harmondsworth: Penguin.

Vila, P. 1992. 'Rock Nacional and Dictatorship in Argentina', in R. Garofalo (ed.) *Rockin' the Boat: Mass Music and Mass Movements.* Boston: South End Press, pp.209–29

Žikić, A. 1999. *Fatalni ringišpil: Hronika beogradskog rokenrola 1959–1979* [Fatal Carousel: A Chronicle of Belgrade Rock and Roll 1959–1979]. Belgrade: Geopoetika.

Žižek, S. 2004. 'Interview', *Mladina* 28: 36–40.

Chapter 9

Being Locked Out and Locked In

The Culture of Homelessness in Hungary

Terézia Nagy

The intention of this chapter is to show how the 'hidden poverty' of state socialism continues to manifest itself in the postsocialist present while the phenomenon of 'new poverty' is being simultaneously created. Part of this new poverty is homelessness, a topic which did not officially exist during the socialist period and was considered taboo. Social scientists, however, began studying poverty during the mid to late 1980s, years that have often been referred to as 'soft communism' (Bokor 1987; Ferge 1982; Gönczöl 1982, 1991; Kemény 1979; Eberstadt 1988; Höjdestrand 2003).

As we will see, the reality of growing poverty became obvious when many forms of unemployment, homelessness and permanent social deprivation were noticed. Since 1990, although scholars have often concentrated on specific aspects of postsocialist economic and social changes, poverty has received little attention from an anthropological perspective. To be fair, some aspects – such as rural poverty, the plight of Roma, or youth in urban housing estates – have been researched but there has been little in depth work on the wider spectrum of poverty that has come to exist as a consequence of capitalist development.

Neither the new poor nor the winners of the postsocialist transformation have gained attention from Hungarian anthropologists, since native ethnographers have conducted almost no fieldwork in urban areas (for a few exceptions, see Kőbányai 1980, 1982; Kürti 2002; Simonyi 1995). Foreign anthropologists, meanwhile, have dealt predominantly with the concerns of the postsocialist economy, such as market transition and the dismantling of agricultural cooperatives. Therefore, being both citizens of Hungary and working as native observers, scholars working at home may bring unique perspectives to the study of homelessness. I am going to apply this insider–outsider device in order to introduce the phenomenon of new poverty through changes in Hungarian history and economy. These are changes that endow new features to the culture of homelessness, which is different than that of countries where this aspect of poverty developed gradually (see Costa Nunez 1996; Hazra 2005).

My interviews revealed the way in which homeless people rationalized the processes that forced them onto the streets. Moreover, my purpose was to examine their exclusion from the general society as they moved into the society of the homeless. My fieldwork was carried out between 2002 and 2004 in Szeged, a city in southern Hungary.[1] During the research I participated in the everyday lives of homeless groups as an observer and I conducted interviews. During this time, I observed people's ways of life and relationships, and at the same time I heard different interpretations of life histories and autobiographical events. Later, besides making observations and talking with people, I conducted some life-history interviews as well. At the beginning of my fieldwork, I faced several problems, because people told me pre-constructed stories, and when I was present they could exclude me by using particular linguistic codes. My attempts to cross this boundary ended in failure for a long time. Later, when this boundary had disappeared, it was the intimacy I shared with people that caused me difficulties, and forced me to keep my distance. Thus, while getting closer to the group, I always remained an outsider. I contextualized these life stories with information from sociological investigations of Hungarian poverty. Moreover, my intention is to demonstrate the unique elements of homeless culture and society and to shed light on the special situation of how and when the phenomena of destitution suddenly became a reality for a large percentage of Hungarian citizens.

Poverty in the Last Days of Socialism: Dossers, Tramps and the 'Criminally Idle'

Under socialism, poverty was rarely, if ever, discussed and the concept of impoverishment basically meant departure from the average income and lifestyle (Szalai 1997: 1403). For scholars, this usually did not entail any obvious distress although it appeared in suburbs and farmsteads which were on the brink of collapse. On the other hand, impoverishment certainly implied deprivation of power and personal rights, as well as a departure from the average standard of living and a proper, respectable manner of life (Bokor 1987). Alcohol consumption, misuse of income, poor health, careless hygiene and low levels of education were all noticeable aspects of the culture of poverty in Hungary under socialism. Obviously, education had low prestige for the poor, while establishing a family and getting a job had more importance. At the same time, alcohol consumption had greater significance than maintaining a certain standard of living, a trap which often led to crime or domestic abuse directed at consort (man or woman) or child.

The destruction of dwelling places could also be observed in suburban districts, due partly to the occupiers being unable to maintain or renovate these buildings. All these topics did not generate public discussion because most of these poor people – who had the above mentioned problem – had jobs, and relatively respectable lives. Consumption of alcohol was generally accepted by family members (as well as researchers) while violence or paying debts were of no importance to them. During the last decade of socialist rule, poverty as such was still considered a shameful and invisible aspect of social life (Bokor 1987). Nevertheless, deprivation was often observed to be a phenomena occurring largely among marginal groups described as hobos, tramps and 'dangerous' idlers. Others successfully concealed their deprived status by seclusion or withdrawal from society, such as those, for example, who managed to hold a job but lived in workers' hostels.

Although homelessness as such was known during the socialist regime, it was not defined as such. In the literature one can find negative labels used to describe homeless people, such as hobos, tramps[2] and criminal idlers.[3] A tramp is a person who wanders between settlements and roams the countryside occasional accepting menial work but basically preferring easier ways of earning money. Some of them – mainly younger ones – armed themselves with a specific ideology as they left home, saying that they were escaping from obligations authority figures, such as parents and the workplace as well as schools. The sweet taste of freedom appealed to them, particularly in the summertime when many of them moved out temporarily to sleep under the stars. Many of these former hobos now have respectable homes and employment. Dossers[4] had also changed their lifestyle, although they appeared predominantly in the squares and parks of larger towns and were visible at rock concerts. Their Hungarian name (*csöves*) may derive from the large pipe at construction sites which they frequently slept in (Utasi 1987: 181). A few youngsters were recruited to live in grounds from among the ranks of criminals and school drop-outs who had chosen to escape from parental authority but they were living outside periodically when they wanted. Finally, there were those who were brought to the same fate by having a disability which prevented them from being integrated into homeless society hereby they lived alone in that time.

Youngsters managed to get by by a number of means, doing odd jobs, pickpocketing, stealing, begging, forging prescriptions, pimping and prostitution. Older homeless people lived on collecting litter or even cheating by selling counterfeit gold. Naturally, these activities were regarded as illegal by both the homeless as well as the state. Indeed, government policy regarded unemployment a dangerous menace to society and those youngsters who did not start work immediately after finishing school – putting off becoming employed for a while so that they could live a vagrant life, or just living without working – were seen as parasites, maniacs or criminally idle (Ferge

1982). The status of the homeless did not only draw social disapproval; the military could intervene and set them to work (interview with M.R., a former criminal idler 1998/2[5]).

Almost none of them slept in the street; perhaps at most they slept on park benches in the summer. They preferred to live in summer cottages which were temporarily unsettled, condemned buildings, cabins built without authorization, or bed-shares.[6] Some of them intended to spend the winter in labour hostels, hospitals or lunatic asylums, while others looked on prisons as a possible solution to their seasonal accommodation needs (for all these, see Kőbányai 1980; Utasi 1987; interview with Malac 2002/5).

Hiding Places: Workplaces and Workers' Hostels

Workplaces and workers' hostels[7] both produced hidden unemployment and homelessness (Spéder 2002: 45), as their institutionalizing appeared at the end of the socialist era when many of workplaces and almost all of workers' hostels ceased. Workplaces had a surplus of labour, a phenomenon well-known from the era of state socialism, which created problems for both employers and employees. These were not obvious at first, however, because no one in the workplace seemed idle. Everyone worked – socialist ideology was one of full employment – but surplus workers produced an unused surplus of goods that piled up in warehouses (Ferge 1982).

For labourers, cheap workers' hostels provided temporary accommodation but in reality these were the permanent or only homes for many (Láng and Nyilas 1987: 33; Veres 1979). As Mátyus (1978) pointed out, hostels helped for the present but they did not provide a future. Hostel dwellers worked long hours in order to earn more money, but they did not save and instead spent considerable amounts on entertainment, and often got into disastrous personal relationships that produced an ever greater cultural gap between the homeless (Mátyus 1978). The majority of hostel residents were from a peasant background; consequently their former community could not protect them in the city, as Kürti describes for the workers in Csepel (2002). Becoming an urban factory worker meant that most of the time these formerly rural dwellers abandoned social ties with their home communities. Despite the fact that alienation and helplessness was a characteristic feature of this world it still left an empty space when hostels were closed. Those who had hostel accommodation provided by the state, or who had neglected their relationships with the communities from which they came, had no place to go (Láng and Nyilas 1987). If they had a job or savings they could rent accommodation. Those who did not, or lost their jobs, had no other choice but to live on the street. The argument that hostels concealed homelessness is not entirely true, however. Rather, they were an institution that helped migration toward urban centers, especially for those who originally had homes in the countryside. However, emerging social, cultural or generational conflicts inside the family led to a situation where rural youth could not return and remained instead powerless urban dwellers.

The Challenges of Postsocialism

With the collapse of socialism, the pseudo-system of security offered by the state vanished instantly. Poorer people had to contend with serious changes in the early postcommunist years. Meanwhile, they saw a change in those values that had seemed obvious before: self-identity, ideology and faith in their own ability (Šiklová 1996: 537, 539; cf. Laki 2003: 129).

As full employment ended, due to the closing of large factories, mines and state enterprises during the transformation to a market economy, there emerged a need for highly trained and educated professionals. However, as there was much less of a need for manual labourers, blue-collar workers could no longer expect job security nor find new jobs, and the threat of unemployment suddenly became a much-discussed topic in public discourse (Laki 2003).

Similarly, the socialist housing system went through some basic changes. City council houses were no longer built, and consequently prices jumped sky-high. Mortgage repayments became difficult for many, as was the acquisition of first flats for young family members. Workers' hostels and workplaces closed down at the same time. Those people who were not allowed to go home suddenly found themselves in a very uncertain position. Contractors in the 'second economy'[8] adjusted to the unstable market conditions by frequently employing workers illegally whose futures remained uncertain (Borboly et al. 2003: 195; Simonyi 1995: 65–66; see also Jancius 2002: 63–66) because anytime they can lose their job and livelihood on same time they have many kind of problem by illegality (for example they have not got health care benefit and social security pension). After the socialist era, alcohol abuse increased during working hours, and this became grounds for dismissal. Those who could not adjust or adopt to the new employment standards obviously faced unemployment.

During the socialist period, workers' incomes were not high but one could still survive on them. People of a lower social class could utilize more of their earning because the state subsidized some consumer durables. Moreover, payday could be celebrated with small events such as dining at a restaurant, going for a drink, or celebrating name days[9] and anniversaries. Holidays and travel, meanwhile, were supported by trade union holiday vouchers which could be used at the union's own holiday resort for labourers.

It was a particular feature of Hungary at the time that income was untaxed and contributions to trade unions was set at a low amount. To balance the losses of badly run state enterprises, the government taxed profitable companies. Thus there was neither enough funds in the state budget for the recreation of labourers at trade union resorts nor financial aid for travelling. All this state support – subsidized consumer goods, trade union benefits and so on – ceased immediately after the fall of socialism. At the same time, incomes remained at the same level (Laki 2003: 128–29), prospects became uncertain, and spending on recreation and leisure ceased.

Formerly, moonlighting for secondary incomes[10] provided a reliable supplement to salaries, but as numerous companies closed in the new economic climate this sort of money became the sole means of support for many people. They had to use all their knowledge and experience to adapt to the market economy. Formerly, raw materials, tools, warehouse stock 'wandered off' into the second economy or to agricultural cooperatives' household plots. Moonlighting employees could use both their knowledge and their 'borrowings' to their benefit. But afterwards this system did not operate in the real market economy, a time when a person's knowledge of this sort of thing could help them with the transition to the new system. By 1995, those who could not adapt often found themselves unemployed or at risk of unemployment, while those who had gained practical experience from moonlighting were much more successful in the new economy.

Without a job one becomes unemployed; without a home one becomes homeless. The existence of such phenomena came as a shock to people in the first early years of postsocialism. To gain employment or secure accommodation for oneself is not so easy if there is none to be had. Change brings losers as well as winners. Winners could adapt their experiences to a market economy. Their mental skills and ability to accept changes meant they were able to preserve their former standard of living; some even managed to improve their position. For people touched by unemployment, economic uncertainty and decline gradually created a new, tangible poverty that combined aspects of the invisible poverty of socialism with factors affecting the new class of the poor.

Postsocialist Poverty in Hungary

Postsocialist poverty could be found among two groups of people. One group comprised the poor and deprived from the socialist era who carried this status into the postsocialist period. Unemployment and loss of social status began to have an impact on them during the 1990s. Some of them lived in workers' hostels which closed, leaving them nowhere to go at night, not even to their families in their home towns because of conflicts. The second group was made up of those who fell into poverty from relatively good, lower-middle-class positions. The main reasons behind this fall were either retirement or failure as an entrepreneur in the market economy (see Spéder 2002: 103). Their position was much harder because deprivation reached them first. Hopelessness and isolation led to family and social conflicts. To survive, they needed to save or take out mortgages. The poverty of retired people and children have both been the subject of sociological investigation (Spéder 2000, 2002), though we still lack firsthand accounts of their lives.

Wherever they came from, main concerns of poor's majority were saving and living from day to day, lack of medicines, casual work and illegal labour (Laki 2003; Simonyi 1995). Newly impoverished members of the middle class experienced how family cooperation disintegrates; people from workers' hostels already knew all about it. People who were subject to multigenerational deprivation continued to live in their special cooperation. If there was money, everyone benefited; if there was none, then people would seek better opportunities. This kind of benefit-culture[11] – which had been unknown for the Hungarian social policy in socialist era – developed firstly among the multigenerational deprivated groups, chiefly because labour had value during socialism.

The sudden threat of unemployment impacted people both materially and emotionally. The mass reduction of the workforce, which peaked between 1992 and 1995 (Laki 2003), and the fact that the formerly 'hidden' unemployment problem of the socialist era had become common knowledge, combined to heighten the alarm over economic and social instability. The problem was so widespread that mutual assistance became almost impossible; people could not spare money or possessions. If a serious matter cropped up, they were not able to turn to anyone or anything (Laki 2003: 119). Those who were employed exploited themselves by hard work to preserve their jobs and support their families. Those who could find it undertook casual work and for many this was the only kind available. Some even worked illegally (*feketemunka, svarc*) to earn a living, even though the wages were low, the work was hard, health benefits non-existent. Still, it was better than nothing.

This new kind of poverty bred a new lifestyle as well: the culture of idleness. Daily meetings to kill time, involving long discussions, were part of this culture. The scene of these meetings was the public domain for young people, while the older generation went to pubs on council estates or in outlying neighborhoods. A better way to spend time did not exist for them, for their flats in council estates did not allow it (it was lack of space and it was not habitual how they spend of leisure time), and furthermore the estates were full of conflicts (see Corrigan 1976; Rácz 1998; interview with Malac, Gyufi, Zsolesz, 2002/2).

At this time, the chances of obtaining or maintaining a flat continually worsened. Those who had bought flats with loans could not be sure that they could meet the repayments. From the early 1990s, paying utility bills also generated problems for many because they could not manage to pay both the bills and the loan repayments. If they could sell their flat at even a small profit, some purchased rural cottages without any utilities. The only solution for the rest was to rent. Some who could not continue to pay rent moved in with other family members. Others went to homes for the elderly, if they could. The remainder had to live on the street.

A New Phenomenon: Homelessness

Homelessness was an unknown category in the socialist era. People who integrated into society had jobs (Ferge 1982: 91), and those who had jobs had a place to live. People who chose homelessness were despised by society. Macro-economic and macro-social processes generated by the collapse of socialism meant that many people who became homeless also lost their possessions. Predominantly these were people who had lost their job and with it a place in a hostel, those who had nowhere to go after the hostels closed, and those whose lack of proper qualifications or physical limitations (disabilities and another kind of inaptitude for work) made them unable to find jobs. The winter of 1992 brought the first widespread notice of, and concern for, homelessness (Iványi 1997). The first civil initiatives – shelters for the homeless, temporary and daytime homes, food distribution – began at this time. Homeless people had to contend with the problem that socialism had suppressed the truth concerning homelessness, defencelessness and want. In fact, this situation made it clear to people that the state would not rescue citizens from this fate.

Poverty and Homelessness: The Way to Homelessness

According to representative surveys, 11 per cent of the population was deprived of essential goods and 20 percent was endangered by poorness in the last decade of the socialist era (Bokor 1987). Bokor herself also emphasizes that 'poverty' could not be truly examined: in addition to its 'forbidden' political status there was a lack of 'poverty identity', or a means of identifying the poor.[12] By creating new definitions of poverty after socialism ended, sociologists have attempted to interpret it with objective statistics (Spéder 2002). By 1997, poverty had increased to 13 per cent, but financial difficulties concerned 30 per cent of the population (Spéder 2002: 57). By this time, a generally accepted idea of poverty had emerged, and statistical surveys using self-evaluation were used. Approximately 25 per cent of the Hungarian population defines itself as poor, though not all the processes of impoverishment or its associated subcultures have been investigated. Different surveys applied different definitions of poverty and by so doing it became difficult to ascertain whether the 13 per cent or the 25 per cent figure is the most accurate. Some statistics, for instance, reveal some people with low income but such data do not offer information on people living on the margins of society.

Similarly, obtaining an accurate number of the homeless is difficult. The first census of homelessness, conducted in 2005, recorded approximately 10,000 homeless people. Even if this census served a good purpose, it was not accepted by the scholarly community because fieldworkers used different working definitions. For instance, in Szeged, my home town, there were said to be only thirteen homeless people because only those with a homeless 'lifestyle' – those who actually lived on the street without governmental support – were counted as 'homeless'. Consequently, more than 560 homeless people were left out by the census takers because these people had contacts with social institutions or simply because they had not participated in the census. The expert estimate for mid 2005 Szeged is that between 800 and 1,200 people live on the streets or in the surrounding forests (K.J., executive of the home for the homeless, verbal communication), which is less than one per cent of the city's population. Neither the number of homeless people in other communities nor the ratio of counted to uncounted people is known.

Through in-depth life-history interviews, my homeless informants recounted many well-constructed stories about their past experiences. Several recurring motifs became obvious: reflecting on society's morals and indirectly a desire to sensationalize their histories. Nevertheless, all stories reveal the main points of their trajectory to homelessness. Most of the homeless in Szeged referred both to the transition to the postsocialist society and economy, and the conflicts and conflict-resolution mechanisms of their way of life as the main reasons for becoming homeless. They referred to the uncertainty that dominated the life-ways of industrial and agricultural labourers as well as how their adjustment to new conditions failed.

Iványi (1997: 9–14) has identified four major groups of the homeless in Hungary. The first lost everything during the transformation of the economy – they became penniless mostly because their inexperience undermined their attempts to establish themselves as entrepreneurs. Some of them invested all their assets but failed eventually, sometimes because others exploited them. The second group comprises those whose general impoverishment led towards total homelessness (Iványi 1997: 10). As they were living below the subsistence level, they could not even dream of having their own flats. Their utility bills and other debts continued to accumulate, further decreasing their standard of living until becoming homeless. Unemployment meant a great burden as they could not cope with it without family, social and cultural support. The third group is made up of direct and indirect victims of divorce, alcoholism and drug abuse. A recent survey revealed that ten per cent of the population has alcohol problems (Elekes 2000). Finally, the fourth group includes those who left various health and social care institutions (such as state orphanages, mental homes, homes for the elderly). In addition, former prison inmates or convicts belong to this last category especially if their families cast them aside.

As narratives of homelessness amply demonstrate, becoming homeless is often a tragedy compiling characteristic features from all four groups. One 46–year-old homeless man recounted his story highlighting how a wrong decision in life resulted in a series of mishaps. He was divorced and his wife and children remained together. As a loner, he was forced to purchase a small rural cottage about 60 kilometres away from the city. This proved to be a poor decision as his new home was too far away from his place of work and there was no reliable transportation. He tried to rent a place but his landlady in the city stole his possessions. After he lost his job he began drinking at a small pub – called 'The Knife-thrower', in Hungarian *késdobáló*[13] – then joined a homeless gang and finally found himself begging in front of a church. He had everything he wanted in the beginning as a homeless man: money, alcohol and friends. It was summer and he did not miss the cottage either, he said. All it took was an accident and a bad decision to start his slide into permanent homelessness: he had several operations but did not wait until he had recovered from them before he went back to begging. Today, he cannot stand, he has lost possession of his cottage, he has not seen his home for years, and alcohol has become his close companion.

'We are human, we are being seen as such', writes a 30–year-old homeless man in one of his poems. He had four short marriages and three children. He goes to work from the street. He claims he chose this freedom – 'freedom gives wings, and nothing else is needed'. Another man has an aggressive attitude, which he often cannot control, and he has been treated several times for schizophrenia. As a result, no one will employ him. The confession of a sixty-year-old beggar properly depicts isolation by society: 'I killed a man in a sudden rage, and ... I do not regret anything ... except that my hand has been hurt so now I am on the street'. After he was released from prison he did not have a place to go, so now he lives on the streets in what others refer to as his 'pigsty'.

There are people who have been ended up on the streets because of their pursuit of ideals. One example is a middle-aged man, known as Malac ('Porky') to his friends, who left his wife and daughter to go to live near Lake Balaton 'to be free', as he said. He started to drink excessively, treating everyone as a drinking-buddy while he still had some money. After spending all his cash he returned to Szeged but he did not go home: 'I got used to being in the open air; no one can force me to live between walls. I have spent enough time between walls in prison. If I want, I take a job. There is enough money on the streets'. In his stories, he details how he supported himself with the help of some homeless gangs who, in accordance with the rules of their alliance, helped him in the belief that he would also help them when necessary.

In some stories, long-lasting unemployment forced my informants into illegal work, and some had the sad experience of being cheated out of what little money they could earn. They became victims of hideous dwelling conditions, working conditions, family problems and illegal activities. Some attempted to start a new life with friends, thinking they will be more successful if they worked together. They took jobs, they paid rent together but these arrangements usually did not last for long. One homeless person explained: 'You cannot go to work from the street. People watch me asking when I last had a bath, or if I steal ... If someone has to be fired, it is certain that I will be the first one'.

Most victims of the political reforms emphasize two main reasons for homelessness. Most of them were untrained workers and lived in workers' hostels but lost their jobs and their homes at the same time. Others say that they invested much work and effort in their small enterprises, but tough conditions made them uncompetitive in the new market economy. As all their assets were invested in the business, everything was lost when their business went under. Emotional damage, loss of physical strength, and uncompetitive skills have forced these people over the edge and into the streets.

In the socialist era, untrained employees were also considered as part of the work force. Since wages and promotion were not dependent on an employee's training, there was no reason to try to acquire more skills or knowledge. One was simply a 'worker', a position one held between being a student and being retired, and it was this that largely determined an individual's social status. Living standards could be enhanced, first of all by 'cheating' (*simlisség*), but with the end of socialism cheating and the possibility of keeping one's status despite lack of skills and knowledge disappeared.

During the socialist era, mental illness and obvious mental breakdown were considered shameful, both for the individuals concerned and for their families. This view changed somewhat after the fall of socialism, and the tradition of solving problems within the family remains strong, particularly in rural areas. However, at difficult moments, members of the family can easily be neglected. The postsocialist period has been one where uncertainty has conquered the lives of industrial and agricultural workers. This fact of life can easily be seen in the narratives of young homeless people who have just left state institutions. One young man's story is particularly instructive:

> My parents were young when they let me be fostered. When I left the orphanage I had nowhere to go. The money I received from the state was not enough to buy a flat. I went and lodged with some friends (*haverok*). I could not get a job because my profession was not wanted. Even if we got jobs they did not last long because of our lazy and free attitude. There were times when I did not go to work for days. Selling something meant more money than working. There are some dealers (*orgazda*) who take what I have on stock and they tell me what they need (*adják a drótot*). [In other words, he sold stolen goods to receivers who would even place orders with him for goods which he would then steal and sell to them.] I have money and regular clothes and I am not like those other homeless people. If I have money I book a room, but mostly I am on the street. In fact, I have just come out of prison.

Former prisoners (*priuszos*) often become homeless as very few businesses wish to employ or lodge them. Rehabilitation, in this case, does not work at all as ex-prisoners do not like to keep contact with their patrons – their attitude is 'at last I am free; I do not have to be under anyone's control any more'.

As the above story illustrates, most foster children ended up living in workers' hostels. However, when these were closed they found themselves on the streets in their forties or fifties (Kőbányai 1980). A workers' hostel is not exactly the place for building a future and this theme is more often than not highlighted in most descriptions dealing such lodgings. This sense of being stuck with 'no way out' also occurs in most homeless shelters that will be described below.

The elderly and the sick, especially those without family to rely on, may easily end up living on the streets. Two elderly homeless people described the lack of family cohesion that has led to family members not taking care of each other:

> When we became pensioners we lived quite normally but our pension did not keep up with price increases. When my wife died I could not pay the bills alone as well as buy medicines. I sold our flat and when I ran out of that money, I came out here ... My children are grown up and they do not bother with me at all. But even if they did, I would be ashamed and I do not wish to be introduced to my grandchildren as a beggar.

This explanation by a 74–year-old homeless man from Budapest is tragic but illustrates that both financial difficulties and lack of family cohesion contribute to their desperate situation. In many cases, careless family members are also responsible for their elderly relatives ending up on the streets. Sometimes young couples make a verbal agreement to support elderly family members, a contract that is subsequently broken so the elderly are forced to give up their flats or houses because of the use of emotional pressure or even physical terror.

The Culture of Being Homeless

We have seen some of the ways that people end up living on the streets, and in the following I would like to discuss how homeless people describe their own lives. It turns out from talking to the homeless that they see themselves as a separate society which lives on the margins of mainstream society, within which there is a ranking according to people's source of livelihood. The lowest category consists of those who live on digging through rubbish, collecting food and cigarette butts; some find goods that can be sold at a secondhand market. The next group consists of two kinds of homeless people who collect money illegally: beggars, and those who cheat, steal or bully others at pubs. There is a distinction between these two based on honesty. Beggars say they are at least honest while others say they would never shame themselves by begging on the streets. Above them are those homeless people who make a little money by passing on useful information such as the location of a new charity, an empty building for shelter, or someone who is hiring labourers for odd jobs.

There is another distinction among homeless people between those who live in homeless shelters and those who do not. The latter group assert that they are able to live on their own and do not need charity. They also fear that others will steal their few belongings. During interviews many people mentioned shelter rules that they found unbearable, such as not wishing to stand in queues for food, or giving up drinking in order to get into a shelter for a night. Since 1990, beggars have reappeared on the city streets in increasing number. Organized gangs of 'imported beggars' have also arrived in Hungary from Romania and the Ukraine as well. They have spread out all over the city of Szeged and have divided it into separate territories. Different begging techniques have been developed by them: they address people in different ways and learn urban customs and movement patterns. Knowing urban pathways, they are also familiar about where it is worth begging. This knowledge additionally includes shelters, morning food distributions from churches, suburban shelters during the day, as well as the city center (Dugonics Square) on Tuesdays. On Wednesdays in Szeged, charity is available at Dóm Square and the Knights of Malta dispense food for indigents on Thursdays. Beggars end their 'workday' – as they refer to their day of collecting and begging – by returning to the homeless shelter for the night.

The major part of the day is spent on cultivating useful relationships: greeting each other, common encounters and events, listening to each other's stories, criticizing people and planning new actions (Rácz 1998: 120). Rácz writes in connection with poverty theory that poverty: 'involves open and hidden forms of aggression, self-destruction, self-restriction, misery, self-denial, hopelessness, images of no way out and no future. Sometimes the feeling of waiting for a miracle or waiting for the intervention of authorities (ministry, municipal government) is desired' (Rácz 1998: 125). I have met two types of beggars waiting for some sort of miracle to happen, those who are actively trying to make the desired miracle occur, and those who are passive. Passivity involves waiting for the state and local government to intervene, or receiving family or larger financial aid (which is considered by them to be a natural and a civil right). The more active group envisage getting themselves out of their current situation by, for example, getting a farm with others where they can make their own living space together in peace. However, many do give up on such ideas, arguing that they will not work out: 'I know the type. Everything would be quickly carried away in a week's time. There is no point in starting it at all'.

Women have a particular status in the world of the homeless: they enjoy others' protection because they are seen as vulnerable (Tamási 2004). Usually women attempt to find a man's protection though he usually forces them into prostitution. If they have a child, the man usually concentrates on the child and the woman is sent to a women's shelter which of course means the break up of the family. Children are socialized into begging, rubbish collecting or committing crimes. There are also families where only one member lives on the street, but this type experiences the same problems as if the whole family were homeless. Among them, conflicts and fights are daily occurences.

As maintaining bodily hygiene is difficult, the homeless may have parasites and tuberculosis. Fresh wounds and scars, skin diseases, missing limbs, frostbite and injuries from fights are common among the homeless. Alcoholism is also widespread, as they rationalize: 'Cheap wine (*pillepalackos*)[14] and strong alcoholic beverages are needed to survive and bear the consequences of such a lifestyle'.

A wide range of homeless aid institutions were established at the beginning of the 1990s, with temporary homes, health and social-service institutions, and warm, winter daytime shelters with food facilities. From the middle of the 1990s, more and more religious and charitable organizations have provided services with regular food and help. This is quite an enormous project for organizations that have only recently been established. Currently, particularly in the nation's capital, several service institutes run at various aid sites. Fewer homeless service organizations are open outside the capital and these cannot provide all the necessary services. In Szeged, for instance, accommodating homeless women and providing extra services in winter are longstanding problems. Social work on the streets is carried out with great difficulty. There is no programme either for solving matters of housing, or for rehabilitation. The majority of the homeless escape the attention of supply local government institutions. Aside from the homeless, many people possessing homes but living under extreme conditions are also forced to make use of the same services.

There is one common problem for homeless shelters: street people do not like to sleep in shelters because they regard all rules as a burden, but also because of a fear of theft. In addition, shelters do not allow intoxicated persons to enter. Another problem mentioned by my informants is the separation of men and women in shelters, a rule which discriminates against those who are married. Great responsibility falls on health care and social workers who often find the ill and unaided homeless only at the last moment.

As I mentioned earlier, the world of the homeless is rarely seen by society at large, yet takes place inside it. It possesses a unique, separate set of values that embrace the need for survival, the idea of freedom, and a variety of lifestyles without responsibilities. These are criticized by some of the beggars themselves: 'We say that we are free, but what [is freedom] for if we starve to death in the meantime?' There are some rules that cannot and must not be disobeyed such as mutuality, protection and the rule that aspects of the past are not open to discussion. Some homeless people have committed many crimes – beginning with pickpocketing and stealing and progressing to blackmarketeering, rape or murder – but talking about these is prohibited among homeless people. If someone breaks these rules they will be beaten without warning. Crimes of less significance committed by the gang are discussed only behind each other's back. Conversely, ex-prisoners display the symbols of their crimes and punishments as tattoos on the forearm and wrist.

Throughout my fieldwork with the homeless, I have come to realize that the so-called strong family relations that exist among homeless people tend to erode and are increasingly conflict ridden. Weak ties like friendships, colleagiality, formal or informal relationships refer only to present situations. Old relationships have totally fallen apart while present ones refer only to those in a similar situation, that of homelessness. Relationships outside the homeless world involve only those who can help contribute toward raising the status of the homeless person. At the same time, homeless people usually state that escape from their circumstances is considerably hindered by many of their fellows. If one has some money, others begin to beg for it, and manipulate one's feelings. If one has accommodation, others will move in to it. And if one is able to find a job, other homeless people will surely loiter around the workplace and cause one trouble. Soon any changes in lifestyle are lost; an 'achiever' will finds themselves back on the street again within a few weeks.

The world of the homeless is based on personal ties, often in the forms of pairs and couples who try to protect each other. Usually, there is a vow of 'blood brotherhood' (*vértestvérség*) between each person that is also extended to the entire group, and a vow that they will help each other to the last. Besides sharing everything, they also share the problem of being unable to find the way out of their predicament on their own. Through differences in opportunities, a patron–client relationship develops among people who are homeless. Thus escaping the homeless subculture is made more difficult because of these strong bonds: the more unfortunate tend to pull back those who are more successful in getting out of the homeless predicament.

There are two types of patron–client relationship. The first kind is generally between a patron who is not homeless and a client who is. Patrons may be temporary or permanent. Most permanent patrons do not contact homeless people through civil organizations but associate with them through personal interactions. According to the homeless, they benefit from patrons' emotional needs. In the daily routine, the patron helps the beggar by giving them small amounts of money, clothes or food, exchanges during which they have a superficial conversation. As this relationship mostly depends on the patron, it is chiefly one-sided: the patron satisfies their desire to help the less fortunate, but the homeless recipient does not feel a special personal bond or emotional attachment.

The second type is almost unknown in real life situations: the patron is homeless and the client is not. This usually involves occasional child support – such as giving a computer or a greater amount of money – deriving from illegal or semi-illegal activities (for example he steals or begs and sends the takings to the children). These relationships are rarely mutual, so this does not assist someone in finding their way out of homelessness.

Relationships that help physical survival or reduce deprivation are of great importance. To the homeless these are highly valued but when both patron and client are homeless or both of a low social status they are even more precious. If the balance becomes unequal it is quite hard to restore it. Among the homeless there is a rule: 'if you help others, you will be helped in return. Share what you have, do not horde for yourself!' Those who intentionally break this rule lose prestige and are expelled from their circle of associates. Necessity and mutuality go hand in hand because homeless people depend on each other for survival: needs carry mutuality, and mutuality helps fulfil needs. These require and result in a constant presence in each others' lives as they share all the food, drink, tobacco and dwelling space; they also protect each other. This mutual dependency leads to inescapable homelessness, which cannot be interpreted without understanding the context of being excluded (Nagy 2004).

Being homeless not only means a physical exclusion from society but also exclusion from regular social processes. Homeless people are considered to be outside mainstream society and culture, members of which leave the homeless on their own both symbolically and literally (Caldeira 1999: 102–105; Frankfurt 1997; Jordan 1996: 81). Being penniless and lacking property is not just powerlessness per se but also means being denied access to basic food, shelter, work and a normal social identity. To make up for this, those excluded build new social groups with new preferences and create a value system of their own that is far from that of the majority. Living on the street, and phenomena associated with it such as alcohol abuse, results in social disapproval but even social institutions engender their own prejudice and create a bad reputation for social institutions who helped the homeless.

Houses and homes – the centre of everything according to the majority – symbolize a world of order by providing security and a feeling of importance. Without these, a person is considered insecure, insignificant, defenseless and deprived. The homeless are deprived of their security and of the means for fulfilling their own desires. In addition, they are deprived of their civil rights. Although, theoretically, homeless people can vote, they often cannot exercise this right as they have no registered permanent address or they have sold their ID cards. As a result, essential civil rights are severely lacking for the homeless. Some homeless people's narratives recount being unable to get any social support or subsidy because they could not arrange for them individually. Social workers could help with these problems, but only if the homeless would accept their help, which they often reject.

Enclosure of Areas

Not having a place of their own, the homeless live in public spaces, a fact that is worth examining in more detail. How is it possible to live on the street? If they live on the street, how much of the street belongs to them? Legally speaking public spaces do not belong to homeless. But if one considers that places used by the homeless are seen as being different and that the majority population refuses to use them, it can be argued that there is a different interpretation of territoriality. Public spaces are technically open to everyone, but from the moment someone marks a public space as their own domestic space majority citizens turn away from it. This appropriation marks the space as intimate both for regular citizens and the homeless as well; the space becomes someone's home. Through this illegal occupation, living in public areas becomes a kind of legitimate homesteading. From the perspective of the homeless it is easy to see this special kind of public territoriality. A 43–year-old explains:

> This place is ours, me and my brother's. If another tramp turns up, we tell him to leave as this place is ours. All who help us come back here for they know they find us here. It's been ours since last year. Formerly no one was here, only a beggar, no one else. The promenade belongs to the Csibaks, and Tibor is there, too. Sometimes we come around, but we never work [i.e. beg] in their place.

There are some protected areas belonging to old homeless people. Public squares and streets of the city have already been appropriated by the homeless; these are the spaces in which the homeless attempt to earn some money. Territorial challenges often lead to skirmishes or even violent fights. From the Szeged example it is obvious that the majority of the city's inhabitants do not accept this colonization of public spaces and tey often ask local government to intervene and expel the homeless. For example, two elderly ladies who lived at a bus station were forcefully sent to an elderly people's facility. After a time, people forgot that the bus station was once the old ladies' home and it could be used again as a public space. Cemetery crypts and suburban parks have also gone through this process of colonization and reclamation. According to homeless people, many areas of public space have been developed according to the business concerns and desire for an orderly everyday life of citizens. Cities are notorious for carving out new zones (see Caldeira 1999), those places where the homeless can establish their own shelters and those spaces where they cannot. Among the former there can be spaces, sometimes the busiest market areas of town, which the homeless utilize for begging and generally hanging out (Bridge and Watson 2001; Sassen 1999).

Conclusion: Being Locked into a Homeless Life

I have discussed here the phenomenon of postsocialist poverty by focusing especially on the culture of homelessness in Hungary. As we have seen from the above, poverty in the postsocialist era is the result of two interrelated factors. State socialism developed its own poverty, and had its own kind of homelessness, and this was carried into the new era after the socio-economic and political reforms of 1990. To this was added a new group of homeless who could not manage under the new economic conditions that pertained after the fall of socialism. The new culture of homelessness is characterized by the feeling of uncertainty and hopelessness. No doubt the visibility and the size of the homeless population has shocked most of the citizens of Hungary, but they have lacked the power to help these people off the streets and solve their problems. To be sure, all Hungarian citizens had to face new problems as the result of the transition to a capitalist economy and multi-party democracy. However, assistance and help cannot be expected from anybody other than the society itself. Eventually, we must face the fact that the homeless are part of our society; we must see an end to the enormous resentment harboured by the majority of citizens, who only see exclusion as a solution to the problem.

In Szeged, like anywhere else in Hungary, the homeless are excluded from the normal way of life. It can be argued that they are 'locked' in a separate society. While exclusion implies being kept out of something, being 'locked in' implies that the status of the homeless derives from their lifestyle. Sometimes homeless people perceive these issues in a matter of fact way. Porky has this to say:

> If I worked again ... everything would be fine, but I have got used to living without the same old song: 'Eight hours of work, eight hours of rest and eight hours of amusement'. I am not able to get up in the morning and leave for work. I have got used to getting up when I want, then looking around and going back to sleep again. It could not be the same any more and it would not work at all I suppose.

The regular scheduling of everyday life changes according to daily concerns: sleep is often interrupted because of the need to monitor one's surroundings. Daytime consists of doing nothing or begging, and obtaining food and keeping clean are irregular if not neglected altogether. All these would not be enough to get locked into the homeless lifestyle. Instead, being locked in is a result of a particular culture of homelessness: being dependent on each other for survival and the cohesion of homeless groups means that the condition of homelessness is virtually inescapable. As most social relationships involve other homeless people, it is almost impossible to overcome being locked in.

Although many shelters and social workers could help homeless people establish a new lifestyle for themselves, by finding them a job or retraining programmes, many of the homeless do not wish to change as they fear being deprived of what little they still have. Serious and countrywide plans and programmes for rehabilitation are also missing from government and local government policy and those missed by some of homeless. Losing faith in the future, physical and mental deterioration, all support the homeless in choosing to stick with the homeless lifestyle. As time passes, all these factors become more and more serious: the more time they spend on the street, the less chance they have of escaping and starting a new life.

Notes

1. Szeged is one of the large cities in Hungary. On a local scale, it counts as a large city, but as for its characteristics, it could be considered a small town. Historically, Szeged was an agricultural and commercial town until the building of a university in the first third of the twentieth century. In the socialist era, industrial estates were built by the municipality; these were closed down after the end of the socialist era.. The city, however, still plays an important role in the region, both from an economic and cultural point of view. As regards homelessness, it is apparent that impoverished individuals from nearby settlements believe they can find a solution to their problems by moving to Szeged, where they become homeless in the public places of the city.

2. Tramps (*csavargó*). Like dossers, tramps lived on the streets; however, unlike dossers, they had no homes to return to. Tramps often finished school, became unemployed, begged and lived by casual labour. Some dossers and tramps tried to live 'outside' society, drawing on an ideology against the established order.

3. Criminally idle, criminal idler (*közveszélyes munkakerülő*). During the socialist era, a person's status was dependent on their employment. Those who did not seek employment, or did not find a job in a short time, were considered penal idlers. According to the opinion of the time they were a threat to the existing order and the building of socialism as they would not participate in it. This label was noted on their identity papers, and policemen checking their identities could march them away, or from time to time the local government offered them work.

4. Dosser (*csöves*). In the socialist era, youths living on the streets were called dossers. Many of them escaped from parental supervision to the streets, while some of them began living in public spaces as truants. Their name originates from the drainage tubes (*csövek*), found on building sites, in which they took shelter. Most of them lived only temporarily on the streets. Their characteristic clothing also separated them from other youth subcultures: 'tube-like' trousers, long pullovers, studded leather jackets, gas mask shoulder bags.

5. The numbers after the citation of interview means the year and the serial number of interview with marked person.

6. Bed share (*ágybérlet*). The severe housing shortage made it impossible for all workers to find places in hostels or to rent a room in a flat. People desperate for some kind of shelter could rent a bed in a room holding 10 to 15 beds, with no access to cooking or other privileges.

7. Workers' hostels (*munkásszállás*). In order to satisfy the labour demands of rapidly developing industrial production, companies established hostels which provided accommodation for workers 'enticed' away from the countryside. There were separate hostels for men and women. People living in these considered them a temporary solution, but sometimes a temporary solution became long term one. On workers' hostels in Budapest, see Kürti (2002).

8. Second economy (*második gazdaság*). The second economy was based on work outside working hours. Lots of workers used to run a farm or take small jobs at home to supplement their family's income. They saved up their strength during work time for the second economy. It was not illegal, because at the time there was no income tax or laws about market production; however, these activities reduced the productivity of the first economy.

9. Every single day in calendar is attached to a name (previously a name of a saint) and whoever wears that name, celebrates the day on the certain date by inviting separately colleagues and family members to drink and eat.

10. Secondary incomes (*mellékes* or *mellékes jövedelem*) were derived from work undertaken as part of the second economy.

11. It means that instead of work there were the live from social benefits. This means they create the right conditions for getting continuous allowances.

12. Poverty identity. Researchers had to construct a concept from questions and answers about a poor person's life. Informants often would not respond through feelings of shame, distrust of authority, and a fear that if they complained they might be punished. Nevertheless,

through questions of what a person did or did not have (such as access to cooking facilities or sufficient food) the researchers could determine a general minimum standard of living. Instead of working with a concept of 'the poor', researchers asked 'what do people lack from an acceptable standard of living?'
13. The Knife-thrower (*késdobáló*). This is a disreputable pub where brawls are commonplace and often occur so that customers can show their own strength. Drinks are cheap and regular customers often pull knives.
14. *Pillepalackos* (or *pillepalackos bor, kannás bor*). The name refers to the plastic bottle, with a twist-off top, which holds cheap wine made from grapes of questionable quality and other ingredients.

References

Bokor, Á. 1987. *Szegénység a mai Magyarországon*. Budapest: Magvető Kiadó
Borboly, I., G. Horváth, I. Kovách, and R. Nagy. 2003. 'A feketegazdaság: érdekek és szereplők', in I. Kovách (ed.) *Hatalom és társadalmi változás. A posztszocializmus vége. Szociológiai tanulmányok*. Budapest: Napvilág Kiadó, pp.183–215.
Bridge, G. and S. Watson. 2001. 'Retext(ur)ing the city', *City* 5(3): 350–62.
Caldeira, T. 1999. 'Fortified Enclaves: The New Urban Segregation', in S. Low (ed.) *Theorizing the City: The New Urban Anthropology Reader*. New Brunswick, NJ: Rutgers University Press.
Corrigan, P. 1976. 'Doing Nothing', in S. Hall and T. Jefferson (eds), *Resistance through Rituals*. London: Hutchinson, pp.103–5
Costa Nunez, R. 1996. *The New Poverty: Homeless Families in America*. New York: Plenum.
Diósi, Á. 1978. 'Szövőlányok', *Kultúra és Közösség* 4(4): 56–74.
Eberstadt, N. 1988. *The Poverty of Communism*. New Brunswick, NJ: Transaction Books.
Elekes, Zs. 2000. 'Alkoholprobléma az ezredvégi Magyarországon', in Zs. Elekes and Zs. Spéder (eds), *Törések és kötések a magyar társadalomban*. Budapest: Andorka Rudolf Társadalomtudományi Társaság: Századvég Kiadó, pp.152–69.
Ferge, Zs. 1982. *Társadalmi újratermelés és társadalompolitika*. Budapest: Közgazdasági és Jogi Kiadó.
Frankfurt, H. 1997. 'Equality and Respect', *Social Research* 64(1): 3–15.
Gönczöl, K. 1982. 'A hátrányos helyzet és a bűnözés', *Valóság* 24(8): 61–72.
———— 1991. *Bűnös szegények*. Budapest: Közgazdasági és Jogi Kiadó.
Hazra, A. 2005. 'Poverty and Politics: Some Empirical Observations'. Unpublished conference paper. Retrieved 19 February 2005 from www.anthrobase.com/ txt/H/Hazra_A_01.htm.
Höjdestrand, T. 2003. 'The Soviet-Russian Production of Homelessness: Propiska, Housing, Privatisation'. Retrieved 19 February 2005 from www.anthrobase. com/txt/H/Hoejdestrand_T_01.htm
Iványi, G. 1997. *Hajléktalanok*. Budapest: Sík Kiadó.
Jancius, A. 2002. 'Social Markets and the Meaning of Work in Eastern Germany', in U. Kockel (ed.) *Culture and Economy: Contemporary Perspectives*. Hampshire: Ashgate. pp.60–70.
Jordan, B. 1996. *A Theory of Poverty and Social Exclusion*. Cambridge: Polity.

Kemény, I. 1979. 'Poverty in Hungary', *Social Science Information* 18(2): 247–267.

Kőbányai, J. 1980. 'A „csöves kérdés"', *Kultúra és Közösség* 6(4): 95–101.

———— 1982. 'A margón', *Valóság* 24(1): 93–101.

Kürti, L. 2002. *Youth and State in Hungary: Capitalism, Communism and Class*. London: Pluto.

Laki, L. 2003 'A szegénység közelebbről', in I. Kovách (ed.) *Hatalom és társadalmi változás. A posztszocializmus vége. Szociológiai tanulmányok*. Budapest: Napvilág Kiadó, pp.113–31.

Láng, K. and G. Nyilas. 1987. 'Ideiglenes állandóság. Tanulmány a munkásszálláson élők életkörülményeiről és rétegződéséről', in Á. Utasi (ed.) *Peremhelyzetek. Műhelytanulmányok. Rétegződés-modell vizsgálat VIII*. Budapest: Társadalomtudományi Intézet, pp.33–100.

Mátyus, A. 1978. 'Lakóhely és életmód', *Kultúra és Közösség* 4(4): 49–55.

Nagy, T. 2004. 'Kapcsolatháló elemzés egy szegedi hajléktalancsoportban', in I. Pászka (ed.) *A látóhatár mögött. Szociológiai tanulmányok*. Szeged: Belvedere Meridionale, pp.91–139.

Rácz, J. 1998. 'Semmittevés. Lakótelep és szegénynegyed mentalitás', in J. Rácz (ed.) *Ifjúsági (szub)kultúrák, intézmények, devianciák.Válogatott tanulmányok. Scientia Humana*. Budapest: Scientia Humana, pp.117–29

Sassen, S. 1999. 'Whose City Is It? Globalization and the Formation of New Claims', in J. Holston (ed.) *Cities and Citizenship*. Durham, NC: Duke University Press

Šiklová, J. 1996. 'What Did We Lose After 1989?' *Social Research* 63(2): 531–41.

Simonyi, Á. 1995. 'Munka nélkül. Családi alkalmazkodási stratégiák és hiányuk', *Szociológiai Szemle* 1995(1): 55–70.

Spéder, Zs. 2000. 'Az inaktívak tagolódása az 1990–es évek Magyarországán', in Zs. Elekes and Zs. Spéder (eds), *Törések és kötések a magyar társadalomban*. Budapest: Andorka Rudolf Társadalomtudományi Társaság – Századvég Kiadó, pp.69–96.

———— 2002. *A szegénység változó arcai. Tények és értelmezések*. Budapest: Andorka Rudolf Társadalomtudományi Társaság – Századvég Kiadó.

Szalai, J. 1997. 'Power and Poverty', *Social Research* 64(4): 1403–22

Tamási, E. 2004. 'Egy férfinyira a hajléktalanságtól. Nőpolitika és hajléktalan nők az Európai Unióban', *Esély* 15(3): 26–57.

Utasi, Á. 1987. 'Hajléktalanok, csavargók', in Á. Utasi (ed.) *Peremhelyzetek. Műhelytanulmányok. Rétegződés-modell vizsgálat VIII*. Budapest: Társadalomtudományi Intézet, pp.181–213.

Veres, S. 1979. 'A munkásszálló – kérdőjelekkel', *Valóság* 21(4): 66–79.

Chapter 10

Political Anthropology of the Postcommunist Czech Republic: Local–National and Rural–Urban Scenes

Peter Skalník

In the Czech Republic, post-1989 social change has been strongly informed by politics on all levels. The introduction of democracy has been accompanied by serious contradictions which make many people question the meaning of the transformation from communism to democracy and a market economy. The egalitarian model prevailing in the past is being challenged, and the aggrandizement of managers and politicians leads to the perception of a deep cleavage between citizens and the political elite. Research[1] on the postcommunist[2] nature of national and local political culture, and on the content of rural political life, shows that whereas local politics is actively embraced, because it is based on individual qualities of local public figures, national and to some extent urban politics is devoid of the participation of citizen–voters. The youngest generation of adults tends to be apolitical while older generations are disappointed by the empty content of representative democracy. The result is a widespread recourse to populist, nationalist or celebrity figures who introduce substitute images of politics resulting in a preference for passive political behaviour.

The Czech Republic emerged at the end of 1992 as a result of the break up of federal Czechoslovakia into two successor states. This break up was a by-product of the demise of communist rule which occurred towards the end of 1989 because ethnically based politics, kept under control under communism, re-entered the political scene almost immediately after the shift to liberal democracy.[3] Whereas the first free elections of 1990 can be understood as a spontaneous negation of communism which swept to power a quasi-party rejecting communism,[4] the postcommunist political elites which emerged victorious in the 1992 elections were much more politically sophisticated as well as being ethnically pronounced.[5] By emphasizing an ethno-nationalist agenda,[6] the newly elected leaders – Václav Klaus (of the Civic Democratic Party, or ODS) in the Czech-speaking western part of Czechoslovakia and Vladimír Mečiar (of the Movement for a Democratic Slovakia, or HZDS) of the Slovak-speaking eastern part – were unable to agree on the formation of a viable federal government. Instead, they became prime ministers of the Czech Republic and Slovak Republic respectively and thus made Czechoslovakia and its President and Federal Assembly obsolete. Mečiar's symbolic declaration of sovereignty for Slovakia provoked the resignation of Václav Havel, until then President of the federal Czechoslovakia, in July 1992. The federal parliament then had to prepare and approve a smooth and legal division of Czechoslovakia into two sovereign independent states and thus also seal its own demise and oblivion. Instead, the Czech National Council and the Slovak National Council, parliaments of the two republics of the federation and composed up until then of deputies of secondary political importance, suddenly became parliaments of the successor states, the Czech Republic and the Slovak Republic, which each declared independence on 1 January 1993.

Whereas sociologists and political scientists have attempted to grasp the political changes, which led to the disappearance of Czechoslovakia from the map and its confinement to history (Musil 1995), anthropologists have concentrated instead on the role of people's perception of politics, especially during the revolutionary changes. Czech-born and trained British anthropologist Ladislav Holy, whose book *The Little Czech and the Great Czech Nation* (1996) is based on the author's research sojourn in Prague during the last two years of Czechoslovakia, tried to explain the symbolism of the demise of communism by the elevation of a nation (the Czech ethnic nation) and its alienation from the state. On the other hand, Ernest Gellner, a Czech who trained in Britain as a philosopher, sociologist and social anthropologist, and who spent the last few years of his life in Prague, saw Czech nationalism as culminating in the quest for statehood (Gellner 1997). Both Holy and Gellner agreed that the disappearance of Czechoslovakia would not be such a tragedy if it was replaced by a viable Czech state (pers.comm.).[7] Holy believed that Czech nationalism existed but that it was hidden from the Czechs themselves. During the almost seventy-five years of Czechoslovakia's existence, Czechs identified themselves almost automatically with Czechoslovakia as their nation state. Their identification with Czechoslovakia was superior to that of Slovaks. Czech nationalism was autonomous, without need of comparison to any other nation (more than forty years of the communist system with its proverbial isolationism only strengthened this self-perception). Unfortunately Holy did not undertake any comparative study of socialism as it manifested itself in other countries, nor did he analyse Czech culture by comparing it with German or Slovak culture. His conceptualization of culture is political. Czech political culture for Holy is a complex of tacitly shared signs and symbols which allow members of the Czech nation to communicate among themselves.

The Czech ethnic nation (*český národ*) is obviously a modern society which believes firmly in its inherent democratic nature. The Czech society which produced this political culture is united by its belief in (its own) high culture, in the Gellnerian sense. An innate desire for democracy combines with egalitarianism and the allegedly typical Czech quest for freedom. Czechs were, therefore, fully entitled to be embraced by an (advanced) Europe to which they have belonged from time immemorial. However, this self-centered national pride is devalued by the humbleness of each and every Czech person. Gellner, in contrast to Holy, was influenced by the Czech phenomenological philosopher Jan Patočka, author of *Who are the Czechs?* (1992). Gellner looked critically at views of Tomáš G. Masaryk, a realist philosopher and the founding president of Czechoslovakia, who is largely responsible for the Czech national self-image, according to which Czechs are democrats and fighters against the conservatism of both feudalism and the papacy since the Hussite religious pre-reformation of the fifteenth century. It was Masaryk who implanted a historical 'navel' onto the body of the Czech nation and prompted modern Czech nationalism to culminate in its eventual demand for independent statehood (Gellner 1994a, 1997).

The Importance of Political Culture

Anthropologists interested in postcommunist politics soon realize that it is the question of political culture which they must examine before arriving at conclusions about the nature of the changes which have occurred in postcommunist countries such as the Czech Republic or Slovakia following the Velvet Revolution of 1989. Even the 'velvetness' of the Revolution will have to be analysed in these terms. The main problem, however, concerns the nature of the politicization of people, the very quality of citizenship in the postcommunist era. Has the subject type of political culture, undeniably dominant during the communist period, continued to be dominant during the postcommunist years or has it started to disappear? In other words, are we witnessing the (re-) emergence of the citizens or the continuation of the subjects bending their back before new power holders?

More than forty years ago, when Almond and Verba (1963) developed their tripartite typology of parochial, subject and participant political culture, they displayed, perhaps unwittingly, a tendency toward evolutionist thinking. Their sample was limited to four 'developed' countries (the U.S., the U.K., West Germany and Italy) and one 'less developed' (Mexico). It is well known that since the appearance of the book, Western writers in the 1970s and 1980s looked closely at the political culture of the 'Second World' (that is, communist states). Political anthropologists can do a lot of highly useful work here, provided they fully recognize that their locally gathered 'micro-data' must be related to 'macro-data' from other social sciences. They should also clearly distinguish between power and authority (see Skalník 1999b). Political anthropology rejects the isolationism of cultural circles or civilizations. Its methodology is comparative, and not limited to the study of one country. For example, comparisons of seemingly incomparable situations – such as between African states and those of East-Central Europe or the post-Soviet world – are possible and desirable (see, e.g., Skalník 1999a, 2001a, 2001b; Beissinger and Young 2002). Through concrete studies and comparisons, we can arrive at a deeper understanding of political culture which does not limit itself to evolutionist (and quasi-racist) typologies. Unlike the rather psychological definition employed by Pye and Verba (1965), my own definition views political culture as an objectively existing phenomenon which can be empirically studied as both behaviour and cognition:

> political culture is the values, attitudes and practices, usually derived from the past, which cause political processes to vary from country to country, region to region, group to group. [It] is a social complex of notions and practices which presuppose a certain consensus between the actors of a certain country or cultural area; it has to be recognized as common for a certain number of people. (Skalník 2000: 65)

Political culture changes more slowly than everyday politics and economics. Political culture belongs to the ideology of a concrete social collective and therefore cannot be seen as a tactical instrument of politics. But it is omnipresent in political behaviour: there is no politics without political culture. Those politicians who underestimate political culture, ignore it or do not try to change it in accordance with their political goals, are not successful. Political culture, like a proverbial boomerang, would then return the practical strivings of politicians, parties and movements back to the spot from which they started. It is widely recognized that the notion of political culture was developed originally in anthropology and later adopted by political science. Political anthropology emphasizes qualitative research in the field where practical political behaviour is observed, and this enables anthropologists to test hypotheses about political attitudes and values. The quest of political anthropologists is to postulate universal qualities of politics by way of analyses of individual case studies without presupposing the existence of closed cultures, whether they be tribal, national, professional or local. Cultures, if we can speak of them in the plural, are always semi-autonomous social fields, interconnected with the rest of social relations in the world. Because the world of today is globalizing very fast, one can see a counter-process of particularism, enhanced by identity politics and propelled by culturalist mythologies.[8]

The resurgence of political culture was precipitated by the fall of communist regimes in Europe and Mongolia, by the disintegration of Yugoslavia, the Soviet Union and Czechoslovakia, and by radical economic transformations in China and Vietnam.[9] Hardly anyone would deny that the adoption of democracy in formerly communist countries sparked pro-democratic turnabouts in many African, Latin American and Asian countries. However, this change was easier to carry out at a rhetorical level than in terms of the reality of political behaviour and the lives of ordinary people. Democracy became a fashion, often being limited to rituals of regular voting. During the recent process of real and seeming democratization in the world it also became apparent that there are considerable differences in political culture among well-established liberal democracies, as well as in the newly democratic countries of East-Central Europe and beyond. By adhering to democracy in their political rhetoric and even their laws, people do not necessarily practice democratic principles nor consider democracy a cornerstone of their value system. The whole world now claims to adhere to democracy. However, understandings of this concept differ considerably from country to country, even from one social group to another. We can suppose that the practice of so-called postcommunism is rightly designated 'post-communist' exactly because elements of political culture of the communist period continue to be relevant during the transitional period. It may even be argued that the length of the transition will be dependent to a large extent on the conservative character and adjustment of political culture.

If one looks at political culture in Western European countries, in comparison with the tenacity of communist and postcommunist political culture as well as the continuity of political culture outside Europe, one has to admit that the widely and loosely used concept 'Western democracy' actually represents an unusually varied social phenomenon which, depending on the historical background of each country, imprints different characteristics on the political processes of different Western European countries. Indeed, the point is also valid for the four traditional liberal democracies outside Europe, the U.S.A., Canada, Australia and New Zealand. In all other non-European countries, whether they were once colonies or not, Western models of democracy, however internally structured, have to be reconciled with the existence of stronger or weaker elements of local political tradition or equally imported autocratic forms of politics. In my opinion the question is not whether Western liberal democratic model(s) supersede other models but rather how successful is the combination of imported factors and local ones. In other words, a lot depends on the admission that a compromise must be reached whereby autochthonous forces and models of non-Western origin, as well as hybrid political arrangements, are recognized as legitimate expressions of political creativity. If this is not allowed to happen, there is a serious danger of a return to non-democratic politics.

One of the ways of doing anthropological research on the meaning of politics is through the study of folk models. It is significant that the majority of respondents in a limited research project, which I carried out in 2000 with the help of my political anthropology students at Charles University, were convinced that political culture concerns the way politicians behave in the political arena and not the attitudes of a class or the population of a country or region. Respondents understood political culture as the culture of politicians, that is, their decency, honesty, how they fulfil their promises, and so on. Political culture in the Czech Republic appeared to them to be largely negative because politicians 'lack culture' in their disputes. Politicians, in their view, put the interests of their respective parties before more general, regional or national interests. 'A politician should be first of all a human being before being a party member', said one respondent. Another maintained that truth is the cornerstone of political culture. An ideal political culture should consist of decent, direct and non-conflictual behaviour. Many respondents believed that changing the political culture of politicians is nearly impossible. A truly participant political culture in which power would be equally shared is according to them impossible in a large modern society such as that of the Czech Republic. Power must be centralized and centralized power inevitably leads to non-democratic practices, to oligarchy. Even though they admitted that each society has politics and therefore also a political culture, some respondents even went as far as denying altogether the existence of political culture in the Czech Republic. For others, while political culture was seen to possibly exist in the Czech Republic, it was seen as having insufficient prestige: 'Politicians think that once they are voted in voters should shut up. Citizens have no confidence in politics and politicians. It is Czech smallness which is the problem', wrote one of the student respondents. The same student included voters within the concept of political culture, but she argued that civil society is poorly developed. According to her, the politicians do not want to accept civil society because it prevents politicians' monopolization of politics. They do not want to allow non-governmental structures. According to one respondent, political culture is 'a style of work (cooperation) among politicians led in the form of discussion and listening', whereas another believed that it means 'relations of politicians to the citizens (voters)'. Politicians should represent and fight for the interests of voters and not for their own interests or those of companies or organizations which support them.

Others suggested that political culture is formed by the way politicians behave in public and how they relate to each other. This has a direct bearing on the question about the relationship between representative and direct forms of democracy. One of the researchers concluded that representative democracy is comfortable for both voters and politicians because voters do not need to do more than vote and politicians do whatever they like. Therefore some young people do not vote. Czech respondents also contrasted their country and the 'West' (an emic concept deserving analysis in itself). Whereas Czech political culture was a 'catastrophe' for one respondent, it stands in stark contrast to 'political culture in countries where it could develop for centuries without interruption ... rich countries where people do not fear to engage themselves, to stand up'. Still another respondent had no illusions about 'culture in politics'. While criticizing the public behaviour of the then Prime Minister, Miloš Zeman, she believed that 'politicians in the West have a different style, a kind of greater respect for citizens, they are not that reckless'. A 23–year-old university-educated person dismissed the level of political culture in the Czech Republic: 'When I sometimes follow how politicians express themselves, I feel a mixture of stupefaction and shame for "what we have voted for"'. A student analyst added that voters are also responsible for the low level of political culture. Public opinion goes against the accumulation of offices or the theft of public funds. Still another opinion was expressed by another student researcher, who considered political culture being 'a dialogue between coalition and opposition or within the opposition itself'. Political culture, the student added, should involve the 'distinguished behaviour of all politicians in public, without attacks, half-truths and misleading citizens'. She also believed that this concerns the mass media. A male respondent understood political culture as 'a measure of participation of the citizen in politics and simultaneously her or his consciousness about political developments in her or his country'. Another young male respondent with secondary education expected from political culture 'decency, correctness, no low class'. He required decency among politicians and of politicians towards voters. He accused leading politicians of 'spitting in our face'. He also demanded better transparency and stronger pressure from citizens, who should say to the politicians what they dislike. A middle-aged female respondent complained about the vulgar behaviour of politicians among themselves.

That respondents to the questions posed by my students cared more for the 'cultured' behaviour of politicians rather than political culture overall became clear with the pinpointing of Miloš Zeman as the quintessence of immaturity in Czech political culture, a man whose attitudes were seen to represent 'political puberty'.[10] Politicians' morality, ethics and sensitivity is what matters. Political culture is the correct behaviour of politicians who do not lie, do not politick, and fulfil their election programme, asserted a 50–year-old accountant. She demanded that politicians 'behave in a cultured way, meaning that they do not abuse their position and do not work on … the boards of various firms and take money for it instead of caring for people'. A 42–year-old shop assistant even considered political culture a contradiction in terms because, she said, politics lacks culture. Taking this for granted, she suggested that, nevertheless, politicians should behave decently towards others, and they should have good relations with the media. Meanwhile, one student researcher concluded that politicians such as deputies should be left to do what they like: 'We voted them in and now they rule. We fulfilled our task and now we should leave them to do their work, which is their task'. Another student researcher directly asserted that political culture is something that has not been achieved in the Czech Republic. What was been achieved is chaos and with few exceptions politicians are profiteers.

Cynicism was also found. According to one student of history, politics was never a cultured activity. In the Austro-Hungarian Imperial Council deputies for the Young Czech Party slammed tables and used trumpets to disturb the proceedings, they pointed out, while during the first

Czechoslovak republic deputies brawled and stole. The communist era, they added, does not require comment. 'What do we not like about the cultivated liars and poseurs of today?' the student asked rhetorically, adding that those who criticize politicians in beer halls are the same as the subjects of their criticism; the only difference is that they lack the chance to perpetrate the same misdemeanours. According to this respondent, politics lacks all those attributes which could be seen as part of culture: openness, truth, honesty and fair play.

We could continue citing many of the other responses recorded in this small research project. The common denominator of all remarks is the unusual degree of scepticism about the very existence of political culture in the postcommunist Czech Republic. Most interviewees discounted the possibility of citizens influencing and informing political culture, the latter being seen as the work of politicians, not of society. One respondent even doubted that the phrase 'political culture' made sense, for the two words seemed to be incompatible.

The Question of Direct Democracy

In addition to the research outlined above, the possibility of direct democracy in the Czech Republic was studied with students of political anthropology at the University of Pardubice. However, even the students did not connect this question to the problem of political culture. According to them direct democracy was not part of political culture. Politicians should be decent, responsible but it was not clear who or what should compel them to be so. Democratic participatory political culture in particular can be democratic if it concerns all people who thus assume power directly. People do not rule simply on the basis of votes cast in elections but also through the political responsibility and alertness which they show incessantly, between elections as well as during them, by way of the press and through internet forums and speaking in public. It appears that without much doubt the main problem of Czech political culture is the low degree of development of civil society, viewed not only as a collection of non-governmental organizations and civic associations but also as a politically active citizenry. Spontaneity of political expression does not herald a lack of political culture, but rather the opposite. It seems that this was well grasped by the author of one student essay on the question of direct and indirect democracy researched for my course on political anthropology. She argued that representative democracy is not leading to an even distribution of power in society and thus it limits the degree of freedom of its members. In contrast, direct democracy makes possible broader distribution of power and participation in the political process. She pleaded for the implementation of instruments of direct democracy at community level, such as local referendums, and then the application of these to the wider society. However, these were not enough in themselves. The referendum on European Union membership in the Czech Republic, for example, was not an exercise in direct democracy because the voters were not given the chance of understanding what they were voting for. They did not have access to the relevant facts; instead of a reasoned argument, their votes were wooed by charismatic faces on posters. Thus, she suspected that the results of the referendum were predictable because manipulated in advance.

Representative democracy was preferred by fourteen out of twenty respondents in another student research project. However, the researcher's respondents stated that democratic elections do not promote meritocratic principles but rather candidates of a party irrespective of their qualification for office, or those people who attract attention by various techniques of voter manipulation. Citizens cannot control those elected representatives who do not fulfil their promises, nor parties which do not keep to their manifestos, because there is no feedback between elected politicians and their voters. When important questions are discussed and decisions taken, voters have to rely on their representatives, whether or not they respect them, and vice versa. In contrast, young people in particular favoured the potential of direct democracy, which allows them to co-decide, to vote about substantial questions concerning their country and thus influence their future without having to rely on politicians. The same young respondents were aware of the danger of lack of information, demagogy, blind party propaganda or other misleading factors which might influence decisions in direct democracy. Questions in referendums also tend to be too unambiguous, allowing only yes or no answers, with the result that they exclude deeper understandings of the problem and the possibility of further comment. This does not, however, mean that citizens should not decide in referendums. The same research showed that two-thirds of respondents wanted to participate in the politics of the state by way of referendums. They wanted to submit to referendums questions such as the prohibition of abortion, same-sex marriages, the adoption of children by homosexuals or an increase in the retirement age. Again, however, three-quarters of the same respondents admitted that they might not be competent to vote on such issues because of a lack of information. The researcher concluded that she was against a greater use of referendums because although ideally all citizens should participate, many would not because they either disagreed or felt too ill-informed to be able to decide responsibly. She argued that an ordinary citizen who is not a professional can hardly decide about complex issues. People are easily influenced by the media, she said, and see things in terms of personal advantage rather than seeing the consequences for others. She concluded that people would easily succumb to the most persuasive campaign and believe unrealistic promises because they did not understand the problem to be decided upon enough. On the other hand, elections rarely reach 100 per cent participation and those politicians who manage to gain support by pompous pre-election promises are voted in instead of better-qualified specialists.

Another student researcher considered direct democracy in modern populous states impossible, with the exception of referendums and plebiscites. Indeed, at the local level of communes, referendums and thus direct democracy can and should play a more important role. Still, there is a possible problem concerning the expert knowledge needed for decisions about particular problems. People who do not know the relevant issues would end up making ill-informed decisions. Manipulation is another pitfall because charismatic individuals could gain support without having any real merit or sensible ideas of relevance. But the main advantage of direct democracy, according to this researcher, is its democratic character. Everyone gets to decide, not just an elite of chosen (though elected) representatives. 'For people this form of governance is more acceptable because they speak and act directly for themselves'. Technical feasibility speaks in favour of indirect representative democracy because direct democracy in modern states is possible only exceptionally, for example in infrequent referendums or plebiscites. Parliamentarianism is a concrete form of indirect democracy. It is difficult, writes the researcher, to decide which kind of democracy is better and which worse. 'The most ideal solution would be to give larger (but not entire) autonomy to communes because people in the framework of a smaller region have a far better understanding of problems which obtain there than people in "higher places"'. Everyone in the country should decide directly about such important things as EU membership or the election of the president of the country. Those issues which require expert knowledge, and about which an ordinary citizen understands little, should be left to elected representatives, especially to experts among them – for example, parliamentarians who are also physicians should have a greater voice in decisions about health care.

However, I would like to make an objection to this assertion. It is true that politicians seek expert knowledge from specialists, but then they often suppress this knowledge in favour of the political position of their party. Very clear expert knowledge may thus be ignored. The discussion of whether a foetus is a human being can serve here as an illustration. A Christian Democrat doctor or lawyer could ignore the expert scientific knowledge of their profession and instead repeat the dogma of their party's leadership who, in this case, follow the viewpoint of the Pope.

The other example to consider is the direct election of a head of state. Respondents argue that a president elected by popular vote is likely to have a stronger mandate and legitimacy. The student researcher, however, shows that the mandate of an indirectly elected (by parliament) Italian president is, according to the constitution, very weak, but that by way of his personal authority President Ciampi gave his leadership an unprecedented weight. Popular election does not guarantee that a president's personality has as much of an integrating effect as when the office is assumed by great men such as Masaryk or Havel. Some express the view that a strong and charismatic person should become president. But such a person might be a populist, either with wealth or with the backing of the media. 'People are easily manipulated and it is difficult to resist a perfectly staged campaign'. It is also unclear whether the direct election of a president suppresses the influence of political parties. In the case of the Czech Republic direct election of a president would be welcome because political parties are unpopular. But direct election does not automatically guarantee the election of an apolitical or non-party candidate. Direct election of the head of state might enhance a person's legitimacy but this does not mean much unless president's legal powers are also enhanced. A presidential election campaign is financially demanding, and it can lead to 'voter fatigue' and with it a diminished turnout. Besides, a direct election could lead to the election of a popular but entirely unqualified and hence unsuitable person.

Nonetheless, this student researcher obtained results which showed that most people (94 per cent!) preferred direct voting about important questions concerning the state. However, almost half of these were aware of pitfalls, such as the manipulation of voters through the media, the bizarre decision making of citizens, as well as voters' ignorance or limited access to information. These respondents preferred a combination of the two forms of democracy. For which kind of issue one or the other was suitable was, however, uncertain. In the case of direct popular elections for the presidency, 67 per cent of respondents were in favour, 22 per cent were not sure, and a mere 11 per cent were against. Another student researcher suggested keeping the present forms of representative democracy but adding to them the right of people to come up with legislative initiatives and decide in referendums about substantial questions. The same student pointed out that a Movement for Direct Democracy had been started in the Czech Republic and the first international conference on direct democracy was held in the Czech town of Příbram in 1998, the same year in which a worldwide Direct Democracy Newsletter was launched in the Czech Republic. Meanwhile, 67 per cent of the student's respondents clearly preferred an increase in direct democracy and agreed that they believed that representative democracy in the Czech Republic was in crisis. More than three quarters of the respondents also believed that direct democracy would be strengthened after the Czech Republic joined the EU. Most of them knew about the instruments of direct democracy such as national referendums, petitions, local referendums and direct voting. At the same time, 78 per cent of respondents claimed that representative democracy was dominant in the Czech Republic. The researcher believed that the implementation of elements of direct democracy in the Czech Republic would take time while keeping representative forms of democracy would cause a further loss of trust in politicians. The latter would result in a fall in participation in elections, the reason being that the present coalition and opposition have been dominant in Czech politics for too long.

A democratic political culture is democratic only when it concerns all people, some may even say, a little bit demagogically, 'the people', in the singular. The people directly assume power and rule not only because of the votes they cast in elections but because of the political responsibility and alertness they show to all that happens in politics between elections. 'The people' rule through the free press, petitions, activities of various associations, through internet forums, and through public mass protest. The main problem of Czech political culture is that there has been an inadequate development of civil society, understood not only as a set of non-governmental organizations or civic associations but also spontaneous politically active individuals. Spontaneity of political expression is not a sign of a lack of political culture. Rather, it shows that people think politically and are prepared to engage in political issues, locally, nationally and even internationally. It is however necessary to behave in a cultivated way, without resort to violence, blackmail or terror.

Local Politics and National Political Issues: The Example of Dolní Roveň

'A free commune is the foundation of a free state', stipulates the 1849 temporary law 170 on communal self-rule. Is this statement also valid for the commune of Dolní Roveň, which was studied by a team from the University of Pardubice between 2002 and 2004 (see Skalník 2004b)? Rural villages in the present day Czech Republic, founded in the twelfth and thirteenth centuries and occupied today by a mostly agricultural population, once submitted to the rule of secular or ecclesiastical feudal lords. Hussite opposition to the papacy in the fifteenth century and the emergence of Protestantism in the sixteenth century were both defeated in Central Europe. The Counter-Reformation and so-called Second Serfdom followed in the seventeenth century. During the Enlightenment, in the absence of revolutionary pressures in the Austrian multi-ethnic monarchy, it was the reforms of Emperor Josef II which first abolished serfdom in 1781 and reintroduced religious pluralism. It took the monarchy a further sixty years or so to abolish corvée labour and recognize the need for constitutional rule.

Beginning at the time of the revolutionary upheavals of 1848, a modern political society began to develop in the territory of today's Czech Republic, and subjects gradually turned into citizens. By 1907, all the adult male population could vote. In principle this development was a move towards democracy, following the example of the French and American revolutions. However, the development of a democratic political culture among Czechs was complicated by outside forces. The period between 1848 and 1918 was decisively marked by foreign rule. The Kingdom of Bohemia was less and less respected as an autonomous entity during the eighteenth and nineteenth centuries. The last but one Austrian emperor, Franz Josef I (who ruled from 1848 to 1916), did not let himself be crowned as King of Bohemia, a fact which the inhabitants of the kingdom did not find quite fair. The Austrian monarchy first tried to resist the call for constitutionalism and democratic representation on all fronts but eventually allowed the formation of political parties in 1861 and the gradual expansion of the right to select political representatives in elections. Czech political life was further complicated by the fact that in the second half of the nineteenth century it was ever more divided along ethnic lines. Bohemian Czechs and Germans competed in all walks of life, in politics, education, culture and the economy. The Vienna government finally allowed certain reforms that led to Hungary being put on an equal footing with Austria and becoming an independent composite part of the monarchy; Bohemia and Moravia, however, remained integrated parts of the Austrian, western part of the dual monarchy. Czech modern political aspirations were thus frustrated. Nevertheless, Czech politicians were elected as deputies to the Reichsrat (the Imperial Council in Vienna), among them František Udržal (1866–1938), a native of Dolní Roveň and scion of a centuries-old wealthy peasant family, who became one of the leaders of the Agrarian Party.

At the village level, in the post-1848 period, feudal administration gave way to an increasing degree of village autonomy leading towards self-rule. The lowest unit of administration was the political district, subordinated to regional and land administration. The formation of the Czechoslovak Republic in 1918 removed the last obstacles to self-rule by village communes, and these units, along with their elected communal assembly, became the basic unit of self-rule. The state supplied most of the finances for local development, even though communes were by law autonomous parts of the independent state. At this time the Agrarian Party (republicans) dominated village politics in Czech-speaking Bohemia and later Czechoslovakia. Udržal served as Minister of Defence in the 1920s and Prime Minister between 1929 and 1932. The German occupation in 1939 curbed the autonomy of communes through their subordination to the German military command. Looking from the outside, however, the commune existed as if undisturbed. The establishment of national committees (*národní výbor*) in every commune led to a decline in self-rule in village communes and a transfer of power to the state structures of district, regional and central government. This structure was subsequently strengthened after 1948 by the Communist Party hierarchy which became firmly implanted at all administrative levels, including that of the village. The practice of self-rule by village communes was suspended for more than forty years. During the periods of German occupation and communist rule, citizens living in the countryside learnt to be very prudent, and avoided getting involved in public affairs.

Only in 1990 was village self-rule restored, at which point communal elections regained their importance. To date, five communal elections have taken place in the Czech Republic (in 1990, 1994, 1998, 2002 and 2006). Data from our research in the commune of Dolní Roveň show that local residents have a different attitude towards national political affairs than to those of their commune. Whereas participation in the elections for the lower chamber or assembly (*sněmovna*) of parliament of the Czech Republic dropped in 2002 to a mere 55.43 per cent, down from 80.93 per cent in 1996, participation in communal elections has remained stable: in 1994 it was 55.8 per cent, 48.55 per cent in 1998, and finally 55.81 per cent in 2002. In the case of elections to the assembly, villagers vote mainly for parties and not for individuals, whom they usually do not know. In communal elections the list of candidates is also nominally a list of party representatives – for example in 2002 there were four parties competing: the Christian Democratic Party, the Communists, the Civic Democratic Party, and the Czech Social Democratic Party – but in fact individuals matter much more than parties in these elections (cf. Řechková 2005). It is noteworthy that in 2002 preferential votes were cast for respected and well-known people rather than for the more high-profile candidates who led their party's list. Even the list of the traditionally dominant Christian Democrats contained fewer genuine party members than sympathizers who agreed to stand for election (or re-election) as de facto independents.

In a way it is coincidental that the Christian Democrats have won all Roveň communal elections of the postcommunist period because most of their candidates do not particularly care for the party's policies. What matters is the meritocratic quality of the candidates and not their party political membership or relation to the Roman Catholic Church. For example, the present mayor of Dolní Roveň joined the Christian Democrats only when it appeared that she was elected. The political culture of Dolní Roveň is primarily focused on commune affairs, while the external political scene holds less interest for the villagers. During the 2002 communal elections, which took place simultaneously with elections for the national senate, many voters eagerly participated in communal voting while ignoring, and in some cases actively undermining, the senate elections. While villagers showed a high degree of civic competence (a readiness to engage in public affairs) in matters such as a local bird reserve or a national road which directly concerned the commune and its territory, many boycotted the vote on national issues. One could somewhat paradoxically conclude that the people of Dolní Roveň displayed a participant political culture towards parochial issues but showed a parochial attitude towards national issues.

The Inertia of Political Culture

In post-1989 Czechoslovakia, and especially the western part which became the Czech Republic in 1993, the communist regime was removed by a movement that was both pro-democracy and pro-Europe. Both 'democracy' and 'Europe' were seen as panaceas, medicaments for all ills. A kind of cargo cult emerged, whereby a combination of liberal democracy and an orientation towards Western Europe would function as an automatic springboard to wealth, prosperity, transparency and the rapid development of all branches of society. Nobody seemed to realize that there can be no real return; that we cannot go back to what once was, or was said to have existed.

The only way was to go forward, into the unknown. However, the extent to which the burden of fifty or so years of aberrant totalitarianism[11] had fatally infected things was completely underestimated. Moreover, those who used to be members of the Communist Party of Czechoslovakia – at one time up to one seventh of the population – and the thousands of members and confidants of the secret police were vitally connected to the defeated regime. But these people, the stalwarts and collaborators of the communist era, were not really excluded from influencing the character of the new postcommunist system. In fact, they often infiltrated newly created democratic political parties, and used their network of connections and ill-acquired wealth as social and economic capital; capitalist entrepreneurs were sometimes yesterday's communists. Whereas dissidents of the communist era founded the Civic Forum as a non-party movement which adhered to liberal values, and learnt lessons from the older ones among them about the infamous prewar party politicking which had been a major negative factor in interwar Czechoslovakia, technocrats active during the last years of communism (the so-called prognostics) first jumped on the Civic Forum bandwagon and then (within 18 months of the Velvet Revolution) founded their own party, the Civic Democratic Party (ODS). The ODS, which ruled the Czech Republic between 1992 and 1997, remains one of the two strongest political forces in the Czech Republic. In fact it regained power after the 2006 election. The other currently strong party is the Czech Social Democratic Party (ČSSD), which has held power between 1998 and 2006. As with the ODS, it also harbours quite a few former communists. Although the programmes of these two leading parties differ – in that the former advocates openly liberal values while the latter adheres to the values of the social market economy – when in government they have differed little. Neither was able to privatize state assets without huge losses, stop corruption and embezzlement, form a reliable state administration, or foster in citizens trust in the fair conduct of judicial proceedings. In fact neither of these two parties has managed to create a new political culture. One could argue, seen from an ordinary citizen's viewpoint, political culture has declined in the postcommunist period.

One of the most blatant cases of the corruption of power was the so-called opposition treaty between the ODS and ČSSD, represented respectively by Václav Klaus and Miloš Zeman, which was in force between 1998 and 2002. This was a highly pragmatic, even cynical, document allowing the ČSSD minority government to 'rule', but only within the limits set by the ODS which at the time ostensibly assumed the role of the opposition. In practice the ODS dictated which parts of the ČSSD's programme would and would not be implemented. For example, the privatization of major companies and banks accelerated during the Zeman years because it was in accord with the general political goals of the ODS. However, proposals for registered civil partnerships between homosexual couples, the draft of which took many years to complete, did not make it into law until recently because there was no joint will between the deputies representing the two parties to make it happen.[12]

The goal of the liberal democrats of the ODS was representative democracy understood as an 'electocracy' (cf. Dawisha 1999), by which I mean that people are seen not so much as the ultimate source of power but rather voters who are periodically courted by political parties at the time of an election. Once they have used their civic right to vote their usefulness to parties is exhausted until the next election. In this system there is no interdependence between citizens and their representatives, for one ceases, in effect, to be a citizen between elections.

This lack of direct democracy in postcommunist politics can be illustrated by the events that led to the division of Czechoslovakia into two federal states. In 1992, approximately two-and-a-half million citizens of Czechoslovakia (out of ten million voters) signed a petition against the division of the country into two independent states. The petition, which also called for a popular vote on this crucially important issue, was, however, in vain. The two main parties, referring to the absence of a law on referendums and arguing that there was a lack of time, ignored this expression of the people. The Federal Assembly hastily approved a long series of laws and voted at the end of November 1992 for the division of the state. To this day there is no general law on referendums in the Czech Republic. The only use of a referendum has been when people were asked to approve accession to the European Union, but that referendum was possible only because a special one-off law was adopted. Similarly, the new constitution of the Czech Republic was not submitted to public discussion, let alone a popular vote. Instead, the 1920 constitution of Czechoslovakia was taken as a blueprint and the Czech National Council, composed of second-rate deputies, approved the hastily compiled text just in time so that the new state, proclaimed on 1 January 1993, had a constitution.

This kind of uncritical adoption of statutes and so forth from the first Czechoslovak republic was common during the Czech Republic's first years. For many the 'return to Europe' was equal to the return to the idealized prewar Czechoslovak democracy. This took place at a time when there was hardly anyone alive who had experienced the prewar political system as an adult. After fifty years of totalitarian and semi-totalitarian regimes, the problem of shaky coalitions, the closed-door politics of the so-called 'Fiver' (*Pětka*), the sacred cult of 'President-Liberator' Tomáš G. Masaryk (voted in four times between 1918 and 1935), and the dominance of party-political politics over direct popular democracy, were all as if forgotten and ignored (cf. Holy 1996). As a result, since 1993 the Czech Republic has had a limited representative democracy without popular democracy.[13] In practice, representative democracy of the postcommunist type means the hegemony of leaders of political parties. There is no representative democracy within parties, let alone direct democracy, but rather the strong hand, one might even say dictatorship, of leaders. These sometimes resemble hereditary chiefs or military commanders, whose leadership is not to be questioned. Instead of the will of the people, free elections in the Czech Republic corroborate Michels's Iron Law of Oligarchy (Michels 1999).

Does the idea of political culture make sense of this kind of phenomenon? I am convinced that we can observe here a high degree of political continuity. Some observers believe that the main problem of Czech postcommunism lies in the attitude to the communist past typified by the Velvet Revolution. According to these analysts, this 'handshake transition' (Haraszti 1999) made possible the survival of communists, who came to hold behind-the-scene positions in economic and political life. I would contend, however, that the main problem of post-1989 developments is the fact that communist political culture, strongly rooted in all segments of the population, continues to dominate the whole of society and each individual to such an extent that the citizens, facing the falsity of politicians, feel as helpless as they did during the period of communist dictatorship. Masaryk's famous maxim, 'lest you fear and lest you steal', remains a matchless ideal in the postcommunist Czech Republic. Czech political culture is a multi-layered complex in which each layer is quite unlike the others. The layer formed during the period of the interwar republic is entirely different to the one formed by the communist era which followed it.

Today's uncritical attitude to the pre-totalitarian era's supposedly democratic system emphasizes elements of voluntarism and parochial subjection. It was Jan Patočka, the Czech phenomenological philosopher, who saw in parochialism the main Czech problem of modern times (Patočka 1992). One must challenge the naivety of contemporary epigones of Masaryk: prewar political culture was not really participatory but rather a combination of its parochial and subject types..[14] Czech national character, succinctly described by Patočka and more recently by Holy (1996), is a consequence of the defeat, at the battle of White Mountain in 1620, of the attempt to establish an independent protestant polity. Czech smallness, the little Czech man, plebeian and servile attitudes: these qualities are not 'small is beautiful' à la Schumacher (cf. Gellner 1994b: 134) but a linguistic patriotism instead of territorial. They expound egalitarianism, particularism, building of society from below by way of small steps and without great visions, in other words, parochialism. Patočka's analysis stands in contrast to Masaryk's conception of the Czech question, in which Hussitism as a pre-modern democratism sits at the root of the Czech claim to world fame. Preferring freedom and democracy to obscurantism and the medieval theocratic ossification of the Habsburg monarchy was, according to Masaryk, the main Czech asset. Why this purported asset was not used to the profit of the Czechs can be explained by the political culture of smallness among Masaryk's compatriots. It appears that this political culture was closer to Patočka's conception, and Masaryk's Czechoslovak project did not last mainly because of his blind belief in the inherent democratic nature of the Czechs, and an unrealistic vision of a fusion of Czech and Slovak political cultures (Nosál 1998; Skalník 2001a; Williams 1997).

Western political scientists have dealt in the not too distant past with Czechoslovak political culture. They have mainly been interested in its continuity and in political pluralism. Canadian scholar Gordon Skilling, decorated in the 1990s by President Havel for his analyses, saw the question of political pluralism and political culture in the Czech political environment as a dialectics of continuity and discontinuity. At one pole there was a remarkable degree of continuity during the seven decades of pluralism between 1867 and1938. This development was interrupted by the Munich Agreement of September 1938 which, for Skilling, was a turning point in Czechoslovak political culture. A gradual loss of pluralist qualities paralleled by the growth of authoritarianism followed (Skilling 1984: 122), although authors such as Paul (1984) and Brown and Wightman (1977) believed that pluralist political values, combined with the rejection of foreign rule, survived under the surface. Both Paul and Skilling called this 'Švejkism', a mixture of collaboration and resistance for the sake of 'survival'.[15] Czech politicians and political scientists seem to agree that after 1990 a change of political system took place in what is now the Czech Republic. Indeed, one has to accept that among political parties, alliances and coalitions are freely formed as well as easily ended. In a mechanistic sense a new pluralist political system has been put in place.

However, unless we pose questions about the qualities of the people who form or join these parties, what political culture they bring to them, and what kind of politics this creates, we will not understand to what degree there has or has not been a change of political system. How can we explain why the country's 'new' politicians, despite being democratically elected and brandishing ideals of moral and transparent politics, have not been deterred from the blatant abuses of power and economic aggrandizement so typical of communist rule? How is it possible that while these people reject communist misrule they simultaneously, and without shame, abuse their position for the irregular acquisition of property, assume key posts in the management structure of privatized companies, and adopt laws and regulations which enable them – not to speak of their family, acquaintances and professional partners – to gain access to financial packages which allow them not to pay back what they have borrowed? The answer is that they learnt under the totalitarian system, or from those who experienced it, the principle that what belongs to the state potentially belongs to anybody, and it all depends on one's skill at grabbing it. In the political sphere this attitude can be summarized as follows: 'Vote for me and I will handle your mandate as I see fit. If you do not like how my colleagues and I in government do things then that's your tough luck. All you can do is look on, mutely, and observe how I rule and how I do what I like with the state's assets'. This is possible for two reasons. Firstly, voters are swayed by irresponsible bombastic promises, such as 'in just two years we will reach the standard of living found in Austria' (Prime Minister Čalfa), and 'by the year 2000 wages will have doubled' (Prime Minister Klaus). Secondly, citizens not only believe such transparent propaganda and vote for it, but they even accept and admire these reckless lies because the politicians who make them are popular and rich.[16]

The Parameters of the Czech Postcommunist Political Class

Only naive idealists believed that following the democratic and pluralist takeover an era of virtue would prevail in Czech politics, whereby the citizen–voter would be able to control politicians by way of the free press, petitions and the right to assemble, and the state would serve as guarantor of an honest political gamesmanship. However, a truly active civil society has not developed in the Czech Republic; the majority of the population does not respect meritocratic principles and live instead according to the principle of giving little and taking much. What kind of political culture can emerge in a society which does not know any more the concept of fellowship, and where relatives, neighbours and work colleagues do not trust each other, plot against each other and strive to attain advantage for themselves at the cost of the other by whatever means? The answer to this question cannot be only moralistic, for political anthropology aims to be more precise and concrete. In this section we will look at Czech political culture as a system of asymmetric reciprocity between politicians and voters. In fact there is a certain reciprocity: politicians pretend that they care for the lives of voters, while in fact their personal material gain stands at the centre of their political life; voters in turn pretend to be interested in public affairs and to want to participate in the political process.

One of the foremost students of Czech political culture, Igor Nosál, has argued persuasively that as far as local political culture is concerned it is non-participatory and clientelistic. Political initiative, Nosál suggests, is in the hands of a limited number of anti-elites, which formed or reconstituted themselves soon after the end of the popular protests of 1989/90. Civic competence and self-consciousness, meanwhile, is less than half that of Western European democracies such as Britain, the Netherlands and the western part of Germany (Nosál 1999, 2004). According to Nosál, in the two years that followed the Velvet Revolution, power was grabbed by a new political class of 'democratic' technocrats and political self-appointees on the one hand, and managers recruited from so-called 'old structures' – or former communist cadres – on the other. This unholy alliance has pushed the anti-totalitarian dissidents who led the Velvet Revolution from power. Since then, former dissidents have regrouped. Some have become civic cultural activists, while others have joined political parties such as the ecologically-minded Greens who, because they have not reach the threshold of 5 per cent of votes, have not been able to enter parliament (in 2006 elections they made it to the parliament and formed a coalition with Civic Democrats and Christian Democrats). Meanwhile, the ruling political class has been trying to co-opt remnants of other elites, intellectuals or political opportunists of the social-democratic type. The above mentioned treaty between the Civic Democrats (ODS) and the Social Democrats (ČSSD), which provided the framework for the running of the country for four years (1998–2002), should be seen as a success for this new political class.

The general election of 2002 gave the ČSSD, in coalition with the Christian Democrats (KDU-ČSL) and Freedom Party (US), a majority of one seat, consequently ending the pragmatic alliance between the ČSSD and ODS. However, a weak (Špidla) and corrupt (Gross) premiership brought the ruling ČSSD into crisis with a year to go before the 2006 general election. This crisis brought to power an eloquent and forceful, if authoritarian, politician, Jiří Paroubek, who promised to win the election. The question is whether the ODS, with their 'blue chance' (i.e. neo-liberal) programme, will win over or antagonize voters. If they do, then Czech citizens will witness the establishment of a stable but alternating political system based on a complementary 'electocratic' (Dawisha 1999) opposition of two seemingly different political parties.[17] If the ČSSD win, Czech political culture might be enriched by a kind of Peronist leadership, combining authoritarianism and populism, and a system of redistributive politics favouring those less endowed millions who fear a diminishment of the state control of housing, public transport, education, and the heavily subsidized public health system (cf. Tismaneanu 1998). In the case of a close result, another unholy alliance is possible, this time enabling a minority government with the ODS. However, much will depend on the percentage of votes gained by the Communists (KSČM) and Greens (SZ), who might prove to be, in Lenin's terms, 'uselful idiots' as coalition partners or tacit supporters of either of the strongest parties. ODS leaders have constantly accused the ČSSD under Paroubek of being prepared to join forces with the Communists, but I would not exclude the emergence of a grand coalition or quasi-coalition inspired by the recent post-election developments in Germany, where, after a narrow victory, the Christian Democrats agreed to let some Social Democrats run important ministries in the Angela Merkel government[18].

In 2002, a year before his presidential term was up, Václav Havel warned that Czech society was at risk from a 'mafia-like concept of capitalism' which would make life easier for all 'tunnelers'[19] and other cheats (Havel 2002). However frightening, this will only complement the formation of a postcommunist political class and a system of alternating government involving power-sharing parties. The new political system will be a logical consequence of the inertia of political culture of parochial and subject type.

This rather gloomy assessment might look better if we examine the experience of the formation of political classes in historically more stable states than the Czech Republic. In these democratic states, political classes have been in place for decades, if not centuries, and have developed particular attitudes, relations and values which many participants in our research would without hesitation call a positive political culture. However, at their inception, these political classes had members who were usurpers, parvenus and illicit profiteers. With time they refined themselves into law-abiding leaders with responsibility for the well-being of their country. We can only hope that under the controlling eye of civil society and a free press that the political jungle of postcommunism will be civilized within two or more generations. However, one should not think that this process is automatic. For example, the political class of Lebanon is so dependent on individual personalities, families, religion and economics that there is hardly any connection between political ideology on the one hand and the behaviour of leaders, blocs and parties on the other (Skalník 2004a). In Soviet bloc-type regimes, such as that of Czechoslovakia, the communist political class was far better organized than today's pluralist one, which is to my mind still in the formative period of its existence.

Igor Nosál (2000, 2004) has successfully analysed the problem of the postcommunist political class in the Czech Republic. According to Nosál the new power bloc of politicians and managers, which is parasitic on the state and and the emergent group of large capitalists, are locked in mutually internal fights for the control of privatized property and for the dominant political myth (i.e. the winning ideology). The gulf between these and the emergent middle class not speaking about working class deepens. In this sense it is not yet clear who will eventually be included in the Czech political class. The role of social and cultural capital today, a fact which Nosál stresses so much, is better understood when we identify the ruins from which the new class comes into being. According to Nosál, grassroots autonomous political elites do not emerge in this messy situation. They are suppressed by 'coagulated' social networks and clientelism. The new political class emerging from three basic elements – the managerial elite, the politicians and a section of the humanist intelligentsia – imposes a dominant ideology, or 'new ideocracy', from above. Consequently, the emergence of an open society, formed from below, becomes impossible, and what emerges instead is its virtual image, a picture of liberal capitalism plagiarized from Marxist-Leninist brochures. Nosál suggests that the unstable and conflict-ridden politics of postcommunism can better be explained from 'the perspective of an ideocratic *umma* than the perspective of Western liberal society' (Nosál 2004: 84). Political systems may, therefore, have similar forms and institutions but different cultural logics and different meanings. Gellner's (1994b) remarks about communist and Muslim *umma*, and his ideas about the conditions of liberty, as well as the conclusions of Eyal, Szelenyi and Townsend (1998) about postcommunist ruling elites, could have been sources of inspiration here. It is, however, not easy to prove the ideocratic character of the new political class in the Czech Republic. Nosál asserts that the ODS strive for power without attributes, whereby they negate the liberating 'sacral form of the new myth' of Open Society (Nosál 2004:

85). The privatization of major companies during the eight years of ČSSD rule would also suggest that it too is fighting for power without attributes, i.e without any moral ideology. The question, therefore, is whether the ideocratic *umma* and the three-member political class really exists.

Notes

1. Research for this chapter was supported by the Grant Agency of the Academy of Sciences of the Czech Republic (grant no. A8111001) and the Grant Agency of the Czech Republic (grant no. 403/02/0255).
2. The choice of the term 'postcommunist' here is intentional as the terms 'socialist' and 'postsocialist' seem to me inadequate for the description of the social and political issues relating to communism (cf. Hann 2002). 'Really existing socialism' was an ideological term coined in order to cover up the impotence of communist regimes and their failure to create a truly socialist system.
3. Removal of the word 'Socialist' from the state's name led to the so-called 'dash war' (Czechoslovakia was to be written with a hyphen, i.e., Czecho-Slovakia) which was finally resolved in April 1990 with the adoption of the fairly absurd state appellation Czech and Slovak Federal Republic (Česká a Slovenská federativní republika), a phrase which had to be written with a capital 'S' for Slovenská, a practice unacceptable in both Czech and Slovak orthography.
4. This quasi-party was tellingly called the Civic Forum (Občanské forum) in the Czech-Moravian part of the state and Public Against Violence (Verejnosť proti násiliu) in Slovakia. In the 1990 elections these two groups received almost 100 per cent of the vote, which reminded many of the results from the staged elections of the communist era.
5. Electoral victory in the Czech Republic went to the Civic Democratic Party (Občanská demokratická strana, ODS), founded by the present-day President of the Czech Republic, Václav Klaus. In the Slovak Republic, the Movement for a Democratic Slovakia (Hnutie za demokratické Slovensko, HZDS) won; this was less a political party than a broad gathering of followers of the populist leader Vladimír Mečiar.
6. For a better understanding of ethno-nationalism, the term coined by Walker Connor, see Conversi 2001.
7. I heard these remarks when Holy and Gellner met during the Second Biennial Conference of the European Association of Social Anthropologists, held in Prague in August 1992.
8. Chabal and Daloz (2006) have made a thorough analysis of this resurgence of culture.
9. This has prompted the emergence of coordinated research on the anthropology of Eurasia; see Hann (2005).
10. Zeman ostensibly went into retirement in 2002, after having served as Prime Minister for the preceding four years. From his base in the Czech-Moravian highlands he continues to influence Czech politics in a number of ways; for example, by inviting politicians to his house, attending widely publicized gatherings and publishing critical memoirs. Though his influence is indirect, influential Social Democratic politicians consider Zeman's views important.
11. To forty-one years of communist rule one should add the preceding nine years: six years of German dictatorship between March 1939 and May 1945, plus a very limited period of democracy between October 1938 and March 1939, and between May 1945 and February 1948.
12. The Communist Party of Bohemia and Moravia, which consequently supported the adoption of the law, is not considered democratic by the other parties. During the thirteen years of his presidency (1989–2003), Václav Havel never received or consulted Communist politicians because of the widespread belief that the Communist Party was not a democratic political force. It was of course Havel who agreed with the party's leaders, such as Prime Minister

Adamec, to the transfer of power in November/December 1989. Although its abolition has been proposed from time to time, the Communist Party has continued to exist and has normally participated in all free elections to the lower chamber of the Czech parliament as well as other elections (senate, regions, communes). Its candidates usually receive not less than 10 per cent of the vote. Labelled 'non-democratic', Communists nevertheless often play a decisive role in parliamentary deliberations. Self-appointed democratic parties opportunistically use the Communists' support in getting through laws and policies. For example, in 2003, Václav Klaus was elected President of the Czech Republic in the third round of voting by a tiny margin thanks to the votes of the Communists.

13. When mentioning popular democracy (Ake 1996; Gellner 1994b) I would like to make a clear distinction between this kind of desired direct democracy and people's democracy. The latter was a hallmark of the communist period when so-called 'people's democracies' (in fact utterly undemocratic Soviet satellites) were contrasted with the 'bourgeois democracies' of the West which were purportedly democratic only for members of the ruling class.

14. It is worth emphasizing that there is no guarantee that the three types of political culture proposed by Almond and Verba (1963) are related as an evolutionary sequence.

15. The term 'Švejkism' is derived from Jaroslav Hašek's well-known novel *The Good Soldier Švejk* (1923). In her ethnography of Czech NATO membership, Hana Červinková (2006) has shown persuasively that Švejkism is far from dead.

16. A comparison of the Czech Republic and the Republic of South Africa reveals that the former lags behind in various parameters of transformation, especially those concerning dealing with the authoritarian past and the degree and pace of development of civil society (Skalník 1999a: 14).

17. The ODS ruled between 1992 and 1997. Then followed almost one year of technocratic government, substituted by eight years of rule by the ČSSD, the first four years in connivance with the ODS.

18. As I mentioned above the 2006 election ended up with the victory of Civic Democrats (ODS) who since rule in the coalition with Christian Democracts and the Greens.

19. To 'tunnel' a bank or enterprise means to strip it of assets by supposedly 'borrowing' those assets and transferring them to newly founded companies; however, although legally 'borrowed', these assets are never returned. In this manner the Czech state lost up to 600 billion Czech crowns (€20 billion) to 'tunnelers'. However, the 'tunnelers' did not invest their ill-gained assets in the Czech economy but instead spent the money in acts of conspicuous consumption, both at home and abroad, as well as investing it in foreign enterprises.

References

Ake, C. 1996. *Democracy and Development in Africa*. Washington, DC: Brooking Institute.

Almond, G. and S. Verba (eds). 1963. *The Civic Culture: Political Attitudes and Democracy in Five Nations*. Princeton, NJ: Princeton University Press.

Beissinger, M. and C. Young (eds). 2002. *Beyond State Crisis? Postcolonial Africa and Post-Soviet Eurasia in Comparative Perspective*. Washington, DC: Woodrow Wilson Center Press.

Brown, A. and G. Wightman. 1977. 'Czechoslovakia: Revival and Retreat', in A. Brown and J. Gray (eds), *Political Culture and Political Change in Communist States*. London: Macmillan, pp.159–96.

Červinková, H. 2006. *Playing Soldiers in Bohemia: An Ethnography of NATO Membership*. Prague: Set Out.

Chabal, P. and J.-P. Daloz. 2006. *Culture Troubles: Politics and the Interpretation of Meaning*. London: Hurst.

Conversi, D. (ed.) 2002. *Ethnonationalism in the Contemporary World: Walker Connor and the Study of Nationalism.* London: Routledge.

Dawisha, K. 1999. 'Electocracies and the Hobbesian Fishbowl of Postcommunist Politics', *East European Political Studies* 13(2): 256–70.

Eyal, G., I. Szelenyi and E. Townsley. 1998. *Making Capitalism Without Capitalists: The New Ruling Elites in Eastern Europe.* London: Verso.

Gellner, E. 1994a. 'Reborn from Below: The Forgotten Beginning of the Czech National Revival' [review of Patočka 1992], in *Encounters with Nationalism.* Oxford: Blackwell, pp.130–44

———— 1994b. *Conditions of Liberty: Civil Society and Its Rivals.* London: Hamish Hamilton.

———— 1997. *Nationalism.* London: Weidenfeld and Nicolson.

Hann, C. 2005. 'The Anthropology of Eurasia in Eurasia'. in P. Skalník (ed.) *Anthropology of Europe: Teaching and Research.* Prague: Set Out, pp. pp.51–66.

Hann, C. (ed.) 2002. *Postsocialism: Ideals, Ideologies and Practices in Eurasia.* London: Routledge.

Haraszti, M. 1999. 'Decade of Handshake Transition', *East European Politics and Society* 13(2): 288–92.

Havel, V. 2002. Volební rok 2002 bude přelomový. Novoroční projev prezidenta České republiky Václava Havla. *Lidové noviny,* 2 January 2002, p.8.

Holy, L. 1996. *The Little Czech and the Great Czech Nation: National Identity and the Post-communist Social Transformation.* Cambridge: Cambridge University Press.

Michels, R. 1999. *Political Parties: A Sociological Study of the Oligarchical Tendencies of Modern Democracy.* New Brunswick, NJ: Transaction.

Musil, J. (ed.) 1995. *The End of Czechoslovakia.* Budapest: Central European University Press.

Nosál, I. 1998. 'Česká politická kultura a stabilita demokracie v České republice', in *Sborník příspěvků z celostátní konference 'Osudy české společnosti 1918–1998', Praha 19.února 1998.* Prague: Masarykova česká sociologická společnost., pp.57–65.

———— 1999. 'Politická kultura a lokální politika v České republice', *Cahiers du CeFReS* 16: 21–30.

———— 2000. 'Zrození nové politické třídy a její politické kultury: mezi otevřenou společností a dědictvím leninismu', *Sociální studia* 5: 207–22.

———— 2004. 'Zrození české postkomunistické politické kultury', in P. Skalník (ed.) *Politická kultura: antropologie, sociologie, politologie.* Prague: Set Out, pp.71–88.

Patočka, J. 1992. *Co jsou Češi? Was sind die Tschechen?* Prague: Panorama.

Paul, D. 1984. 'Czechoslovakia's Political Culture Revisited', in A. Brown (ed.) *Political Culture and Communist Studies.* London: Macmillan, pp.134–48.

Pye, L. and S. Verba (eds). 1965. *Political Culture and Political Development.* Princeton, NJ: Princeton University Press.

Řechková, K. 2005. 'Politická kultura a obecní politika v Dolní Rovni', in P. Skalník (ed.) *Sociální antropologie obce Dolní Roveň.* Scientific Papers of the University of Pardubice, Series C, Supplement 13. Pardubice: Univerzita Pardubice, pp.73–106.

Skalník, P. 1999a. 'Czech Republic and South Africa: Comparisons with Special Emphasis on Political Culture in the Nineteen Nineties', in P. Skalník (ed.)

    Transition to Democracy: Czech Republic and South Africa Compared.
    Prague: Set Out, pp.1–16.
————— 1999b. 'Authority versus Power: A View from Social Anthropology',
    in A. Cheater (ed.) *The Anthropology of Power. Empowerment and
    Disempowerment in Changing Structures.* London: Routledge, pp.163–74.
————— 2000. 'Anthropological Dimensions of Political Culture', in P. Skalník (ed.)
    *Sociocultural Anthropology at the Turn of the Century: Voices from the
    Periphery.* Prague: Set Out, pp. 61–68.
————— 2001a. 'Masaryk, Smuts, Nkrumah i Havel', in E. Voráček (ed.) *T.G.
    Masaryk, idea demokracie a současné evropanství*, Part 1. Prague: Filosofia,
    pp.239–47.
————— 2001b. 'Explaining the State in Africa: Bayart, Chabal and Other Options',
    in L. Kropáček and P. Skalník (eds), *Africa 2000: Forty Years of African
    Studies in Prague.* Prague: Set Out, pp.145–55.
————— 2004a. 'Politická kultura na asijském pomezí: srovnání Libanonu a Papua
    Nové Guineje', in P. Skalník (ed.) *Politická kultura: antropologie, sociologie,
    politologie.* Prague: Set Out, pp.157–69.
————— 2004b. 'Re-study of Dolní Roveň; A Combination of Anthropology and
    Sociology of Rural Bohemia at the Beginning of the Third Millennium',
    in P. Skalník (ed.) *Dolní Roveň: poločas výzkumu/Dolní Roveň, Research
    at Half-time.* Scientific Papers of the University of Pardubice, Series C,
    Supplement 8. Pardubice: Univerzita Pardubice, pp.17–34.
Skilling, H. 1984. 'Czechoslovak Political Culture: Pluralism in an International
    Context', in A. Brown (ed.) *Political Culture and Communist Studies.*
    London: Macmillan, pp.115–33.
Tismaneanu, V. 1998. *Fantasies of Salvation: Democracy, Nationalism, and Myth in
    Post-communist Europe.* Princeton, NJ: Princeton University Press.
Williams, K. 1997. 'National Myths in the New Czech Liberalism', in G. Hosking
    and G. Schöpflin (eds), *Myths and Nationhood.* London: Hurst, pp.132–40.

Chapter 11

Comparative Cultural Aspects of Work in Multinational Enterprises

Gabriel-Ionut Stoiciu

Introduction: Postsocialist Europe in the 'Age of Integration'

The political, economic, geographical and spiritual opening up that was part of the post-1989 changes in Central and Eastern Europe was seen as a logical attitude after the decline of Soviet control over the entire region. The new 'free citizens' felt that they could finally choose countries to visit, information to believe and learn and – maybe the most important – people to represent them. Besides social and political changes, economic restructuring had the most dramatic impact on these new democracies. The rules of competition and profit, the altering of pre-1989 internal and external commercial agreements, as well as pressure from the International Monetary Fund and World Bank, led the new regimes to pursue liberalization and privatization.

In the 1980s, Central and East European countries reacted to the deepening crisis of the 'communist dream' in very different ways. Poland and Czechoslovakia, for example, initiated political changes before 1989 and implemented economic reforms afterwards. In contrast, economic reforms in Hungary were shaped by more competitive principles while, at the same time, the Kádár regime had a loose control over political and social life of the country until its fall. Meanwhile, Bulgaria, and more especially Romania, were ruled by the most severe totalitarian regimes of the time in Europe, and the state exercised a great degree of economic and political control in both countries.

Until recently, the process of transformation from a socialist, autarchic economy to a market economy in Romania has been a painfully slow process. While Poland and the Czech Republic introduced 'shock therapy' reforms, and while Hungary, Latvia, and Estonia opened up their economies to foreign investment and competition, Romania seriously lagged behind. Because of the lack of the legal and institutional infrastructure necessary to support the workings of a modern market economy – such as bankruptcy and competition laws and a stock exchange – foreign investment was a negligible aspect of Romania's economic transformation. The irresolute privatization program showed a government with only a weak commitment to reform. The financial losses from trade boycotts with Iraq and the former Yugoslavia (with whom Romania had enjoyed a good deal of trade) added to the rising economic troubles: 'Over 40 years of Communism destroyed many basic values, such as a respect for law and public institutions. The inherited value system is a product of the double standards of socialism, where formal principles, such as equality and solidarity co-existed with less-principled pragmatic behaviours which developed to survive in the conditions of a shortage economy and political oppression' (Ruminska-Zimny 1999: 14).

The experience of almost twenty years of postsocialism has proved that emerging market forces cannot substitute for the governmental management of the transition process, especially in the area of institution building, social security and investment in human capital. Liberalization and privatization have dramatically increased the need for some kind of social security, while the post-1999 recession constrained public finances and imposed cuts in social expenditures. At the same time, institutional weakness and structural constraints prevented the opening and channelling of capital flows through market mechanisms.

European integration, as well as globalization, is not a naturally occurring phenomenon that would have happened without people's determination. It is meant to fulfil aspirations to a higher level of socio-economic life. A businessman may see opportunities for the expansion of markets, while others may see European integration as a threat to local traditions unable to compete with the 'aggressive' Western cultures introduced by media and technology. It is an unpredictable process leading people into a postindustrial information age. Although geographical and political borders still separate Europe's populations, increasingly available information and communication technologies make these borders permeable.

The main interests motivating the process of European integration are economic (profit-related), political (power-related) and cultural (exploring other identities). These are managed by the three institutional actors of internationalization: transnational businesses and capital flow, intergovernmental organizations, and non-governmental organizations. Among these, transnational businesses are the main promoter of the process of integration, while the other two (along with the nation state) negotiate this process. Many transnational businesses succeed in eluding local regulations and the supervision of national governments. In 'the new spirit of competition' these businesses are not interested in protecting even their original plant or their headquarters if this may affect the profit. The interaction of different cultures is now more than ever facilitated by these businesses, along with the appearance of the Internet. But will this enhance cross-cultural understanding and empathy? Cooperation may be enhanced, but so too chauvinism. Through the Internet fugitives from justice can be identified, but the Internet also provides the most dangerous terrorist with a safe means to send messages worldwide. We cannot say in good faith that the Internet is generating global social capital rather than empowering fanatic groups.

Enterprises, Markets and States in the New 'Integrative' Economy

The modern market economy has developed around three types of institution: enterprises (firms), markets and states, with currency being the binding instrument. Enterprises and markets are the key places of action for major changes that lead to the structural homogenization processes necessary to global integration. This 'integrative' economic system's efficiency is bound to the balance between two forms of organization: the stability of the business and the fluidity of the market. This balance is not steady by default. The state, by monitoring enterprises and market activity, plays a central role in the establishment of an optimal balance between the competitive dynamics of markets and the monopolistic logic of (multinational) enterprises.

Today the contrast between the market, state and business seems to become less pronounced. Within state institutions, managers introduce market-like relations with clients and suppliers to eliminate bureaucratic numbness. Simultaneously, markets increasingly apply the principles of long-term contracts to commercial relationships. These changes lead to an increased unification of the productive system with the establishment of an immense network that functions in a more and more uniform manner. The borders of what is or is not enterprise seem to lose their significance with talk of rights and profitable 'employment' conditions (Laval n.d.: 40). Nowadays, a brand's quality standards are imposed all over the world to a similar level and this results in the development of similar technological requirements, such that two plants that produce the same goods – in South America and Western Europe, for example – make their products in the same way by using similar machines. And this is not only valid for activities of manufacture in the classical sense but for the whole administrative organization of businesses. The widespread use of management programs represents an increased standardization of structures and business coordination. The same rationale is even found in the successful distribution of services networks acting as independent small enterprises. One sells at the same time both an image of a brand and a uniform, optimized working ethos.

However, at the present moment, contrary to other dimensions of the productive activity of firms, working conditions for labourers do not have a tendency to become standardized according to some global scale. In a world where investment and profit tend to override state borders, businesses maintain regional inequalities through uneven budget allocations for salaries and safety measures at work.

Multinationals were sometimes considered by nation states as potentially dangerous because they could threaten national sovereignty. Eventually these businesses became potential allies because they made possible the development of local employment, technological transfers and economic growth. The nation state lost one of their main features, as Manuel Castells states (2001), to one 'world network' of enterprises and transnational groups. The concept of 'national territory' was replaced by one of 'implantation' site. For the leaders of nation states, the priorities of economic policy shifted from a concern with generating the maximum amount of employment towards maximizing inward investment. They encouraged those businesses which had the fastest rates of growth, an international monopoly, and which – as sources of prosperity – brought steady economic and social advantages.

In a local economic environment, the decision of major shareholders to appoint a general manager could be biased by the national origin of the company. But when the major shareholder is a multinational firm with equal involvement, the nationality of the company becomes irrelevent. Certainly, the style of management can define the nationality of the company. But in a world of increasing competition, if it is more profitable to employ a manager or management system from abroad, the pragmatic view replaces any patriotic tendency. Nevertheless, it remains clear for the time being that Siemens and Nokia are European firms, Motorola is American and Samsung is Asian. The nationality of enterprises in which various cultures and interests cohabit still counts even though it may be becoming less important.

In the language of economists, nation states remain 'blocks of production factors'. Every nation state must participate in the global economy and to succeed it needs its citizens as labour. Workers' actions reflect value systems, traditions, rules of conduct and systems of management. Governments in countries of 'implantation' exercise overt influence at times on multinational enterprises' technological choices and, particularly, the strategies of innovation they employ locally. While arbitrating between multinationals and local enterprises, governments play a legal role through the enforcement of national laws and regulations – concerning such things as competition, monopolies, taxation and so on – and through their own economic policies.

The Cultural Dimension of Multinational Enterprises and Collective Identities

General Considerations

Claude Lévi-Strauss expressed decades ago the fear that worldwide modernization and the development of communication, exchanges and contacts between human groups had started a process of cultural homogenization (Lévi-Strauss 1983: 128). Regarding the collective form of culture, there is a corresponding understanding of the concepts 'identity' and 'resemblance' through which members of one group perceive themselves as alike and in relation to which they differ from other people outside the group (Smith 1991: 74). But both the individual and the collective are territorially bound, the connectedness with location being central in both cases. No matter if the individual has to fit into society or if individuals have to have a place in society, society has always been territorially bound. The de-territorialization of culture creates a situation in which the context of identity is both in the territory and outside, which marks a shift away from 'traditional' frames of reference. Still, we have to remember that the traits of identification have to be divided into non-voluntary – such as gender, race or ethnic origin – and voluntary – such as cultural or national identification – the latter being predominantly chosen by the logic of what society commonly considers to be positive (Miscevic 2001: 215). Gender, race and ethnicity can of course be regarded as being achieved through voluntary action. There are numerous examples of this, though a discussion of 'acquired' versus 'natural' characteristics is beyond the scope of this chapter.

Mead, in his discussion on the 'genesis of self', implies that, besides the relation to others, identity is constructed as a result of interplay with a person's surroundings. The construction of one's identity often depends on the positive acceptance of these surroundings, implying that if identifications are not approved the construct's validity starts to diminish (Mead 1962: 153). What Mead means by 'surroundings' are all other people 'in the outside world', in what he defines as 'the generalized other'.

As Enriquez (1988) states, enterprises offer a culture – a structure of values and norms, a way of thinking and a means to apprehend the world – that orients actors. This cultural system is a set of social, historically organized representations. It is a mixture of traditions, customs, rituals and beliefs that give specificity to a working group. Enterprises 'develop a process of learning and the differential socialization of actors so that each of them can define themselves in relation to the proposed ideal. Every model of socialization has as its goal, to select "good behaviour", "good attitudes", and it thus plays a role in recruitment to or in exclusion from ... the organization' (Enriquez 1988: 211).

According to Sainsaulieu (1988), collective identities in enterprises have been explored along three dimensions. Firstly, in terms of *spaces of identification*, which focuses on spheres of adherence and reference for individuals. Secondly, in terms of *representations about authority*: issues here include ideas about the hierarchical organization of a business, the locus of decision-making processes, the space for individual and collective action, staff development, and representations of the enterprise itself and its economic performance. Thirdly, in terms of *sociability outcomes*, the aggregate of relationships that institutes itself within a group at work and the behavioural norms that are constructed there.

Sainsaulieu also describes four spaces of identification. The first of these concerns work content as the interlude of professional improvement; the second concerns the enterprise as a place of adherence that ensures integration to a collective; the third concerns careers as projects linking the acquired identity with that aimed for; and the fourth concerns external society as the explicit reference point for the action invested in work.

Taking all this into consideration, it is pertinent to say that the social scientist who analyses organizational environments must, as Paradeise points out, pay attention 'on the one hand to individuals, [and] on the other hand to interactions, to relations in which individuals define themselves, define the identity of others and participate in the construction of the social world' (Paradeise 1991: 31).

An interesting study of cultures, a quantitative one – more specific to social psychology, was made in 67 countries (at their IBM plants) by Geert Hofstede, who identified five dimensions of analysis – which he named 'Power Distance', 'Insecurity avoidance', 'Masculinity', 'Individualism' and 'Long term orientation' (added later) and proposed a personal definition of culture as 'the collective programming of human mind which allows us to distinguish members of a category of people from another one' (Hofstede 1980: 9).

An insightful and qualitative approach was realised by Philippe d'Iribarne and his colleagues Alain Henry, Jean-Pierre Segal, Sylvie Chevrier and Tatjana Globokar, who have done several comparative ethnological surveys in enterprises in different countries (Europe, Africa and North America) in order to analyse the adequacy of the match between the economy of enterprises and the culture of individuals, characterised by "la logique de l'honneur" as Iribarne described in his works (see Iribarne et al. 1993; Iribarne 1998).

The Comparative Aspects of Employment in Multinational Enterprises

Cultural differences among salaried employees in multinational enterprises can make for important difficulties in the productive and administrative activities of the enterprise. The research I discuss here compares different perceptions of work conditions related to the speeding up of the globalization process and is based on several interviews with salaried employees in French and Romanian multinational enterprises. France has been confronted with anti-globalization movements (ATAC) and the relocation of factories to lower-wage countries like Romania, where foreign direct investment is rejected by 'old-fashioned' workers.

László Kürti (2002) has recently described the way this phenomenon has been encountered with different tempos all over postcommunist Eastern Europe. Csepel, a working-class suburb of Budapest, faced different stages of industrialization from the communist era to the current discontent towards foreign investment. How globalization and Europeanization took place in Hungary's capital can easily be seen from Kürti's ethnography of workers:

> Still more important for workers and their families were the consequences of these supranational transformations as they made themselves felt in their own lives. The development of joint ventures in Csepel took at first look an unexpected turn: the celebrations of the socialist collapse did not subside even when the first appeared on the horizon. The first East–West joint ventures did not and could not save the traditionally skilled industrial working class, causing enormous resentment among workers and their families. (Kürti 2002: 234)

A similar but cross-cultural comparative analysis (between ex-centralized Romania and a stable democracy like France), focusing on employees' representations concerning their position in multinational enterprises seems extremely useful. I argue that such an analysis of employees in a multinational enterprise can have several useful dimensions and variables:
1) cultural – looking at cultural exchanges, cross-cultural interactions;
2) economic – looking at ideas of the market, competition, profitability, technologies, strategies;
3) individual – looking at adaptation/resistance to changes (innovations), representation of self employment (career), of the employee's own place in the enterprise, of attitudes to unemployment;
4) social – looking at education (professional formation), socialization, unions, the state.

These dimensions and variables lead to different indicators like: prestige conferred by the company's brand, organizational pressure, autonomy,

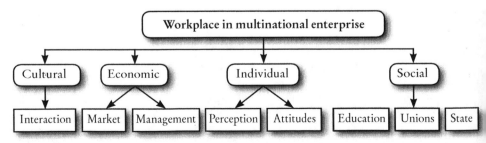

Figure 11.1

collective identity and identification with the enterprise, individualism, resistance to a foreign business culture and modernization, work conditions, risk of unemployment or the plant's relocation, cultural stereotypes, social and professional status inside the organization and the perception of one's career. We may see these factors at work in the diagram presented here.

Objectives and methodology of research

[T]echnique performances in labour culture are primary means through which workers express themselves to knowledgeable insiders within the work group.... Put more simply, people interact with tools and machines based on the precedents of inherited knowledge, yet their social positions within the work group may be altered through their representations of self through both work performance and narrative critics of that performance.

—McCarl (1992: 69)

The main object of this research is to take McCarl's view more seriously and present the way in which an employee in a multinational enterprise (MNE) sees his professional and social position and future related to the cultural adaptation of work habits to foreign managerial styles and imported technologies, in other words to globalization and its inherent modernizing features. I envisaged several aspects regarding the perception of decisional autonomy concerning assignments of employment in a MNE and the specificity of horizontal and vertical relationships in a multicultural organization. I also tried to extract a correlation between the basic concept of working in a MNE and the level of difficulty and complexity of tasks, working conditions, salaries and advancement opportunities.

My main hypothesis was that, depending on decisions and innovations brought from abroad, an increased sense of employment insecurity, unacceptable to some people even if it means efficiency, profit and bigger income, has been experienced by workers themselves. If workers are unaware of incentives and innovations their resistance tends to increase. However, possibilities of retraining may in time decrease this resistance.

In order to better illustrate the different aspects that a topic like this one can offer, a qualitative approach seemed appropriate. I used both semi-directive group interviews and individual interviews. Group interviews have the advantage of a more vivid engagement during discussions but, at the same time, they are more difficult to moderate. Individual, more personal, interviews helped us to delve more deeply into problematic areas and to uncover people's motivations. Workers interviewed were unionized, salaried employees from several MNEs in France, and Romanian firms privatized through foreign direct investment.

Before we turned to the actual interviews I asked the following questions of all interviewees:

- What were the age, the profession, the qualification and the seniority of the subject?
- Did the subject work in another enterprise than the present one?
- How did they manage to work in the concerned enterprise?
- What was their general perception of their own employment (the level of satisfaction)?

The French and Romanian groups were not at all homogeneous. They were both composed of workers ranging from elementary school to postgraduate skilled engineers. Throughout the research it was the intention to illustrate how similar is their perception on multinational status of their enterprises and the consequences of this status. In Romania, I studied the cases of two companies – Pipera and Miorita – in the fields of furniture and dairy production which were privatized after 1990. They both used to be parts of communist 'mammoth' enterprises called 'combinats', employing an enormous number of workers (labour hoarding) and forming a complete technological chain allowing Romanian industrial production to become more and more autarchic. After 1990, these combinats were split into several relatively autonomous plants and privatized separately. The work force in both companies decreased to twenty per cent once new machines were brought and the management was changed. Before 1989, the furniture company used to export to the USSR and the German Democratic Republic, but between 1992 and 1999 production decreased due to a lack of demand. After 2001, the furniture company engaged new external contracts and now it is well on its way to normality. The other company, Miorita, was one of the sad losers of privatization in Romania. After being one of the main dairy factories in the country, privatization and bad management allowed it to be wiped out almost entirely (since 2004 its land has been rented to a giant supermarket).

The workers of both Romanian companies were a bit reluctant to answer questions; with sarcasm they replied, 'Even the walls have ears' (a reference to the communist secret police – the Securitate). This common fear has not vanished in Romania, even fifteen years since the fall of the communist regime. Another reason for their reluctance had to do with continual worry about the social problems resulting from Romania's shaky economy.

French workers employed in companies like Alsthom (a French engine manufacturer), Becton-Dikinson (a pharmaceutical instruments manufacturer of U.S. origin), Caterpillar (a U.S.-based technological equipment manufacturer) Rossignol (a French sports equipment manufacturer), Rhodia (part of the French chemical industry), and Schneider Electric (a French manufacturer of electrical equipment) had a tendency to exaggerate and over-dramatize their situation. Most of all they feared unemployment as a serious social and occupational consequence of globalization. They also expressed worry about the global cultural homogenizing of labour. Given the fact that there were union representatives at the plants studied (registered in the two most important French confederations CGT and CFDT), the French employees were not afraid to invite me to their workplaces and visit their factories.

Results and New Directions for Research

The French and the Romanian groups were selected not only according to blue- and white-collar criteria but also according to age (that is with a seniority of ten years or more). The interviews in France took place at factory sites in Grenoble between 15 April and 15 May 2002. The research in Romania had been undertaken one year previously. All interviews – which I carried out all by myself – took place in a leisurely fashion, in a free ambiance, and without the interference that would have been caused by a possible linguistic barrier, likely to be caused by the fact that French is not my mother tongue. The people interviewed were kind and useful with up-to-date information; therefore, I consider both Romanian and French experiences extremely rich.[1]

In order to facilitate the analysis of the linkage with the assumed objectives, I asked questions in four thematic groups:
- the prestige given by the firm (brand) & work conditions,
- unemployment and social reassurance,
- relations of work, relations within the hierarchy

The Prestige Given by the Firm (Brand) and Work Conditions

The majority of French workers interviewed consider working in a MNE to be prestigious. This prestige is given by not only the size of the firm, the products marketed, and the special organization of activities (the management), but also by the specific measures of social policies adopted and applied inside the enterprise. A technician from Schneider recounted:

> MNEs have a rather positive influence on the career of an individual: the diversification of functions. The more the company is important and is well-established, the more differences of internal promotion arise. Yes, there is the possibility to develop the polycompetency: more internal training, better human resources and project management, also the possibility to acquire knowledge about other cultures.

'Caterpillar increase the feeling of pride, the prestige of employees,' said a 48–year-old engineer. 'American multinational enterprises have a better capacity to react to different problems,' argued a worker at Becton-Dikinson.

Romanians associate the prestige attached to an enterprise like an objective entity in itself. They have a feeling of pride when they speak of what they produce. 'The renown is won and maintained easier in a multinational enterprise than in a local one,' said a 29–year-old worker at

Pipera. 'Prestige, for me personally no, for others it is possible to be more valuable,' commented an old technician from the same company. 'There is an influence given by the international recognition of the multinational, there is also a stronger pressure and more elevated requirements to fight international competition, and all that gives a specific way of working,' stated an engineer from Miorita.

All these features of the multinational enterprise represent what Sainsaulieu calls 'spaces of identification that determine spheres of adherence and reference for individuals' (1984: 259). They bind the individual identity to their enterprise's renown in a dome of prestige in front of employees of other enterprises. French workers do appreciate the conditions of work and their permanent improvement (the exception is a worker from Schneider – 'encore travail taylorisé' – with a reference to the famous F. W. Taylor and his model of "scientific organisation of work"). They consider that the important changes occur in the medium term. 'Changing of work conditions every 5–10 years according to the competition, machines are evolving even more rapidly. Technological renewal at maximum every 10 years,' stated a worker at Alsthom. They feel a kind of organizational pressure that the majority of them assign to the multinational aspect of the enterprise, its competitive character – 'evolution according to the competition [between] Rossignol [and] Salomon'– to the fact that a change in a plant placed somewhere in the world can generate a change in all countries of implantation. 'Things become even more pyramidal than before', even closures or relocations are 'externalizing to countries with worse conditions ... in particular toward countries of the East', employees from Rossignol, Rhodia and Electricité de France (EDF) suggested in group interviews. According to informants, in a MNE work has the following characteristics: dynamism, polyvalence, change of tasks – sometimes unforeseen, fluctuating supervision by the hierarchy. An important gain attached to the multinational character is the possibility to acquire a lot of information on the shop floor. 'To inform us on novelties there is a program of technological overview and also magazines and Internet,' commented a 38–year-old engineer from Schneider.

Conditions of work improved considerably after the fall of communism in 1989, but they are still precarious in Romania. As one worker commented: 'Technological renewal is necessary. One could not continue with old machines'. In spite of this, a resistance to change, especially among old workers, is still present: 'We have problems of adaptation to the new machines. There were many accidents. Machines are complicated and demanding. Better to work with the old "made in Romania" machines', argued a 55–year-old worker at Pipera. There is a lot of organizational pressure to learn and to adjust to the new technologies. Accordingly it is necessary to get used to foreign styles of management and the requirements of competition and profitability. A technician from Miorita remarked: 'It is not necessary to reinvest all the profit in technology and other things. It is also necessary to give money to people'. One said: 'better to work with the hammer while winning money in addition, than to work with the machine and wait'.

The Romanian salaried employees complained about the intensification of work, fatigue, insufficient wages, the menace of unemployment and unpaid overtime: 'The quotas are not good. A lot of contracts and few workers', said an engineer from Pipera. According to the workers at Miorita the situation is similar: 'Some of us have to work Saturdays or even ten hours and more', said one of them. 'Not so much physical effort, but a psychological one. We are supervized all the time', continued another. 'Wages are less than last year. They go down every month. Lot of work. Little money', replied a third one.

Work conditions are objective aspects that are easy to evaluate, and an object of innumerable studies. The representation of these conditions is, however, subjective. It gives a more lucid picture on the ways in which people are employed in MNEs versus the local ones. Both French and Romanian groups acknowledged an external influence in terms of business culture and management style. While the French strongly supported the idea of forcing their foreign managers to act 'à la française', the Romanians refrained, fearing the bosses' retaliation. Both groups claimed the instability of tasks and the arrogance of hierarchy.

Unemployment and Social Reassurance

The power of workers against site closures, the relocation of plants or massive layoffs is considered an imperative goal by the French workers. On the other hand, they appreciate that public authorities must not be involved in any way in the management decisions of a company except in the case of public contracts or transgression of laws. 'The authorities must not intervene except to punish illegal actions', argued a technician at Caterpillar. 'Public powers must only intervene in the case of the threat of massive layoffs or relocation', added a worker at Becton.

French employees made some useful contextual comments about unemployment in France. They had a cautious attitude with regard to their professional future, considering it quite possible to find themselves unemployed in the medium term: 'Unemployment is normal for society, and could be a tragedy for the individual', said an engineer from Becton. 'For about twenty years unemployment has been something quite usual. Today when someone starts in an enterprise he won't necessarily accomplish his entire career there', explained a worker from Alsthom. 'No unemployment during the *"trente glorieuse"* ["the glorious thirty" – reference to the period of continuous economic growth between 1946 and 1973 – n.a.]. Then we had *"chômage endémique"* ["endemic unemployment"] in certain areas', remarked an engineer at Rossignol. 'Once unemployment in France passed three million, then the government succeeded by its measures and social policies in reducing it to nine hundred thousand', added a technician at

Rhodia. 'When metallurgy and the mines closed, a new poverty occurred; that is why the government enforced the Minimum Income Guarantee law' [a law which ensures that every French citizen receives a minimum clearly stated monthly income], continued the engineer from Rossignol.

Romanian workers are increasingly more and more worried about the status of their jobs. They see unemployment as a permanent threat used against them by management, and as an instrument used against possible salary claims or other complaints about benefits. That is why Romanian workers are adamant about a permanent state control over firms. 'The shares are in hands of managers, they decide our fate', said a worker at Miorita. 'They [the owners] can say: it is my enterprise, my machines, if I want to give you a job I will', commented a worker at Pipera.

All the people questioned find it very difficult to preserve their jobs when working in a MNE because of possible dislocation. Privatization and massive foreign investment are seen negatively by Romanian salaried employees. They view shareholders with scepticism. 'If the enterprise had remained state owned, it would have been better. Workers would have been more powerful. Nobody would have told us, "From tomorrow you don't work here anymore". Investors don't raise our salaries any more', said a technician from Pipera.

As they do not have reliable information on takeovers, workers feel exploited and their power in decline. All in all, Romanian workers seem to prefer the state as a permanent boss: 'Under Ceausescu's regime we had good wages. They remained good too after the revolution [December 1989], until the privatization', commented a worker from Miorita. These interviews support my hypothesis that economic incentives (profitability) are rather marginal in the face of social incentives (facing job insecurity). Internal training and the other measures to improve workers' qualifications reduce their fear of losing their job.

The image of unemployment as a tragedy for the professional evolution of an individual, sometimes having consequences for the very existence of an individual, is common to Romanian and French salaried employees. However, French employees see unemployment as a common feature of society, acceptable as long as it does not turn into a mass phenomenon.

Relations in Work and within the Hierarchy

Individualism is an increasing phenomenon, particularly in Western countries. Even if they appreciate the relationships with their colleagues as good and they discuss the conditions and the organization of work collectively, French workers acknowledge the 'shortage' of *team spirit* at their workplaces: 'Good work is done individually, but colleagues give themselves a helping hand if necessary,' said a technician from Rossignol. 'Some valorise collaboration in a multinational enterprise but this tends to disappear. There is more team spirit in local enterprises', added an engineer from EDF. His fellow union colleague from Rhodia added with sarcasm: 'The collective (group) of work does not exclude individualism; there is a "collective individualism"'.

On the other hand friendly relations and a warm social ambiance are among the strongest incentives and sources of work satisfaction for Romanians. 'The needs made us closer. We speak between us, but each has their own grief', commented a worker from Pipera.

The French workers consider that there is an autonomy of task execution in MNEs, but this no way influence the overall power of decision making. They consider this situation as both a cause and consequence of the wide gap between management and personnel. 'The hierarchy is distant from the reality on the ground', a worker from Alsthom told me. 'There is a lack of mutual confidence. Managers have adapted; once they were jail wardens, now they listen to us'. An engineer from Caterpillar remarked: 'Yes, one can express one's opinion if it is only about work, [but there is] no real freedom of speech'.

A similar situation exists in Romania concerning the rigid relations with management (even more than in France); a hierarchy is viewed as creating strains in the enterprise. 'There were times when we came with pleasure to the job. Now we come with fear. The chiefs should be closer to us. They use bad language'. Autonomy is nearly non-existent in most enterprises in Romania. The intermediate hierarchy (team leaders) indicates to the workers all the operations and procedures on a daily basis. In general, Romanian workers have very good relationships with their colleagues, but strained ones with managers in the upper levels. Therefore, the incentive and the satisfaction of work is gradually replaced by fear of unemployment, leading to a perverted spirit of competition among colleagues. 'When one complains, we are told: you can always look elsewhere for work if this doesn't satisfy you. The boss threatens us that there are ten people who are waiting to be hired for each job', said a technician at Miorita.

Relationships that are settled within a group of workers give the most essential characteristic of work identity. The distance from the hierarchy (submissiveness, obedience or autonomy) and to workmates (friendship, collaboration, individualism) structures the social dimension among salaried employees.

Conclusions

'The transition from socialism is defined by two major changes: a shift to a multiparty system, and the reintroduction of a market economy' (Lampland 1995: 341). However, I would like to stress here an additional point when market globalization, of multinationalization of products or transnationalization of enterprises, is discussed, namely that there is an enormous gap between the economic and social reality and peoples' mentalities, which remain ethnocentric. The culture of the enterprise is taken as a fundamental element but the impact of national culture is very often disregarded by researchers. Therefore, it is important to examine simultaneously national cultures, the social environment of enterprises and the culture of the enterprise itself when studying such organizations. By focusing on firms in their national settings, one of the most important lessons I learned concerns the theory of globalization, now even more popular than in the 1980s. If in fact there is an acceleration of the globalization process, and an increased standardization of goods and services, this does not seem to erase cultural differences. A unique global cultural identity, a monocultural world, would be an impoverishment of our lives and even considerably disruptive for business.

On the contrary, cultures resist, and persons responsible for marketing give more and more value to this important dimension of consumption. Today national culture is of particular concern in human resource management studies, generating the concept and theories of intercultural management. An enterprise – no matter how global – must structure its strategy and organizational matters according to the way in which it conceives the world in its local – that is, national – context. Therefore, if it perceives the world as a unique market, an enterprise will adopt a global strategy, and this will lead to a very well structured organization worldwide which will give consistently less space to individuals' freedom of choice in the different countries where the respective enterprise is doing business.

Managers of multinational enterprises have a tendency to say that their foreign investment is dictated by the imperatives of market competition; in other words, by global factors to which they are forced to adjust if they want to maintain the efficiency of their production and their very existence. On the other hand we can easily assume that the search for profit is the real cause of these changes. According to Blim: 'The world is becoming a global factory. The rise of this new global factory is marked not simply by the spread of industrialization throughout the world but also by the incorporation of vast new populations of workers in novel production and labour processes manufacturing goods for the world capitalist market' (1992: 1).

The multinational enterprises presented here seem to have a tendency to be more sensitive to changes of economic pressure in the world market than do national businesses. This was mentioned in several of the interviews quoted above, with the possible corollary that MNEs have a tendency also to react more quickly in the case of slow economic growth, for instance by adjusting the labour force accordingly. However, it does not seem that employment security is markedly different in MNEs than is the case for national companies. No matter how global in their scope, MNEs must also comply with national labour legislation.

For multinationals, as for other enterprises, to adjust their labour force plans to national policy as much as possible; to give sufficient notice in advance of job restructuring; and to consult in good faith all stakeholders regarding employment policy will in years to come constitute very important social principles. In short, the phenomenon of MNEs appears all over the world, and the analysis of its effects on employment in industrialized countries must necessarily find its complement in an analysis of the effects on employment in developing countries.

The evolution toward a society in which multinationals adjust their current major tendencies concerning the labour force will have some serious consequences for the number of professions and for qualification standards. This situation can have two effects on MNEs. One is the continuous search for polyvalent skills that can extend from technical tool mastering to PR qualities. The other one is the capacity to face the individualization of tasks generated by the lack of classic hierarchical relations, which had the role of transmitting information and orders. The new management would have to refocus on the mobilization and maintenance of team spirit, on keeping vivid a 'working network', which would become probably more and more virtual.

For these reasons, from a macroeconomic perspective, we can say that these transformations are leaving room for important complex changes. If the currents of modernization and the technological revolutions of the 1950s and 1960s were accompanied by the gradual deskilling of the labour force, present global tendencies indicate a considerable reverse phenomenon in developed countries. It is difficult to say if these are long-term tendencies, indications in terms of employment practices of a new era of economic growth. Or if it is just that enterprises act cautiously, by hiring a limited number of people but with high qualifications, in order to face the unforeseen tendencies of a 'shaky' economic environment (with potential evolution of markets, and the need to react to the competition).

Romania is also confronted with a gap with regard to qualifications at all levels, excepting some branches of research. Hence, a yearly decrease in productivity occurred along with a decrease in the quality of life as reflected by economic recession and national currency inflation. Displacements in occupational structure in different areas reveal a simultaneous process of de-industrialization and re-agrarianization, due to incapacity of the services sector – in East European countries – to generate employment for the population available after industrial closings and lay-offs. As Blim stated (1992: 2), even most complex socio-economic theories and programmes can 'overlook cultural diversity and the potential for resistance' of less influent actors in society. Following Blim, we can assume that when people discover that the state does not answer their needs or cannot act in their name, some choose to regroup at the level of the community, not to regain a certain political control but to claim their own identities. They adopt some common actions to fight the consumption trends potentially induced by multinational enterprises. They produce their own goods to replace those found on the market, and adopt specific policies and actions against the homogenization of a passive media culture, as process that has been named 'glocalisation' (Kürti and Langman 1997: 2–3). For Castells, 'European integration is at the same time a reaction to the process of globalization, but also its most advanced expression' (2001: 112).

The events of 1989/90 opened up Central and Eastern Europe by reinforcing a democratic climate and a widened knowledge of possibilities and ideas of free exchange. It is a cliché to affirm that our society is passing through one of the most volatile periods in its history. Opportunities brought by socio-cultural changes must not result in a convergence in form, nor in content, of the specific traits of any one society or community. The model of the 'cultural melting pot', submitted to the one of the 'common dream', must not replace the existential coordinates given by local collective representations perpetuated along the centuries: '[T]he recognition of a global capitalist system or international network of production, exchange and consumption; that is, the global factory ... and the local context is seen as part of a dynamic global structure' (Rothstein 1992: 238).

Even if they choose by free will other countries in which to earn their living, people – migrants or just expats – continue to blame all the difficulties they encounter not only on socio-economic objective conditions, but also on subjective cultural ones as well. The cultural difference between them and the enterprise's and/or manager's origin is the reason for the state of their misfortune. And these ideas and attitudes are shared across societies even though non-discrimination is a cause that every democracy promotes.

Note

1. I gratefully appreciate here the kindness of the interviewed subjects in France and Romania, who did everything possible to help me by providing comprehensive and pertinent answers to all my questions.

References

Blim, M. 1992. 'Introduction: The Emerging Global Factory', in F. Rothstein and M. Blim (eds), *Anthropology and the Global Factory*. New York: Bergin and Garvey, pp.1–32.

Castells, M. 2001. *Sociétés en réseaux*. Paris: Fayard.

Enriquez, E. 1988. 'L'entreprise comme lien social: un colosse aux pieds d'argile' in S. Renaud (ed.) *L' enterprise: une affaire de societé*. Paris: Presses National de la Fondation des Sciences Politiques, pp.203–28.

Hofstede, G. 1980. *Culture's Consequences*. London: Sage.

Iribarne, P. d'. 1998. *Cultures et mondialisation*. Paris: Seuil.

Iribarne, P. d', A. Henry, J.-P. Segal, S. Chevrier and T. Globokar. 1993. *La logique de l'honeur*. Paris: Seuil.

Kürti, L. 2002. *Youth and the State: Capitalism, Communism and Class*. London: Pluto.

Kürti, L. and J. Langman. 1997. 'Introduction: Searching for Identities in the New East Central Europe', in L. Kürti and J. Langman (eds), *Beyond Borders: Remaking Cultural Identities in the New East and Central Europe*. Boulder, CO: Westview, pp.1–16.

Lampland, M. 1995. *The Object of Labor: Commodification In Socialist Hungary*. Chicago: University of Chicago Press.

Laval, D. *Mondialisation et desindustrialisation*. Paris: SELIO (undated).

Lévi-Strauss, C. 1983. *Le Regard éloigné*. Paris: Plon.

McCarl, R. 1992. 'Exploring the Boundries of Occupational Knowledge', in J. Calgione, D. Francis and D. Nugent (eds), *Workers' Expressions. Beyond Accomodation and Resistance*. Albany: State University of New York Press, pp.68–78.

Mead, G.H. 1962[1934]. *Mind, Self, and Society*. Chicago: University of Chicago Press.

Miscevic, N. 2001. 'National Identities in Transition' in *Studies in East European Thought 53: 197–219*.

Paradeise, C. 1991. 'Les théories de l'acteur', *Cahiers Français* 247: 31–38.

Rothstein, F. 1992. 'Conclusion: New Waves and Old-Industrialization, Labour, and the Struggle for a new World Order', in F. Rothstein and M. Blim (eds), *Anthropology and the Global Factory*. New York: Bergin and Garvey, pp.238–46.

Ruminska-Zimny, E. 1999. 'Globalization with a Human Face', *Human Development Report*, Part 2. New York: United Nations Press.

Sainsaulieu, R. 1984. *Identité au travail*. Paris: Presses National de la Fondation des Sciences Politiques.

———— 1988. *L'enterprise: Une affaire de societé*. Paris: Presses National de la Fondation des Sciences Politiques.

Smith, A. 1991. *National Identity*. Reno: University of Nevada Press.

Chapter 12

Immigrants from Ukraine in the Czech Republic: Foreigners in the Border Zone

Zdeněk Uherek

In this chapter I deal with several types of emigration from Ukraine to the Czech Republic[1] that took place from the early 1990s to the early twenty-first century. The aim of this study is to show some of the specifics, including causes and effects, of postcommunist migration. I take note of the motivations of migrants, their aspirations, how they invest the wealth they have gained, what their attitudes are to the population of the target country and, conversely, how the majority population of the target country views migrant groups. The migrations commented on here are part of migrational movements from East to West. Both the source and target countries are, however, postcommunist. As we will see below, a similar historical experience does not necessarily mean that the populations of the source and target countries had the chance in the past to get to know each other or that they have a positive relationship.

In the first part of the chapter I situate Ukrainian migration in its wider socio-cultural context; next, I concentrate on short-term migration from Transcarpathia in western Ukraine. In the third part, I deal with groups from Ukraine that have migrated to the Czech Republic permanently. In the conclusion I argue that while migration from Ukraine can be characterized as innovative, emigrants do not want to change their lives in all respects. They value some areas of their social life and culture more than those they encounter in the host society.[2]

Migration in the Context of the Socio-cultural Transformations since 1989

According to John Salt, the scope of migration in Europe in the 1990s was comparable only with the migrations associated with the First and Second World Wars (Salt 2001: 1). The reasons are clearly identifiable: firstly, borders became easier to cross after the fall of communist regimes in Eastern and Central Europe; secondly, there were military conflicts which troubled some parts of the former Soviet Union and the Balkans from the early 1990s onwards; and thirdly, there were great economic differences between individual countries of Eurasia, including different conditions in their labour markets. Salt divided the countries involved into three separate regions, based on migration behaviour: Western Europe, Central Europe, and Eastern Europe, excluding the Commonwealth of Independent States (Salt 2001: 1).

Although the fall of the Iron Curtain set some parts of the postcommunist world in motion, Europe exhibits a lower degree of migration in comparison to other continents. As Salt shows, migration activity associated with the collapse of the Communist bloc in Europe reached its highest intensity already in the years 1992/93. At the same time, however, he points out that in Central and Eastern Europe the number of short-term and short-distance movements across state boundaries increased. Several researchers consider short-term migration as typical for Central Europe, whether it is labour migration or involves business activities (Wallace 2001: 45; Okólski 2001: 105–28). The migration situation in the Czech Republic fits this characteristic well. For the year 2003 alone, which was not otherwise remarkable in terms of migration, a total of 260 million people (arrivals and departures) were processed at the borders of the Czech Republic, a country with a population of just over 10 million.[3] Of these border crossings, 71 million were made by citizens of the Czech Republic while 189 million were made by persons of other nationalities.

The relatively high number of border crossings – especially those by foreign nationals – contrasts markedly with the number of foreigners who were long-term or permanent residents of the Czech Republic. At the end of 2004, 254,294 foreigners were resident in the Czech Republic, of whom 154,827 had long-term visas and 99,467 had permanent residence.[4] At 2.5 per cent, the percentage of foreigners resident in the Czech Republic is not high in comparison to figures from Western European states. It is, however, many times higher than it was before 1989. Whereas in the 1980s there was a relatively stable population of between 34,000 and 37,000 foreigners living in Czechoslovakia,[5] from 1991 until the second half of the 1990s we see a sudden increase in their number due to international economic migration, a new phenomenon for the population of the Czech Republic. This large increase in migration has meant an influx of workers from a variety of postcommunist states. At the end of 2005, the largest number of legally resident foreign nationals were Ukrainians (87,789 people), followed by Slovaks (49,446 people), Vietnamese (36,832 people) and Poles (17,810 people). In the case of Slovaks and Poles, these are citizens of states neighbouring the Czech Republic which are also members of the European Union; in the case of Vietnamese and Ukrainians, they are citizens of so-called 'third countries' which are not immediate neighbours and must overcome more obstacles to migration.

In the 1990s, just after the Velvet revolution and removal the communist regime attitudes of the autochthonous population of the Czech Republic towards foreigners were influenced by their experience of citizens from other states from the communist era, by means of media campaigns, by the specific features of Czech nationalism and, of course, by experience from close contact with individual foreigners. These attitudes were full of contradictions. For example, attitudes towards people from the former Soviet Union were fundamentally influenced by Czech citizens' experiences of the occupation of Czechoslovakia in 1968 by the Soviet Union and other Warsaw Pact armies, and by the years following which Czech historians refer to as 'normalization'. Normalization, in their view, means a consolidation after the unsuccessful attempt of members of the Czechoslovak Communist Party at the end of the 1960s to set the country's political course, one which would not be dictated from Moscow, and is associated with the persecution of those citizens of Czechoslovakia who disagreed with the Soviet-led occupation. It is estimated that the purges following the 1968 occupation affected half a million inhabitants of Czechoslovakia (Měchýř 1999: 33).

Czechoslovak society during the 1970s and 1980s was not unified. Jan Měchýř divides it into three groups: normalizers, dissidents and a grey zone. According to Měchýř, the number of dissidents who actively opposed the communist regime was at most between 100,000 and 200,000, while the normalizers – or sympathizers of the communist regime – numbered about 1.5 million people. The remainder of Czechoslovakia's population of 15 million are counted by Měchýř as the so-called grey zone (Měchýř 1999: 39–40).

The grey zone was comprised of citizens who, at least outwardly, conformed to the policy of normalization. After the suppression of the mass demonstrations of 1968 and 1969, they gave up on publicly expressing their opinion of the political situation in the country. The attitudes of this grey zone, which comprised the vast majority of the citizens of Czechoslovakia, are very difficult to reconstruct. A lot is suggested, however, by the findings of Ladislav Holy (1996) who conducted research in Czechoslovakia soon after the Velvet Revolution of 1991/92. One of the issues which attracted Holy's attention was the then constantly emphasized statement that Czechs are an educated and cultured nation, a claim that Holy explained in relation to the specific forms of Czech nationalism. It is possible to agree with his explanation, though it is worth adding that the accentuation of this characteristic at the end of the 1980s and beginning of the 1990s was to a remarkable extent caused by the fact that normalization was an act of passive watching how things are done (supposedly) badly, while every passive watcher had the feeling that they knew a better solution, albeit one that they could not implement. The situation in which Czech society found itself formed the conditions for the grey zone, people who passively watched themselves being governed by a minority appointed by the Soviet Union, who conceptualized themselves as intelligent and cultured individuals who knew better how to organize work, direct the economy and produce and distribute cultural values, but who could not use their knowledge in a totalitarian communist state. On the other hand, they imagined the governing minority as uncultured idiots who could make decisions and make things happen but who had no knowledge, education or proper cultural view. Bearing in mind that official political and social impulses were legitimized by the Soviet Union, the Soviet Union itself was logically conceptualized as a source of backwardness and stupidity.

This discourse of educated and cultured individuals who cannot implement their ideas, and the simpletons who lead them, was also encouraged by the fact that the official media was considered to tell nothing but lies, including information about the Soviet Union, which was almost always positive. Thus it was sufficient to invert all statements from the official media so as to properly understand them, and these inversions became widely distributed, mainly in the form of anecdotes. The grey zone made fun of Soviet inventions,[6] (supposed) economic successes,[7] political leaders,[8] aggressiveness and expansionism.[9] Katherine Verdery (1996: 8) has written that, for her, totalitarianism looked appalling and at the same time fascinating from the distant perspective of the U.S.A.; for the grey zone of Czechoslovakia in the period of normalization, totalitarianism was boring, mind-numbing, ridiculous and bizarre. Yet at the same time it gave citizens the scope for creating myths about their own sophistication and individuality, because what they read, listened to and discussed with friends as often as not seemed to them to exist at a much higher cultural level than what was on offer by way of official propaganda.

The inhabitants of Czechoslovakia were, however, rarely in direct contact with those people who they were laughing at. Only a few citizens of Czechoslovakia visited the Soviet Union. Travel around the Soviet Union was possible only along approved routes, and border crossings were allowed only on the basis of officially authenticated invitations. Interactions with soldiers of the Soviet Army stationed in Czechoslovakia were also uncommon as they were stationed on military bases that were out of bounds for Czechoslovak citizens. Apart from this, Soviet presence was visible while transporting military equipment along public roads. The mediated experience and strong stereotyping of the inhabitants of the Soviet Union on the part of the Czech population led to, among other things, inhabitants of the Soviet Union being perceived as one unified mass. Czechs usually did not distinguish between the various nations of the Soviet Union and collectively referred to its citizens as Russians or 'Ruskies'.

At the beginning of the 1990s, the situation changed markedly. On the one hand, the occupying army started to pull out, and on the other hand the Czech population started to come into direct contact with 'Ruskies'. The initial reaction was more or less positive. Just after 1989, Czech society was only just formulating its attitude toward its neighbours. Its new representatives leaded by Václav Havel aspired to open the state "to the world", build new image of Czechoslovakia on a broad international co-operation and cultivate cultural and humanitarian ideals. It agreed on a kind of negation of the Soviet communist regime applied in the Czechoslovakia before 1989 that was conceptualized like a close, paranoid, based on hypocrisy, hostile against the surrounding world and disregarding basic human values. In his speeches, Václav Havel called the former communist Soviet Union an empire of evil. The November 1989 slogan against violence used by participants of mass meetings in Prague against communist regime 'We are not like them' (e.g. communists) could be accepted by wide public also meant openness an respect to moral values. The perceived orientation to openness and respect to moral values was also demonstrated in the first free election in 1990. In addition to the economist Václav Klaus, voters mostly opted for popular actors, such as Rudolf Hrušínský, Jan Kačer or Daniela Kolářová (Měchýř 1999: 194–5), people who had never been seriously involved in politics but who, thanks to their media presence, represented peoples' cultural and moral ideals. The slogan 'return to Europe', often heard among the adherents of non-left-wing parties, presupposed openness, not only towards the West but also towards the East. An example of this openness was the speed with which the Czechoslovak government reacted to the request for repatriation of Czech descendents and their Ukrainian and Russian family members living in the area affected by the Chernobyl nuclear disaster, who desired to move to Czechoslovakia. The descendents of Czech emigrants to tsarist Russia, often already children of mixed Czech-Ukrainian marriages, were passed the request on to President Havel in 1990. The reaction of the Czechoslovak government was immediate. Between 1991 and 1993 almost 2,000 people moved to Czechoslovakia and these were guaranteed adequate housing in Bohemia, plus interest-free loans and jobs. As I was at the time a member of a research team that studied the transfer and adaptation of migrants,[10] I can describe the varied behaviour of Czechs towards each wave of immigrants. The most accommodating behaviour towards immigrants was noticed in 1991, but the attitude towards foreigners from the East rapidly worsened in 1992 and the situation got even worse in 1993. A group of ethnic Czechs from Belarus and their Belarussian family members who migrated at the end of 1993 found that social isolation was only overcome with great difficulty (Uherek, Valášková and Brouček 1997).[11]

Variations in helpfulness and openness towards the world are also clear in the asylum policies of Czechoslovakia. In 1991, one year after opening its borders to asylum seekers, Czechoslovakia granted 776 people asylum. This, however, was to be the year in which asylum figures peaked in Czechoslovakia and later in the Czech Republic, and by 1992 there was already a marked decrease in the number of granted asylum cases.[12] The reasons for this change in behaviour included the rising number of labour migrants, a rising fear of criminality and organized crime, and competition from migrants in the labour market. Until 1990, Czechoslovakia had not known unemployment. On the contrary, there was a shortage of workers, especially of unqualified labourers. Foreign labourers were therefore seen in a positive light. In the same way that openness and a humane approach were seen as a demonstration of the fact that Czechoslovakia had not been part of the Communist bloc of its own will and that it wished to distance itself from its totalitarian past, the notion that the movement towards Europe would lead to the ending of its isolation was a prominent idea in Czech society in the first years after the communist era ended. However, with rising numbers of immigrants from the East, fears emerged among the population and with them the stereotype that people from the East were second-class people – that is, uncultured, uneducated and dangerous – started to accelerate again.

This change in the social climate can be demonstrated by the results of the 1992 elections. Twelve political parties were elected to the Czechoslovak Federal Assembly, whose political spectrum was quite varied. The central-right coalition of the Civil Democratic Party (ODS) and Christian Democratic Union (KDU-ČSL) won. The same coalition also won the election for the Czech National Council, the predecessor of the Czech Republic's current parliament. Meanwhile, Občanské hnutí (a successor to Civic Forum), a grouping based on humanity and culture which had been the leading political force in 1990, disappeared from the scene. The opposite pole of the right-wing ODS became the Levý blok (Left Bloc). It is symptomatic of this time, when the Czechoslovak Republic fell apart, that the extreme right-wing and nationalist political party Association for the Republic – Republican Party of Czechoslovakia, connected with the skinhead movement, was elected for the first and only time into both the Czechoslovak Federal Assembly and the Czech National Council for one election period (1992–1996).

Access to the Czech labour market by migrants from the East remained unregulated at this time. Ukrainian workers in particular were able to carve out a niche as a result of transformational changes in the Czech economy during the 1990s, a point made clear by the sociologists Jiří Večerník and Petr Matějů:

Because the overall tempo of modernization is quite slow, and while demands for qualifications and productivity grow equally slowly, human resources and their level of skill have only played a minor role in the dynamics of labour productivity and salary differences. Their adaptation to market changes and the reorientation towards new markets led to the situation that Czech companies, which were suffering from an insufficiency of financial means for modernization, were building on the comparative advantage of a cheap labour force. Overall economic growth was then founded mainly on the intensity of labour. This strategy to a certain extent ensured a lack of technological development of ... factories. (Večerník and Matějů 1998: 22)

Ladislav Holy in his book *The Little Czech and the Great Czech Nation* (1996)shows exactly how, in 1989, nationalism was able to unite a wide mass of citizens in the fight against the communist government. National rhetoric, national slogans and national symbols were clearly most common at anti-government demonstrations (Holy 1996: 16–54). After 1989, an exalted declaration of national unity was replaced by openness which allowed the anchoring of Czech society in a wider European context. Thus the grounds were laid for nationalists to be able to legitimately strive for a Czech nation state.

Transcarpathian Ukraine as a Labour Reservoir for the Czech Republic

Many theoreticians of migration avoid dealing with the problems of temporary labour migration and do not include it among migration themes. However, as Claire Wallace (2001: 45) notes, it is necessary to understand even this type of migration. The reason why it is so important to deal with various types of short-term labour migration is that often the autochthonous population do not perceive the migration as a temporary phenomenon – that is as individual arrivals and departures of migrants – but as the permanent presence of foreigners who do not integrate but constantly cause the same adjustment problems. On the other hand, in the countries where the migrants come from, the migration experience, shared among a large number of people, and the notion of the close connection between the source and target areas, are thus accumulated.

Although other areas of Ukraine are also sources of migration to the Czech Republic, the largest number of people migrating there come from Transcarpathia (Drbohlav 1997: 36). For this reason, I carried out field research in this westernmost part of Ukraine in 2001 and continued to do so until the beginning of 2005.[13]

Transcarpathia – known before the Second World War as Subcarpathian Ruthenia – is that part of Ukraine which is geographically closest to the Czech Republic. From 1919 until 1938 it formed the easternmost part of the Czechoslovak state, and from 1945 to 1992, as part of the Soviet Union, it directly neighboured the then state of Czechoslovakia. It is a mountainous region of about 12,000 square kilometres covered with vast, deep forests and with a belt of lowlands in the south along the Tisa River.

There were limited possibilities of making a living in this territory and extensive economic migration was recorded mainly from the last third of the nineteenth century.[14] In the period between the two world wars, when Ruthenia was part of Czechoslovakia, the first wave of labour migration to Bohemia and Moravia took place, and Ruthenians were employed there mainly as farm labourers and lumberjacks. The younger generation, meanwhile, received high school and even university education. In Prague, for example, Ruthenian students could choose between two Russian and one Ukrainian grammar school (Zilynskyj 1995: 36–38), which had been established by the Czechoslovak state as part of a campaign for post-revolutionary emigrants from Russia who were seeking a democratic environment in Czechoslovakia or a refuge from persecution on the part of the Soviet regime.

In 1939, Subcarpathian Ruthenia fell under the control of Hungary. Then, in 1945, it became part of the Soviet Union on the basis of a treaty between Czechoslovakia and the USSR, when it was renamed Transcarpathian Ukraine.[15] After the Soviet takeover of the territory, migration to and from Czechoslovakia stopped and contacts diminished dramatically. Migration from Ukraine to Czechoslovakia only started again in 1990 and continued to increase after Ukraine became an independent state in 1991 and after Czechoslovakia divided into the Czech Republic and Slovakia in 1993.

According to the census of December 2001, the population of Ukraine stood at nearly 49 million, a decrease of almost 3 million from the level recorded in the 1989 census (when the country was still part of the Soviet Union), a fall which is due to emigration and a diminishing birth rate. In 2001, 1,258,000 inhabitants were recorded as living in the Transcarpathian region, of whom 446,000 lived in towns and 792,000 lived in the countryside. In 2001, the largest city in Transcarpathia was Uzhgorod (population 117,200), followed by Mukachevo (83,300) and Chust (29,100). The predominant nationality recorded by the census was Ukrainian (80.5 per cent of the population), followed by Hungarian (12 per cent) and Romanian (2.5 per cent).

Information obtained from field research allows us to formulate a number of theses about migration from Transcarpathia, and in particular to the Czech Republic.

Firstly, labour migration from Transcarpathia to the Czech Republic from 1990 continued patterns of migrational behaviour which had formed gradually in the past. Migration in search of work did not stop even after the incorporation of Transcarpathia into the Soviet Union, it simply changed direction. Transcarpathian jobseekers started to leave mainly for the industrial regions of the Soviet Union. Seasonal movement in search of work is considered to be a standard way of living in Transcarpathia, and is directed wherever there is a shortage of labour. Workers from Transcarpathia found employment building railways in Slovakia between the world wars, building the border defences in Bohemia before the Second World War, and were employed in a similar way in the Soviet economy between 1945 and 1991.

Secondly, awareness of the possibilities of gaining income in Bohemia and Moravia has been transferred from generation to generation and was partially revived by business practices even during the period of totalitarian isolation. Before my research in Transcarpathia, I had supposed that after 1946 there had been a much more significant reduction in individual economic activities than was actually the case. Apart from the contacts which Ukrainians and Ruthenians living in Bohemia maintained with their relatives, there also existed spontaneous entrepreneurial activities. In Transcarpathia, I heard stories on several occasions about tourist trips which local agricultural cooperatives had organized to Prague and other large cities in Bohemia and Moravia during the communist period. Buses were loaded with local products like woodwork, souvenirs, tanned sheepskins, pot scouring steel wool, and so on. These products were then sold on to middlemen in Bohemia. The trade usually took place in such a way that cooperative members received cash for their goods and then used this to buy other goods (industrial products, electronics, food products) which they subsequently consumed, bartered or sold on their return to Ukraine. Thus an awareness was maintained that it was possible to do business in Bohemia.

Thirdly, since labour migration from Transcarpathia is a long-term continuous phenomenon, and brings migrants a higher economic position than those who do not migrate, migration is not considered to be a sign of social failure here; it does not socially disqualify a person. Actually it is the opposite. Even highly placed functionaries in the cities of Uzhgorod and Rachiv assured me that labour migration had a long list of positive effects. Not only do people gain the means to buy things, they also obtain the means for investing in the local economy as well as experience of life in other countries.

Fourth: Transcarpathian Ukrainians know a lot more about European countries to the West of their borders than inhabitants of the states of Western and Central Europe know about Transcarpathian Ukraine. Transcarpathians are able to judge what the job situation is in Portugal, Italy, the Czech Republic, Slovakia, Australia, Canada and so on. Potential labour migrants discuss which target country is most accessible under current circumstances. The target countries are divided into two categories. The first category is suitable for long-term stays, and even permanent immigration: Australia, Canada, the U.S.A. and some other countries fall into this category. Countries that are suitable for short-term stays fall into the second category: this includes the Czech Republic, Poland, Italy, Spain, Portugal, Germany, Russia and other parts of Ukraine. In 2004, most Ukrainians (the numbers include Transcarpathians) worked in Russia, the estimate being almost 1 million; meanwhile there were an estimated 500,000 in Italy; 300,000 in Poland; 200,000 in the Czech Republic; and 100,000 in Spain.

Fifth: because of the obstacles that the Czech Republic has gradually put in place to prevent labour migration from Ukraine, the popularity of the Czech Republic as a target country for Transcarpathians has declined. On the one hand this is because countries where Ukrainians receive better wages have opened up to migration, and on the other because the cost of gaining access to the Czech labour market has increased. Consequently, to obtain the desired amount of wealth it has become necessary to lengthen one's stay.

When evaluating the situation in the Czech Republic, respondents very opined that the Czech Republic was an optimal target for labour migration until about 1996. All one had to do was find a company willing to hire a worker. Migration was not institutionalized and migration networks were just starting to form from information passed on by family members or neighbours about companies seeking to hire workers. Sometimes jobs were passed on like relay batons, such that a person would work for a company for a certain time period – for example three months, the maximum length of a legal tourist visa – and then they would leave and the post would pass to another family member. Ukrainian workers were very often hired without a work permit or a properly signed contract by businessmen in the Czech Republic.

From the mid 1990s, private legal, semi-legal, and illegal organizations which arranged work and eased migrant's way into the Czech labour market started to play a leading role in the organization of migration flows, replacing spontaneous migration for a number of reasons. The first is that migration is a profitable business and employment agencies can create obstacles for migrants and then charge them for overcoming them. In addition, the labour supply began to exceed demand, and the threat of prosecution for work without work permits by the Czech state began to increase. Especially for large firms in the Czech Republic employing migrants, it started to become advantageous to hire a firm rather than individuals to do the work. At this point stories of mafias and organized crime began to emerge, and others about hiring people for prostitution under the pretext of manual labour and so on.

On the issue of organized crime, respondents said that the mafia is more evident in Poland and in the Czech Republic than in Transcarpathian Ukraine, where people know each other and there is no room for organized crime. In the Czech Republic, however, according to respondents, the police think that what Ukrainians do among themselves is their own business and thus under these conditions the mafia blooms.

On 18 June 2000, visa requirements were introduced between Ukraine and the Czech Republic. In this way the Czech state began to regulate migration from Ukraine more effectively. In addition, it completed the institutionalization of labour recruitment. Labour force is usually recruited directly in Ukraine, through a mediator. The mediator, in Ukraine called the client, deals with all the formalities of travel, work and accommodation, and workers pay for these services with deductions from the salary they earn in the target country. For employment agencies this is a very lucrative business and leads to their great enrichment.

Sixth, one of the ways employment intermediaries get rich is from the fact that foreign workers, such as those from Transcarpathian Ukraine, are less concerned with who they pay than with paying as little as possible. It is not only about the investment of money, but also the investment of time, as well as investment in personal safety. Those Ukrainians interested in work pay where and when it is necessary and those who help them overcome obstacles. If they find that dealing with state institutions is too expensive, protracted or uncertain, they will try to find an employment agency to do it for them. For Ukrainian workers, the workings of the Czech state and its officials are probably even less comprehensible than the activities of employment agencies.

After 2000, a number of Ukrainians tried to lower the entry costs of access to the Czech labour market by applying for asylum there. Between 1990 and 2005, a total of 12,299 Ukrainian citizens requested asylum in the Czech Republic, the highest number of applicants in any one year being 2001 when 4,419 Ukrainians applied.[16] An application for asylum effectively legalized a migrant's stay and, in the period between 1 January 2000 and 1 February 2002, it also made legal employment possible because asylum seekers were granted a work permit for the period when their asylum application was being processed. Processing these applications was relatively protracted and it was often possible to prolong a stay for a period of over a year. The sudden increase in requests for asylum in the Czech Republic, however, motivated the state and the parliament to amend Act No. 325/1999 on asylum, these changes being introduced in the Collection of Laws No. 2/2002.[17] At the same time, changes in Act No. 1/1991 on Employment were implemented. According to the newly amended § 2e in section III into the Employment Act a work permit will not be issued to applicants for asylum for a period of one year commencing from the day of application. Following these measures, the number of applicants for asylum decreased. In 2004, only 1,600 Ukrainian citizens applied for asylum in the Czech Republic, about a third of the number in 2001, in 2005 applications fell further to 987 and in 2007 there were 293 asylum seekers from the Ukraine in the Czech Republic.[18] Even so, Ukrainians comprise the largest group of foreign citizens requesting asylum in the Czech Republic, making up 15.6 per cent of the total number of asylum seekers in 2007.[19]

Seventh: for migrants' households in the Ukraine, migration from Transcarpathia is important as a means of maintaining their standard of living as well as representing a possible means of economic innovation. In interviews, earnings gained in the Czech Republic and other states were often associated with the notion of 'ready money'. The household economy is to a great extent based on subsistence, even in those cases where people are employed. Salaries in a number of Ukrainian companies and institutions have often been irregular, and in some cases remain so today. At the end of 2003, the average salary in Ukraine was in the region of 306 hrivna (UAH) per month; in January 2005 it had reached an average value of 641 UAH.[20] Incomes in agriculture, the most widespread economic activity in Transcarpathia, were the lowest of all, and in January 2005 the average income in agriculture for the whole of Ukraine was approximately 296 UAH.[21] In 2003, pensions did not exceed 80 to 120 UAH.[22] Local government authorities interviewed in 2001 in Transcarpathia estimated unemployment at approximately 50 per cent. It was much more higher compared to number of registered unemployed. Official number of registered unemployed in Ukraine at that time was of less than 4 per cent. That indicated considerable number of people without any income.[23] The cost of medical care and medicines are borne by patients themselves.

At the end of December 2004, the exchange rate of the hrivna to the dollar was 5.3 UAH to $1; in April 2006, the exchange rate was 5 UAH to $1. It follows from this that the average hourly wage in Ukraine in late 2004 and early 2005 was $0.75 per hour, while in Transcarpathia it was $0.59.[24] According to migrants, they received the equivalent of about $1.2 to $2 per hour for unqualified manual labour in the Czech Republic, which means that they could earn two or three times as much per hour in the Czech Republic as they could back home in Transcarpathian Ukraine.

Migrants manage the money they gain in this way, using it when paying in cash cannot be avoided, and they try to invest what they can back home in Transcarpathia where the relative value of the wealth they have obtained increases. It appears from the answers of respondents that they mostly invest in housing in Transcarpathia. After that money is spent on home furnishings, cars and electronics. Money earned abroad is also often used to pay for medicines and medical care for sick parents and other relatives. I have not met anyone who, on the basis of the money they earned during their stay in the Czech Republic, would start to do business in Transcarpathian Ukraine.

Eighth: it is common in Transcarpathian Ukraine for labour migration to influence the organization of family life. Families living without one of the household's adult members on a long-term basis, or households where children are raised by grandparents because both parents are abroad, again on a long-term basis, are not uncommon. I have also recorded cases where families have disintegrated because one of the partners began living with someone else whilst they were abroad.

Finally, I was surprised by how people from Transcarpathia evaluated working in the Czech Republic and their communication with the Czech population. It is known that Ukrainians in the Czech Republic mostly do poorly paid, unqualified, physically demanding work which does not reflect their level of education and qualifications. They often work twelve hours a day, as well as working overtime and on Saturdays and Sundays. Many would think that this is an exhausting and dangerous lifestyle. Respondents from Ukraine, however, did not evaluate their work as such. More often than not they said that work in the Czech Republic is not easy, but in the end that is why they are hired to do it. A large part of the population of Transcarpathia is convinced that they know how to work hard, but this awareness does not correspond to the economic situation in which they find themselves. They probably do not evaluate work conditions in the Czech Republic negatively because they are similar to the experience of working in other countries. Heavy workloads, and working weekends and overtime, are not foisted on migrants by employers but are rather requested by the migrants themselves because it cuts the length of their stay and increases the amount they can earn. In Transcarpathian villages there is widespread work in the form of temporary help without contractual arrangement. It is often hard, physical labour for a low wage, and may involve considerable travelling: a woman might travel eight kilometres on foot just to scythe someone's meadow. Thus Ukrainians do not request contractual guarantees in the Czech Republic, though many have been cheated as a result and have not been properly paid for their work.

People from Transcarpathia who worked in the Czech Republic usually did not complain about contacts with inhabitants of the Czech Republic. Indeed, they rarely had time for lengthy interaction and, with the exception of supervisors, they tend to view Czechs from a distance. They are usually employed with other Ukrainians and also live with them in staff housing. Czechs do not work with them not only because they do not look for the work done by Ukrainians, but also because the companies that employ Ukrainians avoid employing Czechs. In 2003, one student of mine decided to write his master's thesis on foreign workers from Ukraine. He describes, among other things, how difficult it was for a non-Ukrainians to find work in a company that cleans department stores and on construction sites, which mostly employ Ukrainians (Červinka 2004). Such companies also try to keep the Ukrainian workers isolated.

I frequently came across the idea in Transcarpathia that there was not really much of a difference between Transcarpathian Ukraine and the Czech Republic. Inhabitants of Transcarpathia assured each other that Czech people are similar to them and, because Czech is a closely related language, it is easy to make oneself understood in Bohemia. However, once people began to talk about their stay in the Czech Republic more extensively, it became clear that communication problems were part of their experience. Yet despite this very few migrants make preparations for their first stay, precisely because they do not expect communication barriers. In addition, those who have been to the Czech Republic seldom tell others about their experiences. They do not highlight communication problems, and they do not want to create competition for themselves in the labour market by highlighting them. One of our informants was preparing to leave for Bohemia to work in construction. He visited a female friend so that she could give him the basic words he would need (shovel, pick, broom and so on). But rather than giving him the necessary words she gave him vulgar terms, so that when he arrived in Bohemia he would refer to a shovel, pick or broom with these, and so make himself a joke to everyone.

Alongside the discourse about the relative closeness of Czech and Transcarpathian languages and cultures, there is also a discourse about the distance between them. The inhabitants of Transcarpathian Ukraine are patriots: they love their country, their region; they like to talk about how Transcarpathia could be a paradise for tourists from all over the world and that their country could be a place for natural spas, agricultural tourism and similar things. In their discussions, they state that Czechs are not as warm, sensitive and hospitable as Ukrainians from Transcarpathia (the Hucul, Boiko, Lemko people), and they say that they could not adjust to life in Bohemia and would not want to live there permanently. These mutually interconnected discourses about closeness and distance give the inhabitants of Transcarpathia self-confidence; they also help them to understand labour migration as a necessary evil which they conceptualize as a temporary episode. They also comment that many people in the target countries they stay consider them to be second-class beings.

In 2001, Mikuláš Mušinka, a professor of Ruthenian history from Slovakia, asked an official of the Interior Ministry in Uzhgorod what he thought about the fact that, in opinion polls, Czechs placed Ukrainians second only to Romanies as the kind of people they would not want to live next to. The official replied that this must mainly be a result of their economic situation: 'I would not want a second-class neighbour either', he said, and finished his answer by saying, 'Ukraine is the most spiritual country in Europe'.

The inhabitants of Transcarpathian Ukraine say that the border area attracts wealthy people from other parts of Ukraine due to its closeness to the West. My research confirmed that in a number of border villages, such as Storozhnica, there are lots of expensive villas being built which, however, often remained empty or unfinished.

According to Ukrainian statistics, Transcarpathia is witnessing an outflow of population, not only to the West but also to other parts of Ukraine itself. In 2004, Transcarpathia experienced a net population loss of 1,424 people to internal migration and 1,116 to international migration.[25] Figures for international migration are particularly remarkable when compared to those for other regions of Ukraine (Transcarpathia has the third highest level of international migration), especially when one bears in mind that it is a small, sparsely populated region. Overall, these figures clearly indicate that processes of industrialization and urbanization are at work, and that inhabitants of Transcarpathia are being drawn to large cities, both in Ukraine and abroad.

Permanent Migration from Ukraine to the Czech Republic: A Case of Immigrants from Southern Ukraine to a Small Town in Western Bohemia

Although the majority of migration from Ukraine to the Czech Republic is temporary, there is also a significant number of people whose aim is to remain in the Czech Republic permanently. Among those that have the prerequisites for permanent immigration are families from Ukraine in which at least one member has one or more ancestors who originally came from Bohemia, and others who have a deep emotional tie to the lands of the Czech Republic.

I have already mentioned the Czech state's assisted resettlement of those from areas affected by the Chernobyl disaster. This programme ended in 1993, since when Ukrainian citizens of Czech origin have been treated much the same as other foreigners wanting to emigrate to the Czech Republic from outside the EU. Because their native tongue is usually either Ukrainian or Russian, they encounter the same problems as other foreigners because these eastern Slav languages are not readily understood by most Czechs. One such group started to move from the Crimean village of Novgorodkivka (known until 1945 as Chekhograd) and settled with their relatives in Tachov, a town of approximately 12,000 inhabitants which lies about ten kilometres from the Czech border with Bavaria. Part of this group are of Czech origin, descended from Czechs who migrated to tsarist Russia in the second half of the nineteenth century, a move they made because they expected to find favourable conditions for farming and the opportunity to buy land cheaply.

In the village Novgorodkivka, the Czech language, Czech songs and Czech dances have all been maintained up to the present, passed down from generation to generation, although these have recently experienced a degree of innovation on account of the Czech clergymen and teachers who visited the village in the 1990s and the small grants for social development that have been provided by the Czech Ministry of Foreign Affairs. Compatriot and religious institutions from the Czech Republic and the U.S.A. then participated in the building of a new Catholic church in Novgorodkivka, completed in 1994, which replaced the one destroyed by the communists in 1939. These and other activities enhanced the prestige of the Czech community and for this reason even villagers born of mixed marriages describe themselves as Czechs. In 1999, basing his findings on figures obtained from registry offices, Ondřej Klípa worked out that, out of about 1,500 inhabitants, about 500 people in Novgorodkivka were of Czech origin (see Uherek et al. 2000: 331).

The close contact with the Czech Republic that opened up after 1989 resulted in a wave of migration from the village in the second half of the 1990s. This happened in a number of ways. First, there were short visits and study stays, then organized events concerning folklore, and finally attempts at permanent resettlement. I first contacted this group of immigrants in the

Czech Republic in 2003 and then again in 2004 and 2005, at which time they numbered about fifty people in thirteen households. Twelve of these households had come directly from Novgorodkivka, while another came from the Crimean city of Simferopol.[26] In 2003/4 every one of this group was a foreign national.[27]

At the time I conducted interviews, most immigrant households were two generations deep, made up of nuclear families – parents and their children – with the exception of two cases of three-generation families.[28] One of these contained a married couple of pensionable age who had followed their children, and another contained a woman who had come with her adult son and his family. Households most commonly contained two children (on average 1.8 children per family); most of these were aged between 13 and 18 years and born in Ukraine, and younger children who had been born in the Czech Republic (aged between 2 and 5 years) were a minority. Children over 6 years of age currently go to school.

One of the basic factors that motivated this group to migrate from Ukraine to the Czech Republic was economics: they had come in an attempt to find work and gain a reasonable wage. Conversely, lack of prospects in Ukraine was, according to them, the major factor that lay behind their decision to migrate. Families where both parents were of a working age appeared to be very enterprising, and they felt that there were more possibilities open to them than they had left behind in Ukraine.

Although this group had some basic knowledge of the situation they would face on arriving in the Czech Republic, they left Ukraine without knowing how to set about taking up permanent residence. In 1997, four men from the group tried to enter the Czech labour market, which was technically illegal. After a few weeks, the police checked their identity and they were consequently deported to Ukraine. Luckily for them they were only banned from returning to the Czech Republic for one year. In 1998, they made a second attempt. The men went to Bohemia on holiday, secured a promise of work and accommodation at a sawmill, and after returning to Ukraine they successfully applied for a work permit. The sawmill, where they lived and worked, was situated in a small village some eight kilometres from the town of Tachov, where they later started to settle.

The sawmill became the stopgap for at least eight families of the group, each staying for between five months and a year before finding accommodation in town. In the sawmill they lived in makeshift conditions, four people to a room, a set up they considered unsuitable for longer stays. One respondent, a woman, lived at the sawmill during the last months of a pregnancy and then shortly after she had given birth, an episode that she remembers as being very difficult. On the other hand, all respondents appreciated the stopgap offered by the sawmill as one of the few places where they could solve the twin problem of accommodation and employment concurrently and thus fulfil some of the conditions for being granted permanent residence.[29] Following their stay at the sawmill, families gradually moved to Tachov, which became the migrants' second stage of integration into the Czech Republic. Here the migrants were able to find accommodation independently of their employer. For those arriving after 2000, when the visa duty between the Ukraine and the Czech Republic was introduced, the situation became more complicated as they had to get a tourist visa for their first arrival.

The choice of Tachov as the place where the group settled was determined by availability of work and accommodation and the fact that the children had already commuted to school there. Another factor was that one of the men had an aunt (FZ) and uncle in this small district town who had moved there right after the Second World War. The uncle had arrived in Bohemia with the Czechoslovak Army brigade which had fought alongside the Red Army. He did not return to Ukraine after the war and the aunt was able to join him legally. However, the aunt and uncle were not part of a migrational network in the sense of a mediating contact. As far as I know, the immigrant in question did not turn to his relatives to solve his residence problems. Rather, the aunt and uncle were more of an emotional tie and the man felt good about knowing someone in the town. He remembered that he had visited his aunt and uncle in his youth, sometime around 1967, and that he had liked the town at the time.

Only one family had support from relatives in Tachov. Other families gradually moved there because the closeness of related immigrant families helped them overcome the obstacles connected with integration into a new milieu. This behaviour is familiar from migration studies which show that migrants are drawn to a place where there is an already existing network of compatriots from their country of origin. According to my experience, the greater the number of obstacles that have to be overcome, the more valid the theory of migration networks becomes. In this case, the extent of the obstacles changed after the arrival of the first wave of migrants. In 1998, the already existing Act No. 123/1992, on the residence of foreigners in the Czech and Slovak Federal Republic, was altered. These alterations meant that migrants had to submit a document confirming the nature of their accommodation and another detailing the availability of funds to support them as they applied for long-term residence. As a contract of employment was considered a valid substitute for the latter, employment and accommodation at the sawmill fulfilled these legal requirements. From the start of 2000, Act No. 326/1999 on the Residence of Aliens in the Territory of the Czech Republic came into effect, and this contained more stringent regulations than the earlier act. For example, Section 13, paragraph 2 of this Act sets the necessary funds for support at '15 times the Subsistence Minimum for Personal Needs if the period of stay in the Territory is to exceed 30 days while this sum shall be increased to double the subsistence minimum for each whole month of expected stay'.[30] At the time, the already established network of migrants in Tachov was able to help newcomers.

Since the immigrants from Novgorodkivka formed their own network in the small town, they did not need the mediation of other people. We know from advertisements in newspapers for potential migrants in the Ukraine and immigrants in the Czech Republic that other institutional routes existed. Registering and formalizing a foreign firm with the help of the company Merkus cost 500€, and preparing the file of documents for gaining a VC–62 – a visa needed for doing business in the Czech Republic – cost 400€. It was also possible to borrow the necessary funds for support needed to fulfil the requirements of the amended act (Červinka 2004).

Migrant enclaves' integration into a new milieu tends to be through bureaucracy, work and immigration networks, and these help migrants overcome obstacles to residence. Where short-term labour migration is concerned, the individual often does not get out of this relational web. In the case of illegal immigration, individuals are sheltered by the employment companies. Family migration with the prospect of permanent residence, however, involves broadening out from the set of initial contacts concerned with such things as accommodation, work and schooling.

In the present case, problems with school were quickly overcome but those concerning accommodation were not. The rural population of Ukraine is not used to formalized communication by means of written contracts and agreements, and they tend to assume the validity of various informal oral promises which provide a lot of room for interpretation. When asked about their opinion of the majority population, one migrant said that it was good overall, though it was a pity that Czechs had a tendency not to keep their word.[31] The group as a whole was able to solve its housing problems eventually, over a two to five year period, by purchasing flats. Until that time, most of them lived in rented accommodation.

The rental price for a four-room flat in Tachov at the time of the research was about 5,000 koruna (CZK), or 172€, per month. In 2004, a four-room flat on a housing estate in Tachov cost approximately 750,000 CZK (25,862€). Most families were not able to pay this amount in full and so took out a loan. One family was able purchase a family home about six years after arriving in the Czech Republic. At the time of the research the entire group had moved to Tachov; the sawmill, meanwhile, was still working and it is entirely possible that other families from Novgorodkivka will settle in the Czech Republic after working there.

Adult members of the group thus encountered their new milieu mostly through their dealings with the police and as workers, renters of flats, and parents of schoolchildren. During interviews, they did not evaluate Czech society negatively, though they were of the opinion that it was rather 'cold' and formal, that in the town there were few cultural amenities, and that Czechs do not know how to enjoy themselves. As I soon discovered, the core of the group consists of people who were involved in Novgorodkivka folklore groups. These devoted themselves to their artistic activities not only because they were a means of getting closer to other people, but also because they were a means of competing with one another. The families kept videos, photographs and their own and their childrens' diplomas not only as reminders of the events they had lived through, but also as proof their capabilities. In Tachov they have found there are few opportunities of this kind in which to outdo others but also few competitors as the current Czech population does not go in for folklore competitions of the kind fund in Ukraine. In interviews it was often clear that the immigrants from Novgorodkivka consider themselves to be educated and cultured individuals, and they feel that the local population does not possess the qualities and abilities that they themselves have.

People coming to the Czech Republic from Ukraine are mainly economic migrants. They are people who have a preconceived idea about a Western lifestyle, something which they have tried to emulate in Ukraine. Indeed, improving their own living conditions was one of the reasons people gave for moving from Novgorodkivka to Tachov. While still living in Novgorodkivka, members of the migrant group must have thought that they would not be able to contact their relatives in Ukraine regularly, and that they would thus be saying goodbye to a friendly collective. Despite this, they decided to emigrate, prioritizing their material security. Migration to the Czech Republic was definitely done selectively: those who preferred a rural life and a friendly collective to material security certainly did not emigrate.

Material circumstances are the basis by which migrants measure their own success in moving to the Czech Republic and their adaptation to their new milieu. Prominent here is the perceived quality of housing, and the quantity and quality of furnishing, consumer goods and electronics that they own. In addition to a large amount of electronic goods, families also equipped themselves with used cars and bought themselves flats. These expenditures, some large, were paid for with money earned from poorly paid manual work. The entire adult population of the group, except pensioners, worked every weekday. After five or six years of this, some families were so exhausted they began to wonder if it had all been worth it. They said that for the sake of their children it has been. Nonetheless, about one fifth of those questioned stated that they were not prepared to move and resettle somewhere else again as they would not have the strength for it.

The kind of work available to immigrants such as these limits their aspirations and advancement. While the education of children is of a relatively high quality in the Czech Republic, the same cannot be said about adult education. Children's integration into Czech society occurs in a matter of months rather than years, but adults find that language, in particular, limits the extent to which they can integrate themselves. Immigrants from Ukraine, including the group under discussion, reach a stage where they can express themselves in Czech (sometimes with a characteristically 'Russian' accent), and can understand what they hear, but cannot become proficient in writing. Consequently, they are sentenced to unqualified labour and their own education is effectively devalued. In 2004, only one member of the group held a responsible position – he was a team leader in a small firm which made car seats. All this despite the fact that the core of the group consists of high-school graduates, some of whom are also university educated.

Since the group tends to be oriented to making money, many work overtime and on Sundays. The overall situation probably leads to parents projecting their ambitions onto their children. Rarely does one hear as much praise for one's own children as we heard among the immigrants from Novgorodkivka. In this way, they may also be compensating for a certain lack of respect shown by some members of the Czech society which considers itself to be more educated or cultured than people with a Russian or Ukrainian accent – they use the informal addressing without asking, try to hire them without a contract and so on.

After four or five years, it seems that the immigrants have begun to feel at home in their surroundings. Most of them like the countryside in western Bohemia, and they appreciate its moist, temperate climate which has fewer temperature fluctuations than there are in their native land. They also appreciate that the countryside is rolling and forested. Although a large part of the group feel that they are at home here, not all of them have decided to opt for Czech citizenship. Although they usually want to do so for their children, the adults prefer to remain Ukrainian nationals as they have relatives and acquaintances in Ukraine and with a Ukrainian passport they do not need a visa to travel there. Currently they have permanent residence rights in the Czech Republic and this suits them. They have a dual or split identity, feeling themselves to be at home both in the Ukraine and the Czech Republic.

Conclusions

In this chapter I have described a number of kinds of migration from Ukraine to the Czech Republic, part of a more widespread migration flow from the East to the West. Its core is economic, and those who migrate are motivated by a desire to improve their material living conditions. In the foregoing text we have looked at two basic strategies of migrants. In the case of temporary labour migration from Transcarpathian Ukraine, we saw that migrants aimed to improve their material living conditions in the source country after their return from abroad. In the case of permanent migration from Novgorodkivka, the aim is to create corresponding amounts of material wealth in the target country of migration. In the case of temporary migration from Transcarpathia it is often difficult to decide whether the motivation to migrate is of a conservative or innovative character. People need to invest in their house to keep it from collapsing, or pay for a medical operation for their relatives so that they do not die, and so on. They use their money to maintain their original conditions, but also to emulate a Western lifestyle. In the case of permanent emigration from Novgorodkivka, the reasons for migration are more evident: they are not purely of an economic character but have an additional cultural subtext. Migrants want to change their lifestyle, or more precisely to improve their standard of living. As it does for temporary migrants, for those opting to settle permanently in the Czech Republic this mainly means changes in their material circumstances.

In her analysis of postsocialism, Katherine Verdery argues that postcommunist transformation is not a simple shift to Western capitalism. During the transformation new social phenomena emerge which defy easy classification (Verdery 1996: 204–34). The group of migrants from Novgorodkivka behave very capitalistically if we describe capitalism in the categories of Karl Polanyi (1944). Their concept of social status is derived from people's economic success and their notion of integration into the majority society is to a certain extent guided by the idea that 'when we have what they have, we will be what they are'. Despite the importance of other factors – language, entertainment and informal contacts – for adults, integration effectively hinges on the issue of property, a term which, as Chris Hann points out, 'is best seen as directing attention to a vast field of cultural as well as social relations, to the symbolic as well as the material contexts within which things are recognized and personal as well as collective identities made' (Hann 1998: 5). Following Hann, property relations are not primarily relations between people and things but relations between people (1998: 4). But what is the property in question here? Despite privations, the family buys an adequate flat and furnishes it with great effort. This includes buying a satellite dish and home theatre system to be able to watch Ukrainian television programmes in the warmth of their home in the Czech Republic. Thus they can remember life in the village, which they consider to be more cultured and richer than life in Tachov (the Czech inhabitants of Tachov, meanwhile, consider themselves to be more cultured and educated than the immigrants from Ukraine and behave towards them accordingly). Cultural difference is quickly overcome among schoolchildren, but only partly and with difficulty among adults.

The behaviour of both temporary and permanent migrants confirms the arguments a large number of theses of migration theory. Economic differences between Ukraine and the Czech Republic are the basis for the pattern of migration described in the neoclassical theory of migration. It has been noted that immigrants create various forms of chain migration, which allow them to better gain a foothold in the place they migrate to. They create migration networks which allow them to lower their initial investment in the target country of migration. It is also notable that employment institutions, and institutions of so-called clients, are generally seen to help migrants overcome obstacles created by the state in the target country. In the present case, however, immigrants to the Czech Republic overcome such obstacles not only through using the client system but also through using avenues available in the target country intended for other purposes, such as the asylum system.

Finally, the kind of work undertaken by Ukrainian migrants in the Czech Republic would seem to support the dual labour market theory of migration. Regardless of their education and qualifications, immigrants are regularly employed in manual, poorly paid jobs, a situation they can seldom extricate themselves from. Thanks to differences in language, they often remain semi-literate in their new linguistic milieu and thus tend to focus on the success of their children. This fact is especially alarming as adult immigrants are usually relatively young people between twenty and forty years of age.

On the other hand, it is interesting that they do not feel degraded and stigmatized by being categorized as manual, poorly paid labourers; on the contrary, they are proud of being able to work hard and achieve an adequate standard of living under these difficult conditions. One can perhaps see here a type of postsocialist migrant personality emerging, that of a person who almost does not care about what and how much they do, but only about what they can buy. I have shown above that the community from Novgorodkivka is going through the process of integration into a new cultural milieu. It is internally differentiated into those who are more and less economically successful. The less successful usually find it more difficult to identify themselves with their new milieu and it is sometimes the case that only via this confrontation with a different reality can they begin to appreciate the place from which they emigrated.

Notes

1 Historical note: the reader should be aware that the country of Czechoslovakia divided into two states – the Czech Republic and Slovakia – at the start of 1993. The Czech Republic inherited a number of institutions and laws from Czechoslovakia.

2 The text was elaborated on the basis of field enquiries that were realised under the research programmes of the Institute of Ethnology of the Academy of Sciences of the Czech Republic, v.v.i. The final version of the text has been formulated within the research grant IAA700580801 GA AV ČR.

3 Source of information: *Zpráva o situaci v oblasti migrace na území České republiky za rok 2003* (Prague: Ministerstvo vnitra České republiky, 2004), p.106.

4 Source of information: *Migrace na území České republiky za rok 2004* (Prague: Ministerstvo vnitra České republiky, 2005), p.4.

5 Source of information: *Cizinci v České republice* (Prague: Český statistický úřad, 2001), p.14.

6 For example, in the 1980s it was possible to hear the following joke: 'Have you heard that in the Soviet Union they have bred the largest bees on Earth? There is one small problem. They knock over trees'.

7 A joke from the 1980s: 'Czech doctors sent a shipment of medicines to the Soviet Union, but it was sent back. They could not figure out why, as the shipment was OK. After a while they figured it out. On the package was written: "Take after eating"' (Budínský 1990: 5).

8 A joke from Prague in the 1970s: 'Do you know how Lenin conceived the way to Communism? Like a train trip: the train is in a dark tunnel and at the end is a bright light. And so you know how Brezhnev conceived it? Like a flight: one man pilots and the others are sick from it'.

9   A joke from the 1970s: 'Do you know who neighbours the Soviet Union? Whoever they want' (Budinský 1990: 9).

10 The research took place between 1991 and 1997, and the conclusions were published in an independent publication (Valášková, Uherek and Brouček 1997).

11 The reason for the marginalization of the last group, however, included its poor language competence.

12 Source of information: Ministry of Interior of the Czech Republic.

13 This research was undertaken as part of a group made up of Mikuláš Mušinka, Naďa Valášková, Kateřina Plochová and myself.

14 Mass migration to the U.S.A. is considered to have begun in 1877 when a group of Ukrainian villagers from what was then Subcarpathian Ruthenia went to work in the mines of eastern Pennsylvania. Magocsi (1995) estimates that between 1880 and 1914 about 225,000 Subcarpathian Ruthenians moved overseas.

15 About 20,000 people moved from Transcarpathian Ukraine to Czechoslovakia before the territory joined the USSR (Vaculík 1995: 12; 2001: 53).

16 Source of information: http://www.mvcr.cz/statistiky/2005/uprch12/9zpl_12.html. Retrieved 16 April 2006.

17 The Act on Asylum has been amended several times since 2001.

18 Source of data: Ministry of interior of the Czech Republic.

19 Source of information for 2007: http://aplikace.mvcr.cz/archiv2008/statistiky/2007/uprch2007/2nz_2007.html Retrieved 18 February 2008.

20 Source of information: 'Average Wages, By Types of Economic Activity 2005: Wage Accruals Per Pay-roll, UAH'. Electronic document of the State Statistics Committee of Ukraine, available at: www.ukrstat.gov.ua. Retrieved 25 June 2005.

21 By April 2005, the average salary of almost all sectors rose slightly; in agriculture the growth was considerable, by more than 90 UAH.

22 Retail prices at the same time were in the region of the following amounts:
    shirt, shorts and comparable textiles – approximately 13 UAH
    vacuum cleaner – 280–550 UAH
    television – 1,000–1,100 UAH
    stereo system – 1,000 UAH
    shampoo (Panthene pro V) – 10 UAH
    washing powder – 3 UAH
    vodka, 0.5 litre – 4–6 UAH
    fruit juice, 1 litre – 5 UAH
    cooking oil, 1 litre – 4.8 UAH
    shoes – 75–115 UAH

23 In 2007 the number of registered unemployed dwindled to about 2 per cent.

24 In January 2005, the average monthly wage in Transcarpathian Ukraine was 502 UAH. Source of information: 'Average Wages and Salaries by Region, 2005: Wage Accrual Per Pay-roll, UAH'. Electronic document of the State Statistics Committee of Ukraine, available at: www.ukrstat.gov.ua. Retrieved 25 June 2005.

25 Source of information: 'Migration of Population in 2004 01–12, by Oblast'. Electronic document of the State Statistics Committee of Ukraine, available at: www.ukrstat.gov.ua. Retrieved 25 June 2005.

26 I conducted the research together with Kateřina Plochová. I stayed in Novgorodkivka in 2000 and again for a short time in 2002, when we also visited Simferopol. Research in Novgorodkivka and Simferopol involved participant observation and non-standardized interviews, while in western Bohemia we additionally used standardized interviews and questionnaires. At the time of writing we have carried out seventeen such interviews and so have covered more than half of the adult population of the migrant group. Observations have been of the whole community.

27 They were possibly all Ukrainian citizens, though we were uncertain as to whether or not two of them were Russian nationals.

28 In 2004, three-generation families remained atypical of the group, though at the time another pair of grandparents was preparing to follow their children, and they arrived in the Czech Republic in 2005.

29 Permanent residence was gained by the families relatively quickly thanks to the benevolence of Czech bureaucrats who accepted assurances that the families applying had one or more Czech ancestor.

30 Information from: http://www.mvcr.cz/cizinci/z_pc_an2.html. Retrieved 25 June 2005. The act has been amended several times since 2001 and a number of provisions in it have been changed, including the issue of funds for support.

31 A family was interested in buying a garden which also contained a garden house. The owner said that she would sell the immigrants the garden in six months or so after resolving some issues concerning the title to the land. Until then, she said, the immigrants were free to do whatever they liked with it. Thus the immigrants cleared the garden, which had been left idle, a task which involved considerable work. After six months the owner sold it to another party for a higher price without telling the immigrants anything (see also Plochová 2004: 167). Incidentally, the family had a similar experience when trying to purchase a flat. On several occasions they were involved in oral negotiations with owners about buying a flat and each time the owners asked for a higher price than they had previously mentioned, explaining that there was now another interested party and that if they paid the higher price then they could have the flat.

References

Auerhan, J. 1920. *České osady ve Volyni, na Krymu a na Kavkaze*. Prague: A. Hajn.

Budínský, V. 1990. *Anekdoty z trezoru, aneb vtipy o zlatou mříž z období neúspěšného budování socialismu v Československu*. Prague: Svépomoc.

——— 1999. *Anekdoty z trezoru: nejlepší politické vtipy v listopadu a po listopadu 1989*. Pardubice: Filip Trend.

Červinka, O. 2004. 'Ukrajinská pracovní migrace v České republice: případová studie', in Z. Uherek et al. *Migrace do České republiky, sociální integrace a lokální společnosti v zemích původu (prostor bývalého SSSR a slovenští Romové)*. Prague: Etnologický ústav AV ČR, pp.111–61.

Drbohlav, D. 1997. *Imigranti v České republice (s důrazem na ukrajinské pracovníky a ,západní' firmy operující v Praze*. Prague: výzkumná zpráva RSS/HESP No. 662/1995.

——— 2004. *Migration Trends in Selected EU Applicant Countries, Volume II: The Czech Republic*. Vienna: International Organization for Migration.

Drbohlav, D. et al. 1999. *Ukrajinská komunita v České republice*. Unpublished research report. Prague: Přírodovědecká fakulta UK.

Hann, C. 1998. 'Introduction: the Embeddedness of Property', in C. Hann (ed.) *Property Relations: Renewing the Anthropological Tradition*. Cambridge: Cambridge University Press, pp.1–47.

Holy, L. 1996: *The Little Czech and the Great Czech Nation: National Identity and the Post-communist Transformation*. Cambridge: Cambridge University Press.

Hořec, J. 1993. *Země Naděje*. Prague: Česká expedice.

——— 1994. *Podkarpatská Rus – země neznámá*. Jinočany: H & H.

Magocsi, P. 1995. *Karpatskí Rusíni*. Fairview, PA: Karpatorusínske výskumné centrum.

Měchýř, J. 1999. *Velký převrat či snad revoluce sametová?* Prague: Československý spisovatel.

Okólski, M. 2001. 'Incomplete Migration: a New Form of Mobility in Central and Eastern Europe. The Case of Polish and Ukrainian Migrants', in C. Wallace and D. Stola (eds), *Patterns of Migration in Central Europe*. Houndmills: Palgrave, pp.105–28.

Plochová, K. 2004. 'Spontánní migrace z jižní Ukrajiny do České republiky: obyvatelé Čechohradu', in Z. Uherek et al. *Migrace do České republiky, sociální integrace a lokální společnosti v zemích původu*. Prague: Etnologický ústav, pp.162–75.

Polanyi, K. 1944. *The Great Transformation*. New York: Rinehart.

Salt, J. 2001. *Current Trends in International Migration in Europe*. European Committee on Migration (CDMG) No. 33. Brussels: Council of Europe.

Uherek, Z. 2003. 'Cizinecké komunity a městský prostor v České republice', *Sociologický časopis* 39(2): 193–216.

_____ 2004. 'Dílčí poznatky o migraci a integraci imigrantů z bývalého Sovětského svazu v českém prostředí', in *Acta Universitatis Carolinae. Philosophica et historica. Studia ethnologica XII*. Prague: Nakladatelství Karolinum, pp.129–40.

Uherek, Z. and K. Plochová. 2003. 'Migration from the Former Soviet Union to the Czech Republic: Comparing the Cases of Resettlers from Areas Affected by the Chernobyl Nuclear Disaster, Kazakhstan and Labour Migration from Subcarpathian Ukraine', in D. Torsello and M. Pappová (eds), *Social Networks in Movement: Time, Interaction and Interethnic Spaces in Central Eastern Europe*. Šamorín / Dunajská Streda: Forum Minority Research Institute, pp.211–27.

Uherek, Z., N. Valášková and S. Brouček. 1997. 'Češi z Běloruska', *Český lid* 84(3): 177–90.

Uherek, Z. et al. 2000. 'Češi na jižní Ukrajině', *Český lid* 87(4): 307–50.

_____ 2003. *Češi z Kazachstánu a jejich přesídlení do České republiky*. Prague: Etnologický ústav AV ČR.

_____ 2004. 'Pracovní migrace ze Zakarpatské Ukrajiny do ČR', in Z. Uherek et al. *Migrace do České republiky, sociální integrace a lokální společnosti v zemích původu (prostor bývalého SSSR a slovenští Romové)*. Praha: Etnologický ústav AV ČR, pp.91–110.

Vaculík, J. 1995. *Hledali svou vlast*. Prague: Česká expedice.

_____ 2001. *Začleňování reemigratů do hospodářského života v letech 1945–1950*. Brno: Národohospodářský ústav Josefa Hlávky.

Valášková, N., Z. Uherek and S. Brouček. 1997. *Aliens or One's Own People: Czech Immigrants from the Ukraine in the Czech Republic*. Prague: Institute of Ethnology.

Večerník, J. and P. Matějů. 1998. *Zpráva o vývoji české společnosti 1989–1998*. Prague: Academia.

Verdery, K. 1996. *What Was Socialism and What Comes Next?* Princeton, NJ: Princeton University Press.

Wallace, C. 2001. 'The New Migration Space as a Buffer Zone?' in C. Wallace and D. Stola (eds), *Patterns of Migration in Central Europe*. Houndmills: Palgrave, pp.72–83.

Wallace, C., O. Chmouliar and E. Sidorenko. 1996. 'The Eastern Frontier of Western Europe: Mobility in the Buffer Zone', *New Community* 22(2): 259–86.

Zilynskyj, B. 1994. *Ukrajinci v Čechách a na Moravě (1894) 1917–1945*. Prague: X-Egem.

Chapter 13

Afterword – Under the Aegis of Anthropology: Blazing New Trails

Christian Giordano

This book represents the noteworthy and innovative contribution of a small yet authoritative group of scholars in the social and cultural sciences, and sends an important message to the anthropological community. Each article reveals that something new is actually surfacing in Eastern Europe, and gives a clear indication that the discipline there is evolving or may have already undergone an irrevocable modification. The authors, all from Eastern Europe and currently professionally involved in this area of the continent (though for study or research reasons they have stayed in the West for longer or shorter periods), share a common project: each of them seeks to point out, though employing disparate lines of argumentation and themes, that the rationale propounded by anthropology (social and cultural) has a strong scientific legitimacy. In the near future, therefore, anthropology should be instrumental to the modernization of the social sciences in Eastern Europe. Accordingly, this discipline could adequately take the place of others, still deeply embedded in the academic tradition, that are based on very dissimilar epistemological assumptions despite a relative similarity of subject matter.

The texts reveal an undeclared yet still clear desire to turn over a new leaf and confront the new paradigms that, up to the fall of the Berlin Wall, have not been properly acknowledged by the academic community in Eastern Europe (though not totally unknown to field experts, especially in some countries such as Poland and Hungary, who were quite knowledgeable about social science developments in the West). The unmistakable intrinsic enterprise of this collection of articles is first of all to break away from the more traditional approaches – euphemistically speaking – of folkloric research (in one's own national society) and ethnographic research (in *other* societies). These kinds of study had enjoyed a well-established standing in the scientific pantheon of realized socialism. Ironically though, they had been employed to some extent in previous times, times which the regime, in line with its philosophy of history, had stigmatized as reactionary.

Indeed, as far as folkloric research is concerned, there were actually no major breakthroughs in the Soviet bloc countries under socialism; there was, rather, a significant continuity with previously popular methodological and thematic paradigms. With due exceptions,[1] studies linked to the *Volkskunde* in the German area were definitely predominant at least until 1989 and to some extent even later on. Thus, the idea of *Volksgeist* or *Volksseele* was still prevalent, at least implicitly, in most of the research carried out during the socialist era[2]. Such studies clearly drew on the key notions created or inspired by Johann Gottfried Herder, the thinker whose scientific rigor and analytical ability is regarded to this day by the most reliable critics as far less important than that of Immanuel Kant, his contemporary, or of other distinguished exponents of German philosophical idealism (such as Georg Friedrich Wilhelm Hegel). On the contrary, Herder may be reckoned, after due consideration, as the extremely successful creator of formulae with a famed and timeless efficacy precisely because of their superficial catchiness (Giordano 1997: 469).

We ought to bear in mind that Herder was widely renowned in all of Eastern Europe, from the Baltic States to the Balkans, and from Russia to Francophone and Francophile Romania. As such, from the nineteenth century onwards, his ideas exerted a strong influence, which the foreign observer can easily perceive to this day even beyond the limited scope of folkloric research in some attitudes of everyday life. The most distinguished intellectuals, from Russian Slavophiles to several Central and Eastern European historians, philologists, writers and artists, bent on imagining, building and rebuilding their own nation, almost constantly drew inspiration from the organic concept of *Volk* and its derivatives coined by Herder.

Paradoxically, the single regimes of the Soviet bloc, ostensibly internationalist but actually nationalist (Ceausescu's Romania comes to mind), never truly gave up employing the most classic notions of Herder, although the latter were constantly overlapped by the rhetoric of brotherhood and proletarian solidarity which intrinsically transcends both the nation's interests and its narrow confines. As such, however, folkloric research becomes a very useful means to produce a State folklorism based on rurality, which is regarded as the cradle, the essence, or indeed the symbol of *Volksgeist*.

With the clear-cut choice in favour of internationalism and industrialization, communist countries opted to value the worker instead of the peasant, since the latter was a presocialist relic unworthy of belonging to the proletarian vanguard. However, in view of their definitive unification through the assimilation of peasants into the working class, several socialist States defined themselves as the outcome of the alliance between industrial and agricultural workers already predicted by Lenin. Thus, by virtue of its Constitution, the German Democratic Republic regarded itself as the first state of workers and peasants on German land.

The previously mentioned paradox is striking in this case because even in the world of collectivism, and contrary to expectations, the myth of rurality nurtured in presocialist times lived on. In fact, in all countries, the keeping of popular traditions of peasant origin was of major importance for folkloric research and had a highly significant value in ideological discourses. Unsurprisingly, institutions in charge of organizing popular events such as open-air museums (the well-known *Skansen*), more or less accurate reconstructions of village life, arts competitions, the production and exhibition of mainly appallingly uniform and tacky handicrafts, and cheap recordings and publication of books or picture books illustrating various rural paradises, flourished from northern Estonia to southern Bulgaria. A veritable state-run folkloric industry was thus set up with experts on popular traditions as scientific consultants if not actual stage directors. As curators of popular culture, their task was to enhance and reinterpret Herder's conceptual heritage from a Marxist standpoint, highlighting the authenticity of the healthy peasant and thus of national roots. The latter, which, from a genealogical and temporal point of view precedes the contamination from urban and Western capitalism, offers the rising proletariat a source of 'purity of origin'. Ultimately, folkloric research becomes a valid means to manage the proper administration of rural identity and consequently of the national one.

But the role of academics is more far reaching, especially if they study cultural diversity beyond the narrow context of their own national society. By means of theoretical acrobatics and empirical mystifications, they must also guarantee compatibility between the actuality of ethnic or national specificities and the internationalist ideal according to which ethnic diversities are remnants, or, as Friedrich Engels wrote, relics of the past and at best ethnographic monuments (Engels 1971: 13, 225). Internationalism is widely known to prophesy the gradual but relentless cultural homogenization of society marching towards the communist dawn. That being the case, these academics have to reconcile the Marxist-Leninist doctrine, recast by Stalin, with the stubborn persistence of scores of cultural, linguistic and religious affiliations. Actually, what *can* account for the fact that the end of Russian imperialism, together with the elimination of capitalist production relations and thus of class hierarchy after the October Revolution, didn't straighten out the national question within Soviet territory and that of satellite countries?

After Stalin's death, the Soviet ethnographer Julian V. Bromlej, with his *etnos* theory, borrowed from his renowned pre-revolutionary predecessor S. M. Shirokogorov, put forward a compromise that we believe may be somewhat roughly summarized as follows (Skalník 1988: 164; Skalník 1990: 185). The *etnos* has its own innate and thus longlasting unchangeable essence that is unscathed by epoch-making events such as the October Revolution and the Great Patriotic War. According to this essentialist perspective, the growth and expansion of Soviet power irreversibly neutralizes the conflict potential between ethno-national groups. The national question is thus solved ... but the differences persist: this is the Columbus's egg concocted by Bromlej.

By now, the reawakening of ethnic conflicts in the ex-Soviet empire's periphery has extensively proven that Bromlej's theoretical proposition is a sham compromise. An orthodox communist could certainly explain these frequently violent phenomena as a consequence of the breakdown of the harmonious division of labour in the republics of the Soviet Union and the iniquitous restoration of private property and capitalist production relations. However, one could reply that by employing the *etnos* theory Bromlej willfully staged and mythologized interethnic harmony, thus creating a smokescreen concealing the persistence of violent disputes and tensions. Ultimately, this performance, set up by the Soviet *etnografija* scholars dominated by Bromlej, turned out to be very expedient for the Communist Party of the Soviet Union a long-running cover-up to negate the obvious. Peter Skalník is clearly in the right when he stresses that the *etnos* theory developed by Bromlej and his acolytes shouldn't be regarded as a divergence from Marxism-Leninism of Stalinist derivation but rather as a way to create myths for the benefit of the state and party apparatus, in keeping with Soviet totalitarianism (Skalník 1988: 170–2; Cannarsa 1994).

We need to add at this point that *etnos* theory won scarce renown in Soviet Union's satellite countries. However, the relatively few authors who carried out research beyond the European context (in Central Asia, for example) referred to the Soviet *etnografija* experts only in homeopathic doses (Jasiewicz 1969). With due exceptions, these references are quite artificial, betraying some awkwardness when used, and cannot in any way be interpreted as a conclusive acknowledgement of *etnos* theory as a valid epistemological foundation. Consequently, references to Soviet *etnos* theory have the bitter aftertaste of a nearly mandatory and hollow practice, an imposed act of allegiance. Nevertheless, Bromlej's most important book, *Etnos i Etnografja*, was translated into German and became a required university textbook in the German Democratic Republic (Bromlej 1977). Finally, *etnos* theory was sporadically adopted in Cuba, though it never reached a high standing (Guanche 1983). Maybe the restraint of socialist field ethnographers outside the USSR can be somewhat explained by the fact that, in countries where ethno-cultural differences were held to be far less marked, Bromlej's theoretical approach seemed too imperial, and thus hardly suitable in national contexts which most of these researchers regarded as more homogeneous or, better yet, mono-ethnic.

The intention of this edited volume, however, is not only to do away with how both folkloric studies (in one's own setting) and ethnographic ones (usually beyond one's own narrow national context) were theoretically conceived and empirically carried out during the socialist era. We need to stress that nearly all the articles in this collection are also a critical response to research in the social sciences, more specifically anthropological research, with what might be called an 'Occidental' outlook on the postsocialist period. As such, we are dealing with a variously explicit and implicit groundbreaking critical assessment of those theoretical paradigms that have been prevalent in social and cultural analysis during the fifteen years following the downfall of totalitarian regimes in Eastern Europe. As such, there is a noticeable breakaway project to leave behind the concept of 'transition' and its derivatives, such as the more historicizing and less deterministic 'transformation', or the 'change of system' notion in political science. This critical stance is far from unexpected; actually it is fully justified. Moreover, it proves that Eastern European anthropologists, with more insight than several of their Western colleagues, have more easily perceived the blatant epistemological flaws of these paradigms that were developed and firmly upheld by Western social sciences.

The transitional model and its several related versions have hardly turned out to be cogent, though they brought forth an extensive scientific literature with which, willingly or not, the Western anthropology of postsocialism has had to come to grips. This lack of tenability is due above all to the fact that old interpretative schemes, which the theories of modernization had already put forward in the 1960s for so-called Third World societies, were simply adapted. Modernization theories, in line with a simplistic neo-evolutionistic analysis, defined Third World countries as 'transitional societies' precisely because they were bound for an inevitable and rapid integration in the purportedly 'developed' capitalist world. This nearly prophetic view was, however, clearly wide of the mark, so much so that we wonder how the social sciences (and also anthropology to some extent) could have chosen to use it again to interpret the changes that have occurred in Eastern Europe since 1989. Most probably, Western researchers blamed the transitional model's inapplicability in developing countries on the purported beneficiaries, and their Oriental otherness. They assumed that the cultural proximity with the West of countries previously under Soviet regime would instead ensure their smooth shift from a socialist to a capitalist society.

Accordingly, the transitional model applied to Central and Eastern Europe has become a convention, by now employed without specifications, while the fifty-year period prior to 1989 has been portrayed nearly always as an abnormal hibernation phase or an imposed deviation endured by these societies during their natural advance towards 'progress'.

Other arguments have challenged both the transition concept's suitability and the soundness of its related social theories, though in practice the latter still prevail in political, administrative and technocratic discourses. Firstly, we need to recall the tendency to universalize a single transitional model – that is, the Western one – which leads to a standardization of social values, representations and practices (namely, a 'homologation', as the famed Italian writer Pier Paolo Pasolini styled it). Consequently, there would be no room for other types of socio-cultural changes such as the ones evoked by the sociologist Shmuel N. Eisenstadt through the concept of 'multiple modernities' (Eisenstadt 2002).

Upholding the idea that only one road leads to development obviously implies a value judgment, thus an ethnocentric standpoint: the Western transitional model is not just the sole model but also the best possible one, intrinsically better than all others. Consequently, societies which, due to various historical reasons or psychological factors, could not or would not comply are in a state of both structural and political-cultural backwardness (which, well before 1989, was looked upon as a malignant and obsolete form of nationalism: see, e.g., Kohn 1961; Sugar and Lederer 1969) as well as socio-economic stagnation (which, before the end of socialism, was already perceived as a lack of capitalist rationality: see, e.g., Gerschenkron 1962; Chirot 1989). The notion of transition therefore implies a theory of deficit according to which Eastern Europe's stagnant or backward societies still lack that system of virtues, value orientations, organizational structures and collective action strategies needed to produce 'prosperity', as Francis Fukuyama would have it (Fukuyama 1995).

Ultimately, this means artificially dividing the European continent into a more virtuous part – the Western one – and a rather virtueless part – the Eastern one. This only leads to presenting a modernized version of the invention of Eastern Europe through the outdated Orientalist (or, as it were, Balkanistic) separation between Europe's East and West (Said 1978; Todorova 1997), whose distant origins date back to the eighteenth-century Enlightenment (Wolff 2003).

In this afterword I have deliberately delved into the characteristics of folkloric and ethnographic studies during socialism (and to some extent after its end), as well as the type of discourse common within the transitional model proposed by Western social sciences after the end of communism (but already devised by then), to draw attention to the weighty legacy that this volume's authors have had to cope with. Above all, it seemed particularly appropriate to highlight the importance of these articles, which show a deep-seated resolve to break away from a burdensome past. Aptly enough, the authors' course of action was not to simply reassess the scientific background, but rather to establish links with the more current paradigms proposed by anthropology by supplementing them with distinctive and fresh thematic as well as methodological suggestions.

I have noticed that all contributors have endeavoured consistently to avoid the *Gemeinschaft* discourse so typical of traditional folkloric and ethnographic studies of a still lingering past; consequently, they have employed the *Gesellschaft* model. As such, the social configurations and types of sociability researched have been finally rid of that fictitious aura of organicism and unalterability attributed especially in the primordialist perspective to ethno-national groups. By contrast, the society conceived as being *Gesellschaft* in this volume's chapters takes on more dynamic, differentiated, and ambivalent aspects that take into account the swift changes in social structures, roles, positions, as well as breaches, confrontations, tensions, latent conflicts and negotiation practices between collective and individual agents.

The articles by Vytis Čiubrinskas and Zdeněk Uherek are definitely indicative of this focus on *Gesellschaft*. Employing a transnational approach, these two authors address issues linked to immigration and emigration in two countries that, for historical reasons, have had dissimilar experiences in the field of social mobility. The phenomena of emigration (both historical and current) and immigration (especially after the downfall of the borders imposed by the socialist system) is one of the most crucial themes for understanding new social structures, the workings of transnational networks, and the renewed relations between diasporas and society of origin in the societies that emerged from the Soviet bloc's collapse. Westbound emigration from Central Europe along with immigration from the former Soviet empire's peripheries and the world's underdeveloped South towards Central Europe are a major challenge that societies that emerged from socialism in 1989 are currently coping with. Unsurprisingly, the above-mentioned authors' articles display perspectives of anthropological analysis that will certainly have a strong influence on future researches in this field.

The significance of the transnational context also emerges in Gabriel-Ionuț Stoiciu's article, in which he compares two different entrepreneurial cultures, French and Romanian, the latter developing after 1989 but still firmly affected by its socialist past. Interestingly, data reveals that cultural differences between the actors of the two countries' multinational enterprises persist despite the strong globalization drive typical of this sector of the economy. Globalization's outcome is not a unified worldwide *Gesellschaft*. Consequently, it neither leads to the utopian end of history (Fukuyama 1992), nor to the dreaded Mcdonaldization of society (Ritzer 1996), but rather, as the author shows empirically, to 'glocalized' (Robertson 1990) arrangements in which work relations and entrepreneurial styles specific to the local *Gesellschaft* maintain their *raison d'être*.

Hana Červinková's article also deals with a transnational scenario in which a U.S. moviemaking team and Czech Republic air-force pilots interact. This situation, paradoxical for the reader and described with a keen sense of humour, offers an excellent opportunity to analyse the radical role and status changes that took place in this country's armed forces after the downfall of socialism. The analysis of the military system as an important segment of the *Gesellschaft* in Eastern Europe has, for obvious reasons, never been a major anthropological topic in the West, as the author herself aptly stresses. Instead, the question of changes that took place in Eastern European formerly socialist countries' armed forces and their consequences, such as a curtailed prestige and a concurrent increase in training and professionalization, has been rightly detected only by other Eastern European anthropologists, such as Tanja Petrović in Serbia and Venelin Stoichev in Bulgaria. Following in her wake, these two young researchers, who are affiliated with a project of the Centre for Advanced Study in Sofia headed by Aleksander Kiossev, are respectively studying the current social memory of the Federal Yugoslavian armed forces, born of the partisan war, and the sensitive issues facing Bulgarian armed forces' officers, of redefining their identity after the country recently joined NATO. Apparently, the armed forces have become a specific and major topic of anthropological research in Eastern Europe.

Peter Skalnik, on the one hand, and Alexandra Bitušíková with Katarína Koštialová, on the other, examine the various political expressions of the postsocialist *Gesellschaft*. In his overview of the various political scenarios in the Czech Republic, Skalník highlights the need for multisited, or rather 'translocal', research (Marcus 1998; Hannerz 1998: 246 ff.), capable of stretching beyond the local dimension. The local, however, is not totally discarded, but rather is contextualized and integrated in the broader frame of *Gesellschaft*. Therefore, the exhortation of Boissevain and Friedl (1975) to go 'beyond the community' is still viable. But Skalník also shows the need for interdisciplinarity, of political anthropology in general and that of postsocialist countries in particular. This discipline, drawing on major concepts of other related social sciences, such as that of political culture employed by the author himself, can enrich others through its own self-assessment, providing a vigorous drive towards developing new theoretically relevant proposals, fruitful for political science and political sociology as well. Alexandra Bitušíková and Katarína Koštialová comment on a theme that will become an increasingly topical issue in the region's *Gesellschaften*. Drawing inspiration from local politics, they show that, despite major difficulties, women in Slovakia play less marginal roles in the public sphere compared to the period before 1989. In a field where men are traditionally predominant, female participation in civil and political life has increased, suggesting a possible budding shift in gender relations, especially in ones involving power relations, in Central and Eastern Europe.

At first glance the two subjects discussed by Michał Buchowski and László Kürti in this volume could seem the more traditional ones, since they analyse respectively the question of property relations in rural Poland and the activities and influence of a relatively small transnational business in Hungary. In the first case, Michał Buchowski examines the Polish specificity, in which private property, unlike the case in other socialist countries, was still predominant in the agricultural sector. Due to this peculiarity, an increasingly precarious class relationship took shape in the Polish farmlands after 1989 between those who already owned the land in the past and farmed it personally and those who were suddenly jobless and forced to seek employment because the collectivized farms where they had worked had been wound up. The aftermath of this process has been a heightening of social differences that in the past were more egalitarian, on paper at least. In the second case, László Kürti, against the current critical trend of some Western academic circles, argues that the delocalization and, consequently, the foreign capitalist penetration of enterprises in the peripheries of Eastern Europe did not always have a negative influence on local economies and culture. In fact, the case he studied can actually be called a success story, though, as the author himself acknowledges, some caution must be exercised in the eagerness to generalize.

After the impressive number of studies and research dealing with resurgent nationalism on the one hand, and the age-old problem regarding ethnic minorities' more or less precarious standing on the other, readers will be glad to find that this volume has contributions that also discuss other groups on the *Gesellschaft's* outer edge. In fact, Grażyna Kubica's article on the condition of gays and lesbians in Poland, Terézia Nagy's on the culture of the homeless in Hungary, and Rajko Muršič's on the long-term activities of a rock band tackle with assurance and insight an array of major social questions and burning political issues in Central and Eastern Europe (and not only here). Ultimately, the thorny issues of discrimination, labelling processes and, last but not least, the difficult and tangled recognition of what may be called social minorities and groups that produce alternative cultures, come to the fore. In following the examples of these three authors, anthropology can uncover a broad field of research, undoubtedly challenging but very fruitful and important as well.

By mentioning only some of what I see as the key points tackled by each chapter, I may not have fully illustrated the richness and liveliness of anthropological reflection found amongst Central and Eastern European researchers. However, the remarkable variety of subjects and theoretical and methodological arguments also reveals the considerable gap between these approaches and past folkloric and ethnographic studies, as well as the contrast with the unilineal reductionism of classic transition theories. Thanks to the various chapters, such a single-minded idea of transition conjures up a process that ended precisely because it never began. On the whole, I have a clear feeling that this volume will not only further an interest in anthropology but also reliably help reassess the overrated obstacles that hindered this discipline's swift development in Central and Eastern Europe for so long.

(Translated from Italian by Lura Ann Munsel)

Notes

1. Such as Wolfgang Jacobeit in the German Democratic Republic, Edit Fél and Tamás Hofer in Hungary, Józef Burszta in Poland and Henri H. Stahl in Romania: see Jacobeit, 1985–95; Fél and Hofer 1969; Burszta 1979; Stahl 1969.
2. *Folk spirit* and *folk soul* are the English terms for *Volksgeist* and *Volksseele* coined by Herder.

References

Boissevain, J. and J. Friedl (eds). 1975. *Beyond the Community: Social Process in Europe.* The Hague: Department of Educational Science of the Netherlands.

Bromlej, J. 1977. *Ethnos und Ethnographie.* Berlin: Akademie Verlag.

Burszta, J. 1979. 'Methoden und Resultate der ethnologischen Untersuchungen lokaler Gemeinschaften in Polen', in G. Wiegelmann (ed.) *Gemeinde im Wandel. Volkskundliche Gemeindestudien in Europa.* Münster: F. Coppenrath Verlag.

Cannarsa, S. 1994. *Etnografia ed etnos. L'etnografia sovietica di fronte alle questioni delle nazionalità e delle religioni.* Milan: Edizioni Unicopli.

Chirot, D. (ed.) 1989. *The Origins of Backwardness in Eastern Europe: Economics and Politics from the Middle Ages until the Early Twentieth Century.* Berkeley: University of California Press.

Eisenstadt, S. (ed.) 2002. *Multiple Modernities.* New Brunswick, NJ: Transaction.

Engels, F. 1971. 'Po und Rhein', in K. Marx and F. Engels, *Werke.* Berlin: Institut für Marxismus-Leninismus beim ZK der SED, Dietz Verlag, Vol. 13 pp.225–68.

Fél, E. and T. Hofer. 1969. *Proper Peasants: Traditional Life in a Hungarian Village.* New York: Aldine.

Fukuyama, F. 1992. *The End of History and the Last Man.* New York: Macmillan.

——— 1995. *Trust, the Social Virtues and the Creation of Prosperity.* New York: Free Press.

Gerschenkron, A. 1962. *Economic Backwardness in Historical Perspective.* Cambridge, MA: Harvard University Press.

Giordano, C. 1997. 'La penséé ethnologique de Max Weber' *Ethnologie Française, (L'Allemagne: L'interrogation)* 27(4): 463–78.

Guanche, J. 1983. *Procesos etnoculturales de Cuba.* Havana: Editorial Letras Cubanas.

Hannerz, U.. 1998. 'Transnational Research', in B. Russell (ed.) *Handbook of Methods in Cultural Anthropology.* Walnut Creek, CA: Altamira, pp.235–56.

Jasiewicz, Z. 1969. *Uzbecy. Studia nad Przeobrażeniami społeczno-kulturowymi w XIX i XX wieku.* Poznań: Adam Mickiewicz University of Poznan, Works of the philosophic-historic Department, Ethnographic Series Nr. 6.

Jacobeit, W. 1985–1995. *Illustrierte Sozialgeschichte des Deutschen Volkes.* Berlin: Akademie Verlag.

Kohn, H. 1961. *The Idea of Nationalism.* New York: Macmillan.

Marcus, G. 1998. *Ethnography through Thick and Thin.* Princeton, NJ: Princeton University Press.

Ritzer, G. 1996. *The Mcdonaldization of Society.* Rev. edn. Thousand Oaks, CA: Pine Forge Press.

Robertson, R. 1990. 'Mapping the Global Condition: Globalization as the Central Conception', in M. Featherstone (ed.) *Global Culture: Nationalism, Globalization, Modernity.* London: Sage, pp.15–30.

Said, E. 1978. *Orientalism.* New York: Pantheon.

Skalník, P. 1988. 'Union soviétique-Afrique du Sud: les *théories* de l'*etnos*', *Cahiers d'Etudes africaines* 28(2): 157–76.

——— 1990. 'Soviet *etnografiia* and the national(ities) question', *Cahiers du monde russe et soviétique* 31(2–3): 183–91.

Stahl, H. 1969. *Les anciennes communautés villageoises roumaines. Asservissement et pénetration capitaliste.* Bucharest: Editions de l'Académie de la Republique Socialiste de Roumanie, Paris: Editions du Centre National de la Recherche Scientifique.

Sugar, P. and I. Lederer (eds). 1969. *Nationalism in Eastern Europe.* Seattle: University of Washington Press.

Todorova, M. 1997. *Imagining the Balkans.* Oxford: Oxford University Press.

Wolff, L. 1994. *Inventing Eastern Europe: The Map of Civilization on the Mind of Enlightenment.* Stanford, CA: Stanford University Press.

——— 2003. 'Die Erfindung Osteuropas: Von Voltaire zu Voldemort', in K. Kaser, D. Gramshammer-Hohl and R. Pichler (eds), *Europa und die Grenzen im Kopf, Wieser Enzyklopädie des Europäischen Ostens*, Volume II. Klagenfurt: Wieser Verlag, pp.21–34.

Notes on Contributors

Alexandra Bitušíková received a Ph.D. in ethnology/ social anthropology from Comenius University in Bratislava. Since 1991 she has been working at the Research Institute of Matej Bel University in Banská Bystrica as a senior research fellow and in 1993–2000 as the director of the institute. She is the author of *Urban Anthropology: Trends and Perspectives* (in Slovak), a number of publications focused on urban anthropology, post-socialist social and cultural change in Central Europe, identities, minorities, diversity and gender. In 2001–2002 she worked in the European Commission, Directorate General Research, in Brussels. Now based in Brussels, she works as a research program manager at the European University Association and continues working for Matej Bel University in Banská Bystrica in Slovakia as a senior researcher. Her latest research projects include the EU funded projects: 'Enlargement, Gender, Governance: Civic and Political Participation of Women in the EU Candidate Countries' (FP5) and 'Sustainable Development in a Diverse World' (FP6 Network of Excellence).

Michał Buchowski is a Professor of Social Anthropology at the University of Poznań and of Comparative Central European Studies at European University Viadrina in Frankfurt/Oder. He lectured and was Visiting Professor at the University of Kansas, Humboldt University, Rutgers University and Columbia University. He was a Fellow of the British Council, Fulbright Foundation, Kosciuszko Foundation and the Humboldt Foundation, and worked as a research fellow in the Centre Marc Bloch in Berlin and CNRS in Paris. His scientific interest is in modes of thought and in Central European social and cultural transformations. He has published several books, among them most recently in English *Reluctant Capitalists* (1997), *The Rational Other* (1997), *Rethinking Transformation* (2001), as well as *To Understand the Other* (in Polish); and he is the co-editor of *Poland Beyond Communism* (2001) and *The Making of the Other in Central Europe* (2001). Currently he is working on issues related to the encounter of the free market and democracy with the realities of post-socialist Poland at the grass-roots level in Poland and Central Europe

Hana Červinková received her Ph.D. in anthropology from New School for Social Research in New York (2003). In her research, she focused on the changing institution of the military and its place in Czech society upon the Czech Republic's entry into NATO (published as *Playing Soldiers in Bohemia: An Ethnography of NATO Membership*, 2006). Červinková has also published articles on post-socialist transformation, cultural memory, anthropology in education and translated anthropological texts from English into Czech. She works and lives in Wrocław, Poland where she teaches anthropology and works as the Director of the International Institute for the Study of Culture and Education at the University of Lower Silesia.

Vytis Čiubrinskas is currently director of the Center of Social Anthropology at the Vytautas Magnus University, Lithuania. He received his Ph.D. from Vilnus University in 1993. From 2002 to 2006 he conducted research in the USA on transmigration and transnationalism among Lithuanian diasporas and repatriates focusing especially on cultural identity, cultural politics and cultural heritage maintenance. He has published numerous books and articles in Lithuanian, his English-language publications include 'Lithuanian Transnationalism: Constructed, Imagined and Contested Identity of the Lithuanian – Americans', in *Beginnings and the Ends of Emigration* (2005), 'Transnational Identity and Heritage : Lithuania Imagined, Constructed and Contested', in Craith, Mairead N., Kockel, Ullrich (eds.) *Communicating Cultures* (2004), and 'Europe, Cultural Construction and Reality' (review article), – *Ethnologia Scandinavica*, (2003).

Christian Giordano, born 1945 in Lugano (Switzerland); Italian citizen. Studies in Bern and Heidelberg; 1973 Ph.D. in Sociology, University of Heidelberg; 1987 Habilitation in Cultural Anthropology and Anthropology of Europe, University of Frankfurt/M.. Assistant Professor of Cultural Anthropology 1980–86, University of Frankfurt/M. 1988–89. Associate Professor of Sociology, University of Munich. Since 1989 Full Professor of Social Anthropology at the University of Fribourg (Switzerland). Doctor honoris causa of the University of Timişoara (Romania). President of Ethnobarometer, International Research Network on Minorities and Migrations, Italian Council for the Social Sciences; Rome. President of the Interfaculty Institute of East and Central Europe, University of Fribourg. Member of the Evaluation Pool, European Science Foundation. Publications: *Die Betrogenen der Geschichte. Überlagerungsmentalität und Überlagerungsrationalität in mediterranen Gesellschaften*, Frankfurt/M., 1992; (ed.) *Constructing Risk, Threat, Catastrophe: Anthropological Perspectives*, Fribourg, 2002, (ed.) *Terre, Territoire, Appartenances*, Paris 2003.

Katarína Koštialová studied at the Constantine the Philosopher University in Nitra, Slovakia and specialises in ethnology, social anthropology and folk culture. She carried out research on cultural transformations of the Zvolen region at the Museum in Zvolen, Slovakia. Nowadays she conducts her fieldwork at the Research Institute of Matej Bel University in Banská Bystrica focusing on study of social and professional groups in an urban environment. She teaches ethnology at the University of Matej Bel. She is a member of the Slovak Ethnological Society.

Grażyna Kubica studied sociology at the Jagiellonian University and specialized in social anthropology. Her fieldwork site is Cieszyn Silesia and Kraków. She is also interested in the history of anthropology, Polish-Jewish relations, nationalism, gender, queer theory and visual anthropology. Her books are: *Lutherans of Cieszyn Silesia*, 1994; the comprehensive edition of Malinowski's diaries, 2002; *Malinowski's sisters, modern women at the beginning of the XX century*, 2006 (all in Polish). She co-edited a volume *Malinowski: Between Two Worlds*, Cambridge 1988 and two others in Polish. She is also a photographer. From 2000 to 2004 she was a member of the Executive Committee of EASA.

László Kürti received his Ph.D. in cultural anthropology from the University of Massachusetts in 1989. He taught anthropology at The American University in Washington DC, and the Eötvös University in Budapest, and presently teaches at the University of Miskolc, Hungary. He conducted fieldwork in North America, Romania and Hungary. His English-language books include: *The Remote Borderland* (2001), *Youth and the State in Hungary* (2002), and served as co-editor for *Beyond Borders* (1996), and *Working Images* (2004). From 2001 to 2006 he served as the Secretary of the European Association of Social Anthropologists.

Rajko Muršič studied ethnology, philosophy (BA) and cultural anthropology (Ph.D., 1998) at the University of Ljubljana. There he teaches basic methodological courses, social structure and popular culture at undergraduate and postgraduate level. He did fieldwork in Slovenia, Poland, Macedonia, Serbia, Germany and Japan. His professional interests comprise methodology of anthropological research, theory and philosophy of science, theory of culture, popular music and anthropology of music, philosophy of music, popular culture and material culture, cultural complexities and transnational studies, and political anthropology. He has published four monographs in Slovene and co-edited MESS: *Mediterranean Ethnological Summer School*, Vol. 3/1999; *Cultural Processes and Transformations in Transition of the Central and Eastern EuropeanPost-Communist Countries*, 1999, and Mess, Vol. 5/2003 (all in English, published in Ljubljana).

Terézia Nagy received her MA in ethnology (2002) and sociology (2004) from the University of Szeged. Currently, she is Ph.D. student at Corvinus University in Budapest. She works at the Centre for Regional Studies at Hungarian Academy of Sciences. Her interests include culture of refugees, migrants, homelessness and theoretical approaches of postmodern anthropology and city dwellers. Her articles in English include: 'The appearance of an underground electro-music subculture in the cultural sphere of the city' (2003), 'Conversion and (re)construction of identity – converts in a Hungarian Islam fellowship' (2006).

Peter Skalník (b. 1945) studied in Prague, Leningrad and Cape Town and specializes in political anthropology (state and chiefdom, political culture). He conducted fieldwork in four continents and interests include anthropology of Europe, diplomacy, media and anthropology. He taught social anthropology at Charles University of Prague, Comenius University of Bratislava, University of Leiden, University of Cape Town and presently University of Pardubice. He was an extraordinary professor at University of Wroclaw, Poland, in 2005–2007. He was ambassador of his country in Lebanon (1992–1997). His publications (only edited or co-edited books): *The Early State* (Mouton 1978), *The Study of the State* (Mouton 1981), *Outwitting the State* (Transaction 1989), *The Early Writings of Bronislaw Malinowski* (Cambridge 1993), *Sociocultural Anthropology at the Turn of the Century* (Set Out 2000), *Africa 2000: Forty Years of African Studies in Prague* (Set Out 2001), *The Post-communist Millennium: The Struggles for Sociocultural Anthropology in Central and Eastern Europe* (Set Out 2002), *Ernest Gellner: Special Memorial Issue* (Social Evolution and History 2/2, 2004), *Dolní Roveň: poločas výzkumu/Dolní Roveň: Research at Half-time* (University of Pardubice 2004), *Anthropology of Europe: Teaching and Research* (Set Out 2005), *Studying Peoples in People's Democracies: Socialist Era Anthropology* (LIT 2005). He is a Vice-President of the International Union of Anthropological and Ethnological Sciences (2003–present).

Gabriel Ionut Stoiciu has a BA (2000) in psychology and sociology from the University of Bucharest. He holds two Master's Degrees: one in Social Anthropology (2001) from the University of Bucharest and another one in Industrial Sociology (2002) from Pierre Mendes France University in Grenoble (France). Presently, he is a Ph.D. candidate at Bucharest University writing his thesis on the anthropology of work. He conducted fieldwork in France and Romania and published several articles in Romanian scientific journals. He is currently employed as junior researcher at the Anthropological Institute of the Romanian Academy.

Zdenek Uherek received his Ph.D. in ethnology from the Czechoslovak Academy of Sciences in Prague in 1992. Between 1993 to 1995 he was a research fellow at the Central European University, Centre for the Study of Nationalism under supervision of Professor Ernest Gellner. Currently, he is a director of the Institute of Ethnology of the Academy of Sciences of the Czech Republic and is chair of the Department of Ethnic Studies there. He is the president of the Czech National Committee of the International Union of Anthropological and Ethnological Sciences, representative of the Czech Republic in the Intergovernmental Council of the UNESCO programme MOST, member of RAI and EASA. He is the first president of Czech Association for Social Anthropology. He teaches at Charles University

(Prague), at the University of West Bohemia (Plzeň) and University of Pardubice. His fields of interest are migration studies, theory of ethnicity, anthropology of Europe, and urban anthropology. He conducted field research in the Czech Republic, Kazakhstan, Russia, Ukraine, Slovakia, Bosnia and Herzegovina and Croatia. His English-language books include monographs: *Aliens or One's Own People: Czech Immigrants from the Ukraine in the Czech Republic* (with N. Valášková and S. Brouček 1997), *Bosnia, Bosnian Czechs, and Migratory Bridges* (with P. Lozoviuk and M. Toncrová 2000). He edited and co-edited publications *Urban Anthropology and the Supranational and Regional Networks of the Town* (1993), *Ethnic Studies and the Urbanized Space in Social Anthropological Reflections* (1998), *Roma Migration in Europe: Case studies* (2004), and *Fieldwork and Local Communities* (2005).

Name Index

Subject Index